500 CAKES AND BAKES

500 CAKES AND BAKES

A mouth-watering collection of recipes ranging from traditional teatime treats and fun party and celebration cakes to luxurious gateaux and tarts, shown in 500 photographs

Contributing Editor
Martha Day

HERMES HOUSE

This edition is published by Hermes House,
an imprint of Anness Publishing Ltd,
Blaby Road, Wigston,
Leicestershire LE18 4SE

Email: info@anness.com

Web: www.hermeshouse.com; www.annesspublishing.com

Publisher: Joanna Lorenz
Editorial Director: Judith Simons
Project Editor: Lucy Doncaster
Copy Editor: Jan Cutler
Design: SMI
Photographers: Karl Adamson, Edward Allwright, David Armstrong, Steve Baxter, James Duncan, John Freeman, Michelle Garrett, Amanda Heywood, Tim Hill, Don Last, Michael Michaels
Recipes: Alex Barker, Carole Clements, Roz Denny, Christine France, Shirley Gill, Patricia Lousada, Norma MacMillan, Sue Maggs, Janice Murfitt, Annie Nichols, Louise Pickford, Katherine Richmond, Hilaire Walden, Steven Wheeler, Elizabeth Wolf-Cohen
Food for Photography: Carla Capalbo, Carole Handslip, Wendy Lee, Sarah Maxwell, Angela Nilsen, Jane Stevenson, Liz Trigg and Elizabeth Wolf-Cohen
Stylists: Madeleine Brehaut, Maria Kelly, Blake Minton, Kirsty Rawlings, Fiona Tillett
Editorial Reader: Rosie Fairhead
Production Controller: Steve Lang

A CIP catalogue record for this book is available from the British Library.

Previously published as *500 Fabulous Cakes and Bakes*

Main front cover image shows *Tia Maria Gateau* – for recipe, see page 215

Notes

Bracketed terms are intended for American readers.
For all recipes, quantities are given in both metric and imperial measures and, where appropriate, in standard cups and spoons. Follow one set of measures, but not a mixture, because they are not interchangeable.
Standard spoon and cup measures are level. 1 tsp = 5ml, 1 tbsp = 15ml, 1 cup = 250ml/8fl oz.
Australian standard tablespoons are 20ml. Australian readers should use 3 tsp in place of 1 tbsp for measuring small quantities.
American pints are 16fl oz/2 cups. American readers should use 20fl oz/2.5 cups in place of 1 pint when measuring liquids.
Electric oven temperatures in this book are for conventional ovens. When using a fan oven, the temperature will probably need to be reduced by about 10–20°C/20–40°F. Since ovens vary, you should check with your manufacturer's instruction book for guidance.
The nutritional analysis given for each recipe is calculated per portion (i.e. serving or item), unless otherwise stated. If the recipe gives a range, such as Serves 4–6, then the nutritional analysis will be for the smaller portion size, i.e. 6 servings. The analysis does not include optional ingredients, such as salt added to taste.
Medium (US large) eggs are used unless otherwise stated.

Contents

Introduction

Baking is one of the most satisfying of all the culinary arts. It fills the house with the most wonderful aroma, gives ample reward for minimal effort and always meets with approval,

especially from younger members of the family. Bake a batch of brownies, a fresh fruit pie, a crusty loaf of bread or a luxurious gateau, and watch your rating rise!

This bonanza collection – over five hundred of the finest recipes – is all you need to earn your champion baker's badge. It ranges from simple teatime treats, such as drop scones and basic cookies, to elaborate cakes for special celebrations, such as Coconut Lime Gateau or Easter Egg Nest Cake. Each recipe is illustrated by a beautiful colour photograph of the finished bake, and the step-by-step instructions are so simple and straightforward that even a beginner will find them easy to follow.

In fact, novice cooks often make the best bakers, preheating the oven in plenty of time, taking care to measure ingredients accurately and following recipe methods to the letter. All of these elements are important in baking, which demands more precision than many other types of cooking. With a soup or stew you can happily add extra ingredients or cheat a little when it comes to exact quantities, but the balance of ingredients, the temperature and the timing are all very important when you are baking a cake or pastry. It is well worth reading the chosen recipe carefully before you begin baking, as well as doing any preparation, such as browning almonds or softening butter, in advance, then setting out the measured ingredients in the style of the TV cook.

Advice on lining tins (pans) is given in individual recipes. Baking parchment is easy to use and gives excellent results, as it has a non-stick surface and it comes cleanly away from baked foods. To line a tin cut a piece of baking parchment a little longer than the circumference of the pan and 2.5cm/1in deeper. Fold over 2.5cm/1in along the long edge and snip up to the fold every 4cm/1½in or so. Use a pencil to draw round the base of the tin, then cut out a circle which is exactly the correct size to fit in the base of the tin. Grease the tin and line the side with the paper, so that the snipped edge lies on the base of the tin. Place the paper circle in the base. For some recipes you will only need to line the base of the tin.

Whether or not to grease tins used for pastry is a matter of choice. If the pastry is high in fat, such as shortcrust, flaky or puff, it is not usually necessary; however, spills from fillings may stick. When in doubt, grease the tins lightly. When using shortcrust pastry in a flan tin (tart pan), give the greased tin a light dusting of flour.

If you are a novice baker, start with some of the simpler recipes, such as Chocolate-chip Cookies, Chive and Potato Scones or a Quick-mix Sponge. If you are feeling a bit more confident, try making one of the many delectable breads, which range from a traditional Braided Loaf to the contemporary Saffron Focaccia.

You'll find every occasion amply catered for, from Valentine's Day through to Christmas. There are special cakes for christenings, anniversaries and birthdays, from novelty teddies and pirate's hats to an Eighteenth Birthday Cake and even a Pizza Cake! The collection also includes wonderful ways of keeping the cake tin and cookie jar brimming with healthy snacks suitable for lunchboxes and family treats, including a selection for those with dietary restrictions. With vegans in view, there's a special chocolate gateau and a Dundee cake, and an entire chapter is devoted to low-fat cakes and bakes.

In this book there's a sweet or savoury treat for every taste and every moment of the day, from breakfast Blueberry Muffins to a late-night slice of wickedly indulgent Pecan Tart. Tempted to embark on an immediate baking session? Go right ahead. Baking is a wonderfully therapeutic occupation – with sheer indulgence as the reward!

Farmhouse Cookies

Delightfully wholesome, these melt-in-the-mouth farmhouse cookies are ideal to serve with morning coffee.

Makes 18

115g/4oz/½ cup butter or margarine, at room temperature
90g/3½oz/7 tbsp soft light brown sugar
65g/2½oz/5 tbsp crunchy peanut butter
1 egg
50g/2oz/½ cup plain (all-purpose) flour
2.5ml/½ tsp baking powder
2.5ml/½ tsp ground cinnamon
1.5ml/¼ tsp salt
175g/6oz/1½ cups muesli
50g/2oz/½ cup raisins
50g/2oz/½ cup chopped walnuts

1 Preheat the oven to 180°C/350°F/Gas 4. Grease a large baking sheet.

2 Cream the butter or margarine and sugar until light and fluffy. Beat in the peanut butter and then beat in the egg.

3 Sift the flour, baking powder, cinnamon and salt over the peanut butter mixture and stir to blend. Stir in the muesli, raisins and walnuts. Taste the mixture to see if it needs more sugar, as the sugar content of muesli varies.

4 Drop rounded tablespoonfuls of the mixture on to the prepared baking sheet about 2.5cm/1in apart. Press gently with the back of a spoon to spread each mound into a circle.

5 Bake until lightly coloured, about 15 minutes. With a metal spatula, transfer to a wire rack to cool. Store the cookies in an airtight container.

Cook's Tip

Make these cookies extra wholesome by using a good-quality, rich-tasting peanut butter from your health-food store. You can also use luxury muesli with exotic fruits to make them even tastier.

Energy 165kcal/688kJ; Fat 10g, Saturated Fat 4.1g; Carbohydrate 16.9g, Fibre 1.1g

Crunchy Oat Cookies

Home-made biscuits like these crunchy cookies are always a favourite, and the variations are endless.

Makes 14

175g/6oz/¾ cup butter or margarine, at room temperature
175g/6oz/generous ¾ cup caster (superfine) sugar
1 egg yolk
175g/6oz/1½ cups plain (all-purpose) flour
5ml/1 tsp bicarbonate of soda (baking soda)
2.5ml/½ tsp salt
50g/2oz/⅔ cup rolled oats
50g/2oz/⅔ cup small crunchy nugget cereal

1 Cream the butter or margarine and sugar together until light and fluffy. Mix in the egg yolk.

2 Sift over the flour, bicarbonate of soda and salt, then stir into the butter mixture. Add the oats and cereal, and stir to blend. Chill for at least 20 minutes.

3 Preheat the oven to 190°C/375°F/Gas 5. Grease a large baking sheet.

4 Roll the mixture into balls. Place them on the baking sheet and flatten with the base of a floured glass.

5 Bake until golden, about 10–12 minutes. Then, with a metal spatula, transfer to a wire rack to cool. Store the cookies in an airtight container.

Variations

- *Add grated orange rind to the mixture to give a delicate citrus taste.*
- *You can substitute 50g/2oz/¼ cup chopped walnuts or pecan nuts for the cereal to make nutty oatmeal cookies, or try chocolate chips, raisins or sultanas instead.*
- *Other dried fruits, such as papaya, also transform the cookies and can be substituted for all or part of the cereal.*

Energy 220kcal/923kJ; Fat 11.9g, Saturated Fat 6.8g; Carbohydrate 27.6g, Fibre 0.8g

Apricot Yogurt Cookies

These soft-textured cookies are useful to give children in their lunchboxes, as they are low in fat and full of wholesome ingredients.

Makes 16

175g/6oz/1½ cups plain (all-purpose) flour
5ml/1 tsp baking powder
5ml/1 tsp ground cinnamon
75g/3oz/scant 1 cup rolled oats
75g/3oz/⅓ cup light muscovado (brown) sugar
115g/4oz/½ cup chopped ready-to-eat dried apricots
15ml/1 tbsp flaked (sliced) hazelnuts or almonds
about 150g/5oz/scant ⅔ cup natural (plain) yogurt
45ml/3 tbsp sunflower oil
demerara (raw) sugar, to sprinkle

1 Preheat the oven to 190°C/375°F/Gas 5. Lightly oil a large baking sheet.

2 Sift together the flour, baking powder and cinnamon. Stir in the oats, sugar, apricots and nuts.

3 Beat together the yogurt and oil, then stir evenly into the cookie mixture to make a firm dough. If necessary, add a little more yogurt.

4 Use your hands to roll the mixture into about 16 small balls, place on the baking sheet and flatten with a fork.

5 Sprinkle with demerara sugar. Bake for 15–20 minutes, or until firm and golden brown. Transfer to a wire rack to cool. Store in an airtight container.

Cook's Tip
As these cookies have a moist texture they do not keep well, so it is best to eat them within 2 days. However, they freeze well. Pack them into plastic bags and freeze for up to 4 months. You can simply take one or two out to pop into a child's lunchbox as you need them.

Energy 104kcal/439kJ; Fat 3.2g, Saturated Fat 0.4g; Carbohydrate 17.6g, Fibre 0.7g

Oat and Apricot Clusters

These uncooked treats are full of flavour. You can change the ingredients according to what's in your cupboard – try peanuts, pecan nuts, raisins or dates.

Makes 12

50g/2oz/¼ cup butter or margarine
50g/2oz/4 tbsp clear honey
50g/2oz/½ cup medium oatmeal
50g/2oz/¼ cup chopped ready-to-eat dried apricots
15ml/1 tbsp banana chips
15ml/1 tbsp dried coconut shreds
50–75g/2–3oz/2–3 cups cornflakes or crispy cereal

1 Place the butter or margarine and honey in a small pan and warm over a low heat, stirring until well blended.

2 Add the oatmeal, apricots, banana chips, coconut and cornflakes or crispy cereal, and mix well.

3 Spoon the mixture into 12 paper cases, piling it up roughly. Transfer to a baking sheet and chill until set and firm.

Fruit and Nut Clusters

Children will love to help make these tasty morsels.

Makes 24

225g/8oz white chocolate
50g/2oz/⅓ cup sunflower seeds
50g/2oz/½ cup flaked (sliced) almonds
50g/2oz/½ cup sesame seeds
50g/2oz/⅓ cup seedless raisins
5ml/1 tsp ground cinnamon

1 Break the white chocolate into small pieces and melt in a heatproof bowl over a pan of simmering water.

2 Stir the melted chocolate until smooth and glossy. Mix in the sunflower seeds, flaked almonds, sesame seeds, raisins and cinnamon, and stir well. Using a teaspoon spoon the mixture into paper cases and leave in a cool place to set.

Top: Energy 97kcal/407kJ; Fat 5.4g, Saturated Fat 3.5g; Carbohydrate 11.7g, Fibre 0.9g
Above: Energy 93Kcal/386kJ; Fat 6.3g; Saturated fat 2.1g; Carbohydrate 7.5g; Fibre 0.5g

Nutty Nougat

Makes about 500g/1¼lb
225g/8oz/generous 1 cup granulated sugar
225g/8oz/⅔ cup cup clear honey
1 large (US extra large) egg white
115g/4oz/1 cup flaked (sliced) almonds or chopped pistachio nuts, roasted

1 Line an 18cm/7in square cake tin (pan) with rice paper. Gently heat the sugar and honey with 60ml/4 tbsp water in a heavy pan, stirring until the sugar has completely dissolved.

2 Boil the syrup, without stirring, until soft crack stage (151°C/304°F on a sugar thermometer). Remove from the heat and cool slightly. Whisk the egg white until stiff, then drizzle over the syrup while still whisking. Stir in the nuts. Pour into the tin and leave to cool completely. Cut into squares before it hardens.

Oaty Coconut Cookies

The coconut gives these cookies a wonderful texture.

Makes 48
175g/6oz/generous 2 cups quick-cooking oats
75g/3oz/1 cup desiccated (dry unsweetened shredded) coconut
225g/8oz/1 cup butter
115g/4oz/generous ½ cup caster (superfine) sugar
50g/2oz/¼ cup soft dark brown sugar
2 eggs
60ml4 tbsp milk
7.5ml/1½ tsp vanilla extract
115g/4oz/1 cup plain (all-purpose) flour, sifted
2.5ml/½ tsp bicarbonate of soda (baking soda)
2.5ml/½ tsp salt
5ml/1 tsp ground cinnamon

1 Preheat the oven to 200°C/400°F/Gas 6. Spread the oats and coconut on a baking sheet. Bake for 8–10 minutes.

2 Cream the butter and sugars. Beat in the eggs, milk and vanilla. Fold in the dry ingredients, and the oats and coconut. Drop spoonfuls of mixture on to two greased baking sheets, and bake for 8–10 minutes. Cool on a wire rack.

Top: Energy 2250Kcal/9511kJ; Fat 64.2g; Saturated fat 5.1g; Carbohydrate 415g; Fibre 8.5g
Above: Energy 84kcal/352kJ; Fat 5.4g, Saturated Fat 3.4g; Carbohydrate 8.3g, Fibre 0.5g

Crunchy Jumbles

For even crunchier cookies, add 50g/2oz/½ cup walnuts, coarsely chopped, with the cereal and chocolate chips.

Makes 36
115g/4oz/½ cup butter or margarine, at room temperature
225g/8oz/generous 1 cup caster (superfine) sugar
1 egg
5ml/1 tsp vanilla extract
150g/5oz/1¼ cups plain (all-purpose) flour, sifted
2.5ml/½ tsp bicarbonate of soda (baking soda)
1.5ml/¼ tsp salt
50g/2oz/2¼ cups crisped rice cereal
175g/6oz/1 cup chocolate chips

1 Preheat the oven to 180°C/350°F/Gas 4. Grease two baking sheets. Cream the butter or margarine and sugar until fluffy. Add the egg and vanilla extract. Add the flour, bicarbonate of soda and the salt, and fold in.

2 Add the cereal and chocolate chips and mix thoroughly. Drop spoonfuls 5cm/2in apart on to baking sheets and bake for 10–12 minutes. Transfer to a wire rack to cool.

Cinnamon Balls

Makes 126
175g/6oz/1½ ground almonds
75g/3oz/scant ½ cup caster (superfine) sugar
15ml/1 tbsp ground cinnamon
2 egg whites
icing (confectioners') sugar, for dredging

1 Preheat the oven to 180°C/350°F/Gas 4. Grease a large baking sheet. Mix the almonds, sugar and cinnamon in a bowl. Whisk the egg whites until stiff and fold into the almond mixture.

2 Roll small spoonfuls of the mixture into balls and place on the baking sheet. Bake for 15 minutes, then cool on a wire rack. Roll the cooled balls in some sifted icing sugar until completely covered.

Top: 95kcal/398kJ; Fat 4.2g, Saturated Fat 2.5g; Carbohydrate 14.2g, Fibre 0.3g
Above: Energy 15Kcal/63kJ; Fat 0.8g; Saturated fat 0.1g; Carbohydrate 1.8g; Fibre 0.1g

Ginger Cookies

So much tastier than store-bought varieties, these ginger cookies will disappear quickly, so be sure to make a large batch!

Makes 60

275g/10oz/2½ cups plain (all-purpose) flour
5ml/1 tsp bicarbonate of soda (baking soda)
7.5ml/1½ tsp ground ginger
1.5ml/¼ tsp ground cinnamon
1.5ml/¼ tsp ground cloves
115g/4oz/½ cup butter or margarine, at room temperature
350g/12oz/1¾ cups caster (superfine) sugar
1 egg, beaten
60ml/4 tbsp treacle (molasses)
5ml/1 tsp fresh lemon juice

1 Preheat the oven to 160°C/325°F/Gas 3. Lightly grease three to four baking sheets.

2 Sift the flour, bicarbonate of soda and spices into a small bowl. Set aside.

3 Cream the butter or margarine and two-thirds of the sugar together. Stir in the egg, treacle and lemon juice. Add the flour mixture and mix in thoroughly with a wooden spoon to make a soft dough.

4 Shape the dough into 2cm/¾in balls. Roll the balls in the remaining sugar and place about 5cm/2in apart on the prepared baking sheets.

5 Bake until the cookies are just firm to the touch, about 12 minutes. With a metal spatula, transfer the cookies to a wire rack and leave to cool. The biscuits will firm up as they cool.

Variation
Coarsely chop 150g/5oz drained preserved stem ginger. Add 115g/4oz to the cookie mixture at the end of step 3, and press the remaining pieces into the top of each of the cookies at the end of step 4.

Energy 57kcal/239kJ; Fat 1.7g, Saturated Fat 1g; Carbohydrate 10.3g, Fibre 0.1g

Cream Cheese Spirals

These spirals look so impressive and melt in the mouth, yet they are surprisingly easy to make.

Makes 32

225g/8oz/1 cup butter, at room temperature
225g/8oz/1 cup cream cheese
10ml/2 tsp caster (superfine) sugar
225g/8oz/2 cups plain (all-purpose) flour
1 egg white, beaten with 15ml/1 tbsp water, for glazing
caster sugar, for sprinkling

For the filling
115g/4oz/1 cup finely chopped walnuts
115g/4oz/¾ cup soft light brown sugar
5ml/1 tsp ground cinnamon

1 Cream the butter, cream cheese and sugar until soft. Sift over the flour and mix until combined. Gather into a ball and divide in half. Flatten each half, wrap in baking parchment and chill for 30 minutes.

2 Meanwhile, make the filling. Mix the chopped walnuts with the light brown sugar and cinnamon, stirring well so that the nuts are well coated with the spices. Set aside.

3 Preheat the oven to 190°C/375°F/Gas 5. Grease two baking sheets. Working with one half of the dough at a time, roll out thinly into a 28cm/11in circle. Using a dinner plate as a guide, trim the edges with a knife.

4 Brush the surface with the egg-white glaze, and then sprinkle evenly with half the filling.

5 Cut the circle into 16 triangular segments. Starting from the base of a triangle, roll up the dough to form a spiral. Repeat with the remaining triangles.

6 Place the spirals on the prepared baking sheets and brush with the remaining egg and water glaze. Sprinkle with caster sugar. Bake until golden, about 15–20 minutes. Cool on a wire rack.

Energy 150kcal/621kJ; Fat 11.8g, Saturated Fat 6g; Carbohydrate 9.7g, Fibre 0.3g

Italian Almond Biscotti

Serve biscotti after a meal, for dunking in sweet white wine, such as an Italian Vin Santo or a French Muscat.

Makes 48

200g/7oz/1¼ cups whole unblanched almonds
215g/7½oz/scant 2 cups plain (all-purpose) flour
90g/3½oz/½ cup caster (superfine) sugar
a pinch of salt
a pinch of saffron powder
2.5ml/½ tsp bicarbonate of soda (baking soda)
2 eggs
1 egg white, lightly beaten

1 Preheat the oven to 190°C/375°F/Gas 5. Grease and flour two baking sheets.

2 Spread the almonds on an ungreased baking sheet and bake until lightly browned, about 15 minutes. When cool, grind 50g/2oz/½ cup of the almonds in a food processor, blender, or coffee grinder until pulverized.

3 Coarsely chop the remaining almonds into two or three pieces each. Set aside.

4 Combine the flour, sugar, salt, saffron powder, bicarbonate of soda and ground almonds in a bowl and mix to blend. Make a well in the centre and add the eggs. Stir to form a rough dough. Transfer to a floured surface and knead until well blended. Knead in the chopped almonds.

5 Divide the dough into three equal parts. Roll into logs about 2.5cm/1in in diameter. Place on one of the prepared baking sheets, brush with the egg white and bake for 20 minutes. Remove from the oven. Lower the oven temperature to 140°C/275°F/Gas 1.

6 With a very sharp knife, cut into each log at an angle making 1cm/½in slices. Return the slices on the baking sheets to the oven and bake for another 25 minutes. Transfer the biscotti to a wire rack to cool.

Energy 51kcal/216kJ; Fat 2.6g, Saturated Fat 0.3g; Carbohydrate 5.7g, Fibre 0.4g

Orange Cookies

These classic citrus-flavoured cookies are ideal for a tasty treat at any time of the day.

Makes 30

115g/4oz/generous ½ cup butter, at room temperature
200g/7oz/1 cup caster (superfine) sugar
2 egg yolks
15ml/1 tbsp fresh orange juice
grated rind of 1 large orange
200g/7oz/1¾ cups plain (all-purpose) flour
15ml/1 tbsp cornflour (cornstarch)
2.5ml/½ tsp salt
5ml/1 tsp baking powder

1 Cream the butter and sugar until light and fluffy. Add the yolks, orange juice and rind, and continue beating to blend.

2 In another bowl, sift together the flour, cornflour, salt and baking powder. Add to the butter mixture and stir until it forms a dough. Wrap the dough in baking parchment and chill for 2 hours.

3 Preheat the oven to 190°C/375°F/Gas 5. Grease two baking sheets. Roll spoonfuls of the dough into balls and place 2.5–5cm/1–2in apart on the baking sheets.

4 Press down with a fork to flatten. Bake until golden brown, about 8–10 minutes. Using a metal spatula, transfer to a wire rack to cool.

Variation

These Orange Cookies are ideal for making into Orange Creams. Simply make a butter icing by creaming together 50g/2oz/¼ cup butter and 75g/3oz/¾ cup icing (confectioners') sugar until smooth. Add the grated rind of an orange and moisten to a spreadable consistency with a little freshly squeezed orange juice. Spread a little of the butter icing on to the flat side of a cookie and sandwich with another. Repeat with the remaining cookies. Chocolate butter icing would also go exceptionally well with the orange.

Energy 83kcal/350kJ; Fat 3.6g, Saturated Fat 2.1g; Carbohydrate 12.6g, Fibre 0.2g

Raspberry Sandwich Cookies

These cookies may be stored in an airtight container with sheets of baking parchment between the layers.

Makes 32

175g/6oz/1 cup blanched almonds
175g/6oz/1½ cups plain (all-purpose) flour
175g/6oz/¾ cup butter, at room temperature
115g/4oz/generous ½ cup caster (superfine) sugar
grated rind of 1 lemon
5ml/1 tsp vanilla extract
1 egg white
1.5ml/¼ tsp salt
25g/1oz/¼ cup flaked (sliced) almonds
250ml/8fl oz/1 cup raspberry jam
15ml/1 tbsp lemon juice

1 Process the blanched almonds and 45ml/3 tbsp flour in a food processor or blender until finely ground. Cream the butter and sugar together until light and fluffy. Stir in the lemon rind and vanilla. Add the ground almonds and remaining flour, and mix well. Gather into a ball, wrap in baking parchment, and chill for 1 hour.

2 Preheat the oven to 160°C/325°F/Gas 3. Line two baking sheets with baking parchment. Divide the cookie mixture into four equal parts. Working with one section at a time, roll out to a thickness of 3mm/⅛in on a lightly floured surface.

3 With a 6cm/2½in fluted pastry (cookie) cutter, stamp out circles. Using a 2cm/¾in piping (icing) nozzle or pastry cutter, stamp out the centres from half the circles. Place the rings and circles 2.5cm/1in apart on the baking sheets.

4 Whisk the egg white with the salt until just frothy. Chop the flaked almonds. Brush the cookie rings with the egg white, then sprinkle over the almonds. Bake until lightly browned, about 12–15 minutes. Cool for a few minutes on the baking sheets then transfer to a wire rack.

5 In a pan, melt the jam with the lemon juice until it comes to a simmer. Brush the jam over the cookie circles and sandwich together with the rings.

Energy 133kcal/554kJ; Fat 8.1g, Saturated Fat 3.1g; Carbohydrate 13.9g, Fibre 0.6g

Christmas Cookies

Decorate these delicious cookies with festive decorations or make them at any time of year.

Makes 30

175g/6oz/¾ cup unsalted (sweet) butter, at room temperature
275g/10oz/1½ cups caster (superfine) sugar
1 egg
1 egg yolk
5ml/1 tsp vanilla extract
grated rind of 1 lemon
1.5ml/¼ tsp salt
275g/10oz/2½ cups plain (all-purpose) flour

For decorating (optional)
175g/6oz/1½ cups icing (confectioners') sugar
food colouring
small decorations

1 Preheat the oven to 180°C/350°F/Gas 4. With an electric mixer, cream the butter until soft. Add the sugar gradually and continue beating until light and fluffy.

2 Using a wooden spoon, slowly mix in the whole egg and the egg yolk. Add the vanilla extract, lemon rind and salt. Stir to mix well. Add the flour and stir until blended.

3 Gather the mixture into a ball, wrap in baking parchment and chill for 30 minutes.

4 On a floured surface, roll out the mixture about 3mm/⅛in thick. Stamp out shapes or rounds with cookie cutters. Bake until lightly coloured, about 8 minutes. Transfer to a wire rack and leave to cool completely. The cookies can be left plain, or iced and decorated.

5 To ice the cookies, mix the icing sugar with enough water to make a thick icing consistency. Add a few drops of food colouring to create just one colour, or divide the mixture into small amounts and add different food colouring to each.

6 Fill a piping (icing) bag fitted with a fine nozzle with the icing and pipe dots, lines and patterns on to the cookies. Finish with small decorations such as edible silver balls.

Energy 118kcal/495kJ; Fat 5.3g, Saturated Fat 3.2g; Carbohydrate 17.3g, Fibre 0.3g

Apricot Specials

Walnuts complement the flavour of apricots perfectly in these fruity bars.

Makes 12

90g/3½oz/scant ½ cup soft light brown sugar
75g/3oz/⅔ cup plain (all-purpose) flour
75g/3oz/6 tbsp cold unsalted (sweet) butter, cut in pieces

For the topping

150g/5oz/generous ½ cup ready-to-eat dried apricots
250ml/8fl oz/1 cup water
grated rind of 1 lemon
65g/2½oz/generous ¼ cup caster (superfine) sugar
10ml/2 tsp cornflour (cornstarch)
50g/2oz/½ cup chopped walnuts

1 Preheat the oven to 180°C/350°F/Gas 4. In a mixing bowl, combine the brown sugar and flour. With a pastry blender, cut in the butter until the mixture resembles coarse breadcrumbs, or rub in with your fingertips.

2 Transfer to a 20cm/8in square baking tin (pan) and press level. Bake for 15 minutes. Remove from the oven but leave the oven on.

3 To make the topping, place the apricots and water in a pan and simmer until the fruit is soft; about 10 minutes. Strain the liquid and reserve. Chop the apricots.

4 Return the apricots to the pan and add the lemon rind, caster sugar, cornflour and 60ml/4 tbsp of the soaking liquid. Cook for 1 minute.

5 Cool slightly before spreading the topping over the base. Sprinkle over the walnuts and bake for 20 minutes more. Cool in the tin before cutting into bars.

Cook's Tip
Vary the dried fruit for these bars depending on what you have in your cupboard. Prunes and dried peaches work especially well.

Energy 169kcal/711kJ; Fat 8.1g, Saturated Fat 3.5g; Carbohydrate 23.9g, Fibre 1.1g

Brandy Snaps

You could serve these brandy snaps with rich vanilla ice cream rather than the cream filling.

Makes 18

50g/2oz/¼ cup butter, at room temperature
150g/5oz/¾ cup caster (superfine) sugar
20ml/1 rounded tbsp golden (light corn) syrup
40g/1½oz/⅓ cup plain (all-purpose) flour
2.5ml/½ tsp ground ginger

For the filling

250ml/8fl oz/1 cup whipping cream
30ml/2 tbsp brandy

1 Cream together the butter and sugar until light and fluffy, then beat in the golden syrup. Sift over the flour and ginger, and mix together. Transfer the mixture to a work surface and knead until smooth. Cover and chill for 30 minutes.

2 Preheat the oven to 190°C/375°F/Gas 5. Grease a baking sheet. Working in batches of four, shape the mixture into walnut-size balls. Place well apart on the baking sheet and flatten slightly. Bake until golden and bubbling, about 10 minutes.

3 Remove from the oven and leave to cool for a few moments. Working quickly, slide a metal spatula under each one, turn over, and wrap around the handle of a wooden spoon (have four spoons ready). If they firm up too quickly, reheat for a few seconds to soften. When firm, slide the brandy snaps off and place on a wire rack to cool.

4 When all the brandy snaps are cool, prepare the filling. Whip the cream and brandy until soft peaks form. Pipe into each end of the brandy snaps just before serving.

Cook's Tip
Unfilled brandy snaps will keep well for up to 1 week if stored in an airtight container. However, you should eat filled brandy snaps as soon as they are made, as the cream softens them quite quickly.

Energy 121kcal/505kJ; Fat 7.9g, Saturated Fat 5g; Carbohydrate 11.7g, Fibre 0.1g

Chocolate Pretzels

Pretzels come in many different flavours – here is a delicious chocolate version that is guaranteed to please the tastebuds.

Makes 28

150g/5oz/1¼ cups plain (all-purpose) flour
1.5ml/¼ tsp salt
20g/¾oz/3 tbsp unsweetened cocoa powder
115g/4oz/½ cup butter, at room temperature
130g/4½oz/scant ¾ cup caster (superfine) sugar
1 egg
1 egg white, lightly beaten, for glazing
sugar crystals, for sprinkling

1 Sift together the flour, salt and cocoa powder. Set aside. Cream the butter until light. Add the sugar and continue beating until light and fluffy. Beat in the egg.

2 Add the dry ingredients and stir to blend thoroughly. Gather the dough into a ball, wrap it in clear film (plastic wrap) and chill for 1 hour.

3 Roll the dough into 28 small balls. Chill the balls until needed. Preheat the oven to 190°C/375°F/Gas 5. Lightly grease two baking sheets.

4 Roll each ball into a rope about 25cm/10in long. With each rope, form a loop with the two ends facing you. Twist the ends and fold them back on to the circle, pressing them in to make a pretzel shape. Place on the prepared baking sheets.

5 Brush each of the pretzels with the egg white. Sprinkle sugar crystals over the tops and bake in the oven until firm, about 10–12 minutes. Using a metal spatula, transfer to a wire rack to cool.

Variation
To make mocha-flavoured pretzels, replace 10ml/1 tsp of the unsweetened cocoa powder with instant coffee powder.

Energy 72kcal/303kJ; Fat 3.8g, Saturated Fat 2.3g; Carbohydrate 9.1g, Fibre 0.3g

Iced Ginger Cookies

If your children enjoy cooking with you, mixing and rolling the dough, or cutting out different shapes, this is the ideal recipe to let them practise on.

Makes 16

115g/4oz/½ cup soft light brown sugar
115g/4oz/½ cup soft margarine
a pinch of salt
a few drops of vanilla extract
175g/6oz/1½ cups wholemeal flour
15g/½oz/2 tbsp unsweetened cocoa powder, sifted
10ml/2 tsp ground ginger
a little milk
glacé icing and glacé (candied) cherries, to decorate

1 Preheat the oven to 190°C/375°F/Gas 5. Grease two baking sheets. Cream the light brown sugar, margarine, salt and vanilla extract together until very soft and light.

2 Work in the flour, cocoa and ginger, adding a little milk, if necessary, to bind the mixture. Knead lightly on a floured surface until smooth.

3 Roll out the dough on a lightly floured surface to about 5mm/¼in thick. Stamp out shapes using cookie cutters and place on baking sheets.

4 Bake the cookies for 10–15 minutes, leave to cool on the baking sheets until firm, then transfer to a wire rack to cool completely. Decorate the cooled cookies with the glacé icing and glacé cherries.

Cook's Tip
This mixture is ideal for creating small gingerbread people, which children will love to make. Cut out the cookies using appropriate cutters and decorate with raisins for eyes and glacé (candied) cherries for a smiley mouth. Sesame seeds can be pressed into the mixture to make a pattern or the outline of clothing. Or pipe icing on to the finished cookies to make features, buttons, a bow tie or scarf and clothes.

Energy 119kcal/497kJ; Fat 6.4g, Saturated Fat 3.9g; Carbohydrate 14.7g, Fibre 1.1g

Chocolate Macaroons

Serve these delicious macaroons with coffee.

Makes 24

50g/2oz plain (semisweet) chocolate, melted
175g/6oz/1 cup blanched almonds
225g/8oz/generous 1 cup caster (superfine) sugar
3 egg whites
2.5ml/½ tsp vanilla extract
1.5ml/¼ tsp almond extract
icing (confectioners') sugar, for dusting

1 Preheat the oven to 160°C/325°F/Gas 3. Line two baking sheets with baking parchment and then grease them.

2 Grind the almonds in a food processor. Transfer to a bowl, then blend in the sugar, egg whites, vanilla and almond extracts.

3 Stir in the melted chocolate. The mixture should just hold its shape; if it is too soft, chill for 15 minutes.

4 Shape the mixture into walnut-size balls. Place on the baking sheets and flatten slightly. Brush with a little water and dust with icing sugar. Bake until just firm, 10–12 minutes. With a metal spatula, transfer to a wire rack to cool.

Big Macaroons

Makes 9

2 egg whites
5ml/1 tsp almond extract
115/4oz/1 cup ground almonds
130g/4½oz/1 cup light muscovado (brown) sugar

1 Preheat the oven to 180°C/350°F/Gas 4. Line a large baking sheet with baking parchment. Whisk the egg whites until they form stiff peaks. Add the almond extract and whisk to combine. Fold the almonds and sugar into the mixture.

2 Place nine spoonfuls of the mixture on the baking sheet and flatten slightly. Bake for 15 minutes. Leave to cool on the sheet for 5 minutes before removing to a wire rack to cool completely.

Top: Energy 94kcal/393kJ; Fat 4.7g, Saturated Fat 0.7g; Carbohydrate 11.6g, Fibre 0.6g
Above: Energy 138Kcal/577kJ; Fat 7.1g; Saturated fat 0.6g; Carbohydrate 16g; Fibre 0.9g

Coconut Macaroons

Makes 24

40g/1½oz/⅓ cup plain (all-purpose) flour
1.5ml/1¼tsp salt
225g/8oz/4 cups desiccated (dry unsweetened shredded) coconut
170ml/5½fl oz/scant ¾ cup sweetened condensed milk

1 Preheat the oven to 180°C/350°F/Gas 4. Grease two baking sheets. Sift the flour and salt into a bowl and then stir in the coconut. Pour in the condensed milk and mix, stirring from the centre, to form a thick mixture.

2 Drop tablespoonfuls of the mixture 2.5cm/1in apart on the baking sheets. Bake until golden brown, about 20 minutes.

Chocolate Orange Sponge Drops

Light and crispy, with a zesty marmalade filling, these sponge drops are truly delightful.

Makes 14–15

2 eggs
50g/2oz/¼ cup caster (superfine) sugar
2.5ml/½ tsp grated orange rind
50g/2oz/½ cup plain (all-purpose) flour
60ml/4 tbsp fine-shred orange marmalade
40g/1½oz plain (semisweet) chocolate, melted

1 Preheat the oven to 200°C/400°F/Gas 6. Line three baking sheets with baking parchment.

2 Put the eggs and sugar in a bowl over a pan of simmering water. Whisk until thick and pale. Remove from the pan and whisk until cool. Whisk in the orange rind. Sift the flour over and fold it in gently.

3 Put 28–30 dessertspoonfuls of the mixture on the baking sheets. Bake for 8 minutes, until golden. Cool slightly, then transfer to a wire rack. Sandwich pairs together with marmalade. Melt the chocolate and drizzle over the drops.

Top: Energy 86Kcal/357kJ; Fat 6.6g; Saturated fat 5.5g; Carbohydrate 5.8g; Fibre 1.3g
Above: Energy 58kcal/247kJ; Fat 1.5g, Saturated Fat 0.7g; Carbohydrate 10.5g, Fibre 0.2g

Peanut Butter Cookies

These moreish cookies must come close to the top of the list of America's favourites. They are quick and simple to make with ingredients that you will normally have in the store cupboard or pantry.

Makes 24

150g/5oz/1¼ cups plain (all-purpose) flour
2.5ml/½ tsp bicarbonate of soda (baking soda)
2.5ml/½ tsp salt
115g/4oz/½ cup butter, at room temperature
170g/5¾oz/generous ⅔ cup soft light brown sugar
1 egg
5ml/1 tsp vanilla extract
260g/9½oz/scant 1¼ cups crunchy peanut butter

1 Sift together the flour, bicarbonate of soda and salt, and set aside. In another bowl, cream the butter and sugar together until light and fluffy.

2 In a third bowl, mix the egg and vanilla, then gradually beat into the butter mixture. Stir in the peanut butter and blend thoroughly. Stir in the dry ingredients. Chill for 30 minutes, or until firm.

3 Preheat the oven to 180°C/350°F/Gas 4. Grease two baking sheets. Spoon out rounded teaspoonfuls of the dough and roll into balls.

4 Place the balls on the baking sheets and press flat with a fork into circles about 6cm/2½in in diameter, making a criss-cross pattern.

5 Bake in the oven until lightly coloured, about 12–15 minutes. Using a metal spatula transfer to a wire rack to cool.

Variation
For extra crunch add 50g/2oz/½ cup chopped raw, skinned peanuts with the peanut butter at step 2. (Raw peanuts do not keep well so always buy in small quantities.)

Energy 154kcal/641kJ; Fat 9.9g, Saturated Fat 4g; Carbohydrate 13.7g, Fibre 0.8g

Chocolate Chip Cookies

A perennial favourite with all the family, these cookies contain walnuts as well as chocolate chips.

Makes 24

115g/4oz/½ cup butter or margarine, at room temperature
45g/1¾ oz/scant ¼ cup caster (superfine) sugar
100g/3¾oz/scant ½ cup soft dark brown sugar
1 egg
2.5ml/½ tsp vanilla extract
175g/6oz/1½ cups plain (all-purpose) flour
2.5ml/½ tsp bicarbonate of soda (baking soda)
1.5ml/¼ tsp salt
175g/6oz/1 cup chocolate chips
50g/2oz/⅓ cup walnuts, chopped

1 Preheat the oven to 180°C/350°F/Gas 4. Lightly grease two large baking sheets. With an electric mixer, cream the butter or margarine and both the sugars together until light and fluffy.

2 In another bowl, mix the egg and the vanilla extract, then gradually beat into the butter mixture. Sift over the flour, bicarbonate of soda and salt and stir. Add the chocolate chips and walnuts, and mix to combine well.

3 Place heaped teaspoonfuls of the dough 5cm/2in apart on the baking sheets. Bake in the oven until lightly coloured, about 10–15 minutes. Transfer to a wire rack to cool.

Variations
All chocolate: *substitute 15ml/1tbsp unsweetened cocoa powder for the same quantity of flour, and omit the vanilla.*
Mocha: *Use coffee essence instead of vanilla extract.*
Macadamia nut or hazelnut: *instead of the walnuts add whole or coarsely chopped macadamia nuts or hazelnuts.*
Dried fruit: *instead of the walnuts and chocolate chips add chopped dried fruit, such as rains, sultanas (golden raisins), glacé (candied) cherries, or tropical fruit.*
Banana: *substitute a ripe, mashed banana and 50g/2oz/¼ cup chopped banana chips for the walnuts and chocolate chips.*

Energy 139kcal/582kJ; Fat 7.7g, Saturated Fat 3.9g; Carbohydrate 16.7g, Fibre 0.5g

Almond Tile Cookies

Light and delicate as a feather and truly delicious, these cookies make the perfect accompaniment to a creamy dessert.

Makes about 24

65g/2½oz/scant ½ cup whole blanched almonds, lightly toasted
65g/2½oz/5 tbsp caster (superfine) sugar
40g/1½oz/3 tbsp unsalted (sweet) butter, softened
2 egg whites
2.5ml/½ tsp almond extract
40g/1½oz/⅓ cup plain (all-purpose) flour, sifted
50g/2oz/½ cup flaked (sliced) almonds

1 Preheat the oven to 200°C/400°F/Gas 6. Thoroughly grease two baking sheets. Place the almonds and 30ml/2 tbsp of the sugar in a blender or food processor and process until finely ground, but not forming a paste.

2 Beat the butter until creamy, add the remaining sugar and beat until light and fluffy.

3 Gradually beat in the egg whites until the mixture is well blended, then beat in the almond extract.

4 Sift the flour over the butter mixture and fold in, then fold in the almond mixture.

5 Drop tablespoonfuls of the mixture on to the baking sheets 15cm/6in apart. With the back of a wet spoon, spread each mound into a paper-thin 7.5cm/3in circle. Sprinkle with the flaked almonds.

6 Bake the cookies, one sheet at a time, for 5–6 minutes, or until the edges are golden and the centres still pale.

7 Remove the baking sheet to a wire rack and, working quickly, use a metal spatula to loosen the edges of a cookie. Lift the cookie on the metal spatula and place over a rolling pin, then press down the sides of the cookie to curve it. Repeat with the remaining cookies, and leave to cool.

Energy 59kcal/246kJ; Fat 4.1g, Saturated Fat 1.1g; Carbohydrate 4.5g, Fibre 0.4g

Brittany Butter Cookies

These little cookies are similar to shortbread, but they are richer in taste and texture.

Makes 18–20

6 egg yolks, lightly beaten
15ml/1 tbsp milk
250g/9oz/2¼ cups plain (all-purpose) flour
175g/6oz/generous ¾ cup caster (superfine) sugar
200g/7oz/scant 1 cup lightly salted butter at room temperature, cut into small pieces

1 Preheat the oven to 180°C/350°F/Gas 4. Lightly butter a large baking sheet. Mix 15ml/1 tbsp of the egg yolks with the milk for a glaze. Set aside.

2 Sift the flour into a large bowl and make a central well. Add the egg yolks, sugar and butter and, using your fingertips, work them together until smooth and creamy. Gradually blend in the flour to form a smooth but slightly sticky dough.

3 Using floured hands, pat out the dough to 8mm/⅓in thick and cut out circles using a 7.5cm/3in cookie cutter.

4 Transfer the circles to the baking sheet, brush with egg glaze, then score to create a lattice pattern.

5 Bake for 12–15 minutes, or until golden. Cool on the baking sheet on a wire rack for 15 minutes, then transfer to the wire rack to cool completely.

Variation

To make a large Brittany Butter Cake, pat the dough with well-floured hands into a greased 23cm/9in loose-based cake tin (pan) or springform tin. Brush with the egg and milk glaze, and score the lattice pattern on the top. Bake for 45–60 minutes, or until firm to the touch and golden brown. Cool in the tin for 15 minutes before carefully turning out on to a rack to cool completely.

Energy 170kcal/711kJ; Fat 10g, Saturated Fat 5.7g; Carbohydrate 19g, Fibre 0.4g

Ginger Florentines

These colourful, chewy cookies are delicious served with vanilla or other flavoured ice cream.

Makes 30

50g/2oz/¼ cup butter
115g/4oz/generous ½ cup caster (superfine) sugar
50g/2oz/¼ cup mixed glacé (candied) cherries, chopped
25g/1oz/generous 1 tbsp candied orange peel, chopped
50g/2oz/½ cup flaked (sliced) almonds
50g/2oz/½ cup chopped walnuts
25g/1oz/1 tbsp glacé (candied) ginger, chopped
30ml/2 tbsp plain (all-purpose) flour
2.5ml/½ tsp ground ginger

To finish

50g/2oz plain (semisweet) chocolate, melted
50g/2oz white chocolate, melted

1 Preheat the oven to 180°C/350°F/Gas 4. Beat the butter and sugar together until light and fluffy.

2 Add the glacé cherries, candied orange peel, flaked almonds, chopped walnuts and glacé ginger to the mixture, and blend thoroughly. Sift the plain flour and ground ginger into the mixture and stir well to combine.

3 Line some baking sheets with non-stick baking paper. Put four small spoonfuls of the mixture on to each sheet, spacing them well apart to allow for spreading. Flatten the cookies and bake for 5 minutes.

4 Remove the cookies from the oven and flatten with a wet fork, shaping them into neat rounds.

5 Return to the oven for about 3–4 minutes, until they are golden brown. Work in batches if necessary.

6 Let them cool on the baking sheets for 2 minutes to firm up, and then transfer them to a wire rack. When they are cold and firm, spread plain chocolate on the undersides of half the cookies and white chocolate on the undersides of the rest. Allow the chocolate to set before serving.

Energy 71kcal/298kJ; Fat 3.9g, Saturated Fat 1.3g; Carbohydrate 8.6g, Fibre 0.3g

Festive Cookies

Dainty, hand-painted cookies look delightful served at Christmas. These are great fun for children to make as presents, and any shape of cookie cutter can be used.

Makes about 12

75g/3oz/6 tbsp butter
50g/2oz/½ cup icing (confectioners') sugar
finely grated rind of 1 small lemon
1 egg yolk
175g/6oz/1½ cups plain (all-purpose) flour
a pinch of salt

To decorate

2 egg yolks
red and green food colouring

1 Beat the butter, icing sugar and lemon rind together until pale and fluffy. Beat in the egg yolk, and then sift in the flour and the salt. Knead together to form a smooth dough. Wrap and chill for 30 minutes.

2 Preheat the oven to 190°C/375°F/Gas 5 and lightly grease two baking sheets.

3 On a lightly floured surface, roll out the dough to 3mm/⅛in thick. Using a 6cm/2½in fluted cutter, stamp out as many cookies as you can, with the cutter dipped in flour to prevent it from sticking to the dough.

4 Transfer the cookies to the prepared baking sheets. Mark the tops lightly with a 2.5cm/1in holly leaf cutter and use a 5mm/¼in plain piping (icing) nozzle for the berries. Chill for 10 minutes, until firm.

5 Meanwhile, to make the decoration put each egg yolk into a small cup. Mix red food colouring into one and green food colouring into the other. Using a small, clean paintbrush, carefully paint the colours on to the cookies.

6 Bake for 10–12 minutes, or until they begin to colour around the edges. Let them cool slightly on the baking sheets, then transfer to a wire rack to cool completely.

Energy 118kcal/494kJ; Fat 5.8g, Saturated Fat 3.4g; Carbohydrate 15.7g, Fibre 0.5g

Traditional Sugar Cookies

These lovely old-fashioned cookies would be ideal to serve at an elegant tea party.

Makes 36

350g/12oz/3 cups plain (all-purpose) flour
5ml/1 tsp bicarbonate of soda (baking soda)
10ml/2 tsp baking powder
1.5ml/¼ tsp freshly grated nutmeg
115g/4oz/½ cup butter or margarine, at room temperature
225g/8oz/generous 1 cup caster (superfine) sugar
2.5ml/½ tsp vanilla extract
1 egg
120ml/4fl oz/½ cup milk
coloured or demerara (raw) sugar, for sprinkling

1 Sift the flour, bicarbonate of soda, baking powder and nutmeg into a small bowl. Set aside. Cream the butter or margarine, caster sugar and vanilla extract together until the mixture is light and fluffy. Add the egg and beat to mix well.

2 Add the flour mixture alternately with the milk, stirring with a wooden spoon to make a soft dough. Wrap the dough in clear film and chill for 30 minutes.

3 Preheat the oven to 180°C/350°F/Gas 4. Roll out the dough on a lightly floured surface to a 3mm/⅛in thickness. Cut into circles with a cookie cutter.

4 Transfer the cookies to ungreased baking sheets. Sprinkle each one with sugar. Bake until golden, 10–12 minutes. With a metal spatula, transfer the cookies to a wire rack to cool.

Variation
Transform these cookies into funky flower-power cookies for a children's party by omitting the final sprinkling of sugar and icing them when cold. Spoon a little icing on to the top of each cookie and spread into a circle, then top with a sugared flower. Choose wildly contrasting colours or dainty pastel shades for the icings and flowers.

Energy 85kcal/359kJ; Fat 3g, Saturated Fat 1.8g; Carbohydrate 14.3g, Fibre 0.3g

Spicy Pepper Cookies

Don't be put off by their peppery name – try these warmly spiced cookies and you are sure to be pleasantly surprised by their fabulous flavour. They are also very quick and easy to make.

Makes 48

200g/7oz/1¾ cups plain (all-purpose) flour
50g/2oz/½ cup cornflour (cornstarch)
10ml/2 tsp baking powder
2.5ml/½ tsp ground cardamom
2.5ml/½ tsp ground cinnamon
2.5ml/½ tsp freshly grated nutmeg
2.5ml/½ tsp ground ginger
2.5ml/½ tsp ground allspice
2.5ml/½ tsp salt
2.5ml/½ tsp freshly ground black pepper
225g/8oz/1 cup butter or margarine, at room temperature
90g/3½oz/scant ½ cup soft light brown sugar
2.5ml/½ tsp vanilla extract
5ml/1 tsp finely grated lemon rind
50ml/2fl oz/¼ cup whipping cream
75g/3oz/¾ cup finely ground almonds
50ml/2 tbsp icing (confectioners') sugar

1 Preheat the oven to 180°C/350°F/Gas 4. Sift the flour, cornflour, baking powder, spices, salt and pepper into a bowl. Set aside.

2 Using an electric mixer, cream the butter or margarine and brown sugar until light and fluffy. Beat in the vanilla extract and lemon rind.

3 With the mixer on low speed, add the flour mixture alternately with the cream, beginning and ending with flour. Stir in the ground almonds.

4 Shape the dough into 2cm/¾in balls. Place them on ungreased baking sheets about 2.5cm/1in apart. Bake until golden brown underneath, about 15–20 minutes.

5 Leave to cool on the baking sheets for about 1 minute before transferring to a wire rack to cool completely. Before serving, sprinkle lightly with icing sugar.

Energy 75kcal/314kJ; Fat 5.2g, Saturated Fat 2.8g; Carbohydrate 6.8g, Fibre 0.2g

Sultana Cornmeal Cookies

These little yellow cookies come from the Veneto region of Italy, and contain Marsala wine, which gives them a rich flavour and enhances their regional appeal. Excellent served with a glass of wine.

Makes about 48

65g/2½oz/½ cup sultanas (golden raisins)
50g/2oz/½ cup finely ground yellow cornmeal
175g/6oz/1½ cups plain (all-purpose) flour
7.5ml/1½ tsp baking powder
a pinch of salt
225g/8oz/1 cup butter
200g/7oz/1 cup sugar
2 eggs
15ml/1 tbsp Marsala or 5ml/1 tsp vanilla extract

1 Soak the sultanas in a small bowl of warm water for about 15 minutes. Drain.

2 Preheat the oven to 180°C/350°F/Gas 4, and grease a baking sheet. Sift the cornmeal and flour, the baking powder and the salt together into a bowl.

3 Cream the butter and sugar together until light and fluffy. Beat in the eggs, one at a time. Beat in the Marsala or vanilla extract.

4 Add the dry ingredients to the batter, beating until well blended. Stir in the sultanas.

5 Drop heaped teaspoonfuls of batter on to the prepared baking sheet in rows about 5cm/2in apart. Bake for 7–8 minutes, or until the cookies are golden brown at the edges. Remove to a wire rack to cool.

Cook's Tip

Marsala is a fortified wine with an alcohol level of around 20 per cent. There are sweet and dry types; use the sweet wine to give this recipe an authentic flavour.

Energy 74kcal/311kJ; Fat 4.2g, Saturated Fat 2.5g; Carbohydrate 8.9g, Fibre 0.2g

Mexican Cinnamon Cookies

Pastelitos are traditional sweet shortbreads served at weddings in Mexico, dusted with icing sugar to match the bride's dress.

Makes 20

115g/4oz/½ cup butter
25g/1oz/2 tbsp caster (superfine) sugar
115g/4oz/1 cup plain (all-purpose) flour
50g/2oz/½ cup cornflour (cornstarch)
1.5ml/¼ tsp ground cinnamon
30ml/2 tbsp chopped mixed nuts
25g/1oz/¼ cup icing (confectioners') sugar, sifted

1 Preheat the oven to 160°C/325°F/Gas 3. Lightly grease a baking sheet. Place the butter and sugar in a bowl and beat until pale and creamy.

2 Sift the plain flour, cornflour and ground cinnamon into the butter and sugar mixture, and gradually work in with a wooden spoon until the mixture comes together. Knead the dough lightly until completely smooth.

3 Take tablespoonfuls of the mixture, roll into 20 small balls and arrange on the baking sheet. Press a few chopped nuts into the top of each one and then flatten slightly.

4 Bake the cookies for about 30–35 minutes, or until pale golden. Remove from the oven and, while they are still warm, toss them in the sifted icing sugar. Leave the cookies to cool on a wire rack before serving.

Cook's Tip

Choose two or three types of nut for this recipe. Cashew nuts, walnuts, raw skinned peanuts, almonds or hazelnuts all work well. Or choose from pecan nuts, pistachio nuts or macadamia nuts for a richer flavour. Make sure the nuts are chopped finely if small children are going to eat the cookies. You could even use some sesame seeds with the nuts if you like.

Energy 91kcal/382kJ; Fat 5.8g, Saturated Fat 3.1g; Carbohydrate 9.5g, Fibre 0.2g

Meringues

You can make these classic meringues as large or small as you like.

Makes about 24 small meringues

4 egg whites
1.5ml/¼ tsp salt
275g/10oz/scant 1¼ cups caster (superfine) sugar
2.5ml/½ tsp vanilla or almond extract (optional)

To serve

250ml/8fl oz/1 cup whipping cream

1 Preheat the oven to 110°C/225°F/Gas ¼. Grease and flour two large baking sheets.

2 Beat the egg whites and salt in a metal bowl. When they start to form soft peaks, add half the sugar and continue beating until the mixture holds stiff peaks.

3 With a large metal spoon, fold in the remaining sugar and the vanilla or almond extract, if using.

4 Pipe or spoon the mixture on to the prepared baking sheets. Bake them for 2 hours, then turn off the oven. Loosen the meringues, invert, and set in another place on the baking sheets to prevent them from sticking.

5 Leave the meringues in the oven until they are cool. Whip the cream and use to sandwich the meringues together in pairs.

Variation

To make decorative Meringue Squiggles, line a baking sheet with parchment paper. Make half the amount of meringue mixture given above. Using a large plain nozzle, pipe squiggles about 13cm/5in long on to the baking sheet. Bake for 1 hour. Remove from the oven and leave to cool. Mix the icing sugar with a little water and brush over the meringues. Decorate with sugar sprinkles and serve on their own or with fruit salad and vanilla ice cream.

Energy 78kcal/334kJ; Fat 0.4g, Saturated Fat 0g; Carbohydrate 18.9g, Fibre 0.3g

Toasted Oat Meringues

Try these oaty meringues for a lovely crunchy change.

Makes 12

50g/2oz/generous ½ cup rolled oats
2 egg whites
1.5ml/¼ tsp salt
7.5ml/1½ tsp cornflour (cornstarch)
175g/6oz/¾ cup caster (superfine) sugar

1 Preheat the oven to 140°C/275°F/Gas 1. Spread the oats on a baking sheet and toast in the oven until golden. Lower the heat to 120°C/250°F/Gas ½. Grease and flour a baking sheet.

2 Beat the egg whites and salt until they start to form soft peaks. Sift over the cornflour and continue beating until the whites hold stiff peaks. Add half the sugar; whisk until glossy. Add the remaining sugar and fold in carefully. Fold in the toasted oats.

3 Place tablespoonfuls of the mixture on to the baking sheet and bake for 2 hours, then turn off the oven. Turn over the meringues, and leave in the oven until completely cool.

Chewy Walnut Cookies

Makes 18

4 egg whites
275g/10oz/2½ cups icing (confectioners') sugar
5ml/1 tsp cooled strong coffee
115g/4oz/1 cup finely chopped walnuts

1 Preheat the oven to 180°C/350°F/Gas 4. Line two baking sheets with baking parchment and then grease the paper. Using an electric mixer beat the egg whites until frothy. Sift over the icing sugar and add the coffee.

2 Add 15ml/1 tbsp water, beat on low speed to blend, then on high until thick. Fold in the walnuts. Place spoonfuls of the mixture 2.5cm/1in apart on the sheets. Bake for 12–15 minutes. Transfer to a wire rack to cool.

Top: Energy 87kcal/364kJ; Fat 4.2g, Saturated Fat 2.6g; Carbohydrate 12.3g, Fibre 0g
Above: Energy 107Kcal/449kJ; Fat 4.4g; Saturated fat 0.4g; Carbohydrate 16.2g; Fibre 0.2g

Lavender Cookies

Makes about 30
150g/5oz/⅔ cup butter
115g/4oz/generous ½ cup caster (superfine) sugar
1 egg, beaten
15ml/1 tbsp dried lavender flowers
175g/6oz/1½ cups self-raising (self-rising) flour
leaves and flowers, to decorate

1 Preheat the oven to 180°C/350°F/Gas 4. Grease two baking sheets. Cream the butter and sugar together, then stir in the egg. Mix in the lavender flowers and the flour.

2 Drop spoonfuls of the mixture on to the baking sheets. Bake for 15–20 minutes, or until the cookies are golden. Serve with some fresh leaves and flowers to decorate.

Amaretti

Makes 36
200g/7oz/1¾ cups blanched almonds
plain (all-purpose) flour for dusting
225g/8oz/generous 1 cup caster (superfine) sugar
2 egg whites
2.5ml/½ tsp almond extract
icing (confectioners') sugar, for dusting

1 Preheat the oven to 160°C/325°F/Gas 3. Spread the almonds on a baking sheet and dry them out in the oven, without browning, for 15 minutes. Turn the oven off.

2 Leave the almonds to cool, then dust with flour. Grind with half the sugar. Whisk the egg whites until soft peaks form. Gradually whisk in half the remaining sugar until stiff peaks form. Fold in the remaining sugar, the almonds and the extract.

3 Pipe in walnut-sized rounds on to a greased baking sheet. Sprinkle with icing sugar and leave to stand for 2 hours. Preheat the oven to 180°C/350°F/Gas 4 and bake for 15 minutes. Cool on a wire rack.

Top: Energy 74kcal/310kJ; Fat 4.4g, Saturated Fat 2.7g; Carbohydrate 8.4g, Fibre 0.2g
Above: Energy 59Kcal/249kJ; Fat 3.1g; Saturated fat 0.2g; Carbohydrate 6.9g; Fibre 0.4g

Chocolate Amaretti

Although it is always said that chocolate does not go with wine, enjoy these delightful cookies Italian-style with a glass of chilled champagne.

Makes 24
150g/5oz/scant 1 cup blanched, toasted whole almonds
115g/4oz/generous ½ cup caster (superfine) sugar
15ml/1 tbsp unsweetened cocoa powder
30ml/2 tbsp icing (confectioners') sugar
2 egg whites
a pinch of cream of tartar
5ml/1 tsp almond extract
flaked almonds, to decorate

1 Preheat the oven to 160°C/325°F/Gas 3. Line a large baking sheet with non-stick baking paper or foil. In a food processor fitted with a metal blade, process the toasted almonds with half the sugar until they are finely ground but not oily. Transfer to a bowl and sift in the cocoa and icing sugar; stir to blend. Set aside.

2 Beat the egg whites and cream of tartar until stiff peaks form. Sprinkle in the remaining sugar 15ml/1 tbsp at a time, beating well after each addition, and continue beating until the whites are glossy and stiff. Beat in the almond extract.

3 Sprinkle over the almond mixture and gently fold into the egg whites until just blended. Spoon the mixture into a large piping (icing) bag fitted with a plain 1cm/½in nozzle. Pipe 4cm/1½in rounds, 2.5cm/1in apart, on the baking sheet. Press a flaked almond into the centre of each.

4 Bake the cookies for 12–15 minutes, or until they appear crisp. Remove the baking sheet to a wire rack to cool for 10 minutes. With a metal spatula, remove the cookies to the wire rack to cool completely.

Variation
As an alternative decoration, lightly press a few coffee sugar crystals on top of each cookie before baking.

Energy 66kcal/278kJ; Fat 3.6g, Saturated Fat 0.4g; Carbohydrate 7.2g, Fibre 0.5g

Melting Moments

These cookies are very crisp and light – and they really do melt in your mouth.

Makes 16–20

40g/1½oz/3 tbsp butter or margarine
65g/2½oz/5 tbsp lard or white cooking fat
75g/3oz/scant ½ cup caster (superfine) sugar
½ egg, beaten
a few drops of vanilla or almond extract
150g/5oz/1¼ cups self-raising (self-rising) flour
rolled oats, for coating
4–5 glacé (candied) cherries, quartered, to decorate

1 Preheat the oven to 180°C/350°F/Gas 4, and grease two baking sheets.

2 Beat together the butter or margarine, lard and sugar, then gradually beat in the egg and vanilla or almond extract.

3 Stir the flour into the beaten mixture, with floured hands, then roll into 16–20 small balls. Spread the rolled oats on a sheet of baking parchment and toss the balls in them to coat evenly.

4 Place the balls, spaced slightly apart, on the baking sheets, place a piece of cherry on top of each and bake for about 15–20 minutes, or until lightly browned.

5 Allow the cookies to cool on the sheets for 5 minutes before transferring to a wire rack to cool completely.

Cook's Tips

- *The meltingly short texture for these cookies is achieved by using two different kinds of fat. Lard, made from processed pure pork fat, is often used to make light pastries; use a vegetarian white cooking fat (shortening) if you prefer. The butter adds richness and flavour.*
- *To halve an egg, beat a whole egg in a measuring jug (cup) and then pour off half.*

Energy 88kcal/370kJ; Fat 5g, Saturated fat 2.4g; Carbohydrate 10.9g, Fibre 0.3g

Easter Cookies

Traditionally butter could not be eaten during the Lenten fast, so these cookies were a welcome Easter treat.

Makes 16–18

115g/4oz/½ cup butter or margarine
75g/3oz/scant ½ cup caster (superfine) sugar, plus extra for sprinkling
1 egg, separated
200g/7oz/1¾ cups plain (all-purpose) flour
2.5ml/½ tsp mixed (apple pie) spice
2.5ml/½ tsp ground cinnamon
50g/2oz/¼ cup currants
15ml/1 tbsp mixed chopped (candied) peel
15–30ml/1–2 tbsp milk

1 Preheat the oven to 200°C/400°F/Gas 6. Lightly grease two baking sheets. Cream together the butter or margarine and sugar until light and fluffy, then beat in the egg yolk.

2 Sift the flour, mixed spice and cinnamon over the egg mixture in the bowl, then fold in with the currants and chopped mixed peel, adding sufficient milk to make a fairly soft dough.

3 Turn the dough on to a floured surface, knead lightly until just smooth, then roll out using a floured rolling pin, to about a 5mm/¼in thickness. Cut the dough into circles using a 5cm/2in fluted cookie cutter. Transfer the circles to the baking sheets and bake for 10 minutes.

4 Beat the egg white, then brush over the cookies. Sprinkle with caster sugar and return to the oven for a further 10 minutes, until golden. Using a metal spatula transfer to a wire rack to cool.

Cook's Tip

Cinnamon is one of the exceptions to the rule that you should, if possible, buy spices whole and grind them freshly when you need them. Although cinnamon sticks are widely available, they are difficult – almost impossible – to grind yourself.

Energy 116kcal/485kJ; Fat 5.7g, Saturated Fat 3.4g; Carbohydrate 15.4g, Fibre 0.4g

Shortbread

Once you have tasted this shortbread, you'll never buy a packet from a shop again.

Makes 8

150g/5oz/generous ½ cup unsalted (sweet) butter, at room temperature
115g/4oz/generous ½ cup caster (superfine) sugar
150g/5oz/1¼ cups plain (all-purpose) flour
65g/2½oz/generous ½ cup rice flour
1.5ml/¼ tsp baking powder
1.5ml/¼ tsp salt

1 Preheat the oven to 160°C/325°F/Gas 3. Lightly grease a 20cm/8in shallow round cake tin (pan) or an 18cm/7in square tin and set aside until needed.

2 Cream the butter and sugar together until light and fluffy. Sift over the flours, baking powder and salt, and mix well.

3 Press the mixture neatly into the prepared tin, smoothing the surface with the back of a spoon. Prick all over with a fork, then score into eight equal wedges or into fingers.

4 Bake until golden, about 40–45 minutes. Leave in the tin until cool enough to handle, then unmould and recut the wedges while still hot. Store in an airtight container.

Variation

To make a party sensation for children – Jewelled Shortbread Fingers – bake the shortbread in a greased 18cm/7in square tin (pan). Score the shortbread into fingers when warm and cut when cold. (Use a serrated knife and a sawing action to cut the shortbread neatly.) Make a fairly thin icing using 150g/5oz/1¼ cups icing (confectioners') sugar mixed with 10–15ml/2–3 tbsp lemon juice, and use to drizzle over the shortbread fingers in a random zigzag pattern. Crush some brightly coloured boiled sweets (hard candies) using a rolling pin and sprinkle them over the icing so that they stick. Add a few gold or silver edible balls to each decorated finger.

Energy 290kcal/1212kJ; Fat 15.7g, Saturated Fat 9.8g; Carbohydrate 36.2g, Fibre 0.8g

Flapjacks

For a spicier version, add 5ml/1 tsp ground ginger to the melted butter.

Makes 8

50g/2oz/¼ cup butter
20ml/1 rounded tbsp golden (light corn) syrup
65g/2½oz/scant ½ cup soft dark brown sugar
115g/4oz/⅔ cup rolled oats
1.5ml/¼ tsp salt

1 Preheat the oven to 180°C/350°F/Gas 4. Line and grease a 20cm/8in shallow round cake tin (pan) or an 18cm/7in square tin. Place the butter, golden syrup and sugar in a pan over a low heat. Cook, stirring, until melted and combined.

2 Remove from the heat and add the oats and salt. Stir the mixture to blend. Spoon the mixture into the prepared tin and smooth the surface. Place in the centre of the oven and bake until golden brown, 20–25 minutes.

3 Leave in the tin until cool enough to handle, then unmould and cut into wedges or fingers while still hot. Store in an airtight container.

Variations

Let your imagination go wild with variations on the flapjack theme.
Apricot and Pecan: *substitute maple syrup for the golden (light corn) syrup and add 50g/2oz/½ cup chopped pecan nuts and 50g/2oz/¼ cup chopped ready-to-eat dried apricots.*
Lemon: *substitute Demerara (raw) sugar for the soft dark brown sugar and add the juice and grated rind of 1 lemon.*
Honey and seed: *substitute honey for the golden (light corn) syrup and add 30ml/2 tbsp sesame or sunflower seeds.*
Fruit: *add 50g/2oz/scant ½ cup raisins, sultanas (golden raisins) or dried tropical fruit.*
Chocolate: *add 50g/2oz chocolate drops or chopped chocolate with some dried fruit as well, if you like.*
Apple: *add a peeled and cored apple cut into small pieces for a softer flapjack.*

Energy 144kcal/604kJ; Fat 6.4g, Saturated Fat 3.3g; Carbohydrate 21g, Fibre 1g

Chocolate Delights

Simple and delicious, this method of making cookies ensures they are all of a uniform size.

Makes 50

25g/1oz plain (semisweet) chocolate
25g/1oz dark (bittersweet) cooking chocolate
225g/8oz/2 cups plain (all-purpose) flour
2.5ml/½ tsp salt
225g/8oz/1 cup unsalted (sweet) butter, at room temperature
225g/8oz/generous 1 cup caster (superfine) sugar
2 eggs
5ml/1 tsp vanilla extract
115g/4oz/1 cup finely chopped walnuts

1 Melt the chocolate in the top of a double boiler, or in a heatproof bowl set over a pan of gently simmering water. Set aside. In a bowl, sift together the flour and salt. Set aside.

2 Cream the butter until soft. Add the sugar and continue beating until the mixture is light and fluffy. Mix the eggs and vanilla extract, then gradually stir into the butter mixture. Stir in the chocolate, then the flour. Finally, stir in the nuts.

3 Divide the mixture into four equal parts, and roll each into a 5cm/2in diameter log. Wrap tightly in foil and chill or freeze until firm.

4 Preheat the oven to 190°C/375°F/Gas 5. Grease two baking sheets. With a sharp knife, cut the logs into 5mm/¼in slices. Place the circles on the baking sheets and bake until lightly coloured, about 10 minutes. Using a metal spatula, transfer to a wire rack to cool.

Variation

Try other nuts in this recipe, such as almonds, or use 50g/2oz/scant ½ cup chopped ready-to-eat dried apricots, peaches or dates and halve the amount of nuts used. Almonds and apricots make a particularly pleasing combination, or try dates and pecan nuts.

Energy 90kcal/377kJ; Fat 5.8g, Saturated Fat 2.7g; Carbohydrate 8.9g, Fibre 0.2g

Cinnamon Treats

Place these cookies in a heart-shaped basket, as here, and serve them up with love.

Makes 50

250g/9oz/2¼ cups plain (all-purpose) flour
2.5ml/½ tsp salt
10ml/2 tsp ground cinnamon
225g/8oz/1 cup unsalted (sweet) butter, at room temperature
225g/8oz/generous 1 cup caster (superfine) sugar
2 eggs
5ml/1 tsp vanilla extract

1 Sift the flour, salt and ground cinnamon together in a bowl. Set aside.

2 Cream the butter until soft. Add the sugar and continue beating until the mixture is light and fluffy. Beat the eggs and vanilla extract together, then gradually stir into the butter mixture. Stir in the dry ingredients.

3 Divide the mixture into four equal parts, then roll each into a 5cm/2in diameter log. Wrap the mixture tightly in foil and chill or freeze until it is firm.

4 Preheat the oven to 190°C/375°F/Gas 5. Grease two baking sheets. With a sharp knife, cut the logs into 5mm/¼in slices. Place the rounds on the baking sheets and bake until lightly coloured, about 10 minutes. Using a metal spatula, transfer to a wire rack to cool.

Variation

Transform these treats into sandwiched creams by making a chocolate orange butter icing. Cream together 50g/2oz/¼ cup butter and 75g/3oz/¾ cup icing (confectioner's) sugar until smooth. Add the grated rind of an orange. Blend 15ml/1 tbsp unsweetened cocoa powder with 15ml/1 tbsp water and add to the icing. Blend until smooth. Spread a little of the butter icing on to the flat side of a cookie and sandwich with another. Repeat with the remaining cookies.

Energy 71kcal/298kJ; Fat 4g, Saturated Fat 2.4g; Carbohydrate 8.6g, Fibre 0.2g

Chunky Chocolate Drops

Do not allow these cookies to cool completely on the baking sheet or they will break when you lift them.

Makes 18

175g/6oz plain (semisweet) chocolate
115g/4oz/½ cup unsalted (sweet) butter
2 eggs
90g/3½oz/½ cup caster (superfine) sugar
50g/2oz/¼ cup (packed) soft light brown sugar
40g/1½oz/⅓ cup plain (all-purpose) flour
25g/1oz/¼ cup unsweetened cocoa powder
5ml/1 tsp baking powder
10ml/2 tsp vanilla extract
pinch of salt
115g/4oz/⅔ cup pecan nuts, toasted and coarsely chopped
175g/6oz/1 cup plain (semisweet) chocolate chips
115g/4oz fine quality white chocolate, chopped into 5mm/¼in pieces
115g/4oz fine quality milk chocolate, chopped into 5mm/¼in pieces

1 Preheat the oven to 160°C/325°F/Gas 3. Grease two large baking sheets.

2 In a medium pan over a low heat, melt the plain chocolate and butter until smooth, stirring frequently. Remove from the heat to cool slightly.

3 Beat the eggs with the sugars until pale and creamy. Gradually beat in the melted chocolate mixture. Beat in the flour, cocoa, baking powder, vanilla extract and salt, until just blended. Add the nuts, chocolate chips and white chocolate pieces.

4 Drop 4–6 heaped tablespoonfuls of the mixture on to each baking sheet 10cm/4in apart and flatten each to a round about 7.5cm/3in. Bake for 8–10 minutes, or until the tops are shiny and cracked and the edges look crisp.

5 Cool the cookies on the baking sheets for about 2 minutes, or until they are just set, then remove them to a wire rack to cool completely.

Energy 301kcal/1256kJ; Fat 20g, Saturated Fat 9.7g; Carbohydrate 28.4g, Fibre 1g

Chocolate Crackle-tops

These dainty treats are always popular and are best eaten on the day they are baked, as they dry slightly on storage.

Makes 38

200g/7oz plain (semisweet) chocolate, chopped
90g/3½oz/7 tbsp unsalted (sweet) butter
115g/4oz/generous ½ cup caster (superfine) sugar
3 eggs
5ml/1 tsp vanilla extract
215g/7½oz/scant 2 cups plain (all-purpose) flour
25g/1oz/¼ cup unsweetened cocoa powder
2.5ml/½ tsp baking powder
a pinch of salt
175g/6oz/1½ cups icing (confectioners') sugar, for coating

1 Heat the chocolate and butter over a low heat until smooth, stirring frequently. Remove from the heat. Stir in the sugar, and continue stirring until dissolved. Add the eggs, one at a time, beating well after each addition; stir in the vanilla.

2 In a separate bowl, sift together the flour, cocoa, baking powder and salt. Gradually stir into the chocolate mixture until just blended. Cover and chill for at least 1 hour.

3 Preheat the oven to 160°C/325°F/Gas 3. Grease two or three large baking sheets. Place the icing sugar in a small, deep bowl. Using a teaspoon, scoop the dough into small balls and roll in your hands into 4cm/1½in balls.

4 Drop the balls, one at a time, into the icing sugar and roll until heavily coated. Remove each ball with a slotted spoon and tap against the bowl to remove any excess sugar. Place on the baking sheets 4cm/1½in apart.

5 Bake the cookies for 10–15 minutes, or until the tops feel slightly firm when touched with your fingertip.

6 Remove the baking sheets to a wire rack for 2–3 minutes, then remove the cookies to the wire rack to cool.

Energy 102kcal/428kJ; Fat 4.1g, Saturated Fat 2.3g; Carbohydrate 15.8g, Fibre 0.4g

Chocolate and Coconut Slices

These are easier to slice if they cool overnight.

Makes 24

175g/6oz/2 cups crushed digestive cookies (graham crackers)
50g/2oz/¼ cup caster (superfine) sugar
a pinch of salt
115g/4oz/½ cup butter or margarine, melted
75g/3oz/1 cup desiccated (dry unsweetened shredded) coconut
250g/9oz plain (semisweet) chocolate chips
250ml/8fl oz/1 cup sweetened condensed milk
115g/4oz/1 cup chopped walnuts

1 Preheat the oven to 180°C/350°F/Gas 4. In a bowl, combine the crushed digestive cookies, sugar, salt and butter or margarine. Press the mixture evenly over the base of an ungreased 33 x 23cm/13 x 9in baking dish.

2 Sprinkle the coconut over the cookie base, then scatter over the chocolate chips. Pour the condensed milk evenly over the chocolate. Sprinkle the walnuts on top. Bake in the oven for 30 minutes. Unmould and leave to cool before slicing.

Coconut Pyramids

Makes 15

225g/8oz/1 cup desiccated (dry unsweetened shredded) coconut
115g/4oz/generous ½ cup caster (superfine) sugar
2 egg whites

1 Preheat the oven to 190°C/375°F/Gas 5. Grease a baking sheet. Mix together the coconut and sugar. Lightly whisk the egg whites and fold enough into the coconut to make a firm mixture.

2 Form teaspoonfuls of the mixture into pyramids. Flatten the base and press the top into a point. Place on the baking sheet and bake for 12–15 minutes on a low shelf; the tips should be golden. Use a metal spatula to loosen them but let them cool on the baking sheet before transferring to a wire rack.

Top: Energy 55kcal/233kJ; Fat 2.6g, Saturated Fat 1.5g; Carbohydrate 7.8g, Fibre 0.2g
Above: Energy 122Kcal/509kJ; Fat 9.3g; Saturated fat 8g; Carbohydrate 9g; Fibre 2.1g

Chocolate Chip Oat Cookies

Oat cookies are given a delicious lift by the inclusion of chocolate chips. Try caramel chips for a change, if you like.

Makes 60

115g/4oz/1 cup plain (all-purpose) flour
2.5ml/½ tsp bicarbonate of soda (baking soda)
1.5ml/¼ tsp baking powder
1.5ml/¼ tsp salt
115g/4oz/½ cup butter or margarine, at room temperature
115g/4oz/generous ½ cup caster (superfine) sugar
90g/3½oz/scant ½ cup soft light brown sugar
1 egg
2.5ml/½ tsp vanilla extract
75g/3oz/scant 1 cup rolled oats
175g/6oz/1 cup plain (semisweet) chocolate chips

1 Preheat the oven to 180°C/350°F/Gas 4. Grease three or four baking sheets. Sift the flour, bicarbonate of soda, baking powder and salt into a mixing bowl. Set aside.

2 With an electric mixer, cream the butter or margarine and the sugars together. Add the egg and vanilla, and beat until light and fluffy.

3 Add the flour mixture to the egg and vanilla, and beat on low speed until thoroughly blended. Stir in the rolled oats and plain chocolate chips, mixing well with a wooden spoon. The dough should be crumbly.

4 Drop heaped teaspoonfuls on to the baking sheets, about 2.5cm/1in apart. Bake until just firm around the edges but still soft in the centres, about 15 minutes. With a metal spatula, transfer the cookies to a wire rack to cool.

Variation
For an elegant look suitable to accompany a chilled dessert, melt plain (semisweet) chocolate over a pan of hot, but not boiling water, stirring until smooth. Dip each baked cookie into the chocolate to cover one half of the cookie. Leave to set before serving.

Energy 217kcal/907kJ; Fat 14.6g, Saturated Fat 7.5g; Carbohydrate 20g, Fibre 1g

Nutty Lace Wafers

Serve these delicate cookies with smooth and creamy desserts.

Makes 18

65g/2½oz/scant ½ cup blanched almonds
50g/2oz/¼ cup butter
40g/1½oz/⅓ cup plain (all-purpose) flour
90g/3½oz/½ cup caster (superfine) sugar
30ml/2 tbsp double (heavy) cream
2.5ml/½ tsp vanilla extract

1 Preheat the oven to 190°C/375°F/Gas 5. Lightly grease two baking sheets.

2 With a sharp knife, chop the almonds as finely as possible. Alternatively, use a food processor or blender to chop the nuts very finely.

3 Melt the butter in a pan over a low heat. Remove from the heat and stir in the flour, caster sugar, double cream and vanilla extract. Add the finely chopped almonds and mix well.

4 Drop teaspoonfuls 6cm/2½in apart on the prepared sheets. Bake until golden, about 5 minutes. Cool on the baking sheets briefly, just until the wafers are stiff enough to remove. With a metal spatula, transfer to a wire rack to cool.

Cook's Tip
Many cookies, like these ones here, are soft when cooked but crisp up as they cool. Don't allow them to overcook because you expect them to be firm when they come out of the oven.

Variation
Add 40g/1½oz/¼ cup finely chopped candied orange peel to the mixture at step 3.

Energy 78kcal/327kJ; Fat 5.2g, Saturated Fat 2.2g; Carbohydrate 7.2g, Fibre 0.3g

Oat Lace Rounds

These nutty cookies are very quick and easy to make and they taste delicious.

Makes 36

165g/5½oz/⅔ cup butter or margarine
130g/4½oz/1¼ cups rolled oats
170g/5¾oz/generous ¾ cup soft dark brown sugar
155g/5¼oz/generous ¾ cup caster (superfine) sugar
40g/1½oz/⅓ cup plain (all-purpose) flour
1.5ml/¼ tsp salt
1 egg, lightly beaten
5ml/1 tsp vanilla extract
65g/2½oz/generous ⅓ cup pecan nuts or walnuts, finely chopped

1 Preheat the oven to 180°C/350°F/Gas 4. Lightly grease two baking sheets. Melt the butter or margarine in a medium pan over a low heat. Set aside.

2 In a mixing bowl, combine the oats, brown sugar, caster sugar, flour and salt. Make a well in the centre and add the butter or margarine, egg and vanilla. Mix until blended, then stir in the chopped nuts.

3 Drop rounded teaspoonfuls of the mixture about 5cm/2in apart on the prepared baking sheets.

4 Bake in the oven until lightly browned on the edges and bubbling all over, about 5–8 minutes. Cool on the baking sheets for 2 minutes, then transfer to a wire rack to cool completely.

Cook's Tip
Rolled oats are also known as oatflakes and porridge oats. Fine oatmeal is also excellent for making cookies.

Variation
Substitute 5ml/1 tsp ground cinnamon for the vanilla extract for a tasty variation.

Energy 103kcal/432kJ; Fat 5.5g, Saturated Fat 2.5g; Carbohydrate 13.2g, Fibre 0.4g

Nutty Chocolate Squares

These delicious squares are incredibly rich, so cut them smaller if you wish.

Makes 16

2 eggs
10ml/2 tsp vanilla extract
1.5ml/¼ tsp salt
175g/6oz/1 cup pecan nuts, coarsely chopped
50g/2oz/½ cup plain (all-purpose) flour
50g/2oz/¼ cup caster (superfine) sugar
120ml/4fl oz/½ cup golden (light corn) syrup
75g/3oz plain (semisweet) chocolate, finely chopped
40g/1½oz/3 tbsp butter
16 pecan nut halves, to decorate

1 Preheat the oven to 160°C/325°F/Gas 3. Line the base and sides of a 20cm/8in square baking tin (pan) with baking parchment and lightly grease the paper.

2 Whisk together the eggs, vanilla extract and salt. In another bowl, mix together the chopped pecan nuts and flour. Set both aside until needed.

3 In a pan, bring the sugar and golden syrup to the boil. Watch it carefully and remove from the heat as soon as it comes to the boil. Stir in the chocolate and butter, and blend thoroughly with a wooden spoon. Mix in the beaten egg mixture, then fold in the pecan nut mixture.

4 Pour the mixture into the baking tin and bake until set, about 35 minutes. Cool in the tin for 10 minutes before unmoulding.

5 Cut into 5cm/2in squares and press pecan nut halves into the tops while warm. Cool on a wire rack.

Variation
Toasted hazelnuts also taste great in place of the pecan nuts. Simply brown the hazelnuts under a hot grill (broiler), turning them every so often. When toasted all over, leave to cool, then rub them in a clean dish towel until the skins are removed.

Energy 172kcal/719kJ; Fat 11.8g, Saturated Fat 2.9g; Carbohydrate 15.2g, Fibre 0.7g

Raisin Brownies

Cover these divine fruity brownies with a light chocolate frosting for a truly decadent treat, if you like.

Makes 16

115g/4oz/½ cup butter or margarine
50g/2oz/½ cup unsweetened cocoa powder
2 eggs
225g/8oz/generous 1 cup caster (superfine) sugar
5ml/1 tsp vanilla extract
40g/1½oz/⅓ cup plain (all-purpose) flour
75g/3oz/¾ cup finely chopped walnuts
75g/3oz/generous ½ cup raisins

1 Preheat the oven to 180°C/350°F/Gas 4. Line the base and sides of a 20cm/8in square baking tin (pan) with baking parchment and grease the paper.

2 Gently melt the butter or margarine in a small pan. Remove from the heat and stir in the cocoa powder.

3 With an electric mixer, beat the eggs, caster sugar and vanilla extract together until light. Add the cocoa and butter mixture and stir to blend.

4 Sift the flour over the cocoa mixture and gently fold in. Do not overmix.

5 Add the walnuts and raisins, and scrape the mixture into the prepared baking tin.

6 Bake in the centre of the oven for 30 minutes. Leave in the tin to cool before cutting into 5cm/2in squares and removing from the tin. The brownies should be soft and moist.

Cook's Tip
Adding dried fruit makes brownies a little more substantial and adds to their delicious flavour. Try to find Californian or Spanish raisins for the best flavour and texture.

Energy 181kcal/759kJ; Fat 10.5g, Saturated Fat 4.6g; Carbohydrate 20.4g, Fibre 0.7g

Chocolate Chip Brownies

A double dose of chocolate is incorporated into these melt-in-the-mouth brownies.

Makes 24

115g/4oz plain (semisweet) chocolate
115g/4oz/½ cup butter
3 eggs
200g/7oz/1 cup caster (superfine) sugar
2.5ml/½ tsp vanilla extract
a pinch of salt
150g/5oz/1¼ cups plain (all-purpose) flour
175g/6oz/1 cup chocolate chips

1 Preheat the oven to 180°C/350°F/Gas 4. Then line a 33 x 23cm/13 x 9in baking tin (pan) with baking parchment and grease the paper.

2 Melt the chocolate and butter together in the top of a double boiler, or in a heatproof bowl set over a pan of gently simmering water.

3 Beat together the eggs, sugar, vanilla extract and salt. Stir in the chocolate mixture. Sift over the flour and fold in. Add the chocolate chips.

4 Pour the mixture into the baking tin and spread evenly. Bake until just set, about 30 minutes. The brownies should be slightly moist inside. Leave to cool in the tin.

5 To turn out, run a knife all around the edge and invert on to a baking sheet. Remove the paper. Place another sheet on top and invert again. Cut into bars for serving.

Variations

Rich chocolate: use best quality chocolate (at least 70 per cent cocoa solids) cut into chunks to give the brownies a fantastic flavour.
Chunky choc and nut: use 75g/3oz coarsely chopped white chocolate and 75g/3oz/¾ cup chopped walnuts.
Almond: use almond extract, add 75g/3oz/¾ cup chopped almonds and reduce the chocolate chips to 75g/3oz/½ cup.

Energy 161kcal/674kJ; Fat 8.1g, Saturated Fat 4.7g; Carbohydrate 21.3g, Fibre 0.5g

Marbled Brownies

These fancy brownies have an impressive flavour as well as appearance.

Makes 24

225g/8oz plain (semisweet) chocolate
75g/3oz/6 tbsp butter
4 eggs
300g/11oz/1½ cups caster (superfine) sugar
150g/5oz/1¼ cups plain (all-purpose) flour
2.5ml/½ tsp salt
5ml/1 tsp baking powder
10ml/2 tsp vanilla extract
115g/4oz/1 cup chopped walnuts

For the plain mixture

50g/2oz/¼ cup butter, at room temperature
175g/6oz/¾ cup cream cheese
90g/3½oz/½ cups caster (superfine) sugar
2 eggs
25g/1oz/¼ cup plain (all-purpose) flour
5ml/1 tsp vanilla extract

1 Preheat the oven to 180°C/350°F/Gas 4. Line a 33 x 23cm/13 x 9in baking tin (pan) with baking parchment and grease.

2 Melt the chocolate and butter in a small pan over a very low heat, stirring. Set aside to cool. Meanwhile, beat the eggs until light and fluffy. Gradually beat in the sugar. Sift over the flour, salt and baking powder, and fold to combine.

3 Stir in the cooled chocolate mixture. Add the vanilla extract and chopped walnuts. Measure and set aside 475ml/16fl oz/2 cups of the chocolate mixture.

4 For the plain mixture, cream the butter and cream cheese with an electric mixer. Add the sugar and continue beating until blended. Beat in the eggs, flour and vanilla extract.

5 Spread the unmeasured chocolate mixture in the tin. Pour over the plain mixture. Drop spoonfuls of the reserved chocolate mixture on top.

6 With a metal spatula, swirl the mixtures to marble them. Do not blend completely. Bake until just set, 35–40 minutes. Turn out when cool and cut into squares for serving.

Energy 259kcal/1083kJ; Fat 15.1g, Saturated Fat 7.1g; Carbohydrate 28.8g, Fibre 0.6g

Oat and Date Brownies

These brownies are marvellous as a break-time treat. The secret of chewy, moist brownies is not to overcook them.

Makes 16

150g/5oz plain (semisweet) chocolate
50g/2oz/¼ cup butter
75g/3oz/scant 1 cup rolled oats
25g/1oz/3 tbsp wheatgerm
25g/1oz/⅓ cup milk powder
2.5ml/½ tsp baking powder
2.5ml/½ tsp salt
50g/2oz/½ cup chopped walnuts
50g/2oz/⅓ cup finely chopped dates
50g/2oz/¼ cup muscovado (molasses) sugar
5ml/1 tsp vanilla extract
2 eggs, beaten

1 Break the chocolate into a heatproof bowl and add the butter. Place over a pan of simmering water and stir until completely melted.

2 Cool the chocolate, stirring occasionally. Preheat the oven to 180°C/350°F/Gas 4. Grease and line a 20cm/8in square cake tin (pan).

3 Combine the oats, wheatgerm, milk powder and baking powder together in a bowl. Add the salt, walnuts, chopped dates and sugar, and mix well. Beat in the melted chocolate, vanilla and beaten eggs.

4 Pour the mixture into the cake tin, level the surface and bake in the oven for 20–25 minutes, or until firm around the edges yet still soft in the centre.

5 Cool the brownies in the tin, then chill in the fridge. When they are more solid, turn them out of the tin and cut into 16 squares.

Cook's Tip
When melting chocolate always make sure that the water in the pan does not touch the bowl, or it might bubble up the side of the bowl and splash into the chocolate, changing its texture.

Energy 138kcal/577kJ; Fat 8.6g, Saturated Fat 3.6g; Carbohydrate 13.3g, Fibre 1g

Banana Chocolate Brownies

Nuts traditionally give brownies their chewy texture. Here oat bran is used instead, creating a wonderful alternative.

Makes 9

75ml/5 tbsp unsweetened cocoa powder
15ml/1 tbsp caster (superfine) sugar
75ml/5 tbsp milk
3 large bananas, mashed
215g/7½oz/scant 1 cup soft light brown sugar
5ml/1 tsp vanilla extract
5 egg whites
75g/3oz/⅔ cup self-raising (self-rising) flour
75g/3oz/⅔ cup oat bran
icing (confectioners') sugar, for dusting

1 Preheat the oven to 180°C/350°F/Gas 4. Line a 20cm/8in square cake tin (pan) with non-stick baking paper.

2 Blend the cocoa powder and caster sugar with the milk. Add the bananas, soft brown sugar and vanilla extract. Lightly beat the egg whites with a fork. Add the chocolate mixture and continue to beat well. Sift the flour over the mixture and fold in with the oat bran. Pour into the prepared tin.

3 Cook in the oven for 40 minutes, or until firm. Cool in the tin for 10 minutes, then turn out on to a wire rack. Cut into squares and lightly dust with icing sugar before serving.

Cook's Tips
Win a few brownie points by getting to know what makes them great.
- *They should be moist and chewy with a sugary crust on the outside but squidgy on the inside.*
- *True versions contain a high proportion of sugar and fat and most contain nuts. Lighter versions often contain white chocolate and are often referred to as blondies.*
- *Brownies make superb individual cakes but the cooked slab can also be left whole and then served as a larger cake for dessert, decorated with cream and fruit.*

Energy 223kcal/947kJ; Fat 2.9g, Saturated Fat 1.2g; Carbohydrate 46.4g, Fibre 2.2g

White Chocolate Brownies

If you wish, toasted and skinned hazelnuts can be substituted for the macadamia nuts in the topping.

Serves 12
150g/5oz/1¼ cups plain (all-purpose) flour
2.5ml/½ tsp baking powder
a pinch of salt
175g/6oz fine quality white chocolate, chopped
90g/3½oz/½ cup caster (superfine) sugar
115g/4oz/½ cup unsalted (sweet) butter, cut into pieces
2 eggs, lightly beaten
5ml/1 tsp vanilla extract
175g/6oz/1 cup plain (semisweet) chocolate chips

For the topping
200g/7oz milk chocolate, chopped
215g/7½oz/1⅓ cups unsalted macadamia nuts, chopped

1 Preheat the oven to 180°C/350°F/Gas 4. Grease a 23cm/9in springform tin (pan). Sift together the flour, baking powder and salt, and set aside.

2 In a medium pan over a medium heat, melt the white chocolate, sugar and butter until smooth, stirring frequently. Cool slightly, then beat in the eggs and vanilla. Stir in the chocolate chips. Spread evenly in the prepared tin, smoothing the top.

3 Bake for 20–25 minutes, or until a cocktail stick (toothpick) inserted 5cm/2in from the side of the tin comes out clean. Remove from the oven to a heatproof surface, sprinkle chopped milk chocolate over the surface (avoid touching the side of tin) and return to the oven for 1 minute.

4 Remove from the oven and, using the back of a spoon, gently spread out the softened chocolate. Sprinkle with the macadamia nuts and gently press into the chocolate. Cool on a wire rack for 30 minutes, and then chill for 1 hour.

5 Run a sharp knife around the side of the tin to loosen, then unclip and remove. Cut the brownies into thin wedges to serve.

Energy 526kcal/2190kJ; Fat 37.4g, Saturated Fat 16.1g; Carbohydrate 43.8g, Fibre 2.1g

Maple and Pecan Nut Brownies

This recipe provides a delicious adaptation of the classic American chocolate brownie.

Makes 12
115g/4oz/½ cup butter, melted
75g/3oz/scant ½ cup soft light brown sugar
90ml/6 tbsp maple syrup
2 eggs
115g/4oz/1 cup self-raising (self-rising) flour
75g/3oz/½ cup pecan nuts, chopped

For the topping
115g/4oz/⅔ cup plain (semisweet) chocolate chips
50g/2oz/¼ cup unsalted (sweet) butter
12 pecan nut halves, to decorate

1 Preheat the oven to 180°C/350°F/Gas 4. Line and grease a 25 x 18cm/10 x 7in cake tin (pan).

2 Beat together the melted butter, sugar, 60ml/4 tbsp of the maple syrup, the eggs and flour for 1 minute, or until smooth.

3 Stir in the nuts and transfer to the cake tin. Smooth the surface and bake for 30 minutes, or until risen and firm to the touch. Cool in the tin for 10 minutes, then transfer to a wire rack to cool completely.

4 Melt the chocolate chips, butter and remaining syrup over a low heat. Cool slightly, then spread over the cake. Press in the pecan nut halves, leave to set for about 5 minutes, then cut into squares or bars.

Cook's Tips
- *Maple syrup is a sweet sugar syrup made from the sap of the sugar maple tree. It has a distinctive flavour which is delightful in a variety of sweet recipes as well as being added to ice creams and waffles.*
- *Buy a good quality maple syrup as blends are often disappointing.*
- *Store opened maple syrup in the refrigerator, as its delicate flavour will deteriorate once the bottle is opened.*

Energy 285kcal/1189kJ; Fat 19.4g, Saturated Fat 9.4g; Carbohydrate 26.2g, Fibre 0.8g

American Chocolate Fudge Brownies

This is the classic American recipe, but omit the frosting if you find it too rich.

Makes 12

175g/6oz/¾ cup butter
40g/1½oz/⅓ cup unsweetened cocoa powder
2 eggs, lightly beaten
175g/6oz/1 cup soft light brown sugar
2.5ml/½ tsp vanilla extract
115g/4oz/1 cup chopped pecan nuts
50g/2oz/½ cup self-raising (self-rising) flour

For the frosting

115g/4oz plain (semisweet) chocolate
25g/1oz/2 tbsp butter
15ml/1 tbsp sour cream

1 Preheat the oven to 180°C/350°F/Gas 4. Grease a 20cm/8in square shallow cake tin (pan) and line with baking parchment. Melt the butter in a pan and stir in the unsweetened cocoa powder. Set aside to cool.

2 Beat together the eggs, sugar and vanilla extract in a bowl, then stir in the cooled cocoa mixture with the nuts. Sift over the flour and fold into the mixture with a metal spoon.

3 Pour the mixture into the cake tin and bake in the oven for 30–35 minutes, or until risen. Remove from the oven (the mixture will still be quite soft and wet, but it firms up further while cooling) and leave to cool in the tin.

4 To make the frosting, melt the chocolate and butter together in a pan and remove from the heat. Beat in the sour cream until smooth and glossy. Leave to cool slightly, and then spread over the top of the brownies. When set, cut into 12 pieces.

Cook's Tip

Brownies are firm family favourites and, once you find a favourite recipe, you will want to make them regularly. For brownie enthusiasts you can now buy a special pan with a slide-out base, which makes removing the cooked brownies so much easier.

Energy 335kcal/1396kJ; Fat 25.1g, Saturated Fat 11.7g; Carbohydrate 25.6g, Fibre 1.2g

Fudge-glazed Chocolate Brownies

These pecan nut-topped brownies are irresistible, so hide them from friends!

Makes 16

250g/9oz dark (bittersweet) chocolate, chopped
25g/1oz unsweetened chocolate, chopped
115g/4oz/½ cup unsalted (sweet) butter, cut into pieces
90g/3½oz/scant ½ cup soft light brown sugar
50g/2oz/¼ cup caster (superfine) sugar
2 eggs
15ml/1 tbsp vanilla extract
65g/2½oz/9 tbsp plain (all-purpose) flour
115g/4oz/⅔ cup pecan nuts or walnuts, toasted and chopped
150g/5oz white chocolate, chopped
pecan nut halves, to decorate (optional)

For the glaze

175g/6oz dark (bittersweet) chocolate, chopped
50g/2oz/¼ cup unsalted (sweet) butter, cut into pieces
30ml/2 tbsp golden (light corn) syrup
10ml/2 tsp vanilla extract
5ml/1 tsp instant coffee

1 Preheat oven to 180°C/350°F/Gas 4. Line a 20cm/8in square baking tin (pan) with foil then grease the foil.

2 Melt the dark chocolates and butter in a pan over a low heat. Off the heat, add the sugars and stir for 2 minutes. Beat in the eggs and vanilla extract, and then blend in the flour.

3 Stir in the pecan nuts or walnuts and the chopped white chocolate.

4 Pour into the tin. Bake for 20–25 minutes. Cool in the tin for 30 minutes then lift, using the foil, on to a wire rack to cool for 2 hours.

5 To make the glaze, melt the chocolate in a pan with the butter, golden syrup, vanilla extract and instant coffee. Stir until smooth. Chill the glaze for 1 hour then spread over the brownies. Top with pecan nut halves, if you like. Chill until set then cut into bars.

Energy 382kcal/1595kJ; Fat 25g, Saturated Fat 12.4g; Carbohydrate 37.6g, Fibre 1.2g

Chewy Fruit Muesli Slice

The apricots give these slices a wonderful chewy texture and the apple keeps them moist.

Makes 8

75g/3oz/scant ½ cup ready-to-eat dried apricots, chopped
1 eating apple, cored and grated
150g/5oz/1¼ cups Swiss-style muesli
150ml/¼ pint/⅔ cup apple juice
15g/½oz/1 tbsp sunflower margarine

1 Preheat the oven to 190°C/375°F/Gas 5. Grease a 20cm/8in round cake tin. Combine all the ingredients in a large bowl.

2 Press the mixture into the tin and bake for 35–40 minutes, or until lightly browned and firm. Mark the muesli slice into wedges and leave to cool in the tin.

Mincemeat Wedges

Makes 12

225g/8oz/2 cups self-raising (self-rising) wholemeal (whole-wheat) flour
75g/3oz/6 tbsp unsalted (sweet) butter, diced
75g/3oz/⅓ cup demerara (raw) sugar
1 egg, beaten
115g/4oz/⅓ cup good quality mincemeat
about 60ml/4 tbsp milk
crushed brown or white café (sugar) cubes or a mixture, for sprinkling

1 Preheat the oven to 200°C/400°F/Gas 6. Line the base of a 20cm/8in round sandwich tin (layer pan) and lightly grease the sides.

2 Rub the butter into the flour, using your fingertips or a pastry cutter. Stir in the sugar, egg and mincemeat. Add enough milk to make a soft dough. Spread evenly in the prepared tin and sprinkled over the crushed sugar. Bake for 20 minutes, or until firm. Cool in the tin then cut into wedges.

Top: Energy 266kcal/1115kJ; Fat 14.1g, Saturated Fat 5.7g; Carbohydrate 32.1g, Fibre 1.2g
Above: Energy 168Kcal/707kJ; Fat 6.3g; Saturated fat 3.5g; Carbohydrate 26.9g; Fibre 0.7g

Chocolate Raspberry Macaroon Bars

Any seedless preserve, such as strawberry or apricot, can be substituted for the raspberry in this recipe.

Makes 16–18

115g/4oz/½ cup unsalted (sweet) butter, softened
50g/2oz/½ cup icing (confectioners') sugar
25g/1oz/¼ cup unsweetened cocoa powder
a pinch of salt
5ml/1 tsp almond extract
115g/4oz/1 cup plain (all-purpose) flour

For the topping

150g/5oz/½ cup seedless raspberry preserve
15ml/1 tbsp raspberry flavour liqueur
175g/6oz/1 cup milk chocolate chips
175g/6oz/1½ cups finely ground almonds
4 egg whites
a pinch of salt
200g/7oz/1 cup caster (superfine) sugar
2.5ml/½ tsp almond extract
50g/2oz/½ cup flaked (sliced) almonds

1 Preheat the oven to 160°C/325°F/Gas 3. Line a 23 x 33cm/9 x 13in baking tin (pan) with foil and then grease the foil. Beat together the butter, sugar, cocoa and salt until blended. Beat in the almond extract and flour to make a crumbly dough.

2 Turn the dough into the tin and smooth the surface. Prick all over with a fork. Bake for 20 minutes, or until just set. Remove the tin from the oven and increase the temperature to 190°C/375°F/Gas 5.

3 To make the topping, combine the raspberry preserve and liqueur. Spread over the cooked crust, then sprinkle with the chocolate chips.

4 In a food processor fitted with a metal blade, process the almonds, egg whites, salt, caster sugar and almond extract. Pour this mixture over the jam layer, spreading evenly. Sprinkle with almonds.

5 Bake for 20–25 minutes, or until the top is golden and puffed. Cool in the tin for 20 minutes. Carefully remove from the tin and cool completely. Peel off the foil and cut into bars.

Energy 107kcal/453kJ; Fat 2.9g, Saturated Fat 1.1g; Carbohydrate 19.6g, Fibre 1.9g

Blueberry Streusel Slice

If you are short of time, use ready-made pastry for this delightful summer streusel.

Makes 30

225g/8oz shortcrust pastry
50g/2oz/½ cup plain (all-purpose) flour
1.5ml/¼ tsp baking powder
40g/1½oz/3 tbsp butter or margarine
25g/1oz/2 tbsp fresh white breadcrumbs
50g/2oz/¼ cup soft light brown sugar
1.5ml/¼ tsp salt
50g/2oz/½ cup flaked (sliced) or chopped almonds
30ml/4 tbsp blackberry or bramble jelly
115g/4oz/1 cup blueberries, fresh or frozen

1 Preheat the oven to 180°C/350°F/Gas 4. Line an 18 x 28cm/7 x 11in Swiss roll tin (jelly roll pan) with baking parchment. Roll out the pastry on a lightly floured surface and place in the tin. Prick the base evenly with a fork.

2 Rub together the plain flour, baking powder, butter or margarine, breadcrumbs, sugar and salt until very crumbly, then mix in the almonds.

3 Spread the pastry with the jelly, sprinkle with the blueberries, then cover evenly with the streusel topping, pressing down lightly. Bake for 30–40 minutes, reducing the temperature after 20 minutes to 160°C/325°F/Gas 3.

4 Remove from the oven when golden on the top and the pastry is cooked through. Cut into slices while still hot, then allow to cool.

Variations
Another summer fruit that would work well is the strawberry. If using strawberries, substitute a good strawberry conserve for the blackberry or bramble jelly. You could still enjoy this streusel slice in autumn with the season's blackberries, which will go perfectly with the bramble jelly.

Energy 73kcal/304kJ; Fat 4.2g, Saturated Fat 1.4g; Carbohydrate 8.2g, Fibre 0.5g

Sticky Date and Apple Bars

If possible allow these healthy and tempting bars to mature for 1–2 days before cutting – the mixture will get stickier and even more delicious!

Makes 16

115g/4oz/½ cup butter or margarine
50g/2oz/⅓ cup soft dark brown sugar
50g/2oz/4 tbsp golden (light corn) syrup
115g/4oz/⅔ cup chopped dates
115g/4oz/generous 1 cup rolled oats
115g/4oz/1 cup wholemeal self-raising (self-rising) flour
225g/8oz/2 eating apples, peeled, cored and grated
5–10ml/1–2 tsp lemon juice
20–25 walnut halves

1 Preheat the oven to 190°C/375°F/Gas 5. Line an 18–20cm/7–8in square or rectangular loose-based cake tin (pan) with baking parchment. In a large pan, heat the butter or margarine, sugar, syrup and dates, stirring until the dates soften completely.

2 Gradually work in the oats, flour, apples and lemon juice until well mixed. Spoon into the tin and spread out evenly. Top with the walnut halves.

3 Bake for 30 minutes, then reduce the temperature to 160°C/325°F/Gas 3 and bake for 10–20 minutes more, or until firm to the touch and golden.

4 Cut into squares or bars while still warm, or allow to cool uncut then wrap in foil when nearly cold and keep for 1–2 days before eating.

Variation
Oranges and dates are also a favourite and tasty combination. To make Sticky Date and Orange Bars, finely chop half an orange, including the peel. Add to the pan at step 1 with the dates and syrup, and cook with the dates until soft. Continue with the recipe but omit the apple and lemon juice.

Energy 195kcal/815kJ; Fat 10.9g, Saturated Fat 0.4g; Carbohydrate 22.8g, Fibre 1.4g

Spiced Fig Bars

Make sure you have napkins handy when you serve these deliciously sticky bars.

Makes 48

350g/12oz/2 cups dried figs
3 eggs
175g/6oz/scant 1 cup caster (superfine) sugar
75g/3oz/⅔ cup plain (all-purpose) flour
5ml/1 tsp baking powder
2.5ml/½ tsp ground cinnamon
1.5ml/¼ tsp ground cloves
1.5ml/¼ tsp freshly grated nutmeg
1.5ml/¼ tsp salt
75g/3oz/¾ cup finely chopped walnuts
30ml/2 tbsp brandy or cognac
icing (confectioners') sugar, for dusting

1 Preheat the oven to 160°C/325°F/Gas 3. Then line a 30 x 20 x 4cm/12 x 8 x 1½in baking tin (pan) with baking parchment and grease the paper.

2 With a sharp knife, chop the figs roughly. Set aside.

3 In a bowl, whisk the eggs and sugar until well blended. In another bowl, sift together the dry ingredients, then fold into the egg mixture in several batches.

4 Scrape the mixture into the baking tin and bake until the top is firm and brown, about 35–40 minutes. It should still be soft underneath.

5 Leave to cool in the tin for 5 minutes, then unmould and transfer to a sheet of baking parchment lightly sprinkled with icing sugar. Cut into bars.

Cook's Tip
Figs are healthy fruits containing calcium, iron and potassium. They also have antibacterial properties as well as being a laxative. Omit the brandy or cognac and these fig bars will make a good sweet to add to children's lunchboxes – but remember to add a paper napkin for those sticky fingers!

Energy 53kcal/224kJ; Fat 1.6g, Saturated Fat 0.2g; Carbohydrate 8.9g, Fibre 0.7g

Lemon Bars

A surprising amount of lemon juice goes into these bars, but you will appreciate why when you taste them.

Makes 36

50g/2oz/½ cup icing (confectioners') sugar
175g/6oz/1½ cups plain (all-purpose) flour
2.5ml/½ tsp salt
175g/6oz/¾ cup butter, cut into small pieces

For the topping
4 eggs
350g/12oz/1¾ cups caster (superfine) sugar
grated rind of 1 lemon
120ml/4fl oz/½ cup fresh lemon juice
175ml/6fl oz/¾ cup whipping cream
icing (confectioners') sugar, for dusting

1 Preheat the oven to 160°C/325°F/Gas 3. Grease a 33 x 23cm/13 x 9in baking tin (pan).

2 Sift the sugar, flour and salt into a bowl. With a pastry blender, cut in the butter until the mixture resembles coarse breadcrumbs. Press the mixture into the base of the tin.

3 Bake until golden brown, about 20 minutes.

4 To make the topping, whisk the eggs and caster sugar together until well blended. Add the lemon rind and juice, and mix together well.

5 Lightly whip the cream and fold into the egg mixture. Pour over the still warm base, return to the oven, and bake until set, about 40 minutes. Cool completely before cutting into bars. Dust with icing sugar before serving.

Variation
Try orange in this recipe for a change. It will work just as well in the custard topping and will give the bars a delicately scented flavour.

Energy 124kcal/519kJ; Fat 6.6g, Saturated Fat 3.9g; Carbohydrate 15.7g, Fibre 0.2g

Spiced Raisin Bars

If you like raisins, these gloriously spicy bars are for you. Omit the walnuts if you prefer.

Makes 30

100g/3¾oz/scant 1 cup plain (all-purpose) flour
7.5ml/1½ tsp baking powder
5ml/1 tsp ground cinnamon
2.5ml/½ tsp freshly grated nutmeg
1.5ml/¼ tsp ground cloves
1.5ml/¼ tsp mixed (apple pie) spice
215g/7½oz/1½ cups raisins
115g/4oz/½ cup butter or margarine, at room temperature
90g/3½oz/½ cup caster (superfine) sugar
2 eggs
170g/5¾oz/scant ½ cup black treacle (molasses)
50g/2oz/½ cup chopped walnuts

1 Preheat the oven to 180°C/350°F/Gas 4. Line a 33 x 23cm /13 x 9in baking tin (pan) with baking parchment and lightly grease the paper.

2 Sift together the flour, baking powder and spices. Place the raisins in another bowl and toss with a few tablespoons of the flour mixture.

3 With an electric mixer, cream the butter or margarine and caster sugar together until light and fluffy. Beat in the eggs, one at a time, and then add the black treacle. Stir in the flour mixture, raisins and chopped walnuts.

4 Spread evenly in the baking tin. Bake until just set, about 15–18 minutes. Cool in the tin before cutting into squares.

Cook's Tips

- *If you are a real raisin fan, try to use Muscat raisins, as they have a rich and sweet quality.*
- *If you are making bars or cookies that contain nuts to serve to children always chop the nuts finely, as they can be a choking hazard. Although you can omit the nuts completely they are a good source of protein.*

Energy 102kcal/429kJ; Fat 4.7g, Saturated Fat 2.2g; Carbohydrate 14.6g, Fibre 0.3g

Toffee Meringue Bars

Two deliciously contrasting layers complement each other beautifully in these easy-to-make bars.

Makes 12

50g/2oz/¼ cup butter
215g/7½oz/scant 1¼ cups soft dark brown sugar
1 egg
2.5ml/½ tsp vanilla extract
65g/2½oz/9 tbsp plain (all-purpose) flour
2.5ml/½ tsp salt
1.5ml/¼ tsp freshly grated nutmeg

For the topping

1 egg white
1.5ml/¼ tsp salt
15ml/1 tbsp golden (light corn) syrup
90g/3½oz/½ cup caster (superfine) sugar
50g/2oz/½ cup finely chopped walnuts

1 Combine the butter and brown sugar in a pan and heat until bubbling. Set aside to cool.

2 Preheat the oven to 180°C/350°F/Gas 4. Line the base and sides of a 20cm/8in square cake tin (pan) with baking parchment and grease the paper.

3 Beat the egg and vanilla extract into the cooled sugar mixture. Sift over the flour, salt and nutmeg and fold in. Spread into the base of the cake tin.

4 To make the topping, beat the egg white with the salt until it holds soft peaks. Beat in the golden syrup, then the sugar, and continue beating until the mixture holds stiff peaks. Fold in the nuts and spread on top of the base. Bake for 30 minutes. Cut into bars when completely cool.

Cook's Tip

For this recipe, and any recipe that uses a traditional meringue, it is important to use a large grease-free bowl for whisking egg whites. Also, always check that the whisk or beaters are completely clean, as traces of grease will stop the whites from achieving stiff peaks.

Energy 189kcal/797kJ; Fat 6.8g, Saturated Fat 2.5g; Carbohydrate 31.9g, Fibre 0.3g

Chocolate Walnut Bars

These delicious double-decker bars should be stored in the refrigerator in an airtight container.

Makes 24

50g/2oz/⅓ cup walnuts
55g/2¼oz/generous ¼ cup caster (superfine) sugar
100g/3¾oz/scant 1 cup plain (all-purpose) flour, sifted
90g/3½oz/7 tbsp cold unsalted (sweet) butter, cut into pieces

For the topping
25g/1oz/2 tbsp unsalted (sweet) butter
90ml/6 tbsp water
25g/1oz/¼ cup unsweetened cocoa powder
90g/3½oz/½ cup caster (superfine) sugar
5ml/1 tsp vanilla extract
1.5ml/¼ tsp salt
2 eggs
icing (confectioners') sugar, for dusting

1 Preheat the oven to 180°C/350°F/Gas 4. Grease the base and sides of a 20cm/8in square baking tin (pan).

2 Grind the walnuts with a few tablespoons of the caster sugar in a food processor or blender. In a bowl, combine the ground walnuts, remaining sugar and the flour.

3 Rub in the butter using your fingertips or a pastry cutter until the mixture resembles coarse breadcrumbs. Alternatively, use a food processor.

4 Pat the walnut mixture evenly into the base of the baking tin. Bake for 25 minutes.

5 To make the topping, melt the butter with the water. Whisk in the cocoa powder and sugar. Remove from the heat, stir in the vanilla extract and salt, then cool for 5 minutes.

6 Whisk in the eggs until blended. Pour the topping over the baked crust.

7 Return to the oven and bake until set, about 20 minutes. Set the tin on a wire rack to cool, then cut into bars and dust with icing sugar before serving.

Energy 97kcal/407kJ; Fat 6.1g, Saturated Fat 2.9g; Carbohydrate 9.8g, Fibre 0.3g

Hazelnut Squares

These crunchy, nutty squares are made in a single bowl. What could be simpler?

Makes 9

50g/2oz plain (semisweet) chocolate
65g/2½oz/5 tbsp butter or margarine
225g/8oz/generous 1 cup caster (superfine) sugar
50g/2oz/½ cup plain (all-purpose) flour
2.5ml/½ tsp baking powder
2 eggs, beaten
2.5ml/½ tsp vanilla extract
115g/4oz/1 cup skinned hazelnuts, roughly chopped

1 Preheat the oven to 180°C/350°F/Gas 4. Grease a 20cm/8in square baking tin (pan).

2 In a heatproof bowl set over a pan of barely simmering water, melt the chocolate and butter or margarine. Remove the bowl from the heat.

3 Add the sugar, flour, baking powder, eggs, vanilla extract and half of the hazelnuts to the melted mixture and stir well with a wooden spoon.

4 Pour the mixture into the prepared tin. Bake in the oven for 10 minutes, then sprinkle the reserved hazelnuts over the top. Return to the oven and continue baking until firm to the touch, about 25 minutes.

5 Cool in the tin set on a wire rack for 10 minutes, then unmould on to the rack and cool completely. Cut into squares before serving.

Cook's Tip
To remove the skins from the hazelnuts put them on a foil-covered grill (broiling) pan and lightly toast them under the grill on a high heat until the skins loosen. Make sure that the hazelnuts do not brown too much or they will overcook when the Hazelnut Squares are baked in the oven.

Energy 299kcal/1252kJ; Fat 16.9g, Saturated Fat 5.7g; Carbohydrate 34.8g, Fibre 1.1g

Fruity Teabread

Serve this bread thinly sliced, toasted or plain, with butter or cream cheese and home-made jam.

Makes one 23 x 13cm/ 9 x 5in loaf

225g/8oz/2 cups plain (all-purpose) flour
115g/4oz/generous ½ cup caster (superfine) sugar
15ml/1 tbsp baking powder
2.5ml/½ tsp salt
grated rind of 1 large orange
160ml/5½fl oz/generous ⅔ cup fresh orange juice
2 eggs, lightly beaten
75g/3oz/6 tbsp butter or margarine, melted
115g/4oz/1 cup fresh cranberries or bilberries
50g/2oz/½ cup chopped walnuts

1 Preheat the oven to 180°C/350°F/Gas 4. Then line a 23 x 13cm/9 x 5in loaf tin (pan) with baking parchment and grease the paper.

2 Sift the flour, sugar, baking powder and salt into a mixing bowl. Then stir in the orange rind.

3 Make a well in the centre and add the fresh orange juice, eggs and melted butter or margarine. Stir from the centre until the ingredients are blended; do not overmix. Add the berries and walnuts, and stir until blended.

4 Transfer the mixture to the prepared tin and bake until a skewer inserted in the centre of the loaf comes out clean, about 45–50 minutes. Leave to cool in the tin for 10 minutes before transferring to a wire rack to cool completely.

Cook's Tip
Margarine can be used instead of butter for most recipes except those with a high fat content such as shortbread. Margarine will not, however, produce the same flavour as butter but it is usually less expensive so can be useful. Block margarines are better for teabreads, buns and muffins than soft margarines.

Energy 2356kcal/9885kJ; Fat 110.3g, Saturated Fat 45.4g; Carbohydrate 317g, Fibre 12.4g;

Date and Pecan Loaf

Walnuts may be used instead of pecan nuts to make this luxurious and moist teabread.

Makes one 23 x 13cm/ 9 x 5in loaf

175g/6oz/1 cup chopped stoned (pitted) dates
175ml/6fl oz/¾ cup boiling water
50g/2oz/¼ cup unsalted (sweet) butter, at room temperature
50g/2oz/¼ cup soft dark brown sugar
50g/2oz/¼ cup caster (superfine) sugar
1 egg, at room temperature
30ml/2 tbsp brandy
165g/5½oz/generous 1¼ cups plain (all-purpose) flour
10ml/2 tsp baking powder
2.5ml/½ tsp salt
4ml/¾ tsp freshly grated nutmeg
75g/3oz/¾ cup coarsely chopped pecan nuts

1 Place the dates in a bowl and pour over the boiling water. Set aside to cool. Preheat the oven to 180°C/350°F/Gas 4. Line a 23 x 13cm/9 x 5in loaf tin (pan) with baking parchment and then grease the paper.

2 With an electric mixer, cream the butter and sugars until light and fluffy. Beat in the egg and brandy, then set aside.

3 Sift the flour, baking powder, salt and nutmeg together, at least three times. Fold the dry ingredients into the sugar mixture in three batches, alternating with the dates and water. Fold in the chopped pecan nuts.

4 Pour the mixture into the prepared tin and bake until a skewer inserted in the centre comes out clean, about 45–50 minutes. Leave the loaf to cool in the tin for 10 minutes before transferring it to a wire rack to cool completely.

Cook's Tip
Nutmeg is a particularly useful spice for sweet dishes and is used in small quantities in many dishes, as the spice is poisonous in larger quantities.

Energy 2458kcal/10331kJ; Fat 101.7g, Saturated Fat 32.4g; Carbohydrate 356.4g, Fibre 15.6g

Wholemeal Banana Nut Loaf

A hearty and filling loaf, this would be ideal as a winter tea-time treat.

Makes one 23 x 13cm/ 9 x 5in loaf

115g/4oz/½ cup butter, at room temperature
115g/4oz/generous ½ cup caster (superfine) sugar
2 eggs, at room temperature
115g/4oz/1 cup plain (all-purpose) flour
5ml/1 tsp bicarbonate of soda (baking soda)
1.5ml/¼ tsp salt
5ml/1 tsp ground cinnamon
50g/2oz/½ cup wholemeal (whole-wheat) flour
3 large ripe bananas
5ml/1 tsp vanilla extract
50g/2oz/½ cup chopped walnuts

1 Preheat the oven to 180°C/350°F/Gas 4. Line the base and sides of a 23 × 13cm/9 × 5in loaf tin (pan) with baking parchment and grease the paper.

2 With an electric mixer, cream the butter and sugar together until light and fluffy. Add the eggs, one at a time, beating well after each addition.

3 Sift the plain flour, bicarbonate of soda, salt and cinnamon over the butter mixture, and stir to blend. Then stir in the wholemeal flour.

4 With a fork, mash the bananas to a purée, then stir into the mixture. Stir in the vanilla and nuts.

5 Pour the mixture into the prepared tin and spread level. Bake until a skewer inserted in the centre comes out clean, about 50–60 minutes. Leave to stand for 10 minutes before transferring to a wire rack to cool completely.

Cook's Tip
Wholemeal (whole-wheat) flour contains the wheat germ and bran, giving it a higher fibre, fat and nutritional content than white flour. Because of its fat content it is best stored in a cool larder.

Energy 2632kcal/11017kJ; Fat 143.4g, Saturated Fat 66.5g; Carbohydrate 313.4g, Fibre 13.1g

Apricot Nut Loaf

Raisins and walnuts combine with apricots to make a lovely light teabread. Full of flavour, it is also ideal for a morning snack or children's lunchboxes.

Makes one 23 x 13cm/ 9 x 5in loaf

115g/4oz/½ cup ready-to-eat dried apricots
1 large orange
75g/3oz/generous ½ cup raisins
150g/5oz/¾ cup caster (superfine) sugar
85ml/5½ tbsp/⅓ cup oil
2 eggs, lightly beaten
250g/9oz/2¼ cups plain (all-purpose) flour
10ml/2 tsp baking powder
2.5ml/½ tsp salt
5ml/1 tsp bicarbonate of soda (baking soda)
50g/2oz/½ cup chopped walnuts

1 Place the apricots in a bowl, cover with lukewarm water and leave to stand for 30 minutes. Preheat the oven to 180°C/350°F/Gas 4. Line a 23 × 13cm/9 × 5in loaf tin (pan) with baking parchment and grease the paper.

2 With a vegetable peeler, remove the orange rind, leaving the pith. Chop the strips finely.

3 Drain the softened apricots and chop them coarsely. Place in a bowl with the orange rind and raisins. Squeeze the peeled orange over a bowl. Measure the orange juice and add enough hot water to obtain 175ml/6fl oz/¾ cup liquid.

4 Add the orange juice mixture to the apricot mixture. Stir in the sugar, oil and eggs. Set aside.

5 In another bowl, sift together the flour, baking powder, salt and bicarbonate of soda. Fold the flour mixture into the apricot mixture in three batches, then stir in the walnuts.

6 Spoon the mixture into the prepared tin and bake until a skewer inserted in the centre of the loaf comes out clean, about 55–60 minutes. If the loaf browns too quickly, protect the top with a sheet of foil. Cool in the tin for 10 minutes, then transfer to a wire rack to cool completely.

Energy 2904kcal/12229kJ; Fat 109.6g, Saturated Fat 13.6g; Carbohydrate 456.8g, Fibre 20.3g

Bilberry Teabread

A lovely crumbly topping with a hint of cinnamon makes this teabread extra special.

Makes 8 pieces

50g/2oz/¼ cup butter or margarine, at room temperature
175g/6oz/scant 1 cup caster (superfine) sugar
1 egg, at room temperature
120ml/4fl oz/½ cup milk
225g/8oz/2 cups plain (all-purpose) flour
10ml/2 tsp baking powder
2.5ml/½ tsp salt
275g/10oz/2½ cups fresh bilberries or blueberries

For the topping

115g/4oz/generous ½ cup caster (superfine) sugar
40g/1½oz/⅓ cup plain (all-purpose) flour
2.5ml/½ tsp ground cinnamon
50g/2oz/¼ cup butter, cut into pieces

1 Preheat the oven to 190°C/375°F/Gas 5. Grease a 23cm/9in baking dish.

2 With an electric mixer, cream the butter or margarine with the caster sugar until light and fluffy. Add the egg and beat to combine, then mix in the milk until well blended.

3 Sift over the flour, baking powder and salt, and stir the mixture just enough to blend the ingredients. Add the bilberries and stir gently. Transfer the teabread mixture to the prepared baking dish.

4 To make the topping, place the caster sugar, flour, ground cinnamon and butter in a mixing bowl. Cut the butter into the dry ingredients using a pastry blender until the mixture resembles coarse breadcrumbs. Sprinkle the topping over the mixture in the baking dish. Bake until a skewer inserted in the centre comes out clean, about 45 minutes. Serve warm or cold.

Variation

In late summer and early autumn, when blackberries are plentiful, try to gather some to use instead of bilberries for this delicious teabread.

Energy 374kcal/1575kJ; Fat 11.7g, Saturated Fat 6.9g; Carbohydrate 66.2g, Fibre 2.1g

Dried Fruit Loaf

Use any combination of dried fruit you like in this delicious teabread. The fruit is soaked first making the loaf superbly moist.

Makes one 23 x 13cm/9 x 5in loaf

450g/1lb/2¾ cups mixed dried fruit, such as currants, raisins, chopped ready-to-eat dried apricots and dried cherries
300ml/½ pint/1¼ cups cold strong tea
200g/7oz/scant 1 cup soft dark brown sugar
grated rind and juice of 1 small orange
grated rind and juice of 1 lemon
1 egg, lightly beaten
200g/7oz/1¾ cups plain (all-purpose) flour
15ml/1 tbsp baking powder
1.5ml/¼ tsp salt

1 In a bowl, mix the dried fruit with the cold tea and leave to soak overnight.

2 Preheat the oven to 180°C/350°F/Gas 4. Line the base and sides of a 23 x 13cm/9 x 5in loaf tin (pan) with baking parchment and grease the paper.

3 Strain the soaked fruit, reserving the liquid. In a bowl, combine the dark brown sugar, orange and lemon rind, and strained fruit.

4 Pour the orange and lemon juice into a measuring jug (cup); if the quantity is less than 250ml/8fl oz/1 cup, then top up with the soaking liquid.

5 Stir the citrus juices and lightly beaten egg into the dried fruit mixture until combined.

6 Sift the flour, baking powder and salt together into another bowl. Stir the dry ingredients into the fruit mixture until well blended.

7 Transfer to the tin and bake until a skewer inserted in the centre comes out clean: about 1¼ hours. Leave in the tin for 10 minutes before unmoulding.

Energy 2763kcal/11770kJ; Fat 10g, Saturated Fat 2g; Carbohydrate 673.9g, Fibre 14.8g

Herb Popovers

Popovers are especially delicious when they are flavoured with herbs, and served as a snack.

Makes 12

3 eggs
250ml/8fl oz/1 cup milk
25g/1oz/2 tbsp butter, melted
75g/3oz/⅔ cup plain (all-purpose) flour
1.5ml/¼ tsp salt
1 small sprig each mixed fresh herbs, such as chives, tarragon, dill and parsley

1 Preheat the oven to 220°C/425°F/Gas 7. Grease 12 small ramekins or individual baking cups.

2 With an electric mixer, beat the eggs until blended. Beat in the milk and melted butter.

3 Sift together the flour and salt, then beat into the egg mixture to combine thoroughly.

4 Strip the herb leaves from the stems and chop finely. Mix together and measure out 30ml/2 tbsp. Stir the measured herbs into the batter.

5 Half-fill the prepared ramekins or baking cups. Bake until golden, 25–30 minutes. Do not open the oven door during baking time or the popovers may collapse.

6 For drier popovers, pierce each one with a knife after 30 minutes' baking time and then bake for a further 5 minutes. Serve the herb popovers piping hot.

Variation
For basic plain popovers simply omit the herbs. To make a traditional popover heat a knob (pat) of dripping or lard (white cooking fat) in each cup of a patty tin (muffin pan). Heat the tin in the preheated oven and then pour in the batter until the cups are two-thirds full. Bake at the top of the oven as before.

Energy 65kcal/272kJ; Fat 3.5g, Saturated Fat 1.7g; Carbohydrate 5.9g, Fibre 0.2g

Cheese Popovers

Serve these popovers simply as an accompaniment to a meal, or make a filling and serve them as an appetizer.

Makes 12

3 eggs
250ml/8fl oz/1 cup milk
25g/1oz/2 tbsp butter, melted
75g/3oz/⅔ cup plain (all-purpose) flour
1.5ml/¼ tsp salt
1.5ml/¼ tsp paprika
25g/1oz/⅓ cup freshly grated Parmesan cheese

1 Preheat the oven to 220°C/425°F/Gas 7. Grease 12 small ramekins or individual baking cups.

2 With an electric mixer, beat the eggs until blended. Beat in the milk and melted butter.

3 Sift together the flour, salt and paprika, then beat into the egg mixture. Add the Parmesan cheese and stir in.

4 Half-fill the prepared cups and bake until golden, about 25–30 minutes. Do not open the oven door or the popovers may collapse.

5 For drier popovers, pierce each one with a knife after about 30 minutes' baking time and then bake for another 5 minutes. Serve hot.

Cook's Tips
- *Although some believe that batters for pancakes and popovers will be improved by resting for a while before cooking, this is not absolutely necessary. However, if you wish to prepare the batter in advance it can be left to stand for up to 4 hours, or 24 hours in a refrigerator.*
- *Always cook popovers on the top shelf of the oven.*
- *This recipe can be cooked in a well-greased, small baking tin (pan), if you prefer. It will take 35–40 minutes. Cut into wedges and serve warm.*

Energy 74kcal 311 kJ; Fat 4.2g, Saturated Fat 2.1g; Carbohydrate 5.9g, Fibre 0.2g

Sweet Sesame Loaf

Lemon and sesame seeds make a great partnership in this light teabread.

Makes one 23 x 13cm/ 9 x 5in loaf
75g/3oz/6 tbsp sesame seeds
275g/10oz/2½ cups plain (all-purpose) flour
12.5ml/2½ tsp baking powder
5ml/1 tsp salt
50g/2oz/¼ cup butter or margarine, at room temperature
130g/4½oz/scant ¾ cup caster (superfine) sugar
2 eggs, at room temperature
grated rind of 1 lemon
350ml/12fl oz/1½ cups milk

1 Preheat the oven to 180°C/350°F/Gas 4. Carefully line a 23 x 13cm/9 x 5in loaf tin (pan) with baking parchment and then grease the paper.

2 Reserve 25g/1oz/2 tbsp of the sesame seeds. Spread the rest on a baking sheet and bake in the oven until lightly toasted, about 10 minutes.

3 Sift the flour, baking powder and salt into a bowl. Stir in the toasted sesame seeds and set aside.

4 Cream the butter or margarine and sugar together until light and fluffy. Beat in the eggs, then stir in the lemon rind and milk. Pour the milk mixture over the dry ingredients and fold in with a large metal spoon until just blended.

5 Pour into the tin and sprinkle over the reserved sesame seeds. Bake until a skewer inserted in the centre comes out clean, about 1 hour. Cool in the tin for 10 minutes. Turn out on to a wire rack to cool completely.

Cook's Tip
Sesame seeds are nutty flavoured and slightly sweet. Their flavour is enhanced by light toasting in a dry pan. However, because of their high oil content they do not store well and so you should always buy them in small quantities.

Energy 2578kcal/10849kJ; Fat 105.2g, Saturated Fat 39.7g; Carbohydrate 367g, Fibre 14.4g

Cardamom and Saffron Tea Loaf

An aromatic sweet bread ideal for afternoon tea, or lightly toasted for breakfast. The delicate spices of cardamom and saffron give it an unusual flavour.

Makes one 900g/2lb loaf
a generous pinch of saffron threads
750ml/1¼ pints/3 cups lukewarm milk
25g/1oz/2 tbsp butter
1kg/2¼lb/9 cups strong white bread flour
2 sachets easy-blend (rapid-rise) dried yeast
40g/1½oz/generous ¼ cup caster (superfine) sugar
6 cardamom pods, split open and seeds extracted
115g/4oz/scant ¾ cup raisins
30ml/2 tbsp clear honey, plus extra for glazing
1 egg, beaten

1 Crush the saffron straight into a cup containing a little of the warm milk and leave to infuse (steep) for 5 minutes.

2 Rub the butter into the flour using your fingertips or a pastry cutter, then mix in the yeast, sugar, cardamom seeds and raisins.

3 Beat the remaining milk with the honey and egg, then mix this into the flour, along with the saffron milk and threads, until the mixture forms a firm dough. Turn out the dough and knead it on a lightly floured surface for 5 minutes.

4 Return the dough to the mixing bowl, cover with oiled clear film (plastic wrap) and leave in a warm place until doubled in size.

5 Preheat the oven to 200°C/400°F/Gas 6. Grease a 900g/2lb loaf tin (pan). Turn the dough out on to a floured surface, knock back (punch down) and knead for 3 minutes.

6 Shape the dough into a fat roll and fit into the tin. Cover with a sheet of lightly oiled clear film and leave to stand in a warm place until the dough begins to rise again.

7 Bake the loaf for 25 minutes, or until golden brown and firm on top. Turn out on to a wire rack and as it cools brush the top with clear honey.

Energy 4571kcal/19407kJ; Fat 52.3g, Saturated Fat 24.6g; Carbohydrate 956.8g, Fibre 33.3g

Courgette Teabread

Like carrots, courgettes are a vegetable that works well in baking, adding moistness and lightness to the bread.

Makes one 23 x 13cm/ 9 x 5in loaf

50g/2oz/¼ cup butter
3 eggs
250ml/8fl oz/1 cup vegetable oil
285g/10½oz/1½ cups caster (superfine) sugar
2 unpeeled courgettes (zucchini), grated
275g/10oz/2½ cups plain (all-purpose) flour
10ml/2 tsp bicarbonate of soda (baking soda)
5ml/1 tsp baking powder
5ml/1 tsp salt
5ml/1 tsp ground cinnamon
5ml/1 tsp freshly grated nutmeg
1.5ml/¼ tsp ground cloves
115g/4oz/1 cup chopped walnuts

1 Preheat the oven to 180°C/350°F/Gas 4. Line the base and sides of a 23 x 13cm/9 x 5in loaf tin (pan) with baking parchment and grease the paper.

2 In a pan, melt the butter over a low heat. Set aside.

3 With an electric mixer, beat the eggs and oil together until thick. Beat in the sugar, then stir in the melted butter and the grated courgettes. Set aside.

4 In another bowl, sift the flour with the bicarbonate of soda, baking powder, salt, ground cinnamon, grated nutmeg and ground cloves. Sift twice more and then carefully fold them into the courgette mixture. Fold in the chopped walnuts.

5 Pour into the tin and bake until a skewer inserted in the centre comes out clean, about 60–70 minutes. Leave to stand for 10 minutes before turning out on to a wire rack to cool.

Cook's Tip
Sifting the flour and dry ingredients three times helps to make the teabread mixture light. Be careful to fold in the other ingredients gently so that the air that was incorporated is not lost.

Energy 5135kcal/21437kJ; Fat 321.5g, Saturated Fat 59.1g; Carbohydrate 522.8g, Fibre 16.1g

Mango Teabread

This delicious teabread is baked with juicy ripe mango.

Makes two 23 x 13cm/ 9 x 5in loaves

275g/10oz/2½ cups plain (all-purpose) flour
10ml/2 tsp bicarbonate of soda (baking soda)
10ml/2 tsp ground cinnamon
2.5ml/½ tsp salt
115g/4oz/½ cup margarine
3 eggs, at room temperature
285g/10½oz/1½ cups caster (superfine) sugar
120ml/4fl oz/½ cup vegetable oil
1 large ripe mango, peeled and chopped
85g/3¼oz/generous 1 cup desiccated (dry unsweetened shredded) coconut
65g/2½oz/½ cup raisins

1 Preheat the oven to 180°C/350°F/Gas 4. Line the base and sides of two 23 x 13cm/9 x 5in loaf tins (pans) with baking parchment and grease the paper.

2 Sift together the flour, bicarbonate of soda, cinnamon and salt.

3 Cream the margarine until soft. Beat in the eggs and sugar until light and fluffy. Beat in the oil.

4 Fold the dry ingredients into the creamed ingredients in three batches, then fold in the mango, two-thirds of the coconut and the raisins.

5 Spoon the batter into the tins. Sprinkle over the remaining coconut. Bake until a skewer inserted in the centre comes out clean, about 50–60 minutes. Leave to stand for 10 minutes before turning out on to a wire rack to cool completely.

Cook's Tip
A simple way of dicing a mango is to take two thick slices from either side of the large flat stone without peeling the fruit. Make criss-cross cuts in the flesh on each slice and then turn inside out. The cubes of flesh will stand proud of the skin and can be easily cut off.

Energy 2291kcal/9601kJ; Fat 121.2g, Saturated Fat 29.8g; Carbohydrate 292.2g, Fibre 12.7g

American-style Corn Sticks

These traditional corn sticks are quick and simple to make, and can be enjoyed simply spread with butter or with jam.

Makes 6

1 egg
120ml/4fl oz/½ cup milk
15ml/1 tbsp vegetable oil
115g/4oz/scant 1 cup cornmeal or polenta
50g/2oz/½ cup plain (all-purpose) flour
10ml/2 tsp baking powder
45ml/3 tbsp caster (superfine) sugar

1 Preheat the oven to 190°C/375°F/Gas 5. Grease a cast-iron corn-stick mould and heat in the oven.

2 Beat the egg in a small bowl. Stir in the milk and vegetable oil, and set aside.

3 In a mixing bowl, stir together the cornmeal or polenta, flour, baking powder and sugar. Pour in the egg mixture and stir with a wooden spoon to combine.

4 Spoon the mixture into the prepared mould. Bake until a skewer inserted in the centre of a corn stick comes out clean, about 25 minutes.

5 Cool in the mould on a wire rack for 10 minutes before unmoulding.

Cook's Tips

- *The traditional way to make corn sticks is in a cast-iron corn-stick mould, which is heated in the oven before the mixture is added. A new mould needs to be seasoned before use. Grease it well with white vegetable fat (shortening) and then heat it in a hot oven for about 20 minutes. After use wash in warm soapy water and then grease before storing.*
- *If you do not have a corn-stick mould use éclair tins (pans) instead and reduce the cooking time by 10 minutes.*

Energy 167kcal/700kJ; Fat 3.8g, Saturated Fat 0.7g; Carbohydrate 29.3g, Fibre 0.7g

Savoury Corn Bread

This corn bread has the delicious addition of cheese.

Makes 9

2 eggs, lightly beaten
250ml/8fl oz/1 cup buttermilk
115g/4oz/1 cup plain (all-purpose) flour
115g/4oz/scant 1 cup cornmeal
10ml/2 tsp baking powder
2.5ml/½ tsp salt
15ml/1 tbsp caster (superfine) sugar
115g/4oz/1 cup grated Cheddar cheese
225g/8oz/1¼ cups corn, fresh or frozen and thawed

1 Preheat the oven to 200°C/400°F/Gas 6. Grease a 23cm/9in square baking tin (pan).

2 Combine the eggs and buttermilk in a small bowl and whisk until well mixed. Set aside.

3 In another bowl, stir together the flour, cornmeal, baking powder, salt and sugar.

4 Add the egg mixture to the dry ingredients and stir with a wooden spoon to combine thoroughly. Stir in the cheese and corn and combine.

5 Pour the mixture into the baking tin. Bake until a skewer inserted in the centre comes out clean, about 25 minutes.

6 Unmould the bread on to a wire rack and leave to cool. Cut into squares before serving.

Cook's Tip

Buttermilk is made from the skimmed milk which is left over after the fat from full cream (whole) milk has been skimmed off to be used for making butter. This skimmed milk is then soured by bacteria to produce buttermilk. Although the results are not quite the same, yogurt is sometimes mixed with sweet (fresh) milk and works in a similar way to buttermilk.

Energy 206kcal/866kJ; Fat 6.4g, Saturated Fat 3.2g; Carbohydrate 28.9g, Fibre 1g

Corn Bread

Serve this bread as an accompaniment to a meal, with soup, or take it on a picnic.

Makes one 23 x 13cm/ 9 x 5in loaf

115g/4oz/1 cup plain (all-purpose) flour
65g/2½oz/generous ¼ cup caster (superfine) sugar
5ml/1 tsp salt
15ml/1 tbsp baking powder
175g/6oz/1½ cups cornmeal or polenta
350ml/12fl oz/1½ cups milk
2 eggs
75g/3oz/6 tbsp butter, melted
115g/4oz/½ cup margarine, melted

1 Preheat the oven to 200°C/400°F/Gas 6. Then line a 23 x 13cm/9 x 5in loaf tin (pan) with baking parchment and grease the paper.

2 Sift the flour, sugar, salt and baking powder into a mixing bowl. Add the cornmeal or polenta and stir to blend. Make a well in the centre. Whisk together the milk, eggs, melted butter and margarine. Pour the mixture into the well. Stir until just blended; do not overmix.

3 Pour into the tin and bake until a skewer inserted in the centre comes out clean, about 45 minutes. Serve hot or at room temperature.

Cook's Tip
Often a loaf tin (pan) needs only to be greased and have a long strip of baking parchment placed along the base and up the short sides of the tin. At other times, however, it is best to line the whole tin. To do this cut another strip of baking parchment the length of the base of the tin and long enough to come up the long sides of the tin. Grease the paper you have already laid in the base of the tin and then lay the other sheet on top, smoothing both pieces up the sides of the tin. Finally, grease the paper.

Energy 3008kcal/12539kJ; Fat 179.8g, Saturated Fat 46.1g; Carbohydrate 303.3g, Fibre 7.4g

Spicy Corn Bread

An interesting variation on basic corn bread; adjust the number of chillies used according to taste.

Makes 9 squares

3 or 4 whole canned chillies, drained
2 eggs
475ml/16fl oz/2 cups buttermilk
50g/2oz/¼ cup butter, melted
50g/2oz/½ cup plain (all-purpose) flour
5ml/1 tsp bicarbonate of soda (baking soda)
10ml/2 tsp salt
175g/6oz/scant 1½ cups cornmeal or polenta
350g/12oz/2½ cups canned corn or frozen corn, thawed

1 Preheat the oven to 200°C/400°F/Gas 6. Line the base and sides of a 23cm/9in square cake tin (pan) with baking parchment and lightly grease the paper.

2 With a sharp knife, finely chop the canned chillies and set aside until needed.

3 In a large bowl, whisk the eggs until frothy, then whisk in the buttermilk. Add the melted butter.

4 Sift the flour, bicarbonate of soda and salt together into another large bowl. Fold the dry ingredients into the buttermilk mixture in three batches, then fold in the cornmeal or polenta in three batches. Finally, fold in the chillies and corn and gently mix to combine thoroughly.

5 Pour the mixture into the tin and bake until a skewer inserted in the centre comes out clean; about 25–30 minutes. Leave in the tin for 2–3 minutes before unmoulding. Cut into squares and serve warm.

Cook's Tip
Bicarbonate of soda (baking soda) is used with buttermilk in this and many other recipes because the two together produce carbon dioxide to make the dough rise.

Energy 213kcal/892kJ; Fat 7.1g, Saturated Fat 3.4g; Carbohydrate 31.2g, Fibre 1.1g

Sweet Potato and Raisin Bread

Serve buttered slices of this subtly spiced loaf at coffee or tea time.

Makes one 900g/2lb loaf

350g/12oz/3 cups plain (all-purpose) flour
10ml/2 tsp baking powder
2.5ml/½ tsp salt
5ml/1 tsp ground cinnamon
2.5ml/½ tsp freshly grated nutmeg
450g/1lb mashed cooked sweet potatoes
90g/3½oz/½ cup soft light brown sugar
115g/4oz/½ cup butter or margarine, melted and cooled
3 eggs, beaten
75g/3oz/generous ½ cup raisins

1 Preheat the oven to 180°C/350°F/Gas 4. Grease a 900g/2lb loaf dish or tin (pan).

2 Sift the flour, baking powder, salt, cinnamon, and nutmeg into a small bowl. Set aside.

3 With an electric mixer, beat the mashed sweet potatoes with the brown sugar, butter or margarine, and eggs until well mixed.

4 Add the flour mixture and the raisins. Stir with a wooden spoon until the flour is just mixed in.

5 Transfer the batter to the prepared dish or tin. Bake until a skewer inserted in the centre of the loaf comes out clean, about 1–1¼ hours.

6 Let the bread cool in the pan on a wire rack for 15 minutes, then unmould from the dish or tin on to the wire rack and leave to cool completely.

Cook's Tip
Soft light and dark brown sugars are both comprised of white sugar with added molasses, which gives them a moist and delicate flavour. Soft dark brown sugar has more molasses added to give it a richer colour and more intense flavour.

Energy 3220kcal/13567kJ; Fat 117.4g, Saturated Fat 65.7g; Carbohydrate 514.5g, Fibre 23.1g

Lemon and Walnut Teabread

Beaten egg whites give this citrus-flavour loaf a lovely light and crumbly texture.

Makes one 23 x 13cm/9 x 5in loaf

115g/4oz/½ cup butter or margarine, at room temperature
90g/3½oz/½ cup caster (superfine) sugar
2 eggs, at room temperature, separated
grated rind of 2 lemons
30ml/2 tbsp lemon juice
215g/7½oz/scant 2 cups plain (all-purpose) flour
10ml/2 tsp baking powder
120ml/4fl oz/½ cup milk
50g/2oz/½ cup chopped walnuts
1.5ml/¼ tsp salt

1 Preheat the oven to 180°C/350°F/Gas 4. Then line a 23 x 13cm/9 x 5in loaf tin (pan) with baking parchment and grease the paper.

2 Cream the butter or margarine with the sugar until light and fluffy. Beat in the egg yolks. Add the lemon rind and juice, and stir until blended. Set aside.

3 In another bowl, sift together the flour and baking powder three times. Fold into the butter mixture in three batches, alternating with the milk. Fold in the walnuts. Set aside.

4 Beat the egg whites and salt until stiff peaks form. Fold a large spoonful of the egg whites into the walnut mixture to lighten it. Fold in the remaining egg whites carefully until the mixture is just blended.

5 Pour the batter into the prepared tin and bake until a skewer inserted in the centre of the loaf comes out clean, about 45–50 minutes. Cool in the tin for 5 minutes before turning out on to a wire rack to cool completely.

Cook's Tip
Make sure that there is no egg yolk in the white or it will stop it from whisking up properly.

Energy 2490kcal/10413kJ; Fat 144.7g, Saturated Fat 67.5g; Carbohydrate 269.1g, Fibre 8.4g

Date and Nut Maltloaf

Choose any type of nut you like to include in this deliciously rich and fruit-packed teabread.

Makes two 450g/1lb loaves

300g/11oz/2⅔ cups strong plain (all-purpose) flour
275g/10oz/2½ cups strong wholemeal (whole-wheat) bread flour
5ml/1 tsp salt
75g/3oz/⅓ cup soft light brown sugar
1 sachet easy-blend (rapid-rise) dried yeast
50g/2oz/¼ cup butter or margarine
15ml/1 tbsp black treacle (molasses)
60ml/4 tbsp malt extract
scant 250ml/8fl oz/1 cup lukewarm milk
115g/4oz/⅔ cup chopped dates
75g/3oz/½ cup sultanas (golden raisins)
50g/2oz/½ cup chopped nuts
75g/3oz/generous ½ cup raisins
30ml/2 tbsp clear honey, to glaze

1 Sift the flours and salt into a large bowl, then tip in the wheat flakes from the sieve. Stir in the sugar and yeast.

2 Put the butter or margarine in a small pan with the treacle and malt extract. Stir over a low heat until melted. Leave to cool, then combine with the milk.

3 Stir the milk mixture into the dry ingredients and knead thoroughly for 15 minutes, or until the dough is elastic.

4 Knead in the chopped dates, sultanas and chopped nuts. Transfer the dough to an oiled bowl, cover with clear film (plastic wrap) and leave in a warm place for about 1½ hours, or until the dough has doubled in size.

5 Grease two 450g/1lb loaf tins (pans). Knock back (punch down) the dough and knead lightly. Divide the dough in half, form into loaves and place in the tins. Cover and leave in a warm place for 30 minutes, or until risen. Meanwhile, preheat the oven to 190°C/375°F/Gas 5.

6 Bake for 35–40 minutes, or until well risen. Cool on a wire rack. Brush with honey while warm.

Energy 1939kcal/8200kJ; Fat 45.2g, Saturated Fat 16.6g; Carbohydrate 361.7g, Fibre 21.7g

Orange Wheatloaf

Perfect just with butter as a breakfast teabread, and for banana sandwiches.

Makes one 450g/1lb loaf

275g/10oz/2½ cups plain (all-purpose) wholemeal (whole-wheat) flour
2.5ml/½ tsp salt
25g/1oz/2 tbsp butter
25g/1oz/2 tbsp soft light brown sugar
½ sachet easy-blend (rapid-rise) dried yeast
grated rind and juice of ½ orange

1 Lightly grease a 450g/1lb loaf tin (pan). Sift the flour into a large bowl and add any wheat flakes from the sieve to the flour. Add the salt and rub in the butter lightly with your fingertips or a pastry cutter.

2 Stir in the sugar, yeast and orange rind. Pour the orange juice into a measuring jug and use hot water to make up to 200ml/7fl oz/scant 1 cup (the liquid should not be more than hand hot).

3 Stir the liquid into the flour mixture and mix to a soft ball of dough. Knead gently on a lightly floured surface until quite smooth and elastic.

4 Place the dough in the tin and leave it in a warm place until nearly doubled in size. Preheat the oven to 220°C/425°F/Gas 7.

5 Bake the bread for 30–35 minutes, or until it sounds hollow when removed from the tin and tapped underneath. Tip out of the tin and cool on a wire rack.

Cook's Tip

Easy-blend (rapid-rise) yeast is mixed directly with the dry ingredients and is the easiest yeast to use. Don't confuse this with active dried yeast, which needs to be mixed with liquid first and left to become frothy before it is mixed with the dry ingredients.

Energy 1146kcal/4848kJ; Fat 26.6g, Saturated Fat 13.8g; Carbohydrate 204.2g, Fibre 24.8g

Orange and Honey Teabread

Honey gives a special flavour to this teabread. Serve just with a scraping of butter.

Makes one 23 x 13cm/ 9 x 5in loaf

385g/13½oz/scant 3½ cups plain (all-purpose) flour
12.5ml/2½ tsp baking powder
2.5ml/½ tsp bicarbonate of soda (baking soda)
2.5ml/½ tsp salt
25g/1oz/2 tbsp margarine
250ml/8fl oz/1 cup clear honey
1 egg, at room temperature, lightly beaten
25ml/1½ tbsp grated orange rind
175ml/6fl oz/¾ cup freshly squeezed orange juice
115g/4oz/1 cup chopped walnuts

1 Preheat the oven to 160°C/325°F/Gas 3. Line the base and sides of a 23 x 13cm/9 x 5in loaf tin (pan) with baking parchment and grease the paper.

2 Sift the flour, baking powder, bicarbonate of soda and salt together in a bowl.

3 Cream the margarine until soft. Stir in the honey until blended, then stir in the egg. Add the orange rind and combine well.

4 Fold the flour mixture into the honey mixture in three batches, alternating with the orange juice. Stir in the walnuts.

5 Pour into the prepared tin and bake in the oven until a skewer inserted in the centre comes out clean, about 60–70 minutes. Leave for 10 minutes before turning out on to a wire rack to cool completely.

Cook's Tip
Although you can buy beautifully scented honey with the fragrance of wild flowers and herbs, the scents are usually destroyed in cooking, so for recipes such as this a less expensive honey will do perfectly well. Clear honey gradually becomes cloudy, but this can be rectified simply by gently heating it.

Energy 3145kcal/13251kJ; Fat 109.9g, Saturated Fat 8.8g; Carbohydrate 509.6g, Fibre 16.1g

Apple Loaf

The apple sauce in this loaf makes it beautifully moist – it tastes perfect simply sliced and spread with butter.

Makes one 23 x 13cm/ 9 x 5in loaf

1 egg
250ml/8fl oz/1 cup bottled or home-made apple sauce
50g/2oz/¼ cup butter or margarine, melted
100g/3¾oz/scant ½ cup soft dark brown sugar
45g/1¾oz/scant ¼ cup caster (superfine) sugar
275g/10oz/2½ cups plain (all-purpose) flour
10ml/2 tsp baking powder
2.5ml/½ tsp bicarbonate of soda (baking soda)
2.5ml/½ tsp salt
5ml/1 tsp ground cinnamon
2.5ml/½ tsp freshly grated nutmeg
65g/2½oz/½ cup currants or raisins
50g/2oz/½ cup pecan nuts or walnuts, chopped

1 Preheat the oven to 180°C/350°F/Gas 4. Line the base and sides of a 23 x 13cm/9 x 5in loaf tin (pan) with baking parchment and grease the paper.

2 Break the egg into a bowl and beat lightly. Stir in the apple sauce, butter or margarine, and both sugars. Set aside.

3 In another bowl, sift together the flour, baking powder, bicarbonate of soda, salt, cinnamon and nutmeg. Fold the dry ingredients, including the currants or raisins and the nuts, into the apple sauce mixture in three batches.

4 Pour into the prepared tin and bake in the oven until a skewer inserted in the centre of the loaf comes out clean, about 1 hour. Leave to stand in the tin for 10 minutes, then turn out on to a wire rack to cool completely.

Variations
Ring the changes with this moist loaf by using different nuts and dried fruit. Try ready-to-eat dried apricots with hazelnuts, for example.

Energy 2558kcal/10777kJ; Fat 85g, Saturated Fat 30.9g; Carbohydrate 432.4g, Fibre 15.3g

Fruit and Brazil Nut Teabread

Mashed bananas are a classic ingredient in teabreads, and help to create a moist texture as well as adding a full flavour.

Makes one 23 x 13cm/ 9 x 5in loaf

225g/8oz/2 cups plain (all-purpose) flour
10ml/2 tsp baking powder
5ml/1 tsp mixed (apple pie) spice
115g/4oz/½ cup butter, diced
115g/4oz/½ cup light soft brown sugar
2 eggs, lightly beaten
30ml/2 tbsp milk
30ml/2 tbsp dark rum
2 bananas
115g/4oz/⅔ cup dried figs, chopped
50g/2oz/⅓ cup brazil nuts, chopped

For the decoration
8 whole brazil nuts
4 whole dried figs, halved
30ml/2 tbsp apricot jam
5ml/1 tsp dark rum

1 Preheat the oven to 180°C/350°F/Gas 4. Grease and base-line a 23 x 13cm/9 x 5in loaf tin (pan). Sift the flour, baking powder and mixed spice into a bowl.

2 Rub in the butter using your fingertips or a pastry cutter until the mixture resembles fine breadcrumbs. Stir in the sugar.

3 Make a well in the centre and work in the eggs, milk and rum until combined. Peel and mash the bananas. Stir in the mashed bananas, chopped figs and brazil nuts and transfer to the prepared loaf tin.

4 To decorate the teabread press the whole brazil nuts and halved figs gently into the mixture, to form an attractive pattern. Bake for 1¼ hours, or until a skewer inserted in the centre comes out clean. Cool in the tin for 10 minutes, then transfer to a wire rack.

5 Heat the jam and rum together in a small pan. Increase the heat and boil for 1 minute. Remove from the heat and pass through a fine sieve. Cool the glaze slightly, brush over the warm loaf, and leave to cool completely.

Energy 3095kcal/12984kJ; Fat 145.6g, Saturated Fat 72.2g; Carbohydrate 405.9g, Fibre 19.9g

Glazed Banana Spiced Loaf

The lemony glaze perfectly sets off the warm flavours of nutmeg and cloves in this deliciously moist and light banana teabread.

Makes one 23 x 13cm/ 9 x 5in loaf

115g/4oz/½ cup butter, at room temperature
165g/5½oz/¾ cup caster (superfine) sugar
2 eggs, at room temperature
215g/7½oz/scant 2 cups plain (all-purpose) flour
5ml/1 tsp salt
5ml/1 tsp bicarbonate of soda (baking soda)
2.5ml/½ tsp freshly grated nutmeg
1.5ml/¼ tsp mixed spice
1.5ml/¼ tsp ground cloves
175ml/6fl oz/¾ cup sour cream
1 large ripe banana, mashed
5ml/1 tsp vanilla extract

For the glaze
115g/4oz/1 cup icing (confectioners') sugar
15–30ml/1–2 tbsp lemon juice

1 Preheat the oven to 180°C/350°F/Gas 4. Line a 23 x 13cm/ 9 x 5in loaf tin (pan) with baking parchment and grease the paper.

2 Cream the butter and sugar until light and fluffy. Add the eggs, one at a time, beating well after each addition.

3 Sift together the flour, salt, bicarbonate of soda, nutmeg, mixed spice and cloves. Add to the butter mixture and stir to combine well.

4 Add the sour cream, banana and vanilla extract, and mix to just blend. Pour this mixture into the prepared tin.

5 Bake until the top springs back when touched lightly, about 45–50 minutes. Cool in the tin for 10 minutes. Turn out on to a wire rack.

6 To make the glaze, combine the icing sugar and lemon juice until smooth, then stir until smooth. Place the cooled loaf on a rack set over a baking sheet. Pour the glaze over the loaf and allow to set.

Energy 3293kcal/13836kJ; Fat 143.6g, Saturated Fat 85.4g; Carbohydrate 490.2g, Fibre 7.8g

Banana Bread

For a change, add 50–75g/2–3oz/½–¾ cup chopped walnuts or pecan nuts with the dry ingredients.

Makes one 21 x 12cm/8½ x 4½in loaf

200g/7oz/1⅔ cups plain (all-purpose) flour
11.5ml/2¼ tsp baking powder
2.5ml/½ tsp salt
4ml/¾ tsp ground cinnamon (optional)
60ml/4 tbsp wheatgerm
65g/2½oz/5 tbsp butter, at room temperature
115g/4oz/generous ½ cup caster (superfine) sugar
4ml/¾ tsp grated lemon rind
3 ripe bananas, mashed
2 eggs, beaten

1 Preheat the oven to 180°C/350°F/Gas 4. Grease and flour a 21 x 12cm/8½ x 4½in loaf tin (pan).

2 Sift the flour, baking powder, salt and cinnamon, if using, into a bowl. Stir in the wheatgerm.

3 In another bowl, combine the butter with the caster sugar and grated lemon rind. Beat thoroughly until the mixture is light and fluffy.

4 Add the mashed bananas and eggs, and mix well. Add the dry ingredients and blend quickly and evenly.

5 Spoon into the loaf tin. Bake for 50–60 minutes, or until a skewer inserted in the centre comes out clean.

6 Cool the bread in the tin for 5 minutes, then turn out on to a wire rack to cool completely.

Cook's Tip

Wheatgerm is the heart of the wheat grain and contains many nutrients and important vitamins. It must be used fresh and should be stored in an airtight container. Do not store for long periods, as it will become bitter.

Energy 2265kcal/9548kJ; Fat 73.6g, Saturated Fat 38.4g; Carbohydrate 372.4g, Fibre 18.9g

Banana Orange Loaf

For the best banana flavour and a really good, moist texture, make sure that the bananas are perfectly ripe for this cake.

Makes one 23 x 13cm/9 x 5in loaf

90g/3½oz/¾ cup plain (all-purpose) wholemeal (whole-wheat) flour
90g/3½oz/¾ cup plain (all-purpose) flour
5ml/1 tsp baking powder
5ml/1 tsp mixed (apple pie) spice
45ml/3 tbsp flaked (sliced) hazelnuts, toasted
2 large ripe bananas
1 egg
30ml/2 tbsp sunflower oil
30ml/2 tbsp clear honey
finely grated rind and juice of 1 small orange
4 orange slices, halved
10ml/2 tsp icing (confectioners') sugar

1 Preheat the oven to 180°C/350°F/Gas 4. Brush a 23 x 13cm/9 x 5in loaf tin (pan) with sunflower oil and line the base with baking parchment.

2 Sift the flours with the baking powder and spice into a large bowl, adding any bran that is caught in the sieve (strainer). Stir the hazelnuts into the dry ingredients.

3 Peel and mash the bananas in a large bowl. Add the egg, sunflower oil, honey, and the orange rind and juice to the mashed bananas and beat together.

4 Add the banana mixture to the dry ingredients and mix to combine thoroughly.

5 Spoon the mixture into the prepared tin and smooth the top. Bake in the oven for 40–45 minutes, or until the cake is firm and golden brown. Remove from the oven and turn out on to a wire rack to cool.

6 Meanwhile, sprinkle the orange slices with the icing sugar and place on a grill (broiling) rack. Grill until lightly golden. Arrange the glazed orange slices on the top of the loaf.

Energy 1483kcal/6238kJ; Fat 59.9g, Saturated Fat 7g; Carbohydrate 214.3g, Fibre 16.1g

Marmalade Teabread

If you prefer, leave the top of the loaf plain and serve sliced and lightly buttered instead.

Makes one 21 x 12cm/ 8½ x 4½in loaf

200g/7oz/1⅔ cups plain (all-purpose) flour
5ml/1 tsp baking powder
6.5ml/1¼ tsp ground cinnamon
90g/3½oz/7 tbsp butter or margarine
50g/2oz/¼ cup soft light brown sugar
60ml/4 tbsp chunky orange marmalade
1 egg, beaten
about 45ml/3 tbsp milk
60ml/4 tbsp glacé icing and shreds of orange and lemon rind, to decorate

1 Preheat the oven to 160°C/325°F/Gas 3. Lightly butter a 21 x 12cm/8½ x 4½in loaf tin (pan), then line the base with baking parchment and grease the paper.

2 Sift the flour, baking powder and cinnamon together, toss in the butter or margarine, then rub in using your fingertips or a pastry cutter until the mixture resembles coarse breadcrumbs. Stir in the sugar.

3 In a separate bowl, mix together the marmalade, egg and most of the milk, then stir into the flour mixture to make a soft dropping consistency, adding more milk if necessary.

4 Transfer the mixture to the tin and bake for 1¼ hours, or until firm to the touch. Leave the cake to cool in the tin for 5 minutes, then turn on to a wire rack, peel off the lining paper, and leave to cool completely.

5 Drizzle the glacé icing over the top of the cake and decorate with the orange and lemon rind.

Cook's Tip
To make citrus shreds, pare away strips of orange or lemon rind with a vegetable peeler, then cut into fine shreds with a knife.

Energy 1725kcal/7238kJ; Fat 82.5g, Saturated Fat 48.8g; Carbohydrate 209.3g, Fibre 6.2g

Cherry Marmalade Muffins

Muffins are always best served fresh from the oven.

Makes 12

225g/8oz/2 cups self-raising (self-rising) flour
5ml/1 tsp mixed (apple pie) spice
75g/3oz/scant ½ cup caster (superfine) sugar
115g/4oz/½ cup glacé (candied) cherries, quartered
30ml/2 tbsp orange marmalade
150ml/¼ pint/⅔ cup milk
50g/2oz/¼ cup sunflower margarine
orange marmalade, to glaze

1 Preheat the oven to 200°C/400°F/Gas 6. Lightly grease 12 deep muffin cups with oil.

2 Sift together the flour and spice, then stir in the sugar and glacé cherries. Mix the marmalade with the milk and beat into the dry ingredients with the margarine. Spoon into the cups.

3 Bake for 20–25 minutes, or until golden brown and firm. Turn out on to a wire rack, and brush the tops of the muffins with warmed marmalade.

Crunchy Muesli Muffins

Makes 10

150g/5oz/1¼ cups plain (all-purpose) flour
12.5ml/2½ tsp baking powder
30ml/2 tbsp caster (superfine) sugar
200g/7oz/1½ cups toasted oat cereal with raisins
250ml/8fl oz/1 cup milk
50g/2oz/¼ cup butter, melted
1 egg, beaten

1 Preheat the oven to 200°C/400°F/Gas 6. Grease 10 muffin cups or use paper cases.

2 Sift the dry ingredients together into a large bowl. Add the oat cereal and stir. In a separate bowl combine the milk, melted butter and the egg. Add to the dry ingredients, and stir gently. Spoon the mixture into the cups. Bake for 20 minutes.

Top: Energy 162kcal/686kJ; Fat 4.6g, Saturated Fat 0.7g; Carbohydrate 29.8g, Fibre 0.7g
Above: Energy 213Kcal/893kJ; Fat 9.7g; Saturated fat 4g; Carbohydrate 28.1g; Fibre 1.4g

Spiced Date and Walnut Cake

Nuts and dates are a classic flavour combination. Use pecan nuts instead of walnuts, if you wish.

Makes one 900g/2lb cake

300g/11oz/2⅔ cups self-raising (self-rising) wholemeal (whole-wheat) flour
10ml/2 tsp mixed (apple pie) spice
150g/5oz/¾ cup chopped dates
50g/2oz/½ cup chopped walnuts
60ml/4 tbsp sunflower oil
115g/4oz/½ cup dark muscovado (molasses) sugar
300ml/½ pint/1¼ cups milk
walnut halves, to decorate

1 Preheat the oven to 180°C/350°F/Gas 4. Line a 900g/2lb loaf tin (pan) with baking parchment and grease the paper.

2 Sift together the flour and spice, adding back any bran from the sieve. Stir in the dates and walnuts.

3 Mix the oil, sugar and milk in a separate bowl. Add the oil mixture to the dry ingredients and mix to combine thoroughly.

4 Spoon the cake mixture into the prepared loaf tin and arrange the walnut halves on top.

5 Bake the cake in the oven for about 45–50 minutes, or until it is golden brown and firm.

6 Turn out the cake, remove the lining paper, and leave to cool on a wire rack.

Cook's Tip

Dried fruits add natural sweetness as well as moisture to baking. Always chop dried fruits by hand, as a food processor will chop them too finely. Dates bought in a block are ideal for cooking as they have no stones and you can use a sharp knife to slice horizontally through the block in thin slices. The slices can then easily be broken up into small pieces and chopped smaller if you prefer.

Energy 2666kcal/11243kJ; Fat 90.2g, Saturated Fat 12.3g; Carbohydrate 429.6g, Fibre 34.8g

Prune and Peel Rock Buns

These fruity scones are delicious spread with butter.

Makes 12

225g/8oz/2 cups plain (all-purpose) flour
10ml/2 tsp baking powder
75g/3oz/scant ½ cup demerara (raw) sugar
50g/2oz/¼ cup chopped ready-to-eat dried prunes
50g/2oz/⅓ cup chopped mixed (candied) peel
finely grated rind of 1 lemon
50ml/2fl oz/¼ cup sunflower oil
75ml/5 tbsp skimmed milk

1 Preheat the oven to 200°C/400°F/Gas 6. Lightly oil a large baking sheet. Sift together the flour and baking powder, then stir in the sugar, prunes, peel and lemon rind.

2 Mix the oil and milk, then stir into the mixture, to make a dough which just binds together.

3 Spoon into rocky heaps on the baking sheet and bake for 20 minutes, or until golden. Leave to cool on a wire rack.

Traditional Rock Buns

Makes 12

225g/8oz/2 cups plain (all-purpose) flour
10ml/2 tsp baking powder
115g/4oz/½ cup butter
115g/4oz/scant 1 cup mixed dried fruit
115g/4oz/1 cup demerara (raw) sugar
grated rind of half an orange
1 egg, beaten
30ml/2 tbsp milk

1 Preheat the oven to 200°C/400°F/Gas 6. Grease two baking sheets. Sift the dry ingredients into a bowl and rub in the fat using your fingertips or a pastry cutter.

2 Stir in the fruit, sugar and orange rind. Add the egg and enough milk to bind the dough. Place heaps of mixture on the baking sheets and bake for 15–20 minutes, or until golden. Cool on a rack.

Top: Energy 132kcal/559kJ; Fat 3.2g, Saturated Fat 0.4g; Carbohydrate 25.3g, Fibre 1g
Above: Energy 206Kcal/866kJ; Fat 8.7g; Saturated fat 5.2g; Carbohydrate 31.3g; Fibre 0.8g

Raisin Bran Buns

Serve these buns warm or at room temperature, on their own, with butter, or with cream cheese.

Makes 15

50g/2oz/¼ cup butter or margarine
40g/1½oz/⅓ cup plain (all-purpose) flour
50g/2oz/½ cup plain wholemeal (whole-wheat) flour
7.5ml/1½ tsp bicarbonate of soda (baking soda)
1.5ml/¼ tsp salt
5ml/1 tsp ground cinnamon
25g/1oz/generous 1 cup bran
75g/3oz/generous ½ cup raisins
65g/2½oz/generous ¼ cup soft dark brown sugar
50g/2oz/¼ cup caster (superfine) sugar
1 egg
250ml/8fl oz/1 cup buttermilk
juice of ½ lemon

1 Preheat the oven to 200°C/400°F/Gas 6. Lightly grease 15 bun-tray cups. Put the butter or margarine in a pan and melt over a gentle heat. Set aside.

2 In a mixing bowl, sift together the flours, bicarbonate of soda, salt and cinnamon. Add the bran, raisins and sugars, and stir until well blended.

3 In another bowl, mix together the egg, buttermilk, lemon juice and melted butter. Add the buttermilk mixture to the dry ingredients and stir in lightly and quickly until just moistened. Do not mix until smooth.

4 Spoon the mixture into the prepared bun-tray cups, filling them almost to the top. Half-fill any empty cups with water. Bake until golden, about 15–20 minutes. Remove to a wire rack to cool slightly or serve immediately.

Cook's Tip
When you use a bun tray if you half-fill any unused cups with water you will ensure that all the buns will cook evenly.

Energy 89kcal/373kJ; Fat 3.4g, Saturated Fat 1.9g; Carbohydrate 13.4g, Fibre 1.1g

Raspberry Crumble Buns

The crumble topping adds an unusual twist to these lovely fruit buns.

Makes 12

175g/6oz/1½ cups plain (all-purpose) flour
50g/2oz/¼ cup caster (superfine) sugar
45g/1¾oz/scant ¼ cup soft light brown sugar
10ml/2 tsp baking powder
1.5ml/¼ tsp salt
5ml/1 tsp ground cinnamon
115g/4oz/½ cup butter, melted
1 egg
120ml/4fl oz/½ cup milk
150g/5oz/¾ cup fresh raspberries
grated rind of 1 lemon

For the crumble topping

25g/1oz/¼ cup finely chopped pecan nuts or walnuts
50g/2oz/¼ cup soft dark brown sugar
45ml/3 tbsp plain (all-purpose) flour
5ml/1 tsp ground cinnamon
45ml/3 tbsp butter, melted

1 Preheat the oven to 180°C/350°F/Gas 4. Lightly grease 12 bun-tray cups or use 12 paper cases. Sift the flour into a bowl. Add the sugars, baking powder, salt and cinnamon, and stir to blend.

2 Make a well in the centre. Place the butter, egg and milk in the well and mix until just combined. Stir in the raspberries and lemon rind. Spoon the mixture into the prepared bun tray, filling the cups almost to the top.

3 To make the crumble topping, mix the nuts, dark brown sugar, flour and cinnamon in a bowl. Add the melted butter and stir to blend.

4 Spoon some of the crumble over each bun. Bake until browned, about 25 minutes. Transfer to a wire rack to cool slightly. Serve warm.

Variation
Try strawberries or blackberries for a change.

Energy 225kcal/940kJ; Fat 13.3g, Saturated Fat 7.3g; Carbohydrate 25.2g, Fibre 0.9g

Banana and Pecan Muffins

These satisfying muffins are quick and easy to make and contain the winning combination of banana and pecan nuts.

Makes 8

150g/5oz/1 1/4 cups plain (all-purpose) flour
7.5ml/1 1/2 tsp baking powder
50g/2oz/1/4 cup butter or margarine, at room temperature
150g/5oz/3/4 cup caster (superfine) sugar
1 egg
5ml/1tsp vanilla extract
3 bananas, mashed
50g/2oz/1/2 cup chopped pecan nuts
75ml/5tbsp milk

1 Preheat the oven to 190°C/375°F/Gas 5. Lightly grease eight deep muffin cups. Sift the flour and baking powder into a small bowl. Set aside.

2 With an electric mixer, cream the butter or margarine and sugar together. Add the egg and vanilla extract and beat until fluffy. Mix in the banana.

3 Add the pecan nuts. With the mixer on low speed, beat in the flour mixture alternately with the milk.

4 Spoon the mixture into the prepared muffin cups, filling them about two-thirds full. Bake the muffins until golden brown and a skewer inserted into the centre of a muffin comes out clean, about 20–25 minutes.

5 Let the muffins cool in the cups on a wire rack for about 10 minutes. To loosen, run a knife gently around each muffin and unmould on to the wire rack.

6 Leave to cool for another 10 minutes before serving.

Variation
Walnuts also taste good with bananas, so try these instead of pecan nuts for a change.

Energy 277kcal/1164kJ; Fat 10.7g, Saturated Fat 4g; Carbohydrate 43.7g, Fibre 1.3g

Blueberry and Cinnamon Muffins

These moist and "moreish" muffins have great appeal.

Makes 8

115g/4oz/1 cup plain (all-purpose) flour
15ml/1 tbsp baking powder
pinch of salt
65g/2 1/2oz/generous 1/4 cup soft light brown sugar
1 egg
175ml/6fl oz/3/4 cup milk
45ml/3 tbsp vegetable oil
10ml/2 tsp ground cinnamon
115g/4oz/1 cup fresh or thawed frozen blueberries

1 Preheat the oven to 190°C/375°F/Gas 5. Lightly grease eight deep muffin cups.

2 Beat the first eight ingredients together until smooth. Fold in the blueberries. Spoon into the muffin cups, filling them two-thirds full. Bake for 25 minutes, or until lightly coloured. Leave in the cups for 5 minutes then transfer to a rack to cool.

Chocolate-Chip Muffins

Makes 10

115g/4oz/1/2 cup butter or margarine, softened
75g/3oz/1/3 cup granulated sugar
30ml/2 tbsp soft dark brown sugar
2 eggs
175g/6oz/1 1/2 cups plain (all-purpose) flour, sifted twice
5ml/1 tsp baking powder
120ml/4fl oz/1/2 cup milk
175g/6oz/1 cup plain (semisweet) chocolate chips

1 Preheat the oven to 190°C/375°F/Gas 5. Grease ten muffin cups. Cream the butter or margarine with both sugars until fluffy.

2 Add the eggs, one at a time, beating well after each addition. Fold in the flour, alternating with the milk. Divide half the mixture among the muffin cups. Sprinkle the chocolate chips on top, then cover with the remaining mixture.

3 Bake for 25 minutes. Leave in the tin (pan) for 5 minutes then transfer to a rack to cool.

Top: Energy 141kcal/593kJ; Fat 5.4g, Saturated Fat 0.9g; Carbohydrate 21.4g, Fibre 0.9g
Above: Energy 296Kcal/1238kJ; Fat 15.8g; Saturated fat 3.4g; Carbohydrate 36.4g; Fibre 1g

Carrot Buns

Using carrots gives these buns a lovely moist consistency, and a delightful taste too.

Makes 12

175g/6oz/¾ cup margarine, at room temperature
90g/3½oz/generous ½ cup soft dark brown sugar
1 egg, at room temperature
15ml/1 tbsp water
225g/8oz/1½ cups grated carrots
150g/5oz/1¼ cups plain (all-purpose) flour
5ml/1 tsp baking powder
2.5ml/½ tsp bicarbonate of soda (baking soda)
5ml/1 tsp ground cinnamon
1.5ml/¼ tsp freshly grated nutmeg
2.5ml/½ tsp salt

1 Preheat the oven to 180°C/350°F/Gas 4. Grease 12 bun-tray cups or use paper cases.

2 With an electric mixer, cream the margarine and sugar until light and fluffy. Beat in the egg and water, then stir in the grated carrots.

3 Sift over the flour, baking powder, bicarbonate of soda, cinnamon, nutmeg and salt. Stir to blend.

4 Spoon the mixture into the prepared bun tray, filling the cups almost to the top. Bake until the tops spring back when touched lightly, about 35 minutes.

5 Leave the buns to stand for about 10 minutes in the bun tray before transferring to a wire rack to cool completely.

Variation

These mini carrot cakes taste great with a traditional cream cheese topping. Beat 225g/8oz/2 cups icing (confectioners') sugar with 60g/2¼oz/generous 4 tbsp cream cheese and 30g/1¼oz/generous 2 tbsp softened butter. Add 5ml/1 tsp grated orange rind and blend well. Spread over the tops of the cooked and cooled buns.

Energy 193kcal/803kJ; Fat 12.6g, Saturated Fat 0.2g; Carbohydrate 19.2g, Fibre 0.8g

Dried Cherry Buns

Looking for something different? Then try these super little buns with their jewel-like cherries baked inside.

Makes 16

250ml/8fl oz/1 cup natural (plain) yogurt
175g/6oz/¾ cup dried cherries
115g/4oz/½ cup butter, at room temperature
175g/6oz/generous ¾ cup caster (superfine) sugar
2 eggs, at room temperature
5ml/1 tsp vanilla extract
200g/7oz/1¾ cups plain (all-purpose) flour
10ml/2 tsp baking powder
5ml/1 tsp bicarbonate of soda (baking soda)
1.5ml/¼ tsp salt

1 In a mixing bowl, combine the yogurt and cherries. Cover and leave to stand for 30 minutes. Preheat the oven to 180°C/350°F/Gas 4. Grease 16 bun-tray cups or use paper cases.

2 With an electric mixer, cream the butter and sugar together until light and fluffy. Add the eggs, one at a time, beating well after each addition. Add the vanilla extract and the cherry mixture and stir to blend. Set aside.

3 In another bowl, sift together the flour, baking powder, bicarbonate of soda and salt. Fold into the cherry mixture in three batches.

4 Fill the prepared cups two-thirds full. For even baking, half-fill any empty cups with water. Bake until the tops spring back when touched lightly, about 20 minutes. Transfer to a wire rack to cool completely.

Cook's Tip

If you haven't tried dried cherries before, here is the recipe to begin enjoying their special flavour. They are quite unlike glacé (candied) cherries in that they have a wonderful tart taste. The best variety, Montmorency, has a sweet–sour flavour, perfect for this recipe. Dried cherries also make a healthy snack.

Energy 187kcal/787kJ; Fat 7g, Saturated Fat 4g; Carbohydrate 29.9g, Fibre 0.6g

Chelsea Buns

A traditional English recipe, not surprisingly Chelsea buns enjoy wide popularity elsewhere in the world.

Makes 12

225g/8oz/2 cups strong white bread flour
2.5ml/½ tsp salt
40g/1½oz/3 tbsp unsalted (sweet) butter
7.5ml/1½ tsp easy-blend (rapid-rise) dried yeast
120ml/4fl oz/½ cup milk
1 egg, beaten
75g/3oz/½ cup mixed dried fruit
25g/1oz/2½ tbsp chopped mixed (candied) peel
50g/2oz/¼ cup soft light brown sugar
clear honey, to glaze

1 Preheat the oven to 190°C/375°F/Gas 5. Grease a 20cm/8in round tin (pan). Sift together the flour and salt; rub in 25g/1oz/2 tbsp of the butter.

2 Stir in the yeast and make a central well. Slowly add the milk and egg, stirring, then beat until the dough leaves the sides of the bowl clean.

3 Knead the dough for several minutes until smooth. Place in an oiled bowl, cover with oiled clear film (plastic wrap) and set aside until doubled in size.

4 Transfer the dough to a floured surface, gently knock back (punch down) and roll it out to a rectangle 30 x 23cm/12 x 9in.

5 Mix together the dried fruit, peel and sugar in a bowl. Melt the remaining butter and brush over the dough. Sprinkle over the fruit mixture, leaving a 2.5cm/1in border. Roll up the dough from a long side. Seal the edges, then cut into 12 slices.

6 Place the slices, cut sides up, in the greased tin. Cover with clear film and set aside until doubled in size.

7 Bake for 30 minutes, or until a rich golden brown. Brush with honey and leave to cool slightly in the tin before turning out.

Energy 138kcal/582kJ; Fat 3.7g, Saturated Fat 2g; Carbohydrate 25g, Fibre 0.8g

Sticky Nut Buns

These tasty buns will be extremely popular with adults and children alike, so save time by making double the quantity and freezing half for another occasion.

Makes 12

160ml/5½fl oz/generous ⅔ cup lukewarm milk
15ml/1 tbsp active dried yeast
30ml/2 tbsp caster (superfine) sugar
450g/1lb/4 cups strong white bread flour
5ml/1 tsp salt
115g/4oz/½ cup cold butter, cut into small pieces
2 eggs, lightly beaten
finely grated rind of 1 lemon

For the filling

275g/10oz/scant 1½ cups soft dark brown sugar
65g/2½oz/5 tbsp butter
120ml/4fl oz/½ cup water
75g/3oz/¾ cup chopped pecan nuts or walnuts
45ml/3 tbsp caster (superfine) sugar
10ml/2 tsp ground cinnamon
165g/5½oz/generous 1 cup raisins

1 Preheat the oven to 180°C/350°F/Gas 4. Mix the milk, yeast and sugar, and leave until frothy. Combine the flour and salt, and rub in the butter. Add the yeast mixture, eggs and lemon rind.

2 Stir to a rough dough. Knead until smooth, then return to the bowl, cover and leave until doubled in size.

3 To make the filling cook the brown sugar, butter and water in a heavy pan until syrupy, about 10 minutes. Place 15ml/1 tbsp syrup in the base of twelve 4cm/½in muffin cups. Sprinkle a thin layer of nuts in each, reserving the remainder.

4 Knock back (punch down) the dough and roll out to a 45 x 30cm/18 x 12in rectangle. Combine the sugar, cinnamon, raisins and reserved nuts. Sprinkle over the dough. Roll up tightly from a long edge and cut into 2.5cm/1in rounds. Place in the muffin cups, cut sides up. Leave to rise for 30 minutes.

5 Bake until golden, about 25 minutes. Invert the tins on to a baking sheet, leave for 5 minutes, then remove the tins. Cool on a wire rack, sticky sides up.

Energy 439kcal/1844kJ; Fat 18.4g, Saturated Fat 8.6g; Carbohydrate 66.3g, Fibre 1.7g

Oatmeal Buttermilk Muffins

These easy-to-make muffins make a healthy treat for breakfast, or a snack at any time of the day.

Makes 12

75g/3oz/scant 1 cup rolled oats
250ml/8fl oz/1 cup buttermilk
115g/4oz/½ cup butter, at room temperature
75g/3oz/scant ½ cup soft dark brown sugar
1 egg, at room temperature
115g/4oz/1 cup plain (all-purpose) flour
5ml/1 tsp baking powder
1.5ml/¼ tsp bicarbonate of soda (baking soda)
1.5ml/¼ tsp salt
25g/1oz/¼ cup raisins

1 In a bowl, combine the oats and buttermilk, and leave to soak for 1 hour.

2 Grease 12 muffin cups or use paper cases.

3 Preheat the oven to 200°C/400°F/Gas 6. With an electric mixer, cream the butter and sugar until light and fluffy. Beat in the egg.

4 In another bowl, sift together the flour, baking powder, bicarbonate of soda, and salt. Stir into the butter mixture, alternating with the oat mixture. Fold in the raisins. Take care not to overmix.

5 Fill the prepared cups two-thirds full. Bake until a skewer inserted in the centre comes out clean, 20–25 minutes. Transfer to a rack to cool.

Cook's Tips

- *For perfect muffins every time never overbeat the batter. Just mix enough to blend, but don't worry about there being a few lumps. An overbeaten batter will result in tough and rubbery muffins.*
- *If you are not using a tray with muffin cups, use two paper cases for each muffin, to support the batter and stop the sides from collapsing.*

Energy 172kcal/721kJ; Fat 9.1g, Saturated Fat 5.2g; Carbohydrate 20.9g, Fibre 0.8g

Pumpkin Muffins

Molasses adds a delicious flavour to these spicy muffins. For a change, add chopped dried apricots instead of currants.

Makes 14

150g/5oz/10 tbsp butter or margarine, at room temperature
175g/6oz/¾ cup soft dark brown sugar
115g/4oz/⅓ cup molasses
1 egg, at room temperature, beaten
225g/8oz/1 cup cooked or canned pumpkin
200g/7oz/1¾ cups plain (all-purpose) flour
1.5ml/¼ tsp salt
5ml/1 tsp bicarbonate of soda (baking soda)
10ml/1 tsp ground cinnamon
5ml/1 tsp freshly grated nutmeg
50g/2oz/¼ cup currants or raisins

1 Preheat the oven to 200°C/400°F/Gas 6. Grease 14 muffin cups or use paper cases.

2 With an electric mixer, cream the butter or margarine. Add the sugar and molasses, and beat until light and fluffy.

3 Add the egg and pumpkin and stir until well blended.

4 Sift over the flour, salt, bicarbonate of soda, cinnamon, and nutmeg. Fold just enough to blend; do not overmix.

5 Fold in the currants or raisins.

6 Spoon the batter into the prepared muffin cups, filling them three-quarters full.

7 Bake for 12–15 minutes, or until the tops spring back when touched lightly. Serve warm or cold.

Cook's Tip

Strong-flavoured molasses, sometimes called black treacle, is the residue left when cane sugar is refined. Blackstrap molasses, especially, contains small amounts of minerals including iron.

Energy 216kcal/906kJ; Fat 9.4g, Saturated Fat 5.7g; Carbohydrate 32.5g, Fibre 0.7g

Blueberry Muffins

Hot blueberry muffins with a hint of vanilla are an American favourite for breakfast, brunch or tea.

Makes 12

350g/12oz/3 cups plain (all-purpose) flour
10ml/2 tsp baking powder
1.5ml/¼ tsp salt
115g/4oz/½ cup caster (superfine) sugar
2 eggs, beaten
300ml/½ pint/1¼ cups milk
115g/4oz/½ cup butter, melted
5ml/1 tsp vanilla extract
175g/6oz/1½ cups fresh blueberries

1 Preheat the oven to 200°C/400°F/Gas 6. Grease 12 muffin cups or use paper cases.

2 Sift the flour, baking powder and salt into a large mixing bowl and stir in the sugar.

3 Place the eggs, milk, butter and vanilla extract in a separate bowl and whisk together well.

4 Fold the egg mixture into the dry ingredients with a metal spoon, then gently stir in the blueberries.

5 Spoon the mixture into the muffin cups, filling them to just below the top.

6 Place in the oven and bake for 20–25 minutes, or until the muffins are well risen and lightly browned.

7 Leave the muffins in the cups for about 5 minutes, and then turn them out on to a wire rack to cool. Serve warm or cold.

Variation

Most fruit muffin recipes can be varied to use all kinds of different berries. Try blackcurrants or redcurrants instead of the blueberries here, if you like. Remember to stir the fruit in very gently so that the juice does not "bleed" into the batter.

Energy 236kcal/992kJ; Fat 9.6g, Saturated Fat 5.6g; Carbohydrate 34.7g, Fibre 1.4g

Apple and Cranberry Muffins with Walnuts

Not too sweet but good and spicy, these muffins will be a favourite with family and friends.

Makes 12

50g/2oz/¼ cup butter
1 egg
90g/3½oz/½ cup caster (superfine) sugar
grated rind of 1 orange
120ml/4fl oz/½ cup fresh orange juice
150g/5oz/1¼ cups plain (all-purpose) flour
5ml/1 tsp baking powder
2.5ml/½ tsp bicarbonate of soda (baking soda)
5ml/1 tsp ground cinnamon
2.5ml/½ tsp freshly grated nutmeg
2.5ml/½ tsp mixed (apple pie) spice
1.5ml/¼ tsp ground ginger
1.5ml/¼ tsp salt
1 or 2 eating apples
175g/6oz/1½ cups cranberries
50g/2oz/½ cup chopped walnuts
icing (confectioners') sugar, for dusting (optional)

1 Preheat the oven to 180°C/350°F/Gas 4. Grease 12 muffin cups or use paper cases. Melt the butter over a gentle heat. Set aside to cool.

2 Place the egg in a mixing bowl and whisk lightly. Add the melted butter and whisk to combine, then add the sugar, orange rind and juice. Whisk to blend.

3 In a large bowl, sift together the flour, baking powder, bicarbonate of soda, spices and salt.

4 Quarter, core and peel the apples. Use a sharp knife to chop them coarsely.

5 Make a well in the dry ingredients and pour in the egg mixture. With a spoon, stir until just blended. Add the apples, cranberries and walnuts, and stir to blend.

6 Fill the cups three-quarters full and bake until the the tops spring back when touched lightly, about 25–30 minutes. Transfer to a wire rack to cool. Dust with icing sugar before serving, if you like.

Energy 149kcal/624kJ; Fat 6.9g, Saturated Fat 2.6g; Carbohydrate 20.4g, Fibre 0.9g

Yogurt and Honey Muffins

Here is just the recipe for a relaxed Sunday breakfast: fragrant honey muffins served warm – heaven!

Makes 12

50g/2oz/4 tbsp butter
75ml/5 tbsp clear honey
250ml/8fl oz/1 cup natural (plain) yogurt
1 large (US extra large) egg, at room temperature
grated rind of 1 lemon
50ml/2fl oz/¼ cup lemon juice
150g/5oz/1¼ cups plain (all-purpose) flour
175g/6oz/1½ cups wholemeal (whole-wheat) flour
7.5ml/1½ tsp bicarbonate of soda (baking soda)
1.5ml/¼ tsp freshly grated nutmeg

1 Preheat the oven to 190°C/375°F/Gas 5. Grease 12 muffin cups or use paper cases.

2 In a pan, melt the butter and honey. Remove from the heat and set aside to cool slightly.

3 In a bowl, whisk together the yogurt, egg, lemon rind and juice. Add the butter and honey mixture. Set aside.

4 In another bowl, sift together the plain and wholemeal flours with the bicarbonate of soda and nutmeg. Fold them into the yogurt mixture to blend.

5 Fill the prepared cups two-thirds full. Bake until the tops spring back when touched lightly, about 20–25 minutes.

6 Cool in the tin (pan) for 5 minutes before turning out. Serve warm or at room temperature.

Variation
You can make these fabulous muffins more substantial by adding 50g/2oz/½ cup chopped walnuts with the flour at step 4, if you like.

Energy 155kcal/652kJ; Fat 4.6g, Saturated Fat 2.5g; Carbohydrate 25.4g, Fibre 1.7g

Prune Muffins

Prunes bring a delightful moisture to these tasty and wholesome muffins.

Makes 12

1 egg
250ml/8fl oz/1 cup milk
120ml/4fl oz/½ cup vegetable oil
45g/1¾oz/scant ¼ cup caster (superfine) sugar
25g/1oz/2 tbsp soft dark brown sugar
275g/10oz/2½ cups plain (all-purpose) flour
10ml/2 tsp baking powder
2.5ml/½ tsp salt
1.5ml/¼ tsp freshly grated nutmeg
115g/4oz/½ cup cooked pitted prunes, chopped

1 Preheat the oven to 200°C/400°F/Gas 6. Grease 12 muffin cups or use paper cases.

2 Break the egg into a mixing bowl and beat with a fork. Beat in the milk and oil. Stir in the sugars and set aside.

3 Sift the flour, baking powder, salt and nutmeg into a mixing bowl. Make a well in the centre, pour in the egg mixture and stir until moistened. Do not overmix; the batter should be slightly lumpy. Finally, fold in the prunes.

4 Fill the prepared cups two-thirds full. Bake until golden brown, about 20 minutes. Leave to stand for 10 minutes before turning out. Serve warm or at room temperature.

Cook's Tip
Soak the prunes for a few hours before cooking in water to cover. They will take about 20 minutes to cook. Remove the pits from the cooked fruit.

Variation
Try this recipe with dried peaches, soaked and cooked as for the prunes. You could use orange juice instead of water, if you like.

Energy 190kcal/801kJ; Fat 7.8g, Saturated Fat 1.2g; Carbohydrate 28.1g, Fibre 1.3g

Crunchy Muesli Muffins

These muesli muffins are great for breakfast.

Makes 10

150g/5oz/1¼ cups plain (all-purpose) flour, sifted
12.5ml/2½ tsp baking powder
30ml/2 tbsp caster (superfine) sugar
200g/7oz/1½ cups toasted oat cereal with raisins
250ml/8fl oz/1 cup milk
50g/2oz/¼ cup butter, melted, or corn oil
1 egg, beaten

1 Preheat the oven to 200°C/400°F/Gas 6. Grease 10 muffin cups or use paper cases.

2 Mix the flour, baking powder and sugar together in a large bowl. Stir in the oat cereal. In a separate bowl, combine the milk, melted butter or corn oil and the beaten egg. Add to the dry ingredients. Stir until moistened, but do not overmix.

3 Spoon the mixture into the cups, leaving room for the muffins to rise. Bake for 20 minutes, then transfer to a wire rack.

Cheese Muffins

Makes 9

50g/2oz/¼ cup butter, melted
175g/6oz/1½ cups plain (all-purpose) flour
10ml/2 tsp baking powder
30ml/2 tbsp caster (superfine) sugar
a pinch of salt
5ml/1 tsp paprika
2 eggs
120ml/4fl oz/½ cup milk
5ml/1 tsp dried thyme
50g/2oz mature (sharp) Cheddar cheese, cut into 1cm/½in dice

1 Preheat the oven to 190°C/375°F/Gas 5. Grease nine muffin cups or use paper cases. Sift the dry ingredients into a bowl.

2 Whisk the eggs, milk, butter and thyme in another bowl. Add to the dry ingredients and gently stir. Place a spoonful of batter into each cup. Add a few pieces of cheese to each and top with another spoonful of batter. Bake for 25 minutes, or until golden.

Top: Energy 199kcal/841kJ; Fat 7g, Saturated Fat 3.1g; Carbohydrate 30.6g, Fibre 1.8g
Above: Energy 166Kcal/698kJ; Fat 8.1g; Saturated fat 4.6g; Carbohydrate 19.3g; Fibre 0.6g

Raspberry Muffins

Adapt the traditional Cornish cream-tea tradition by serving these fabulous muffins barely warm, split and with a dollop of clotted cream.

Makes 12

50g/2oz/¼ cup butter, melted
115g/4oz/1 cup self-raising (self-rising) flour
115g/4oz/1 cup self-raising wholemeal (whole-wheat) flour
2.5ml/½ tsp salt
45ml/3 tbsp caster (superfine) sugar
2 eggs, beaten
200ml/7fl oz/scant 1 cup milk
175g/6oz/1 cup raspberries, fresh or frozen (defrosted for less than 30 minutes)

1 Melt the butter in a small pan over a low heat and then set it aside until required.

2 Preheat the oven to 190°C/375°F/Gas 5. Lightly grease 12 muffin cups, or use paper cases.

3 Sift the white and wholemeal flours with salt then tip in any wheat flakes left in the sieve. Add the caster sugar.

4 Beat the eggs, milk and melted butter together and stir into the dry ingredients to make a thick batter.

5 Stir the raspberries in gently. If you mix too much the raspberries begin to disintegrate and colour the dough. Spoon into the cups or paper cases.

6 Bake for 30 minutes, or until well risen and just firm to the touch. Leave to cool in the tin placed on a wire rack. Serve warm or cool.

Cook's Tips
Frozen fruits, especially delicate ones like raspberries, are more likely to "bleed" into the batter than fresh soft fruits so just a quick stir will do. Frozen berries will also make the batter solidify so you need to add them and stir immediately.

Energy 132kcal/555kJ; Fat 5g, Saturated Fat 2.7g; Carbohydrate 19g, Fibre 1.5g

Scones

Traditionally, scones should be served warm from the oven, with butter, clotted or whipped cream, and jam.

Makes 10–12

225g/8oz/2 cups plain (all-purpose) flour
15ml/1 tbsp baking powder
50g/2oz/4 tbsp cold butter, diced
1 egg, beaten
75ml/5 tbsp milk
1 beaten egg, to glaze

1 Preheat the oven to 220°C/425°F/Gas 7. Lightly butter a baking sheet. Sift the flour and baking powder together, then rub in the butter using your fingertips or a pastry cutter.

2 Make a well in the centre of the flour mixture, add the egg and milk and mix to a soft dough using a round-bladed knife.

3 Turn out the scone dough on to a floured surface, and knead very lightly until smooth.

4 Roll out the dough to about a 2cm/¾ in thickness and cut into ten or twelve circles using a 5cm/2in plain or fluted cutter dipped in flour.

5 Transfer to the baking sheet, brush with egg, then bake for about 8 minutes, or until risen and golden. Cool slightly on a wire rack before serving.

Cook's Tips

- *For perfectly delicate scones every time, handle the dough as little as possible.*
- *Always have the oven preheated so that once the dough is made and cut into rounds the scones can go straight into the oven.*
- *As well as served warm from the oven, scones taste delicious when cool, and are even tasty the next day split and toasted under a preheated grill (broiler). Butter them while they are still hot.*

Energy 104kcal/437kJ; Fat 4.2g, Saturated Fat 2.4g; Carbohydrate 14.9g, Fibre 0.6g

Drop Scones

If you place the cooked scones in a folded dish towel they will stay soft and moist.

Makes 8–10

115g/4oz/1 cup plain (all-purpose) flour
5ml/1 tsp bicarbonate of soda (baking soda)
5ml/1 tsp cream of tartar
25g/1oz/2 tbsp cold butter, diced
1 egg, beaten
150ml/¼ pint/⅔ cup milk

1 Lightly grease a cast-iron griddle or heavy frying pan, then preheat it.

2 Sift the dry ingredients together, then rub in the butter until the mixture resembles breadcrumbs.

3 Make a well in the centre, then, using a wooden spoon, beat in the egg and sufficient milk to give the mixture the consistency of double (heavy) cream.

4 Drop spoonfuls of the mixture, spaced slightly apart, on to the griddle or frying pan. Cook over a steady heat for 2–3 minutes, until bubbles rise to the surface and burst.

5 Using a metal spatula, turn the scones over and cook for a further 2–3 minutes, or until golden underneath. Serve warm with butter and honey.

Cook's Tip

For best results always cook these traditional scones on a cast-iron griddle. The correct heat is important, as the crust of the drop scones will brown too quickly leaving the centre uncooked if the griddle is too hot. If the griddle is too cool, the scones will take too long to cook and will not be as light. To test the heat, preheat the griddle and then sprinkle a little flour over the surface. If it turns golden in about 3 minutes it is ready for the drop scones.

Energy 72kcal/303kJ; Fat 3g, Saturated Fat 1.6g; Carbohydrate 9.7g, Fibre 0.4g

Wholemeal Scones

Split these wholesome scones in two with a fork while still warm and spread with butter and home-made jam, if you wish.

Makes 16

175g/6oz/¾ cup cold butter
350g/12oz/3 cups plain (all-purpose) wholemeal (whole-wheat) flour
150g/5oz/1¼ cups plain (all-purpose) flour
30ml/2 tbsp caster (superfine) sugar
2.5ml/½ tsp salt
12.5ml/2½ tsp bicarbonate of soda (baking soda)
2 eggs
175ml/6fl oz/¾ cup buttermilk
35g/1¼oz/¼ cup raisins

1 Preheat the oven to 200°C/400°F/Gas 6. Grease and flour a large baking sheet.

2 Cut the butter into small pieces. Combine the wholemeal and plain flours with the sugar, salt and bicarbonate of soda in a bowl. Add the butter and rub in using your fingertips or a pastry cutter until the mixture resembles coarse breadcrumbs. Set aside.

3 In another bowl, whisk together the eggs and buttermilk. Set aside 30ml/2 tbsp for glazing, then stir the remaining egg mixture into the dry ingredients until it just holds together. Stir in the raisins.

4 Roll out the dough to about 2cm/¾in thickness. Stamp out circles with a cookie cutter. Place on the baking sheet and brush with the reserved egg and buttermilk glaze.

5 Bake until golden, about 12–15 minutes. Allow to cool slightly before serving.

Variation
Raisin scones also go particularly well with cheese, so serve them for tea with a mature (sharp) Cheddar, a full-flavoured blue cheese or a creamy soft cheese such as Camembert or Brie.

Energy 207kcal/869kJ; Fat 10.3g, Saturated Fat 6g; Carbohydrate 25.3g, Fibre 2.3g

Orange and Raisin Scones

As well as warm from the oven, these scones are also superb split when cool and toasted under a preheated grill. Butter them while still hot.

Makes 16

275g/10oz/2½ cups plain (all-purpose) flour
25ml/1½ tbsp baking powder
60g/2¼oz/generous ¼ cup caster (superfine) sugar
2.5ml/½ tsp salt
65g/2½oz/5 tbsp butter, diced
65g/2½oz/5 tbsp margarine, diced
grated rind of 1 large orange
50g/2oz/scant ½ cup raisins
120ml/4fl oz/½ cup buttermilk
milk, to glaze

1 Preheat the oven to 220°C/425°F/Gas 7. Grease and flour a large baking sheet.

2 Combine the flour with the baking powder, sugar and salt in a large bowl. Add the butter and margarine, and rub in using your fingertips or a pastry cutter until the mixture resembles coarse breadcrumbs.

3 Add the orange rind and raisins. Gradually stir in the buttermilk to form a soft dough.

4 Roll out the dough to about a 2cm/¾in thickness. Stamp out circles with a cookie cutter. Place on the baking sheet and brush the tops with milk.

5 Bake until golden, about 12–15 minutes. Serve hot or warm, with butter, or whipped or clotted cream and jam.

Cook's Tip
Try these scones the Cornish way (usually reserved for plain scones): split them and spread each half with a little home-made raspberry or strawberry jam (no butter); now add a dollop of real Cornish or Devon clotted cream. Enjoy with a cup of tea, and preferably choose a summer's afternoon so that you can eat them outdoors for the authentic experience.

Energy 145kcal/606kJ; Fat 6.9g, Saturated Fat 2.2g; Carbohydrate 19.8g, Fibre 0.6g

Cheese and Chive Scones

Feta cheese is used instead of butter in these delicious savoury scones, which make a tasty alternative to traditional scones.

Makes 9

115g/4oz/1 cup self-raising (self-rising) flour
150g/5oz/1 cup self-raising (self-rising) wholemeal (whole-wheat) flour
2.5ml/½ tsp salt
75g/3oz feta cheese
15ml/1 tbsp chopped fresh chives
150ml/¼ pint/⅔ cup milk, plus extra to glaze
1.5ml/¼ tsp cayenne pepper

1 Preheat the oven to 200°C/400°F/Gas 6. Sift the flours and salt into a large mixing bowl. Add any bran left in the sieve.

2 Crumble the feta cheese and rub it into the dry ingredients until the mixture resembles breadcrumbs. Stir in the chives, then add the milk and mix to a soft dough.

3 Turn the dough out on to a floured surface and lightly knead until smooth. Roll out to a 2cm/¾in thickness and stamp out scones with a 6cm/2½in cookie cutter.

4 Transfer the scones to a non-stick baking sheet. Brush with milk, then sprinkle with the cayenne pepper. Bake for 15 minutes, or until risen and golden. Cool slightly on a wire rack before serving.

Variation

For Cheddar cheese and mustard scones, add 2.5ml/½ tsp mustard powder to the flours. Dice 50g/2oz/½ cup cold butter, and rub it into the dry ingredients until the mixture resembles breadcrumbs. Stir 50g/2oz/½ cup grated mature (sharp) Cheddar cheese into the mixture, then pour in the milk. Stir gently to make a soft dough. Roll out on a lightly floured surface and cut into triangles. Place on a baking sheet, brush with milk and sprinkle with 25g/1oz/¼ cup cheese. Bake for 15 minutes, or until well risen.

Energy 124kcal/524kJ; Fat 2.5g, Saturated Fat 1.4g; Carbohydrate 21.5g, Fibre 1.9g

Sunflower Sultana Scones

Sunflower seeds give these fruit scones an interesting flavour and texture.

Makes 10–12

225g/8oz/2 cups self-raising (self-rising) flour
5ml/1 tsp baking powder
25g/1oz/2 tbsp soft sunflower margarine
30ml/2 tbsp golden caster (superfine) sugar
50g/2oz/⅓ cup sultanas (golden raisins)
30ml/2 tbsp sunflower seeds
150g/5oz/scant ⅔ cup natural (plain) yogurt
about 30–45ml/ 2–3 tbsp skimmed milk

1 Preheat the oven to 230°C/450°F/Gas 8. Lightly oil a baking sheet. Sift the flour and baking powder into a bowl and rub in the margarine evenly.

2 Stir in the sugar, sultanas and half the sunflower seeds, then mix in the yogurt, with just enough milk to make a fairly soft, but not sticky, dough.

3 Roll out on a lightly floured surface to about a 2cm/¾in thickness. Cut into 6cm/2½in flower shapes or rounds with a cookie cutter and lift on to the baking sheet.

4 Brush with milk and sprinkle with the reserved sunflower seeds, then bake for 10–12 minutes, or until well risen and golden brown. Cool the scones on a wire rack. Serve split, spread with jam or low-fat spread.

Cook's Tip

Sunflower seeds are a wonder food, and a good and tasty way to add nutrients to the diet, especially selenium, which is often lacking. Don't buy too many at one time and source them from a store where they have a quick turnover so that the ones you buy are fresh. As sunflower seeds have a high fat content they don't store well for long periods. Buy small quantities at a time and put them in a sealed container in a cool place – even a refrigerator.

Energy 121kcal/513kJ; Fat 3.3g, Saturated Fat 0.6g; Carbohydrate 21.2g, Fibre 0.8g

Buttermilk Scones

If time is short, drop heaped tablespoonfuls of the mixture on to the baking sheet.

Makes 10

225g/8oz/2 cups plain (all-purpose) flour
5ml/1 tsp baking powder
2.5ml/½ tsp bicarbonate of soda (baking soda)
5ml/1 tsp salt
50g/2oz/¼ cup butter or margarine, chilled
175ml/6fl oz/¾ cup buttermilk

1 Preheat the oven to 220°C/425°F/Gas 7. Sift the dry ingredients into a mixing bowl. Rub in the butter or margarine until the mixture resembles coarse breadcrumbs.

2 Add the buttermilk and combine well to form a soft dough. Turn on to a lightly floured surface and knead for 30 seconds.

3 Roll out to a 1cm/½in thickness. Cut rounds with a floured 6cm/2½in pastry (cookie) cutter. Transfer to a baking sheet and bake for 10–12 minutes. Serve with butter and honey.

Lavender Scones

Makes 12

225g/8oz/2 cups plain (all-purpose) flour
15ml/1 tbsp baking powder
50g/2oz/¼ cup butter
40g/1½oz/3 tbsp caster (superfine) sugar
10ml/2 tsp fresh lavender florets, chopped
about 175ml/6fl oz/¾ cup milk

1 Preheat the oven to 220°C/425°F/Gas 7. Grease a baking sheet. Sift the flour and baking powder into a bowl. Rub in the butter until the mixture resembles breadcrumbs.

2 Stir in the sugar and most of the lavender, reserving a little to decorate. Add enough milk to make a soft dough. Turn on to a floured surface and roll out to 2.5cm/1in thick. Cut 12 rounds with a floured cutter and place on the baking sheet. Brush the tops with milk and sprinkle with lavender. Bake for 10–12 minutes.

Top: Energy 120kcal/503kJ; Fat 4.5g, Saturated Fat 2.7g; Carbohydrate 18.3g, Fibre 0.7g
Above: Energy 115Kcal/484kJ; Fat 3.9g; Saturated fat 2.4g; Carbohydrate 18.8g; Fibre 0.6g

Date Oven Scones

The rich taste of dates gives these scones a full flavour but you can adapt the recipe for use with ready-to-eat dried apricots or peaches as well.

Makes 12

225g/8oz/2 cups self-raising (self-rising) flour
a pinch of salt
50g/2oz/4 tbsp butter
50g/2oz/¼ cup caster (superfine) sugar
50g/2oz/⅓ cup finely chopped dates
150ml/¼ pint/⅔ cup milk
1 beaten egg, to glaze

1 Preheat the oven to 230°C/450°F/Gas 8. Sift the flour and salt into a bowl and rub in the butter using your fingertips or a pastry cutter until the mixture resembles fine breadcrumbs.

2 Add the sugar and chopped dates to the mixture, and stir to blend.

3 Make a well in the centre of the dry ingredients and add the milk. Stir with a fork until the mixture comes together into a fairly soft dough.

4 Turn the dough out on to a lightly floured surface and knead gently for 30 seconds. Roll it out to a 2cm/¾in thickness.

5 Cut out circles with a cookie cutter. Arrange them, not touching, on an ungreased baking sheet, then glaze with the beaten egg.

6 Bake in the oven for 8–10 minutes, or until well risen and golden brown. Using a metal spatula, transfer the scones to a wire rack to cool completely.

Cook's Tip

For light and airy scones don't handle the dough too much and be careful not the roll it out too thinly or the scones will not rise sufficiently.

Energy 128kcal/542kJ; Fat 3.9g, Saturated Fat 2.4g; Carbohydrate 22.4g, Fibre 0.8g

Cheese and Marjoram Scones

A great success for a hearty tea. With savoury toppings, these scones can make a good basis for a light lunch.

Makes 18

115g/4oz/1 cup plain (all-purpose) wholemeal (whole-wheat) flour
115g/4oz/1 cup self-raising (self-rising) flour
a pinch of salt
40g/1½oz/3 tbsp butter
1.5ml/¼ tsp dry mustard
10ml/2 tsp dried marjoram
50–75g/2–3oz/½–¾ cup finely grated Cheddar cheese
120ml/4fl oz/½ cup milk, or as required
50g/2oz/½ cup chopped pecan nuts or walnuts

1 Gently sift the two flours into a bowl and add the salt. Cut the butter into small pieces, and rub into the flour using your fingertips or a pastry cutter until the mixture resembles fine breadcrumbs.

2 Add the mustard, marjoram and grated cheese, and mix in sufficient milk to make a soft dough. Knead the dough lightly.

3 Preheat the oven to 220°C/425°F/Gas 7. Lightly grease two or three baking sheets.

4 Roll out the dough on a floured surface to about a 2cm/¾in thickness and cut it out with a 5cm/2in square cookie cutter. Place the scones, slightly apart, on the baking sheets.

5 Brush the scones with a little milk and then sprinkle the chopped pecan nuts or walnuts over the top. Bake for about 12 minutes. Serve warm, spread with butter.

Cook's Tip
English mustard has been a traditional ingredient in many cheese dishes, as it sharpens the flavour of the cheese making it more pronounced. Always use dry mustard for adding to recipes such as the scones here or to pep up cheese toasts made with grated cheese, and remember: a little goes a long way.

Energy 121kcal/504kJ; Fat 8g, Saturated Fat 2.4g; Carbohydrate 9.8g, Fibre 1.1g

Dill and Potato Cakes

Adding dill to these potato cakes makes them irresistible.

Makes 10

225g/8oz/2 cups self-raising (self-rising) flour
40g/1½oz/3 tbsp butter, softened
a pinch of salt
15ml/1 tbsp chopped fresh dill
175g/6oz/2 cups mashed potato, freshly made
30–45ml/2–3 tbsp milk

1 Preheat the oven to 230°C/450°F/Gas 8. Grease a baking sheet. Sift the flour into a bowl and add the butter, salt and dill. Mix in the mashed potato and enough milk to make a soft, pliable dough.

2 Roll out the dough on a well-floured surface until fairly thin. Cut into circles with a 7.5cm/3in cookie)cutter. Place the potato cakes on the baking sheet and bake them for 20–25 minutes, or until risen and golden.

Savoury Cheese Whirls

Makes 20

250g/9oz frozen puff pastry, thawed
15ml/1 tbsp vegetable extract
1 egg, beaten
50g/2oz/½ cup grated Cheddar cheese

1 Preheat the oven to 220°C/425°F/Gas 7. Grease a large baking sheet. Roll out the pastry on a lightly floured surface to a large rectangle, measuring about 35 x 25cm/14 x 10in.

2 Spread the pastry with vegetable extract, leaving a 1cm/½in border. Brush the edges of the pastry with egg and sprinkle over the cheese. Roll the pastry up quite tightly, starting from a long edge. Brush the outside of the pastry with beaten egg. Cut the pastry roll into slices 4cm/1½in thick and place on the baking sheet. Bake for 12–15 minutes, until the pastry is well risen and golden. Arrange on a serving plate and serve warm or cold with carrot and cucumber sticks.

Top: Energy 121kcal/508kJ; Fat 3.7g, Saturated Fat 2.2g; Carbohydrate 20.6g, Fibre 0.9g
Above: Energy 61Kcal/256kJ; Fat 4.2g; Saturated fat 0.6g; Carbohydrate 4.6g; Fibre 0g

Open Apple Pie

An open pie like this looks attractive and uses less pastry than a double-crust pie. If using eating apples for this pie, make sure they are firm-fleshed rather than soft.

Serves 8

1.3–1.6kg/3–3½lb tart eating or cooking apples
45g/1¾oz/scant ¼ cup caster (superfine) sugar
10ml/2 tsp ground cinnamon
grated rind and juice of 1 lemon
25g/1oz/2 tbsp butter, diced
30–45ml/2–3 tbsp honey, to glaze

For the pastry

275g/10oz/2½ cups plain (all-purpose) flour
2.5ml/½ tsp salt
115g/4oz/½ cup cold butter, diced
60g/2¼oz/4½ tbsp white cooking fat or lard, diced
75–90ml/5–6 tbsp iced water

1 To make the pastry, sift the flour and salt into a bowl. Add the butter and fat and rub in using your fingertips or a pastry cutter until the mixture resembles coarse breadcrumbs.

2 Stir in just enough water to bind the dough. Gather the dough into a ball, wrap in clear film (plastic wrap) and chill for at least 20 minutes.

3 Preheat the oven to 200°C/400°F/Gas 6. Place a baking sheet in the oven.

4 Peel, core and slice the apples thinly. Combine with the sugar, cinnamon, lemon rind and juice.

5 Roll out the pastry to a 30cm/12in circle. Use to line a 23cm/9in pie dish, leaving an overhanging edge. Fill with the apples. Fold in the edges and crimp loosely. Dot the apples with diced butter.

6 Bake on the hot baking sheet until the pastry is golden and the apples are tender, about 45 minutes.

7 Melt the honey in a pan and brush over the apples to glaze. Serve warm or at room temperature.

Energy 418kcal/1755kJ; Fat 22.5g, Saturated Fat 12.2g; Carbohydrate 53.7g, Fibre 4.1g

Apple and Cranberry Lattice Pie

Cranberries and raisins add colour and flavour to this pie.

Serves 8

grated rind of 1 orange
45ml/3 tbsp orange juice
2 large cooking apples
175g/6oz/1⅓ cups cranberries
65g/2½oz/½ cup raisins
25g/1oz/¼ cup chopped walnuts
215g/7½oz/generous 1 cup caster (superfine) sugar
115g/4oz/½ cup soft dark brown sugar
15g/½oz/2 tbsp plain (all-purpose) flour

For the pastry

275g/10oz/2½ cups plain (all-purpose) flour
2.5ml/½ tsp salt
75g/3oz/6 tbsp cold butter, diced
75g/3oz/½ cup cold white cooking fat or lard, diced
50–120ml/2–4fl oz/¼–½ cup iced water

1 To make the pastry, sift the flour and salt, add the butter and fat and rub in well using your fingertips or a pastry cutter. Stir in enough water to bind the dough. Form into two equal balls, wrap in clear film (plastic wrap) and chill for at least 20 minutes.

2 Put the orange rind and juice into a bowl. Peel and core the apples and grate into the bowl. Stir in the cranberries, raisins, walnuts, all except 15ml/1 tbsp of the caster sugar, the brown sugar and flour. Place a baking sheet in the oven and preheat to 200°C/400°F/Gas 6.

3 Roll out one ball of dough to about 3mm/⅛in thick. Transfer to a 23cm/9in pie plate and trim. Spoon the cranberry and apple mixture into the shell.

4 Roll out the remaining dough to a circle about 28cm/11in in diameter. With a serrated pastry wheel, cut the dough into 10 strips, 2cm/¾in wide. Place five strips horizontally across the top of the tart at 2.5cm/1in intervals. Weave in five vertical strips and trim. Sprinkle the top with the reserved sugar.

5 Bake for 20 minutes, then reduce the heat to 180°C/350°F/Gas 4 and bake for about 15 minutes more.

Energy 528kcal/2223kJ; Fat 22g, Saturated Fat 10.1g; Carbohydrate 83.3g, Fibre 2.2g

Peach Leaf Pie

Pastry leaves top this most attractive spiced summer pie.

Serves 8

1.2kg/2½lb ripe peaches
juice of 1 lemon
90g/3½oz/½ cup caster (superfine) sugar
45ml/3 tbsp cornflour (cornstarch)
1.5ml/¼ tsp freshly grated nutmeg
2.5ml/½ tsp ground cinnamon
1 egg beaten with 15ml/1 tbsp water, to glaze
25g/1oz/2 tbsp cold butter, diced

For the pastry

275g/10oz/2½ cups plain (all-purpose) flour
4ml/¾ tsp salt
115g/4oz/½ cup cold butter, diced
60g/2¼oz/4½ tbsp cold white cooking fat or lard, diced
75–90ml/5–6 tbsp iced water

1 To make the pastry, sift the flour and salt into a bowl. Rub in the butter and fat using your fingertips or a pastry cutter until the mixture resembles breadcrumbs. Stir in just enough water to bind the dough. Gather into two balls, one slightly larger than the other. Wrap and chill for at least 20 minutes. Place a baking sheet in the oven and preheat to 220°C/425°F/Gas 7.

2 Drop the peaches into boiling water for 20 seconds, then transfer to a bowl of cold water. When cool, peel off the skins. Slice the flesh and combine with the lemon juice, sugar, cornflour and spices. Set aside.

3 Roll out the larger dough ball to 3mm/⅛in thick. Use to line a 23cm/9in pie plate. Chill. Roll out the remaining dough to 5mm/¼in thick. Cut out leaves 7.5cm/3in long. Mark veins. With the scraps, roll a few balls.

4 Brush the pastry base with egg glaze. Add the peaches and dot with the butter. Starting from the outside edge, cover the peaches with a ring of leaves. Place a second, staggered ring above. Continue until covered. Place the balls in the centre.

5 Brush with glaze. Bake for 10 minutes. Lower the heat to 180°C/350°F/Gas 4 and bake for 35–40 minutes more.

Energy 424kcal/1778kJ; Fat 22.4g, Saturated Fat 12.2g; Carbohydrate 54.2g, Fibre 3.1g

Walnut and Pear Lattice Pie

For the lattice top, either weave strips of pastry or use a special pastry cutter to create a lattice effect.

Serves 6–8

450g/1lb shortcrust pastry, thawed if frozen
450g/1lb pears, peeled, cored and thinly sliced
50g/2oz/¼ cup caster (superfine) sugar
25g/1oz/¼ cup plain (all-purpose) flour
2.5ml/½ tsp grated lemon rind
25g/1oz/generous ¼ cup raisins or sultanas (golden raisins)
25g/1oz/4 tbsp chopped walnuts
2.5ml/½ tsp ground cinnamon
50g/2oz/½ cup icing (confectioners') sugar
15ml/1 tbsp lemon juice
about 10ml/2 tsp cold water

1 Preheat the oven to 190°C/375°F/Gas 5. Roll out half of the pastry and use it to line a 23cm/9in tin that is about 5cm/2in deep.

2 Combine the pears, caster sugar, flour and lemon rind. Toss to coat the fruit. Mix in the raisins, nuts and cinnamon. Put the filling into the pastry case and spread it evenly.

3 Roll out the remaining pastry and use to make a lattice top. Bake the pie for 55 minutes, or until the pastry is golden brown on top.

4 Combine the icing sugar, lemon juice and water in a bowl and stir until smooth. Remove the pie from the oven. Drizzle the glaze evenly over the top, on the pastry and filling. Leave the pie to cool in its tin on a wire rack.

Variation

Try this tasty pie with apples instead of pears or combine fresh peaches or apricots with almonds instead of using pears and walnuts. To skin the peaches or apricots, drop them into boiling water for 20 seconds and then remove them and plunge them into cold water. Peel away the skins.

Energy 366kcal/1536kJ; Fat 18.1g, Saturated Fat 5.1g; Carbohydrate 49.7g, Fibre 2.6g

Lemon Meringue Pie

Crisp on top and soft beneath, here is a classic dish whose popularity never seems to wane.

Serves 8

225g/8oz shortcrust pastry, thawed if frozen
grated rind and juice of 1 large lemon
250ml/8fl oz/1 cup plus 15ml/1 tbsp cold water
115g/4oz/generous ½ cup caster (superfine) sugar plus 90ml/6 tbsp extra
25g/1oz/2 tbsp butter
45ml/3 tbsp cornflour (cornstarch)
3 eggs, separated
a pinch of salt
a pinch of cream of tartar

1 Line a 23cm/9in pie dish with the pastry, folding under a 1cm/½in overhang to give a firm edge. Crimp the edge and chill for 20 minutes.

2 Preheat the oven to 200°C/400°F/Gas 6. Prick the pastry case base, line with baking parchment and fill with baking beans. Bake for 12 minutes.

3 Remove the paper and beans and bake until golden, 6–8 minutes more.

4 In a pan, combine the lemon rind and juice with 250ml/8fl oz/1 cup of the water, 115g/4oz/generous ½ cup of the sugar, and the butter. Bring to the boil.

5 Meanwhile, dissolve the cornflour in the remaining water. Add the egg yolks. Beat into the lemon mixture, return to the boil and whisk until thick, about 5 minutes. Cover the surface with baking parchment and leave to cool.

6 For the meringue, beat the egg whites, using an electric hand whisk, with the salt and cream of tartar until stiffly peaking. Add the remaining sugar a spoonful at a time and beat until glossy.

7 Spoon the lemon mixture into the pastry case. Spoon the meringue on top, sealing it with the pastry rim. Bake until golden, 12–15 minutes.

Energy 254kcal/1067kJ; Fat 12.6g, Saturated Fat 4.7g; Carbohydrate 33.4g, Fibre 0.5g

Blueberry Pie

Serve this tangy blueberry pie with crème fraîche, double (heavy) cream or vanilla ice cream.

Serves 6–8

450g/1lb shortcrust pastry, thawed if frozen
500g/1¼lb/5 cups blueberries
165g/5½oz/generous ¾ cup caster (superfine) sugar
45ml/3 tbsp plain (all-purpose) flour
5ml/1 tsp grated orange rind
1.5ml/¼ tsp freshly grated nutmeg
30ml/2 tbsp orange juice
5ml/1 tsp lemon juice

1 Preheat the oven to 190°C/375°F/Gas 5. On a lightly floured surface, roll out half of the pastry and use it to line a 23cm/9in pie dish that is 5cm/2in deep.

2 Combine the blueberries, 150g/5oz/¾ cup of the sugar, the flour, orange rind and nutmeg. Toss the mixture gently to coat all the fruit.

3 Pour the blueberry mixture into the pastry case and spread evenly. Sprinkle over the citrus juices.

4 Roll out the remaining pastry and use to cover the pie. Cut out small decorative shapes from the top. Use to decorate the pastry, and finish the edge.

5 Brush the top with water and sprinkle with the remaining caster sugar. Bake for 45 minutes, or until the pastry is golden brown. Serve warm or at room temperature.

Cook's Tip

To twist the edge of a double-crust pie hold the edges of the pie between your thumb and index finger and twist the edges together at 1cm/½in intervals. Alternatively, make a scalloped pattern by holding the finger of one hand against the top edge of the pie and squeezing the pastry with the thumb and forefinger of your other hand on the outside edge of the pie.

Energy 371kcal/1559kJ; Fat 16g, Saturated Fat 4.9g; Carbohydrate 55.8g, Fibre 3.2g

Creamy Banana Pie

Do not prepare the topping for this pie too soon before serving or the banana slices will discolour.

Serves 6

200g/7oz/2¼ cups finely crushed ginger cookies
65g/2½oz/5 tbsp butter or margarine, melted
2.5ml/½ tsp freshly grated nutmeg or ground cinnamon
175g/6oz/1 ripe banana, mashed
350g/12oz/1½ cups cream cheese, at room temperature
50ml/generous 3 tbsp thick natural (plain) yogurt or sour cream
45ml/3 tbsp dark rum or 5ml/1 tsp vanilla extract

For the topping

250ml/8fl oz/1 cup whipping cream
3–4 bananas

1 Preheat the oven to 190°C/375°F/Gas 5. For the crust, combine the crushed cookies, butter or margarine and grated nutmeg or ground cinnamon. Mix together thoroughly with a wooden spoon.

2 Press the cookie mixture into a 23cm/9in pie dish, building up thick sides with a neat edge. Bake the crust for 5 minutes, then leave to cool.

3 Beat the mashed bananas with the cream cheese. Fold in the yogurt or sour cream and rum or vanilla extract. Spread the filling in the cookie case. Chill for at least 4 hours or preferably overnight.

4 To make the topping, whip the cream until soft peaks form. Spread over the pie filling. Slice the bananas and arrange on top in a decorative pattern. Serve immediately.

Variation
As banana slices will discolour very quickly, for the decorative top you could use thinly sliced strawberries instead. They will complement the banana cream filling perfectly.

Energy 753kcal/3128kJ; Fat 58.1g, Saturated Fat 35.6g; Carbohydrate 50.4g, Fibre 1.5g

Red Berry Sponge Tart

When soft berry fruits are in season, serve this delicious tart warm, with scoops of vanilla ice cream.

Serves 4

450g/1lb/4 cups soft berry fruits, such as raspberries, blackberries, blackcurrants, redcurrants, strawberries and blueberries
2 eggs
50g/2oz/¼ cup caster (superfine) sugar, plus extra to taste (optional)
15ml/1 tbsp plain (all-purpose) flour
75g/3oz/¾ cup ground almonds
vanilla ice cream, to serve

1 Preheat the oven to 190°C/375°F/Gas 5. Grease and line a 23cm/9in pie plate with baking parchment.

2 Sprinkle the fruit in the base of the plate with a little sugar if the fruits are tart.

3 Beat the eggs and sugar together for 3–4 minutes, or until they leave a thick trail across the surface.

4 Combine the flour and almonds in a bowl, then carefully fold into the egg mixture with a metal spatula, retaining as much air as possible.

5 Spread the sponge mixture evenly on top of the fruit base, bake in the preheated oven for 15 minutes, then turn out on to a serving plate and serve warm.

Variation
For a more substantial tart, line the pie plate, or use a flan tin (tart pan), with 350g/12oz shortcrust pastry. Line the pastry with baking parchment and fill with baking beans. Bake the crust for 15 minutes and then remove the paper and beans and bake for 10 minutes more. Add the fruit as step 1 and continue with the recipe.

Energy 195kcal/816kJ; Fat 10.7g, Saturated 1.3g; Carbohydrate 19.2g, Fibre 2.2g

De Luxe Mincemeat Tart

Fruity home-made mincemeat is the perfect partner to crumbly, nutty pastry in this rich and festive pie.

Serves 8

225g/8oz/2 cups plain (all-purpose) flour
10ml/2 tsp ground cinnamon
50g/2oz/½ cup finely ground walnuts
115g/4oz/½ cup butter
50g/2oz/¼ cup caster (superfine) sugar, plus extra for dusting
1 egg
2 drops vanilla extract
15ml/1 tbsp cold water

For the mincemeat
2 eating apples, peeled, cored and grated
225g/8oz/generous 1½ cups raisins
115g/4oz/½ cup ready-to-eat dried apricots, chopped
115g/4oz/⅔ cup ready-to-eat dried figs or prunes, chopped
225g/8oz/2 cups green grapes, halved and seeded
50g/2oz/½ cup chopped almonds
finely grated rind of 1 lemon
30ml/2 tbsp lemon juice
30ml/2 tbsp brandy or port
1.5ml/¼ tsp mixed (apple pie) spice
115g/4oz/½ cup soft light brown sugar
25g/1oz/2 tbsp butter, melted

1 Process the flour, cinnamon, nuts and butter in a food processor or blender to make fine crumbs. Turn into a bowl and stir in the sugar. Beat the egg with the vanilla extract and water, and stir into the dry ingredients. Form a soft dough, knead until smooth, then wrap and chill for 30 minutes.

2 Mix the mincemeat ingredients together. Use two-thirds of the pastry to line a 23cm/9in, loose-based flan tin (tart pan). Trim and fill with the mincemeat.

3 Roll out the remaining pastry and cut into 1cm/½in strips. Arrange the strips in a lattice over the top of the pastry, wet the joins and press them together. Chill for 30 minutes.

4 Preheat a baking sheet in the oven at 190°C/375°F/Gas 5. Brush the pastry with water and dust with caster sugar. Bake the tart on the baking sheet for 30–40 minutes. Cool in the tin on a wire rack for 15 minutes, then remove the tin.

Energy 434kcal/1822kJ; Fat 19.6g, Saturated Fat 8.1g; Carbohydrate 63.6g, Fibre 1.8g

Crunchy Apple and Almond Flan

Don't put sugar with the apples as this produces too much liquid. The sweetness is in the pastry and topping.

Serves 8

75g/3oz/6 tbsp butter
175g/6oz/1½ cups plain (all-purpose) flour
25g/1oz/¼ cup ground almonds
25g/1oz/2 tbsp caster (superfine) sugar
1 egg yolk
15ml/1 tbsp cold water
1.5ml/¼ tsp almond extract
675g/1½lb cooking apples
25g/1oz/2 tbsp raisins

For the topping
115g/4oz/1 cup plain (all-purpose) flour
1.5ml/¼ tsp mixed (apple pie) spice
50g/2oz/¼ cup butter, cut into small cubes
50g/2oz/4¼ cup demerara (raw) sugar
50g/2oz/½ cup flaked (sliced) almonds

1 To make the pastry, rub the butter into the flour using your fingertips or a pastry cutter until it resembles breadcrumbs. Stir in the almonds and sugar.

2 Whisk the egg yolk, water and almond extract together and mix into the dry ingredients to form a soft dough. Knead until smooth, wrap, and leave to rest for 20 minutes.

3 To make the topping, sift the flour and spice into a bowl and rub in the butter. Stir in the sugar and almonds.

4 Roll out the pastry and use to line a 23cm/9in loose-based flan tin (tart pan). Trim the top and chill for 15 minutes.

5 Preheat a baking sheet in the oven at 190°C/375°F/Gas 5. Peel, core and slice the apples thinly. Arrange over the pastry in overlapping, concentric circles, doming the centre. Sprinkle with the raisins.

6 Cover with the topping mixture, pressing it on lightly. Bake on the hot baking sheet for 25–30 minutes, or until the top is golden brown and the apples are tender (test them with a fine skewer). Leave the flan to cool in the tin for 10 minutes before serving.

Energy 358kcal/1499kJ; Fat 19.3g, Saturated Fat 8.8g; Carbohydrate 42.5g, Fibre 3.2g

Rhubarb and Cherry Pie

The unusual partnership of rhubarb and cherries works well in this fruity pie. Serve it warm, with a scoop of clotted cream or vanilla ice cream.

Serves 8

450g/1lb rhubarb, cut into 2.5cm/1in pieces
450g/1lb canned pitted tart red or black cherries, drained
275g/10oz/scant 1½ cups caster (superfine) sugar
45ml/3 tbsp quick-cooking tapioca
milk, for glazing

For the pastry
275g/10oz/2½ cups plain (all-purpose) flour
5ml/1 tsp salt
75g/3oz/6 tbsp cold butter, diced
50g/2oz/4 tbsp cold white cooking fat or lard, diced
50–120ml/2–4fl oz/¼–½ cup iced water

1 To make the pastry, sift the flour and salt into a bowl. Add the butter and fat and rub in until the mixture resembles coarse breadcrumbs.

2 Stir in enough water to bind. Form into two balls, wrap in clear film (plastic wrap) and chill for 20 minutes.

3 Preheat a baking sheet in the oven at 200°C/400°F/Gas 6. Roll out one pastry ball and use to line a 23cm/9in pie dish, leaving a 1cm/½in overhang.

4 Mix together the rhubarb pieces, black cherries, caster sugar and tapioca, and spoon into the pastry case.

5 Roll out the remaining pastry ball, cut out four leaf shapes using a leaf cutter or a sharp knife, and use to cover the pie, leaving a 2cm/¾in overhang. Fold this overhang under the pastry base and flute to create an attractive edge. Roll small balls from the scraps, mark veins in the leaves and use to decorate the pie.

6 Glaze the top and bake on the baking sheet until golden, 40–50 minutes. Serve with clotted cream.

Energy 442kcal/1868kJ; Fat 14.4g, Saturated Fat 7.5g; Carbohydrate 78.9g, Fibre 2.2g

Festive Apple Pie

Warming spices transform this pie into a special dish.

Serves 8

900g/2lb cooking apples
15g/½oz/2 tbsp plain (all-purpose) flour
115g/4oz/generous ½ cup caster (superfine) sugar
25ml/1½ tbsp fresh lemon juice
2.5ml/½ tsp ground cinnamon
2.5ml/½ tsp mixed (apple pie) spice
1.5ml/¼ tsp ground ginger
1.5ml/¼ tsp freshly grated nutmeg
1.5ml/¼ tsp salt
50g/2oz/¼ cup butter, diced

For the pastry
275g/10oz/2½ cups plain (all-purpose) flour
5ml/1 tsp salt
75g/3oz/6 tbsp cold butter,diced
50g/2oz/4 tbsp cold white cooking fat or lard, diced
50–120ml/2–4fl oz/¼–½ cup iced water

1 To make the pastry, sift the flour and salt into a bowl. Add the butter and fat, and rub it in until the mixture resembles coarse breadcrumbs.

2 Stir in just enough water to bind the pastry. Form into two balls, wrap in clear film (plastic wrap) and chill in the refrigerator for 20 minutes.

3 Roll out one ball on a lightly floured surface, and use it to line a 23cm/9in pie dish. Preheat a baking sheet in the oven at 220°C/425°F/Gas 7.

4 Peel, core and slice the apples. Toss with the flour, sugar, lemon juice, cinnamon, mixed spice, ginger and nutmeg, and the salt. Spoon into the pastry case and dot with butter.

5 Roll out the remaining pastry ball. Place on top of the pie and trim to leave a 2cm/¾in overhang. Fold this under the pastry base and press to seal. Crimp the edge neatly. Form the scraps into leaf shapes and balls. Arrange on the pie and cut steam vents.

6 Bake on the baking sheet for 10 minutes. Reduce the heat to 180°C/350°F/Gas 4 and bake for 40 minutes, or until golden.

Energy 392kcal/1644kJ; Fat 19.6g, Saturated Fat 10.7g; Carbohydrate 53.3g, Fibre 2.9g

Black Bottom Pie

Chocolate and rum make a winning combination over a crunchy ginger base.

Serves 8

10ml/2 tsp powdered gelatine
45ml/3 tbsp cold water
2 eggs, separated
150g/5oz/¾ cup caster (superfine) sugar
15g/½oz/2 tbsp cornflour (cornstarch)
2.5ml/½ tsp salt
475ml/16fl oz/2 cups milk
50g/2oz plain (semisweet) chocolate, finely chopped
30ml/2 tbsp rum
1.5ml/¼ tsp cream of tartar
chocolate curls, to decorate

For the crust

175g/6oz/2 cups ginger nut cookies (gingersnaps), crushed
65g/2½oz/5 tbsp butter, melted

1 Preheat the oven to 180°C/350°F/Gas 4. Mix the crushed ginger nut cookies and melted butter. Press evenly over the base and side of a 23cm/9in pie plate. Bake for 6 minutes. Sprinkle the gelatine over the water and leave to soften.

2 Beat the egg yolks in a large bowl and set aside. In a pan, combine half the sugar, the cornflour and salt. Gradually stir in the milk. Boil for 1 minute, stirring constantly.

3 Whisk the hot milk mixture into the yolks, pour back into the pan and return to the boil, whisking. Cook for 1 minute, still whisking. Remove from the heat.

4 Pour 225g/8oz of the custard mixture into a bowl. Add the chopped chocolate and stir until melted. Stir in half the rum and pour into the pie crust. Whisk the softened gelatine into the plain custard until dissolved, then stir in the remaining rum. Set the pan in cold water to reach room temperature.

5 Beat the egg whites and cream of tartar until they form stiff peaks. Add the remaining sugar gradually, beating thoroughly after each addition. Fold the cooled custard into the egg whites, then spoon over the chocolate mixture in the pie crust. Chill the pie until it is set, about 2 hours. Decorate with chocolate curls and serve immediately.

Energy 248kcal/1040kJ; Fat 13.7g, Saturated Fat 7.6g; Carbohydrate 25.8g, Fibre 0.5g

Pumpkin Pie

A North American classic, this pie is traditionally served at Thanksgiving.

Serves 8

40g/1½oz/scant ⅓ cup pecan nuts, chopped
250g/9oz puréed pumpkin
475ml/16fl oz/2 cups single (light) cream
130g/4½oz/¾ cup soft light brown sugar
1.5ml/¼ tsp salt
5ml/1 tsp ground cinnamon
2.5ml/½ tsp ground ginger
1.5ml/¼ tsp ground cloves
1.5ml/¼ tsp freshly grated nutmeg
2 eggs

For the pastry

165g/5½oz/1⅓ cups plain (all-purpose) flour
2.5ml/½ tsp salt
115g/4oz/⅔ cup lard or white cooking fat
30–45ml/2–3 tbsp iced water

1 Preheat the oven to 220°C/425°F/Gas 7. To make the pastry, sift the flour and salt into a mixing bowl. Rub in the fat until the mixture resembles coarse breadcrumbs. Sprinkle in enough water to bind, then form the mixture into a ball. Wrap in clear film (plastic wrap) and chill in the refrigerator for 20 minutes.

2 Roll out the pastry to a 5mm/¼in thickness. Use to line a 23cm/9in pie plate. Trim and flute the edge. Sprinkle the chopped pecan nuts over the base of the case.

3 Beat together the pumpkin, cream, sugar, salt, spices and eggs. Pour the pumpkin mixture into the pastry case. Bake for 10 minutes, then reduce the heat to 180°C/350°F/Gas 4 and continue baking until the filling is set, about 45 minutes. Leave the pie to cool in the plate, set on a wire rack.

Cook's Tip

For perfect pastry every time, handle the pastry as little and as lightly as you can. There is no need to knead it, just gather it up into a ball before rolling it out. Chill it, and try to keep the working surface cool (a marble slab is ideal) when rolling out the pastry.

Energy 434kcal/1809kJ; Fat 30.8g, Saturated Fat 13.8g; Carbohydrate 35.3g, Fibre 1.2g

Chocolate Nut Tart

This is a sophisticated tart – strictly for grown-ups!

Serves 6–8

225g/8oz sweet shortcrust pastry, thawed if frozen
200g/7oz/1¾ cups dry amaretti
90g/3½oz/generous ½ cup blanched almonds
50g/2oz/⅓ cup blanched hazelnuts
45ml/3 tbsp caster (superfine) sugar
200g/7oz plain (semisweet) cooking chocolate
45ml/3 tbsp milk
50g/2oz/¼ cup butter
45ml/3 tbsp amaretto liqueur or brandy
30ml/2 tbsp single (light) cream

1 Grease a shallow loose-based 25cm/10in flan tin (tart pan). Roll out the pastry on a lightly floured surface, and use it to line the tin. Trim the edge, prick the base with a fork and chill for 30 minutes.

2 Grind the amaretti in a blender or food processor. Tip into a mixing bowl.

3 Set eight whole almonds aside and place the rest in the food processor or blender with the hazelnuts and sugar. Grind to a medium texture. Add the nuts to the amaretti, and mix well to combine thoroughly.

4 Preheat the oven to 190°C/375°F/Gas 5. Slowly melt the chocolate with the milk and butter in the top of a double boiler or in a heatproof bowl over a pan of simmering water. Once the chocolate has melted, stir until smooth.

5 Pour the chocolate mixture into the dry ingredients, and mix well. Add the liqueur or brandy and the cream.

6 Spread the filling evenly in the pastry case. Bake for 35 minutes, or until the crust is golden brown and the filling has puffed up and is beginning to darken.

7 Allow to cool to room temperature. Split the reserved almonds in half and use to decorate the tart.

Energy 644kcal/2685kJ; Fat 42.4g, Saturated Fat 13.4g; Carbohydrate 56.4g, Fibre 3g

Pecan Nut Tartlets

These delightful individual tartlets make an elegant dinner-party dessert.

Serves 6

425g/15oz shortcrust pastry, thawed if frozen
175g/6oz/1 cup pecan nut halves
3 eggs, beaten
25g/1oz/2 tbsp butter, melted
275g/10oz/¾ cup golden (light corn) syrup
2.5ml/½ tsp vanilla extract
115g/4oz/generous ½ cup caster (superfine) sugar
15ml/1 tbsp plain (all-purpose) flour

1 Preheat the oven to 180°C/350°F/Gas 4. Roll out the pastry and use to line six 10cm/4in tartlet tins (pans). Divide the pecan nut halves between the pastry cases.

2 Combine the eggs with the butter, and add the golden syrup and vanilla extract. Sift over the caster sugar and flour, and blend well. Fill the pastry cases with the mixture and leave until the nuts rise to the surface.

3 Bake for 35–40 minutes, or until a skewer inserted into the centre comes out clean. Cool in the tins for 15 minutes, then turn out on to a wire rack to cool completely.

Basic Shortcrust Pastry

Mix together 225g/8oz/1 cups flour, a pinch of salt and 115g/4oz/½ cup butter. Using your fingertips or a pastry cutter, rub the butter into the flour until the mixture resembles fine breadcrumbs. Mix in the water and gather together to form a firm dough. Wrap the dough in clear film (plastic wrap) and chill for 30 minutes. Use this recipe when 350g/12oz pastry is required – enough to line a 23cm/9in flan tin (tart pan). For 425g/15oz pastry you will need 275g/10oz flour to 150g/5oz butter.

- *If you use half butter and half white vegetable fat (shortening) you will have a lighter and less rich crust.*
- *For Sweet Shortcrust Pastry, add 50g/2oz/¼ cup sugar to the flour.*

Energy 828kcal/3463kJ; Fat 47.8g, Saturated Fat 11.2g; Carbohydrate 95g, Fibre 2.9g

Pear and Hazelnut Flan

A delicious flan for Sunday lunch. Grind the hazelnuts yourself if you prefer, or use ground almonds instead.

Serves 6–8

115g/4oz/1 cup plain (all-purpose) flour
115g/4oz/1 cup plain wholemeal (whole-wheat) flour
115g/4oz/½ cup sunflower margarine
45ml/3 tbsp cold water

For the filling

50g/2oz/½ cup self-raising (self-rising) flour
115g/4oz/1 cup ground hazelnuts
5ml/1 tsp vanilla extract
50g/2oz/¼ cup caster (superfine) sugar
50g/2oz/¼ cup butter, softened
2 eggs, beaten
400g/14oz can pears in natural juice
45ml/3 tbsp raspberry jam
few chopped hazelnuts, to decorate

1 For the pastry, stir the flours together, then rub in the margarine using your fingertips or a pastry cutter until the mixture resembles fine breadcrumbs. Mix to a firm dough with the water.

2 Roll out the dough and use to line a 23–25cm/9–10in flan tin (tart pan), pressing it up the sides after trimming, so that the pastry sits a little above the tin. Prick the base with a fork, line with baking parchment and fill with baking beans. Chill for 30 minutes.

3 Preheat the oven to 200°C/400°F/Gas 6. Place the flan tin on a baking sheet and bake blind for 20 minutes. Remove the paper and beans after 15 minutes.

4 To make the filling beat together the flour, hazelnuts, vanilla extract, sugar and eggs. If the misture is too thick, stir in some of the juice from the canned pears.

5 Reduce the oven temperature to 180°C/350°F/Gas 4. Spread the jam on the pastry case and spoon over the filling.

6 Drain the pears and arrange them, cut side down, in the filling. Sprinkle over the nuts for decoration. Bake for 30 minutes, or until risen, firm and golden brown.

Energy 389kcal/1626kJ; Fat 22.8g, Saturated Fat 3.5g; Carbohydrate 40.9g, Fibre 3.6g

Latticed Peaches

When fresh peaches are out of season, make this elegant dessert using canned peach halves instead .

Serves 6

115g/4oz/1 cup plain (all-purpose) flour
45ml/3 tbsp butter or sunflower margarine
45ml/3 tbsp natural (plain) yogurt
30ml/2 tbsp orange juice
milk, to glaze

For the filling

3 ripe peaches
45ml/3 tbsp ground almonds
30ml/2 tbsp natural (plain) yogurt
finely grated rind of 1 small orange
1.5ml/¼ tsp almond extract

For the sauce

1 ripe peach
45ml/3 tbsp orange juice

1 Lightly grease a baking sheet. Sift the flour into a bowl and rub in the butter or margarine. Stir in the yogurt and orange juice to make a firm dough. Roll out half the pastry thinly and stamp out six rounds with a 7.5cm/3in cookie cutter. Place on the baking sheet.

2 Drop the peaches into boiling water for 20 seconds. Remove and plunge into cold water. Remove the skins, halve and remove the stones (pits). Mix together the almonds, yogurt, orange rind and almond extract. Spoon into the hollows of each peach half and place, cut side down, on the pastry rounds.

3 Roll out the remaining pastry thinly and cut into thin strips. Arrange the strips over the peaches to form a lattice, brushing with milk to secure firmly. Trim the ends. Chill for 30 minutes.

4 Preheat the oven to 200°C/400°F/Gas 6. Brush with milk and bake for 15–18 minutes, or until golden brown.

5 To make the sauce, skin the peach as before and halve it to remove the stone. Place the flesh in a food processor or blender, with the orange juice, and purée until the mixture is smooth. Serve the peaches hot, with the peach sauce spooned around them.

Energy 196kcal/822kJ; Fat 10.8g, Saturated Fat 4.3g; Carbohydrate 21.6g, Fibre 1.9g

Surprise Fruit Tarts

Strawberry cream with a dash of liqueur makes a beautiful filling. These delicious and simple little tarts are the perfect summer treat.

Serves 6

4 large or 8 small sheets filo pastry, thawed if frozen
65g/2½ oz/5 tbsp butter or margarine, melted
250ml/8fl oz/1 cup whipping cream
45ml/3 tbsp strawberry jam
15ml/1 tbsp Cointreau or other orange-flavoured liqueur
115g/4oz/1 cup seedless black grapes, halved
115g/4oz/1 cup seedless white grapes, halved
150g/5oz fresh pineapple, cubed, or drained canned pineapple chunks
115g/4oz/⅔ cup raspberries
30ml/2 tbsp icing (confectioners') sugar
6 sprigs fresh mint, to decorate

1 Preheat the oven to 180°C/350°F/Gas 4. Grease six cups of a bun tray. Stack the filo sheets and cut with a sharp knife or scissors into 24 pieces, each 12cm/4½in square.

2 Lay four squares of pastry in each of the six greased cups, rotating them slightly to make star-shaped baskets.

3 Press the pastry firmly into the cups. Brush the pastry baskets lightly with butter or margarine.

4 Bake until the pastry is crisp and golden, about 5–7 minutes. Cool on a wire rack.

5 In a bowl, lightly whip the cream until soft peaks form. Gently fold the strawberry jam and Cointreau into the cream.

6 Just before serving, spoon a little of the cream mixture into each pastry basket. Top with the halved grapes, pineapple and raspberries.

7 Sprinkle with icing sugar, decorate each basket with a small sprig of mint and serve immediately.

Energy 359kcal/1496kJ; Fat 26.1g, Saturated Fat 16.2g; Carbohydrate 28.6g, Fibre 1.6g

Truffle Filo Tarts

The dainty filo pastry cups can be prepared a day ahead and then stored in an airtight container until they are needed.

Makes 24 cups

3–6 sheets filo pastry (depending on size), thawed if frozen
45g/1½oz/3 tbsp unsalted (sweet) butter, melted
sugar, for sprinkling
lemon rind, to decorate

For the truffle mixture

250ml/8fl oz/1 cup double (heavy) cream
225g/8oz plain (semisweet) or dark (bittersweet) chocolate, chopped
50g/2oz/¼ cup unsalted (sweet) butter, diced
30ml/2 tbsp brandy

1 To make the truffle mixture, in a pan over medium heat bring the double cream to the boil. Remove from the heat and add the chocolate, stirring until melted. Beat in the butter and add the brandy. Strain into a bowl and chill for 1 hour.

2 Preheat the oven to 200°C/400°F/Gas 6. Grease a bun tray with 24 cups, each 4cm/1½in. Cut each filo sheet into 6cm/2½in squares. Cover with a damp dish towel. Keeping the other filo sheets covered, place one square on a work surface. Brush lightly with melted butter, turn over and brush the other side. Sprinkle with a pinch of sugar.

3 Butter another square and place it over the first at an angle. Sprinkle with sugar. Butter a third square and place over the first two, unevenly, so that the corners form an uneven edge. Press the layered square into the tray. Continue to fill the tray.

4 Bake the filo cups for 4–6 minutes, or until golden. Cool for 10 minutes on a wire rack in the tray. Remove from the tray and cool completely.

5 Stir the chocolate mixture, which should be just thick enough to pipe. Spoon the mixture into a piping (pastry) bag fitted with a medium star nozzle and pipe a swirl into each cup. Decorate with lemon rind.

Energy 149kcal/621kJ; Fat 11.5g, Saturated Fat 7.1g; Carbohydrate 10.2g, Fibre 0.4g

Apple Strudel

Ready-made filo pastry makes a good substitute for paper-thin strudel pastry in this classic Austrian dish.

Serves 10–12

75g/3oz/generous ½ cup raisins
30ml/2 tbsp brandy
5 eating apples
3 large cooking apples
90g/3½oz/scant ½ cup soft dark brown sugar
5ml/1 tsp ground cinnamon
grated rind and juice of 1 lemon
25g/1oz/scant ½ cup dry breadcrumbs
50g/2oz/½ cup chopped pecan nuts or walnuts
12 sheets filo pastry, thawed if frozen
175g/6oz/¾ cup butter, melted
icing (confectioners') sugar, for dusting

1 Soak the raisins in the brandy for 15 minutes.

2 Peel, core and thinly slice the apples. Combine with the dark brown sugar, cinnamon, lemon rind and juice, half the breadcrumbs, and pecan nuts or walnuts.

3 Preheat the oven to 190°C/375°F/Gas 5. Grease two baking sheets. Unfold the filo pastry and cover with a damp dish towel. One by one, butter and stack the sheets to make two six-sheet piles.

4 Sprinkle half the reserved breadcrumbs over the last sheet and spoon half the apple mixture along the bottom edge. Roll up from this edge, Swiss roll (jelly roll) style. Place on a baking sheet, seam side down, and fold the ends under to seal. Repeat to make a second strudel. Brush both with butter.

5 Bake in the oven for 45 minutes, cool slightly, then dust with icing sugar.

Cook's Tip
Filo pastry is extremely delicate and needs to be kept covered with a damp dish towel when out of the packet and waiting to be used. Otherwise, it will dry out and crack before you are able to use it.

Energy 231kcal/966kJ; Fat 15.2g, Saturated Fat 7.9g; Carbohydrate 21.3g, Fibre 1.5g

Cherry Strudel

A refreshing variation on traditional apple strudel. Serve with whipped cream, if you like.

Serves 8

65g/2½oz/1¼ cups fresh breadcrumbs
175g/6oz/¾ cup butter, melted
200g/7oz/1 cup caster (superfine) sugar
15ml/1 tbsp ground cinnamon
5ml/1 tsp grated lemon rind
450g/1lb/2 cups sour cherries, pitted
8 sheets filo pastry
icing (confectioners') sugar, for dusting

1 In a frying pan, fry the breadcrumbs in 65g/2½oz/5 tbsp of the butter until golden. Set aside.

2 In a large mixing bowl, toss together the sugar, cinnamon and lemon rind. Stir in the cherries.

3 Preheat the oven to 190°C/375°F/Gas 5, and grease a baking sheet.

4 Unfold the filo sheets. Keep the unused sheets covered with a damp dish towel. Lift off one sheet and place on a piece of baking parchment. Brush the pastry with butter. Sprinkle an eighth of the breadcrumbs over the surface.

5 Lay a second sheet of filo pastry on top, brush with butter and sprinkle with breadcrumbs. Continue until you have used up all the pastry.

6 Spoon the cherry mixture along the bottom edge of the strip. Starting at the cherry-filled end, roll up the dough Swiss roll (jelly roll) style.

7 Use the paper to flip the strudel on to the baking sheet, seam-side down. Carefully fold under the ends to seal. Brush the top with melted butter.

8 Bake the strudel for 45 minutes. Cool slightly, then dust with a fine layer of icing sugar.

Energy 370kcal/1553kJ; Fat 18.4g, Saturated Fat 11.4g; Carbohydrate 51.2g, Fibre 1.2g

Strawberry Tart

This tart is best assembled just before serving, but you can bake the pastry case and make the filling ahead.

Serves 6

350g/12oz rough-puff or puff pastry, thawed if frozen
225g/8oz/1 cup cream cheese
grated rind of ½ orange
30ml/2 tbsp orange liqueur or orange juice
45–60ml/3–4 tbsp icing (confectioners') sugar, plus extra for dusting (optional)
450g/1lb/4 cups ripe strawberries, hulled

1 Preheat the oven to 200°C/400°F/Gas 6. Roll out the pastry to about a 3mm/⅛in thickness and use to line a 28 × 10cm/11 × 4in rectangular flan tin (tart pan). Trim the edges, then chill for 30 minutes.

2 Prick the base of the pastry all over with a fork. Line with foil, fill with baking beans and bake for 15 minutes. Remove the foil and beans and bake for a further 10 minutes, or until the pastry is browned. Gently press down on the pastry base to deflate, then leave to cool on a wire rack.

3 Beat together the cheese, orange rind, liqueur or orange juice and icing sugar to taste. Spread the cheese filling in the pastry case. Halve the strawberries and arrange them on top of the filling. Dust with icing sugar, if you like.

Rough-puff Pastry

Cut 175g/6oz/¾ cup butter into small pieces. Sift 8oz/225g/2 cups plain (all-purpose) flour into a bowl and add the butter, 5ml/1 tsp salt, 5ml/1 tsp lemon juice and 150ml/¼ pint/⅔ cup iced water. Mix together with a knife. Turn on to a work surface and gather it together. Roll into a rectangle. Fold up the bottom third to the centre, fold the top third to meet it and then turn the pasty a quarter turn. Repeat the rolling and folding. Wrap and chill for 20 minutes (or pop into the freezer for 5 minutes). Roll, fold and chill twice more.

Energy 434kcal/1805kJ; Fat 32.2g, Saturated Fat 11.1g; Carbohydrate 34.4g, Fibre 0.8g

Alsatian Plum Tart

Fruit and custard tarts, similar to a fruit flan, are typical in Alsace. Sometimes they have a yeast dough base instead of pastry. You can use other seasonal fruits in this tart, or a mixture of fruit, if you like.

Serves 6–8

450g/1lb ripe plums, halved and stoned (pitted)
30ml/2 tbsp Kirsch or plum brandy
350g/12oz shortcrust or sweet shortcrust pastry, thawed if frozen
30ml/2 tbsp seedless raspberry jam

For the custard filling

2 eggs
25g/1oz/4 tbsp icing (confectioners') sugar
175ml/6fl oz/¾ cup double (heavy) cream
grated rind of ½ lemon
1.5ml/¼ tsp vanilla extract

1 Preheat the oven to 200°C/400°F/Gas 6. Mix the plums with the Kirsch or brandy and set aside for about 30 minutes.

2 Roll out the pastry thinly and use to line a 23cm/9in flan tin (tart pan). Prick the base of the pastry case all over with a fork, and line with foil. Add a layer of baking beans and bake for 15 minutes, or until slightly dry and set. Remove the foil and the baking beans.

3 Brush the base of the pastry case with a thin layer of jam, then bake for a further 5 minutes.

4 Remove the pastry case from the oven and transfer to a wire rack. Reduce the oven temperature to 180°C/350°F/Gas 4.

5 To make the custard filling, beat the eggs and sugar until well combined, then beat in the cream, lemon rind, vanilla extract and any juice from the plums.

6 Arrange the plums, cut side down, in the pastry case and pour over the custard mixture. Bake for about 30–35 minutes, or until a knife inserted into the centre comes out clean. Serve the tart warm or at room temperature.

Energy 375kcal/1563kJ; Fat 25.5g, Saturated Fat 11.5g; Carbohydrate 31.7g, Fibre 1.7g

Almond Mincemeat Tartlets

A lemony iced sponge topping encloses mincemeat in a rich almond pastry.

Makes 36

275g/10oz/2½ cups plain (all-purpose) flour
75g/3oz/¾ cup icing (confectioners') sugar
5ml/1 tsp ground cinnamon
175g/6oz/¾ cup butter
50g/2oz/½ cup ground almonds
1 egg yolk
45ml/3 tbsp milk
450g/1lb mincemeat
15ml/1 tbsp brandy or rum

For the lemon filling

115g/4oz/½ cup butter or margarine
115g/4oz/generous ½ cup caster (superfine) sugar
175g/6oz/1½ cups self-raising (self-rising) flour
2 large (US extra large) eggs
finely grated rind of 1 large lemon

For the lemon icing

115g/4oz/1 cup icing (confectioners') sugar
15ml/1 tbsp lemon juice

1 Sift the flour, sugar and cinnamon into a bowl and rub in the butter using your fingertips or a pastry cutter until it resembles breadcrumbs. Add the ground almonds and bind with the egg yolk and milk to a soft, pliable dough. Knead until smooth, wrap in clear film (plastic wrap) and chill for 30 minutes.

2 Preheat the oven to 190°C/375°F/Gas 5. On a lightly floured surface, roll out the pastry and cut out 36 fluted rounds with a pastry cutter. Mix the mincemeat with the brandy or rum and put a small teaspoonful in the base of each pastry case. Chill.

3 To make the lemon sponge filling, whisk the butter or margarine, sugar, flour, eggs and lemon rind together until smooth. Spoon on top of the mincemeat, dividing it evenly, and level the tops. Bake for 20–30 minutes, or until golden brown and springy to the touch. Remove and leave to cool on a wire rack.

4 To make the lemon icing, sift the icing sugar and mix with the lemon juice to a smooth coating consistency. Spoon into a piping bag and drizzle a zigzag pattern over each tart. (If you're short of time, simply dust the tartlets with icing sugar.)

Energy 177kcal/746kJ; Fat 7.8g, Saturated Fat 4.4g; Carbohydrate 26.4g, Fibre 0.6g

Mince Pies with Orange Pastry

Home-made mince pies are so much nicer than shop-bought, especially with this flavoursome pastry.

Makes 18

225g/8oz/2 cups plain (all-purpose) flour
30g/1¼oz/⅓ cup icing (confectioners') sugar
10ml/2 tsp ground cinnamon
150g/5oz/generous 1 cup cold butter, diced
grated rind of 1 orange
about 60ml/4 tbsp iced water
225g/8oz/1½ cups mincemeat
1 egg, beaten, to glaze
icing (confectioners') sugar, for dusting

1 Sift together the flour, icing sugar and cinnamon. Rub in the butter until it resembles fine breadcrumbs. Stir in the grated orange rind.

2 Mix to a firm dough with the water. Knead lightly, then roll out to a 5mm/¼in thickness. Using a 6cm/2½in round cookie cutter, stamp out 18 circles, then stamp out 18 smaller 5cm/2in circles.

3 Line two bun trays with the larger circles. Place a small spoonful of mincemeat into each pastry case and top with the smaller pastry circles, pressing the edges to seal.

4 Glaze the tops with egg glaze and leave to rest in the refrigerator for 30 minutes. Preheat the oven to 200°C/400°F/Gas 6.

5 Bake for 15–20 minutes, or until golden brown. Remove to cool on wire racks. Serve just warm, dusted with icing sugar.

Cook's Tip

This sweet and spicy pastry works for all kinds of sweet pies and tarts. This quantity will line a 23cm/9in flan tin (tart pan) as well as leaving enough for a lattice or cut-out pastry shapes to decorate the top. It is particularly suitable for autumn fruit pies made with apples, plums or pears.

Energy 145kcal/610kJ; Fat 7.6g, Saturated Fat 4.4g; Carbohydrate 19.3g, Fibre 0.6g

Candied Fruit Pie

Use good-quality candied fruits for the best flavour. Try half digestive (graham crackers) and half ginger nut cookies (gingersnaps) for the crust, if you prefer.

Serves 10

15ml/1 tbsp rum
50g/2oz/¼ cup mixed glacé (candied) fruit, chopped
475ml/16fl oz/2 cups milk
20ml/4 tsp powdered gelatine
90g/3½oz/½ cup caster (superfine) sugar
2.5ml/½ tsp salt
3 eggs, separated
250ml/8fl oz/1 cup whipping cream, whipped
chocolate curls, to decorate

For the crust

175g/6oz/2 cups crushed digestive cookies (graham crackers)
75g/3oz/5 tbsp butter, melted
15ml/1 tbsp caster (superfine) sugar

1 To make the crust mix the digestive cookies, butter and sugar. Press evenly over the base and sides of a 23cm/9in pie plate. Chill.

2 Stir together the rum and glacé fruit. Set aside. Pour 120ml/4fl oz/½ cup of the milk into a small bowl. Sprinkle over the gelatine and leave for 5 minutes to soften.

3 In the top of a double boiler or in a heatproof bowl over a pan of simmering water, combine 50g/2oz/4 tbsp of the sugar, the remaining milk and the salt. Stir in the gelatine mixture. Cook, stirring, until the gelatine dissolves. Whisk in the egg yolks and cook, stirring, until thick enough to coat the back of the spoon. Pour the custard over the glacé fruit mixture, set in a bowl of iced water.

4 Beat the egg whites until they form soft peaks. Add the remaining sugar and beat just to blend. Fold a large dollop of the egg whites into the cooled gelatine mixture. Pour into the remaining egg whites and fold together. Fold in the cream.

5 Pour into the pie crust and chill until firm. Decorate with chocolate curls.

Energy 334kcal/1392kJ; Fat 22.3g, Saturated Fat 12.8g; Carbohydrate 29.3g, Fibre 0.4g

Chocolate Chiffon Pie

As the name suggests, this is a wonderfully smooth and light-textured pie.

Serves 8

200g/7oz plain (semisweet) chocolate, chopped
250ml/8fl oz/1 cup milk
15ml/1 tbsp powdered gelatine
90g/3½oz/1 cup caster (superfine) sugar
2 large (US extra large) eggs, separated
5ml/1 tsp vanilla extract
1.5ml/¼ tsp salt
350ml/12fl oz/1½ cups whipping cream, whipped
whipped cream and chocolate curls, to decorate

For the crust

200g/7oz/2⅓ cups crushed digestive cookies (graham crackers)
75g/3oz/6 tbsp butter, melted

1 Place a baking sheet in the oven and preheat the oven to 180°C/350°F/Gas 4. To make the crust, mix the cookies and butter together and press over the base and sides of a 23cm/9in pie plate. Bake for 8 minutes.

2 Grate the chocolate and set aside. Place the milk in the top of a double boiler or in a heatproof bowl over a pan of simmering water. Sprinkle over the gelatine and leave for 5 minutes to soften.

3 In the top of a double boiler or in a heatproof bowl as before, put 40g/1½oz/scant ¼ cup sugar, the chocolate and egg yolks. Stir until dissolved. Add the vanilla extract. Transfer the pan or bowl to a bowl of ice and stir until the mixture reaches room temperature. Remove from the ice.

4 Beat the egg whites and salt until they form soft peaks. Add the remaining sugar and beat just to blend. Fold a dollop of the egg whites into the chocolate mixture, then pour back into the whites and fold in carefully.

5 Fold in the cream and pour into the pie crust. Freeze until just set, about 5 minutes, then chill for 3–4 hours. Decorate with whipped cream and chocolate curls.

Energy 557kcal/2323kJ; Fat 39.3g, Saturated Fat 23.1g; Carbohydrate 47.5g, Fibre 1.2g

Chocolate Pear Tart

Chocolate and pears have a natural affinity, well used in this luxurious pudding that makes an attractive dinner-party dessert.

Serves 8

115g/4oz plain (semisweet) chocolate, grated
3 large firm, ripe pears
1 egg
1 egg yolk
120ml/4fl oz/½ cup single (light) cream
2.5ml/½ tsp vanilla extract
45ml/3 tbsp caster (superfine) sugar

For the pastry

150g/5oz/1¼ cups plain (all-purpose) flour
1.5ml/¼ tsp salt
30ml/2 tbsp caster (superfine) sugar
115g/4oz/½ cup cold unsalted (sweet) butter, diced
1 egg yolk
15ml/1 tbsp lemon juice

1 To make the pastry, sift the flour and salt into a bowl. Add the sugar and butter. Rub in using your fingertips or a pastry cutter until the mixture resembles coarse breadcrumbs.

2 Stir in the egg yolk and lemon juice. Form a ball, wrap in clear film (plastic wrap), and chill for 20 minutes.

3 Preheat the oven to 200°C/400°F/Gas 6. Roll out the pastry and use to line a 25cm/10in flan (tart) dish.

4 Sprinkle the pastry case with the grated chocolate.

5 Peel, halve and core the pears. Cut in thin slices crossways, then fan out slightly. Transfer the pears to the tart using a metal spatula and arrange like spokes of a wheel.

6 Whisk together the egg and egg yolk, cream and vanilla extract. Ladle over the pears and sprinkle with sugar.

7 Bake on a baking sheet for 10 minutes. Reduce the heat to 180°C/350°F/Gas 4 and cook until the custard is set and the pears begin to caramelize, about 20 minutes more. Serve while still warm.

Energy 357kcal/1493kJ; Fat 21.1g, Saturated Fat 12.4g; Carbohydrate 39.5g, Fibre 2.2g

Pear and Apple Crumble Pie

This pie combines the old favourites of fruit pies and crumbles in one delicious treat. You could use just one fruit in this pie if you prefer.

Serves 8

3 firm pears
4 cooking apples
175g/6oz/scant 1 cup caster (superfine) sugar
30ml/2 tbsp cornflour (cornstarch)
1.5ml/¼ tsp salt
grated rind of 1 lemon
30ml/2 tbsp fresh lemon juice
75g/3oz/generous ½ cup raisins
75g/3oz/⅔ cup plain (all-purpose) flour
5ml/1 tsp ground cinnamon
75g/3oz/6 tbsp cold butter, diced

For the pastry

150g/5oz/1¼ cups plain (all-purpose) flour
2.5ml/½ tsp salt
65g/2½oz/5 tbsp cold white vegetable fat (shortening), diced
30ml/2 tbsp iced water

1 To make the pastry, sift the flour and salt into a bowl. Add the fat and rub in using your fingertips until the mixture resembles breadcrumbs. Stir in enough water to bind.

2 Wrap in clear film (plastic wrap) and chill for 30 minutes. Form into a ball, roll out, and use to line a 23cm/9in pie dish, leaving a 1cm/½in overhang. Fold this under for double thickness. Flute the edge, then chill.

3 Preheat a baking sheet in the oven at 230°C/450°F/Gas 8. Peel, core and slice the fruit. Quickly combine in a bowl with one-third of the sugar, the cornflour, salt, lemon rind and juice, and the raisins.

4 For the crumble topping, combine the remaining sugar, flour, cinnamon and butter in a bowl. Rub in until the mixture resembles coarse breadcrumbs. Spoon the filling into the pastry case. Sprinkle the crumbs over the top.

5 Bake on the baking sheet for 10 minutes, then reduce the heat to 180°C/350°F/Gas 4. Cover the pie loosely with foil and bake for a further 35–40 minutes.

Energy 390kcal/1639kJ; Fat 16.3g, Saturated Fat 8.2g; Carbohydrate 61.3g, Fibre 3.1g

Chocolate Lemon Tart

The unusual chocolate pastry is simple to make and complements the tangy lemon filling superbly in this rich tart, generously topped with chocolate curls.

Serves 8–10

245g/8¾oz/1¼ cups caster (superfine) sugar
6 eggs
grated rind of 2 lemons
160ml/5½fl oz/generous ⅔ cup fresh lemon juice
160ml/5½fl oz/generous ⅔ cup whipping cream
chocolate curls, to decorate

For the pastry

180g/6¼oz/generous 1½ cups plain (all-purpose) flour
30ml/2 tbsp unsweetened cocoa powder
25g/1oz/¼ cup icing (confectioners') sugar
2.5ml/½ tsp salt
115g/4oz/½ cup cold butter, diced
15ml/1 tbsp water

1 Grease a 25cm/10in flan tin (tart pan). To make the pastry, sift the flour, cocoa powder, icing sugar and salt into a bowl. Set aside.

2 Melt the butter or margarine and water in a large pan over a low heat.

3 Pour over the flour mixture and stir until the dough is smooth.

4 Press the dough evenly over the base and sides of the flan tin. Chill while preparing the filling.

5 Place a baking sheet on the top shelf of the oven and preheat to 190°C/375°F/Gas 5.

6 Whisk the sugar and eggs until the sugar is dissolved. Add the lemon rind and juice, and mix well. Add the cream.

7 Pour the filling into the pastry case and bake on the hot baking sheet until the filling is set, about 20–25 minutes.

8 Leave the tart on a wire rack to cool completely, then decorate with chocolate curls.

Energy 368kcal/1540kJ; Fat 20.1g, Saturated Fat 11.4g; Carbohydrate 43.1g, Fibre 0.9g

Kiwi Ricotta Cheese Tart

This rich tart makes an elegant dinner-party dessert.

Serves 8

75g/3oz/½ cup blanched almonds, ground
130g/4½oz/scant ¾ cup caster (superfine) sugar
900g/2lb/4 cups ricotta cheese
250ml/8fl oz/1 cup whipping cream
1 egg and 3 egg yolks
15ml/1 tbsp plain (all-purpose) flour
pinch of salt
30ml/2 tbsp rum
grated rind of 1 lemon
30ml/2 tbsp lemon juice
30ml/2 tbsp honey
5 kiwi fruit

For the pastry

150g/5oz/1¼ cups plain (all-purpose) flour
15ml/1 tbsp caster (superfine) sugar
2.5ml/½ tsp salt
2.5ml/½ tsp baking powder
75g/3oz/6 tbsp butter
1 egg yolk
45–60ml/3–4 tbsp whipping cream

1 Mix the flour, sugar, salt and baking powder in a bowl. Add the butter and rub in. Mix in the egg yolk and mix to bind the pastry. Wrap in clear film (plastic wrap) and chill for 30 minutes.

2 Preheat the oven to 220°C/425°F/Gas 7. On a lightly floured surface, roll out the dough to a 3mm/⅛in thickness. Use to line a 23cm/9in springform cake tin (pan). Prick the pastry all over with a fork. Line with baking parchment and fill with dried beans. Bake for 10 minutes. Remove the paper and beans and bake for another 6–8 minutes. Reduce the oven temperature to 180°C/350°F/Gas 4.

3 Mix the almonds with 15ml/1 tbsp of the sugar. Beat the ricotta until creamy then add the cream, egg, yolks, remaining sugar, flour, salt, rum, lemon rind and 30ml/2 tbsp lemon juice. Mix well, add the almonds and mix in. Pour into the pastry case and bake for 1 hour, until golden. Cool and chill.

4 Mix the honey and remaining lemon juice. Halve the kiwi fruit lengthways then slice. Arrange over the tart and brush with the honey glaze.

Energy 688kcal/2865kJ; Fat 48g, Saturated Fat 25.9g; Carbohydrate 47g, Fibre 2.1g

Lime Tart

Fresh limes make a tasty filling for a tart, but you can use lemons instead of limes, with yellow food colouring, if you prefer.

Serves 8
3 large egg yolks
400g/14oz can sweetened condensed milk
15ml/1 tbsp grated lime rind
120ml/4fl oz/½ cup fresh lime juice
green food colouring (optional)
120ml/4fl oz/½ cup whipping cream

For the base
115g/4oz/1⅓ cups crushed digestive cookies (graham crackers)
65g/2½oz/5 tbsp butter or margarine, melted

1 Preheat the oven to 180°C/350°F/Gas 4. To make the base, place the crushed cookies in a bowl and add the butter or margarine. Mix well to combine.

2 Press the mixture evenly over the base and sides of a 23cm/9in pie dish. Bake for 8 minutes, then cool.

3 Beat the egg yolks until thick. Beat in the condensed milk, lime rind and juice and green food colouring, if using. Pour into the pastry case and chill until set, about 4 hours.

4 To serve, whip the cream. Pipe a line of cream around the edge of the tart and then pipe a lattice pattern over the top, or spoon dollops around the edge if you only have enough time to make a quick topping.

Cook's Tip
Crushed cookies make a useful base for all kinds of tarts. You can put the cookies into a food processor and pulse it to make them into crumbs, or put them into a large plastic bag and use a rolling pin to roll over the bag. Make the crumbs as fine or as coarse as you like. There is no need to cook the base if you want to use it for an uncooked cold filling; the case can just be chilled.

Energy 373kcal/1558kJ; Fat 22.6g, Saturated Fat 13g; Carbohydrate 38.1g, Fibre 0.3g

Fruit Tartlets

Glazed fresh fruit on cream and nestled in an individual tart just screams warm summer days. You could make one large fruit tart for an elegant dessert, if you like.

Makes 8
175ml/6fl oz/¾ cup redcurrant jelly
15ml/1 tbsp fresh lemon juice
175ml/6fl oz/¾ cup whipping cream
675g/1½lb fresh fruit, such as strawberries, raspberries, kiwi fruit, peaches, grapes or currants, peeled and sliced as necessary

For the pastry
150g/5oz/10 tbsp cold butter, diced
65g/2½oz/generous ¼ cup soft dark brown sugar
45ml/3 tbsp unsweetened cocoa powder
200g/7oz/1¾ cups plain (all-purpose) flour
1 egg white

1 To make the pastry, melt the butter, brown sugar and cocoa in a large pan over a low heat. Remove from the heat and sift over the flour. Stir, then add enough egg white to bind the dough. Form into a ball, wrap in clear film (plastic wrap), and chill for 30 minutes.

2 Grease eight 8cm/3in tartlet tins (pans). Roll out the pastry between two sheets of baking parchment. Stamp out eight 10cm/4in rounds with a fluted cookie cutter.

3 Line the tartlet tins with the chilled pastry and prick the bases with a fork. Chill for a further 15 minutes. Preheat the oven to 180°C/350°F/Gas 4.

4 Bake the pastry cases until firm, about 20–25 minutes. Cool, then turn out of the tins.

5 Melt the redcurrant jelly with the lemon juice, and brush over the tartlet bases. Whip the cream and spread thinly in the tartlet cases. Arrange the fresh fruit on top. Brush with the jelly glaze and serve when the glaze has set.

Energy 437kcal/1828kJ; Fat 25.6g, Saturated Fat 15.9g; Carbohydrate 49.5g, Fibre 2.4g

Chocolate Cheesecake Tart

You can use all digestive cookies (graham crackers) for the base of this tart, if you prefer.

Serves 8

350g/12oz/1½ cups cream cheese
60ml/4 tbsp whipping cream
225g/8oz/generous 1 cup caster (superfine) sugar
50g/2oz/½ cup unsweetened cocoa powder
2.5ml/½ tsp ground cinnamon
3 eggs
whipped cream and chocolate curls, to decorate

For the base

75g/3oz/1 cup crushed digestive cookies (graham crackers)
40g/1½oz/scant 1 cup crushed amaretti
75g/3oz/6 tbsp butter, melted

1 Preheat a baking sheet in the oven at 180°C/350°F/Gas 4.

2 To make the base, mix the crushed cookies and melted butter in a bowl.

3 Press the mixture over the base and sides of a 23cm/9in pie dish. Bake for 8 minutes. Leave to cool, but keep the oven on.

4 Beat the cream cheese and cream together until smooth. Beat in the sugar, cocoa and cinnamon until blended.

5 Add the eggs, one at a time, beating just enough to blend.

6 Pour into the cookie base and bake on the baking sheet for 25–30 minutes. The filling will sink down as it cools.

7 Decorate the top of the tart with whipped cream and chocolate curls.

Chocolate Curls

For short chocolate curls, run a vegetable peeler against the long side of a bar of chocolate. To make long curls, see p251.

Energy 514kcal/2139kJ; Fat 37.5g, Saturated Fat 22.3g; Carbohydrate 40.8g, Fibre 1g

Frozen Strawberry Tart

When it's a hot summer's day and you want a cooling dessert, but don't fancy ice cream, what could be better than this frozen tart?

Serves 8

225g/8oz/1 cup cream cheese
250ml/8fl oz/1 cup sour cream
500g/1¼lb/5 cups strawberries

For the base

65g/2½oz/5 tbsp butter
115g/4oz/1⅓ cups digestive cookies (graham crackers)
15ml/1 tbsp caster (superfine) sugar

1 To make the base, melt the butter in a large pan. Crush the cookies with a rolling pin, then add to the melted butter. Stir in the sugar and combine thoroughly.

2 Press the mixture over the base and sides of a 23cm/9in pie dish. Freeze until firm.

3 Blend together the cream cheese and sour cream in a large bowl. Reserve 90ml/6 tbsp of the strawberries on one side, and add the remainder to the cream cheese mixture.

4 Scrape the filling into the cookie base and freeze until it is firm, about 6–8 hours.

5 To serve, allow the tart to thaw a little in the refrigerator for 20 minutes and then spoon some of the reserved strawberries on top.

Cook's Tips

- *Raspberries will work equally well instead of strawberries for this tart.*
- *This is an ideal tart to make in advance, as it will be stored in the freezer. If you do this you will need to buy a few extra strawberries to decorate the top when you are ready to serve it.*

Energy 339kcal/1404kJ; Fat 29.2g, Saturated Fat 17.8g; Carbohydrate 16.8g, Fibre 1g

Treacle Tart

Although called Treacle Tart, this old favourite is always made with syrup. It is straightforward to make – even this version with a simple lattice topping.

Serves 4–6

175ml/6fl oz/¾ cup golden (light corn) syrup
75g/3oz/1½ cups fresh white breadcrumbs
grated rind of 1 lemon
30ml/2 tbsp fresh lemon juice

For the pastry

175g/6oz/1½ cups plain (all-purpose) flour
2.5ml/½ tsp salt
75g/3oz/6 tbsp cold butter, diced
40g/1½oz/3 tbsp cold margarine, diced
45–60ml/3–4 tbsp iced water

1 To make the pastry, sift together the flour and salt, add the fats and rub in until the mixture resembles coarse breadcrumbs. Stir in enough water to bind.

2 Form into a ball, wrap in clear film (plastic wrap) and chill for 20 minutes.

3 Roll out the pastry and use to line a 20cm/8in pie dish. Chill for 20 minutes. Reserve the pastry trimmings.

4 Preheat a baking sheet in the oven at 200°C/400°F/Gas 6.

5 In a pan, warm the golden syrup until thin and runny. Stir in the breadcrumbs and lemon rind. Leave for 10 minutes, then stir in the lemon juice. Spread into the pastry case.

6 Roll out the pastry trimmings and cut into 12 thin strips. Lay six strips on the filling, then lay the other six at an angle over them to form a simple lattice.

7 Bake on the baking sheet for 10 minutes. Lower the heat to 190°C/375°F/Gas 5. Bake until golden, about 15 minutes more. Serve warm or cold.

Energy 373kcal/1567kJ; Fat 16.3g, Saturated Fat 7.7g; Carbohydrate 55.5g, Fibre 1.2g

Almond Syrup Tart

Almonds and a rich pastry make a treacle tart with a difference.

Serves 6

75g/3oz/1½ cups fresh white breadcrumbs
225g/8oz/scant 1 cup golden (light corn) syrup
finely grated rind of ½ lemon
10ml/2 tsp lemon juice
225g/8oz rich shortcrust pastry
25g/1oz/¼ cup flaked (sliced) almonds
milk, to glaze (optional)
cream, custard or ice cream, to serve

1 Preheat the oven to 200°C/400°F/Gas 6. Line a 23cm/9in flan tin (tart pan) with the rich shortcrust pastry. Line the pastry with baking parchment and fill with baking beans.

2 Bake for 15 minutes and then remove the beans and paper and cook for 10 minutes more.

3 Combine the breadcrumbs with the golden syrup and the lemon rind and juice.

4 Spoon into the pastry case and spread out evenly. Sprinkle the flaked almonds evenly over the top.

5 Brush the pastry with milk to glaze, if you like. Bake for 25–30 minutes, or until the pastry and filling are golden brown.

6 Transfer to a wire rack to cool. Serve warm or cold, with cream, custard or ice cream.

Rich Shortcrust Pastry

Sift 150g/5oz/1¼ cups plain (all-purpose) flour with a pinch of salt into a bowl. Add 75g/3oz/6 tbsp unsalted (sweet) butter or margarine cut into pieces, and rub in with your fingertips or a pastry cutter. Stir in 1 egg yolk, 7.5ml/1½ tsp caster (superfine) sugar and 15ml/1 tbsp water. Gather the dough together, wrap in clear film (plastic wrap) and chill for 30 minutes.

Energy 407kcal/1712kJ; Fat 16.6g, Saturated Fat 4.6g; Carbohydrate 63g, Fibre 1.5g

Tarte Tatin

A special *tarte tatin* tin is ideal, but an ovenproof frying pan can be used quite successfully.

Serves 8–10

225g/8oz puff or shortcrust pastry, thawed if frozen
10–12 large eating apples
30ml/2 tbsp lemon juice
115g/4oz/½ cup cold butter, diced
115g/4oz/generous ½ cup caster (superfine) sugar
2.5ml/½ tsp ground cinnamon
crème fraîche or whipped cream, to serve

1 On a lightly floured surface, roll out the pastry to a 28cm/11in round less than 5mm/¼in thick. Transfer to a lightly floured baking sheet and chill. Peel, halve and core the apples, and sprinkle with lemon juice.

2 In a 25cm/10in *tarte tatin* tin (pan) or a small frying pan that can go into the oven, cook the butter, sugar and cinnamon until the butter has melted and the sugar has dissolved. Cook for 6–8 minutes, or until the mixture is a medium caramel colour. Remove from the heat and arrange the apple halves, standing on their edges, in the tin.

3 Return the tin to the heat and simmer for 20–25 minutes, or until the apples are tender and coloured. Remove from the heat and cool slightly.

4 Preheat the oven to 230°C/450°F/Gas 8. Place the pastry over the apples and tuck the edges inside the tin around the apples. Pierce the pastry in two or three places, then bake for 25–30 minutes, or until the pastry is golden and the filling is bubbling. Cool in the tin for 10–15 minutes.

5 To serve, run a sharp knife around the edge of the tin to loosen the pastry. Cover with a serving plate and carefully invert the tin and plate together. It is best to do this over a sink in case any caramel drips. Lift off the tin and loosen any apples that stick with a metal spatula. Serve the tart warm with crème fraîche or whipped cream.

Energy 236kcal/986kJ; Fat 15g, Saturated Fat 6g; Carbohydrate 25.8g, Fibre 1g

Rich Chocolate Pie

A delicious rich and creamy pie generously decorated with chocolate curls.

Serves 8

75g/3oz plain (semisweet) chocolate
50g/2oz/¼ cup butter or margarine
45ml/3 tbsp golden (light corn) syrup
3 eggs, beaten
150g/5oz/¾ cup caster (superfine) sugar
5ml/1 tsp vanilla extract
115g/4oz milk chocolate
475ml/16fl oz/2 cups whipping cream

For the pastry
165g/5½oz/1⅓ cups plain (all-purpose) flour
2.5ml/½ tsp salt
115g/4oz/⅔ cup lard or white cooking fat (shortening), diced
30–45ml/2–3 tbsp iced water

1 Preheat the oven to 220°C/425°F/Gas 7. To make the pastry, sift the flour and salt into a bowl. Rub in the fat until the mixture resembles coarse breadcrumbs. Add water until the pastry forms a ball.

2 Roll out the pastry and use to line a 20–23cm/8–9in flan tin (tart pan). Flute the edge. Prick the base and sides of the pastry case with a fork. Bake until lightly browned, about 10–15 minutes. Cool in the tin on a wire rack.

3 Reduce the oven temperature to 180°C/350°F/Gas 4. In the top of a double boiler or in a heatproof bowl over a pan of simmering water, melt the plain chocolate, the butter or margarine, and the golden syrup. Remove from the heat and stir in the eggs, sugar and vanilla extract. Pour the chocolate mixture into the pastry case. Bake until the filling is set, about 35–40 minutes. Cool in the tin on a wire rack.

4 For the decoration, use the heat of your hands to soften the milk chocolate slightly. Use a swivel-headed vegetable peeler to shave off short, wide curls. Chill until needed.

5 Before serving, lightly whip the cream until soft peaks form. Spread the cream over the surface of the chocolate filling. Decorate with the milk chocolate curls.

Energy 712kcal/2962kJ; Fat 52.7g, Saturated Fat 28.9g; Carbohydrate 55.8g, Fibre 1g

Red Berry Tart with Lemon Cream

This jewel-like flan filled with summer fruits is best filled just before serving so that the pastry remains mouth-wateringly crisp.

Serves 6–8

200g/7oz/scant 1 cup cream cheese, softened
45ml/3 tbsp lemon curd
grated rind and juice of 1 lemon
icing (confectioners') sugar, to taste (optional)
225g/8oz/2 cups mixed red berry fruits
45ml/3 tbsp redcurrant jelly

For the pastry

150g/5oz/1¼ cups plain (all-purpose) flour
25g/1oz/¼ cup cornflour (cornstarch)
30g/1½oz/scant ⅓ cup icing (confectioners') sugar
90g/3½oz/7 tbsp cold butter, diced
5ml/1 tsp vanilla extract
2 egg yolks, beaten

1 To make the pastry, sift the flour, cornflour and sugar together. Rub in the butter until the mixture resembles breadcrumbs.

2 Beat the vanilla extract into the egg yolks, then stir into the flour mixture to make a firm dough. Add cold water if the dough is too dry.

3 Roll out the pastry and use it to line a 23cm/9in round flan tin (tart pan). Trim the edges. Prick the base with a fork and leave to rest in the refrigerator for 30 minutes.

4 Preheat the oven to 200°C/400°F/Gas 6. Line the flan with baking parchment and fill with baking beans. Place on a baking sheet and bake for 20 minutes, removing the paper and beans after 15 minutes. Leave to cool, then remove the pastry case from the flan tin.

5 Cream the cheese, lemon curd, and lemon rind and juice, adding icing sugar if you wish. Spread the mixture into the base of the flan. Top with the mixed red berry fruits. Warm the redcurrant jelly and trickle over the fruits just before serving.

Energy 253kcal/1059kJ; Fat 13.8g, Saturated Fat 7.9g; Carbohydrate 30.5g, Fibre 0.9g

Peach and Almond Tart

The delicate flavour of almond goes beautifully with ripe summer peaches.

Serves 8–10

115g/4oz/⅔ cup blanched almonds
15g/½oz/2 tbsp plain (all-purpose) flour
90g/3½oz/7 tbsp unsalted (sweet) butter
115g/4oz/1 cup, plus 30ml/2 tbsp caster (superfine) sugar
1 egg, plus 1 egg yolk
1.5ml/¼ tsp vanilla extract, or 10ml/2 tsp rum
4 large ripe peaches, peeled

For the pastry

185g/6½oz/generous 1½ cups plain (all-purpose) flour
2.5ml/½ tsp salt
90g/3½oz/scant ¼ cup cold unsalted (sweet) butter, diced
1 egg yolk
10–45ml/2–3 tbsp iced water

1 To make the pastry, sift the flour and salt into a bowl. Rub in the butter until the mixture resembles coarse breadcrumbs.

2 Stir in the egg yolk and enough water to bind the pastry. Gather into a ball, wrap and chill for 20 minutes. Preheat a baking sheet in the centre of a 200°C/400°F/Gas 6 oven.

3 Roll out the pastry 3mm/⅛in thick. Transfer to a 25cm/10in pie dish. Trim the edge, prick the base and chill.

4 Grind the almonds with the flour. With an electric mixer, cream the butter and 115g/4oz/scant ¾ cup of the sugar until light and fluffy. Gradually beat in the egg and yolk. Stir in the almonds and vanilla or rum. Spread in the pastry case.

5 Halve the peaches and remove the stones (pits). Cut the fruit crossways in thin slices and fan out. Transfer to the tart, placing the fruit on top of the almond cream and arranging like the spokes of a wheel.

6 Bake until the pastry browns, about 10–15 minutes. Lower the heat to 180°C/350°F/Gas 4 and bake until the almond cream sets, about 15 minutes more. 10 minutes before the end of the cooking time, sprinkle with the remaining sugar.

Energy 376kcal/1569kJ; Fat 24.8g, Saturated Fat 11.4g; Carbohydrate 33.4g, Fibre 2.4g

Pear and Almond Cream Tart

Fanned pears, glazed with brandy, rest on a light almond filling. This tart is equally successful made with other orchard fruits such as nectarines, peaches, apricots or apples.

Serves 6

350g/12oz shortcrust or sweet shortcrust pastry, thawed if frozen
3 firm pears
lemon juice
15ml/1 tbsp peach brandy or cold water
60ml/4 tbsp peach jam, sieved

For the filling

90g/3½oz/generous ½ cup blanched whole almonds
50g/2oz/¼ cup caster (superfine) sugar
65g/2½oz/5 tbsp butter
1 egg, plus 1 egg white
a few drops of almond extract

1 Roll out the pastry and use to line a 23cm/9in flan tin. Chill in the refrigerator while you make the filling.

2 For the filling, put the almonds and sugar in a food processor or blender and pulse until finely ground but not pasty. Add the butter and process until creamy, then add the egg, egg white and almond extract, and mix well.

3 Preheat a baking sheet in the oven at 190°C/375°F/Gas 5.

4 Peel the pears, halve them, remove the cores and rub with lemon juice. Put the pear halves, cut side down, on a board and slice thinly crossways, keeping the slices together.

5 Pour the filling into the pastry case. Slide a metal spatula under one pear half and press the top to fan out the slices. Transfer to the tart, placing the fruit on the filling like the spokes of a wheel.

6 Bake the tart on the baking sheet for 50–55 minutes, or until the filling is set and well browned. Cool on a wire rack.

7 Heat the brandy or water with the jam. Brush over the top of the hot tart to glaze. Serve at room temperature.

Energy 544kcal/2271kJ; Fat 34.7g, Saturated Fat 11.7g; Carbohydrate 51.5g, Fibre 3.9g

Lemon Tart

This tart, a classic of France, has a refreshing tangy flavour.

Serves 8–10

350g/12oz shortcrust or sweet shortcrust pastry, thawed if frozen
grated rind of 2 or 3 lemons
150ml/¼ pint/⅔ cup freshly squeezed lemon juice
90g/3½oz/½ cup caster (superfine) sugar
60ml/4 tbsp crème fraîche or double (heavy) cream
4 eggs, plus 3 egg yolks
icing (confectioners') sugar, for dusting

1 Preheat a baking sheet in the oven to 190°C/375°F/Gas 5.

2 Roll out the pastry and use to line a 23cm/9in flan tin (tart pan). Prick the base with a fork, line with foil and fill with baking beans.

3 Bake for 15 minutes, or until the edges are dry. Remove the foil and beans, and bake for a further 5–7 minutes, or until golden.

4 Beat together the lemon rind, juice and caster sugar, then gradually add the crème fraîche or double cream, beating after each addition until well blended.

5 Beat in the eggs, one at a time, then beat in the egg yolks.

6 Pour the filling into the baked pastry case. Return it to the oven and bake for about 15–20 minutes, or until the filling is set. If the pastry begins to brown too much, cover the edges with foil.

7 Leave the tart to cool, and dust lightly with icing sugar before serving.

Variation
This tart would also taste great made with oranges.

Energy 268kcal/1122kJ; Fat 16.1g, Saturated Fat 5.8g; Carbohydrate 27g, Fibre 0.7g

Maple Walnut Tart

Makes sure you use 100 per cent pure maple syrup in this decadent tart for the truly authentic flavour.

Serves 8

3 eggs
1.5ml/¼ tsp salt
50g/2oz/¼ cup caster (superfine) sugar
50g/2oz/¼ cup butter, melted
250ml/8fl oz/1 cup pure maple syrup
115g/4oz/1 cup chopped walnuts
whipped cream, to decorate

For the pastry

65g/2½oz/9 tbsp plain (all-purpose) flour
65g/2½oz/9 tbsp wholemeal (whole-wheat) flour
1.5ml/¼ tsp salt
50g/2oz/4 tbsp cold butter, diced
40g/1½oz/3 tbsp cold white cooking fat (shortening) or lard, diced
1 egg yolk

1 To make the pastry, mix the plain and wholemeal flours and salt in a bowl. Add the butter and white cooking fat and rub in until the mixture resembles coarse breadcrumbs.

2 Stir in the egg yolk and 30–45ml/2–3 tbsp iced water to bind. Form into a ball, wrap in clear film (plastic wrap) and chill for 20 minutes. Preheat a baking sheet in the oven to 220°C/425°F/Gas 7.

3 Roll out the pastry and use to line a 23cm/9in pie dish. Use the trimmings to stamp out small heart shapes. Arrange on the pastry case rim with a little water.

4 Prick the pastry base with a fork, line with baking parchment and fill with baking beans. Bake for 10 minutes. Remove the paper and beans and bake until golden, about 3–6 minutes more.

5 Whisk together the eggs, salt and sugar. Stir in the butter and maple syrup. Set the pastry case on a baking sheet. Pour in the filling, then sprinkle with the walnuts.

6 Bake until just set, about 35 minutes. Cool on a wire rack. Decorate with piped whipped cream.

Energy 442kcal/1846kJ; Fat 28.1g, Saturated Fat 10.2g; Carbohydrate 43.3g, Fibre 1.5g

Pecan Tart

Serve this tart warm, accompanied by ice cream or whipped cream, if you wish.

Serves 8

3 eggs
pinch of salt
200g/7oz/scant 1 cup soft dark brown sugar
120ml/4fl oz/½ cup golden (light corn) syrup
30ml/2 tbsp fresh lemon juice
75g/3oz/6 tbsp butter, melted
150g/5oz/1¼ cups chopped pecan nuts
50g/2oz/⅓ cup pecan nut halves

For the pastry

175g/6oz/1½ cups plain (all-purpose) flour
15ml/1 tbsp caster (superfine) ugar
5ml/1 tsp baking powder
2.5ml/½ tsp salt
75g/3oz/6 tbsp cold unsalted (sweet) butter, diced
1 egg yolk
45–60ml/3–4 tbsp whipping cream

1 To make the pastry, sift together the flour, caster sugar, baking powder and salt in a bowl. Add the butter and rub in using your fingertips or a pastry cutter until the mixture resembles coarse breadcrumbs.

2 Blend the egg yolk and whipping cream, and stir into the flour mixture.

3 Form the pastry into a ball, then roll out and use to line a 23cm/9in pie dish. Trim and flute the edge neatly and chill for 20 minutes.

4 Preheat a baking sheet in the oven at 200°C/400°F/Gas 6. Lightly whisk the eggs and salt. Mix in the sugar, syrup, lemon juice and butter. Stir in the chopped pecan nuts.

5 Pour into the pastry case and arrange the pecan nut halves in concentric circles on top.

6 Bake on the baking sheet for 10 minutes. Reduce the heat to 160°C/325°F/Gas 3 and bake for 25 minutes more.

Energy 587kcal/2449kJ; Fat 38.3g, Saturated Fat 13.4g; Carbohydrate 56.7g, Fibre 1.9g

Velvety Mocha Tart

A creamy smooth filling tops a dark light-textured base in this wondrous dessert decorated with cream and chocolate-coated coffee beans.

Serves 8

10ml/2 tsp instant espresso coffee
30ml/2 tbsp hot water
175g/6oz plain (semisweet) chocolate
25g/1oz bitter cooking chocolate
350ml/12fl oz/1 ½ cups whipping cream, slightly warmed
120ml/4fl oz/½ cup whipped cream, to decorate
chocolate-coated coffee beans, to decorate

For the base

150g/5oz/2 ½ cups crushed chocolate wafers
30ml/2 tbsp caster (superfine) sugar
65g/2 ½oz/5 tbsp butter, melted

1 To make the base, combine the crushed chocolate wafers with the sugar and butter in a bowl.

2 Press the mixture over the base and sides of a 23cm/9in pie dish. Chill.

3 Dissolve the coffee in the water. Set aside to cool.

4 Melt the plain and bitter chocolates in the top of a double boiler or in a heatproof bowl over a pan of simmering water.

5 Once the chocolate has melted, remove from the double boiler and set the base of the pan in cold water to cool.

6 Whip the cream until light and fluffy. Add the coffee and whip until the cream just holds its shape.

7 When the chocolate is at room temperature, fold it gently into the cream.

8 Pour into the cookie base and chill until firm. Decorate with piped whipped cream and chocolate-coated coffee beans just before serving.

Energy 507kcal/2103kJ; Fat 42.1g, Saturated Fat 26.2g; Carbohydrate 30.3g, Fibre 0.8g

Coconut Cream Tart

Toasted coconut tops this creamy, unusual tart.

Serves 8

150g/5oz/generous 1 ½ cups desiccated (dry unsweetened shredded) coconut
150g/5oz/¾ cup caster (superfine) sugar
25g/1oz/¼ cup cornflour (cornstarch)
1.5ml/¼ tsp salt
600ml/1 pint/2 ½ cups milk
50ml/2fl oz whipping cream
2 egg yolks
25g/1oz/2 tbsp unsalted (sweet) butter
10ml/2 tsp vanilla extract

For the pastry

150g/5oz/1 ¼ cups plain (all-purpose) flour
1.5ml/¼ tsp salt
45g/1 ½oz/3 tbsp cold butter, diced
25g/1oz/3 tbsp cold vegetable fat (shortening) or lard
30–45ml/2–3 tbsp iced water

1 To make the pastry, sift the flour and salt into a bowl, add the fats and rub in until the mixture resembles coarse breadcrumbs. With a fork, stir in just enough water to bind the pastry. Gather into a ball, wrap in clear film (plastic wrap) and chill for 20 minutes. Preheat the oven to 220°C/425°F/Gas 7.

2 Roll out the pastry 3mm/⅛in thick. Line a 23cm/9in pie dish. Trim and flute the edges, prick the base, line with baking parchment and fill with baking beans. Bake for 10 – 12 minutes. Remove the paper and beans, reduce the heat to 180°C/350°F/Gas 4 and bake until brown, 10 – 15 minutes.

3 Spread 50g/2oz/⅔ cup of the coconut on a baking sheet and toast in the oven until golden, 6–8 minutes. Put the sugar, cornflour and salt in a pan. In a bowl, whisk the milk, cream and egg yolks. Add the egg mixture to the pan.

4 Cook over a low heat, stirring, until the mixture comes to the boil. Boil for 1 minute, then remove from the heat. Add the butter, vanilla extract and remaining coconut.

5 Pour into the pre-baked pastry case. When cool, sprinkle toasted coconut in a ring in the centre.

Energy 400kcal/1671kJ; Fat 25.2g, Saturated Fat 17g; Carbohydrate 39.6g, Fibre 2.9g

Orange Tart

If you like oranges, this is the dessert for you!

Serves 8

200g/7oz/1 cup caster (superfine) sugar
250ml/8fl oz/1 cup fresh orange juice, strained
2 large navel oranges
165g/5½oz/scant 1 cup whole blanched almonds
50g/2oz/¼ cup butter
1 egg
15ml/1 tbsp plain (all-purpose) flour
45ml/3 tbsp apricot jam

For the pastry

210g/7½oz/scant 2 cups plain (all-purpose) flour
2.5ml/½ tsp salt
50g/2oz/¼ cup cold butter, diced
40g/1½oz/3 tbsp cold margarine, diced
45–60ml/3–4 tbsp iced water

1 To make the pastry, sift the flour and salt into a bowl. Add the butter and margarine, and rub in using your fingertips or a pastry cutter until the mixture resembles coarse breadcrumbs. Stir in just enough water to bind the dough. Wrap and chill for 20 minutes.

2 Roll out the pastry to a 5mm/¼ in thickness. Use to line a 20cm/8in tart tin. Trim and chill until needed.

3 In a pan, combine 165g/5½oz/¾ cup of the sugar and the orange juice and boil until thick and syrupy. Cut the unpeeled oranges into 5mm/¼in slices. Add to the syrup. Simmer gently for 10 minutes. Put on a wire rack to dry. When cool, cut in half. Reserve the syrup. Place a baking sheet in the oven and heat to 200°C/400°F/Gas 6.

4 Grind the almonds finely in a blender or food processor. Cream the butter and remaining sugar until light and fluffy. Beat in the egg and 30ml/2 tbsp of the orange syrup. Stir in the almonds and flour.

5 Melt the jam over a low heat, then brush over the pastry case. Pour in the almond mixture. Bake on the baking sheet until set, about 20 minutes, then cool. Arrange overlapping orange slices on top. Boil the remaining syrup until thick and brush over the top to glaze.

Energy 500kcal/2093kJ; Fat 27g, Saturated Fat 7.7g; Carbohydrate 59.4g, Fibre 3.1g

Raspberry Tart

A luscious tart of rich custard beneath juicy fresh raspberries.

Serves 8

4 egg yolks
65g/2½oz/generous ¼ cup caster (superfine) sugar
45ml/3 tbsp plain (all-purpose) flour
300ml/½ pint/1¼ cups milk
1.5ml/¼ tsp salt
2.5ml/½ tsp vanilla extract
450g/1lb/2⅔ cups fresh raspberries
75ml/5 tbsp redcurrant jelly
15ml/1 tbsp orange juice

For the pastry

185g/6½oz/1⅔ cups plain (all-purpose) flour
2.5ml/½ tsp baking powder
1.5ml/¼ tsp salt
15ml/1 tbsp sugar
grated rind of ½ orange
75g/3oz/6 tbsp cold butter, diced
1 egg yolk
45–60ml/3–4 tbsp whipping cream

1 To make the pastry, sift the flour, baking powder and salt into a bowl. Stir in the sugar and orange rind. Add the butter and rub in using your fingertips or a pastry cutter until the mixture resembles breadcrumbs. Stir in the egg yolk and cream to bind. Form into a ball, wrap in clear film (plastic wrap) and chill.

2 For the filling, beat the egg yolks and sugar until thick and creamy. Gradually stir in the flour. Bring the milk and salt just to the boil, then remove from the heat. Whisk into the egg yolk mixture, return to the pan and continue whisking over a medium-high heat until just bubbling. Cook for 3 minutes to thicken. Transfer to a bowl. Stir in the vanilla extract, then cover with baking parchment.

3 Preheat the oven to 200°C/400°F/Gas 6. Roll out the pastry and use to line a 25cm/10in pie dish. Prick the base with a fork, line with baking parchment and fill with baking beans. Bake for 15 minutes. Remove the paper and beans, and bake until golden, about 6–8 minutes more. Leave to cool.

4 Spread an even layer of the custard filling in the pastry case and arrange the raspberries on top. Melt the redcurrant jelly and orange juice in a pan and brush over the top to glaze.

Energy 323kcal/1359kJ; Fat 14.6g, Saturated Fat 7.8g; Carbohydrate 44g, Fibre 2.3g

Lattice Berry Pie

Choose any berries you like for this handsome pie.

Serves 8
450g/1lb/about 4 cups berries, such as bilberries, blueberries and blackcurrants
115g/4oz/generous ½ cup caster (superfine) sugar
45ml/3 tbsp cornflour (cornstarch)
30ml/2 tbsp fresh lemon juice
25g/1oz/2 tbsp butter, diced

For the pastry
275g/10oz/2½ cups plain (all-purpose) flour
4ml/¾ tsp salt
115g/4oz/½ cup cold butter, diced
40g/1½oz/3 tbsp cold white cooking fat (shortening) or lard, diced
75–90ml/5–6 tbsp iced water
1 egg, beaten with 15ml/1 tbsp water, for glazing

1 To make the pastry, sift the flour and salt into a bowl. Add the butter and fat and rub in with your fingertips or a pastry cutter until the mixture resembles coarse breadcrumbs. Stir in just enough water to bind. Form into two balls, wrap in clear film (plastic wrap) and chill for 20 minutes.

2 Roll out one ball and use to line a 23cm/9in pie dish, leaving a 1cm/½in overhang. Brush the base with egg.

3 Mix the berries with the caster sugar, cornflour and lemon juice, reserving a few berries for decoration. Spoon this filling into the pastry case and dot with the butter. Brush egg around the pastry rim.

4 Preheat the oven to 220°C/425°F/Gas 7. Roll out the remaining pastry on a baking sheet lined with baking parchment. With a serrated pastry wheel, make 24 thin strips. Use the scraps to cut out leaf shapes, and mark veins.

5 Weave the strips in a close lattice and transfer to the pie. Seal the edges and trim. Arrange the leaves around the rim. Brush with egg and bake for 10 minutes.

6 Reduce the heat to 180°C/350°F/Gas 4 and bake the pie for a further 40–45 minutes. Decorate with the reserved berries.

Energy 384kcal/1607kJ; Fat 19.9g, Saturated Fat 11.2g; Carbohydrate 50.4g, Fibre 1.7g

Plum Pie

When the new season's plums are in the shops, treat someone special with this lightly spiced plum pie.

Serves 8
900g/2lb red or purple plums
grated rind of 1 lemon
15ml/1 tbsp fresh lemon juice
115–175g/4–6oz/generous ½–scant 1 cup caster (superfine) sugar
45ml/3 tbsp quick-cooking tapioca
1.5ml/¼ tsp salt
2.5ml/½ tsp ground cinnamon
1.5ml/¼ tsp freshly grated nutmeg

For the pastry
275g/10oz/2½ cups plain (all-purpose) flour
5ml/1 tsp salt
75g/3oz/6 tbsp cold butter, diced
50g/2oz/4 tbsp cold white cooking fat (shortening) or lard, diced
50–120ml/2–4fl oz/¼–½ cup iced water
milk, for glazing

1 To make the pastry, sift the flour and salt into a bowl. Add the butter and fat and rub in with your fingertips or a pastry cutter until the mixture resembles coarse breadcrumbs.

2 Stir in just enough water to bind the pastry. Form into two balls, wrap in clear film (plastic wrap) and chill for 20 minutes.

3 Preheat a baking sheet in the oven at 220°C/425°F/Gas 7. Roll out a pastry ball and use to line a 23cm/9in pie dish.

4 Halve and stone (pit) the plums, and chop roughly. Mix the lemon rind and juice, the chopped plums, caster sugar, tapioca and salt together in a bowl and mix in the spices, then transfer to the pastry-lined pie dish.

5 Roll out the remaining pastry, place on a baking sheet lined with baking parchment, and stamp out four hearts. Transfer the pastry lid to the pie using the paper.

6 Trim the pastry to leave a 2cm/¾in overhang. Fold this under the pastry base and pinch to seal. Arrange the hearts on top. Brush with milk and bake for 15 minutes. Reduce the heat to 180°C/350°F/Gas 4 and bake for a further 30–35 minutes.

Energy 360kcal/1516kJ; Fat 14.5g, Saturated Fat 7.5g; Carbohydrate 57g, Fibre 2.9g

Dorset Apple Cake

Serve this fruity apple cake warm, and spread with butter if you like.

Makes one 18cm/7in round cake

225g/8oz cooking apples, peeled, cored and chopped
juice of ½ lemon
225g/8oz/2 cups plain (all-purpose) flour
7.5ml/1½ tsp baking powder
115g/4oz/½ cup butter, diced
165g/5½oz/¾ cup soft light brown sugar
1 egg, beaten
about 30–45ml/2–3 tbsp milk, to mix
2.5ml/½ tsp ground cinnamon

1 Preheat the oven to 180°C/350°F/Gas 4. Grease and line an 18cm/7in round cake tin (pan).

2 Toss the apple with the lemon juice and set aside. Sift the flour and baking powder together, then rub in the butter using your fingertips or a pastry cutter, until the mixture resembles breadcrumbs.

3 Stir in 115g/4oz/1 cup of the brown sugar, the apple and the egg, and mix well, adding sufficient milk to make a soft dropping consistency.

4 Transfer the batter to the prepared tin. In a bowl, mix together the remaining sugar and the cinnamon. Sprinkle over the cake mixture, then bake for 45–50 minutes, or until golden. Leave to cool in the tin for 10 minutes, then transfer to a wire rack to cool completely.

Cook's Tips

For successful cakes remember these few golden rules:
- *Heat the oven to the correct temperature in plenty of time.*
- *Measure out the ingredients carefully.*
- *Use the correct size tins (pans) and prepare them before you start combining the ingredients.*

Energy 2436kcal/10244kJ; Fat 103.7g, Saturated Fat 62.2g; Carbohydrate 368.6g, Fibre 10.5g

Parkin

The flavour of this dense and sticky cake will improve if it is stored in an airtight container for several days or a week before serving.

Makes 16–20 squares

300ml/½ pint/1¼ cups milk
225g/8oz/scant ⅔ cup golden (light corn) syrup
225g/8oz/scant ⅔ cup black treacle (molasses)
115g/4oz/½ cup butter or margarine, diced
50g/2oz/¼ cup soft dark brown sugar
450g/1lb/4 cups plain (all-purpose) flour
2.5ml/½ tsp bicarbonate of soda (baking soda)
6.5ml/1¼ tsp ground ginger
350g/12oz/3 cups medium oatmeal
1 egg, beaten
icing (confectioners') sugar, for dusting

1 Preheat the oven to 180°C/350°F/Gas 4. Grease and line the base of a 20cm/8in square cake tin (pan).

2 Gently heat together the milk, syrup, treacle, butter or margarine and sugar in a pan, stirring until smooth. Do not allow the mixture to boil.

3 Stir together the flour, bicarbonate of soda, ginger and oatmeal.

4 Make a well in the centre, pour in the egg, then slowly pour in the warmed mixture, stirring to make a smooth batter.

5 Pour the batter into the tin and bake for about 45 minutes, until firm to the touch. Cool slightly in the tin, then cool completely on a wire rack. Cut into squares or thick slices and dust with icing sugar.

Cook's Tip

This traditional cake is made using the melted cakes method. Melted cakes have a satisfying dense, sticky texture created by using treacle (molasses) or golden (light corn) syrup. Baking powder or bicarbonate of soda (baking soda) are usually used to make melted cakes rise. Melted cakes store well and generally improve with keeping for a few days.

Energy 273kcal/1152kJ; Fat 7.1g, Saturated Fat 3.3g; Carbohydrate 50g, Fibre 1.9g

Banana Ginger Parkin

The combination of banana and ginger give a new slant to the traditional recipe for this delicious cake.

Makes 16–20 squares

200g/7oz/1¾ cups plain (all-purpose) flour
10ml/2 tsp bicarbonate of soda (baking soda)
10ml/2 tsp ground ginger
150g/5oz/1¼ cups medium oatmeal
50g/2oz/¼ cup muscovado sugar (molasses)
75g/3oz/6 tbsp sunflower margarine
150g/5oz/3 tbsp golden (light corn) syrup
1 egg, beaten
3 ripe bananas, mashed
75g/3oz/¾ cup icing (confectioners') sugar
preserved stem ginger, to decorate (optional)

1 Preheat the oven to 160°C/325°F/Gas 3. Grease and line an 18 x 28cm/7 x 11in cake tin (pan).

2 Sift together the flour, bicarbonate of soda and ginger in a bowl, then stir in the oatmeal.

3 Melt the sugar, margarine and syrup in a pan over a low heat, then stir into the flour mixture.

4 Beat the egg and mashed bananas into the flour mixture until thoroughly combined. Spoon the mixture into the prepared tin and bake for about 1 hour, or until firm to the touch.

5 Leave the cake to cool in the tin for 5 minutes, then turn it out on to a wire rack and allow it to cool completely.

6 If you want to keep the cake for a few months, wrap it in foil and put it in an air-tight container without cutting it. If you want to eat it immediately, cut it into squares.

7 Make the icing when you want to serve the cake: sift the icing sugar into a bowl and stir in just enough water to make a smooth, runny icing. Drizzle the icing over each square of cake in a zigzag pattern and top with a piece of stem ginger, if you like.

Energy 157kcal/662kJ; Fat 4.2g, Saturated Fat 0.7g; Carbohydrate 29.2g, Fibre 1g

Gooseberry Cake

This cake is delicious served warm with whipped cream.

Makes one 18cm/7in square cake

115g/4oz/½ cup butter
165g/5½oz/1⅓ cups self-raising (self-rising) flour
5ml/1 tsp baking powder
2 eggs, beaten
115g/4oz/generous ½ cup caster (superfine) sugar
5–10ml/1–2 tsp rose water
pinch of freshly grated nutmeg
115g/4oz jar gooseberries in syrup, drained, juice reserved
caster (superfine) sugar, to decorate
whipped cream, to serve

1 Preheat the oven to 180°C/350°F/Gas 4. Grease an 18cm/7in square cake tin (pan) and line the base and sides with baking parchment. Grease the paper.

2 Gently melt the butter in a pan, then transfer to a large bowl and allow to cool.

3 Sift together the flour and baking powder and add to the butter in the bowl.

4 Beat in the eggs, one at a time, the sugar, rose water and grated nutmeg, until you have a smooth batter.

5 Mix in 15–30ml/1–2 tbsp of the reserved gooseberry juice from the jar, then pour half of the batter mixture into the prepared tin. Sprinkle over the gooseberries and pour over the remaining batter mixture.

6 Bake for about 45 minutes, or until a skewer inserted into the centre of the cake comes out clean.

7 Leave in the tin for 5 minutes, then turn out on a wire rack, peel off the lining paper and allow to cool for a further 5 minutes.

8 Dredge with caster sugar and serve immediately with whipped cream, or leave the cake to cool completely before decorating.

Energy 2080kcal/8719kJ; Fat 108.1g, Saturated Fat 63.3g; Carbohydrate 263.9g, Fibre 7.3g

Crunchy-topped Sponge Loaf

This light sponge makes a perfect tea-time treat.

Makes one 450g/1lb loaf

200g/7oz/scant 1 cup butter, softened
finely grated rind of 1 lemon
150g/5oz/5 tbsp caster (superfine) sugar
3 eggs
75g/3oz/⅔ cup plain (all-purpose) flour, sifted
150g/5oz/1¼ cups self-raising (self-rising) flour, sifted

For the topping

45ml/3 tbsp clear honey
115g/4oz/⅔ cup mixed (candied) peel
50g/2oz/½ cup flaked (sliced) almonds

1 Preheat the oven to 180°C/350°F/Gas 4. Grease and line a 450g/1lb loaf tin (pan) with baking parchment.

2 Beat together the butter, lemon rind and sugar until light and fluffy. Blend in the eggs, one at a time.

3 Sift together the flours, then stir into the egg mixture. Fill the loaf tin with the batter. Bake for 45 minutes, or until a skewer inserted into the centre comes out clean. Leave to cool in the tin for 5 minutes.

4 Turn the loaf out on to a wire rack, peel off the lining paper and leave to cool completely.

5 To make the topping, melt the honey with the mixed peel and almonds. Remove from the heat, stir briefly, then spread over the top of the loaf. Cool before serving.

Cook's Tip

This recipe uses chopped mixed (candied) peel for the topping. To make it extra-special it is worth buying some good quality peel from a delicatessen, as the flavour is far superior. The peel comes in large pieces, so chop it into smaller chunks.

Energy 3768kcal/15772kJ; Fat 212.9g, Saturated Fat 111.5g, Carbohydrate 438.6g, Fibre 16.2g

Irish Whiskey Cake

Other whiskies could be used in this cake.

Makes one 23 x 13cm/9 x 5in cake

175g/6oz/1½ cups chopped walnuts
75g/3oz/generous ½ cup raisins, chopped
75g/3oz/scant ½ cup currants
115g/4oz/1 cup plain (all-purpose) flour
5ml/1 tsp baking powder
1.5ml/¼ tsp salt
115g/4oz/½ cup butter
225g/8oz/generous 1 cup caster (superfine) sugar
3 eggs, separated, at room temperature
5ml/1 tsp freshly grated nutmeg
2.5ml/½ tsp ground cinnamon
75ml/5 tbsp Irish whiskey
icing (confectioners') sugar, for dusting

1 Preheat the oven to 160°C/325°F/Gas 3. Grease a 23 x 13cm/9 x 5in loaf tin (pan) and line the base.

2 Mix the walnuts, raisins and currants with 30ml/2 tbsp of the flour and set aside. Sift together the remaining flour, baking powder and salt into a bowl.

3 In another bowl, cream the butter and sugar together until light and fluffy. Beat in the egg yolks.

4 Mix the nutmeg, cinnamon and whiskey in a small bowl. Fold into the butter mixture, alternating with the flour mixture.

5 Beat the egg whites until stiff. Fold into the whiskey mixture until just blended. Fold into the walnut mixture.

6 Fill the loaf tin and bake for about 1 hour. Cool in the tin.

7 Meanwhile, make a template with which you can create a pattern on top of the cake. Fold a long strip of paper into a concertina and draw two diagonal lines from the bottom to the top. Cut along the lines and open out the strip. Cut it in half to give you two strips and lay these on top of the cake. Once the cake has cooled completely, position the templates and dust with icing sugar. Remove the template and serve in slices.

Energy 4152kcal/17355kJ; Fat 233.2g, Saturated Fat 74.6g, Carbohydrate 433.8g, Fibre 12.6g

Autumn Dessert Cake

Greengages, plums or semi-dried prunes are delicious in this recipe. Serve with cream or ice cream.

Serves 6–8
115g/4oz/½ cup butter, softened
150g/5oz/¾ cup caster (superfine) sugar
3 eggs, beaten
75g/3oz/¾ cup ground hazelnuts
150g/5oz/1¼ cups chopped pecan nuts
50g/2oz/½ cup plain (all-purpose) flour
5ml/1 tsp baking powder
2.5ml/½ tsp salt
675g/1½lb/3 cups plums, greengages or semi-dried prunes
60ml/4 tbsp lime marmalade
15ml/1 tbsp lime juice
30ml/2 tbsp blanched almonds, chopped, to decorate

1 Stone (pit) the plums, greengages or prunes and set aside until they are needed.

2 Preheat the oven to 180°C/350°F/Gas 4. Grease a 23cm/9in round, fluted flan tin (tart pan).

3 Beat the softened butter and caster sugar until light and fluffy. Gradually beat in the eggs, alternating with the ground hazelnuts. Do not overbeat.

4 Stir in the pecan nuts, then sift and fold in the flour, baking powder and salt. Spoon into the tart tin.

5 Bake for 45 minutes, or until a skewer inserted into the centre comes out clean.

6 Arrange the fruit on the base. Return to the oven and bake for 10–15 minutes, or until the fruit has softened. Transfer to a wire rack to cool, then turn out.

7 Warm the marmalade and lime juice gently. Brush over the fruit, then sprinkle with the almonds.

8 Allow to set, then chill before serving.

Energy 481kcal/2007kJ; Fat 34.2g, Saturated Fat 9.7g; Carbohydrate 39g, Fibre 3.2g

Apple Crumble Cake

In the autumn use windfall apples. Served warm with thick cream or custard, this cake doubles as a dessert.

Serves 8–10
75g/3oz/⅔ cup self-raising (self-rising) flour
½ tsp ground cinnamon
40g/1½oz/3 tbsp butter
25g/1oz/2 tbsp caster (superfine) sugar

For the base
50g/2oz/¼ cup butter, softened
75g/3oz/6 tbsp caster (superfine) sugar
1 egg, beaten
115g/4oz/1 cup self-raising (self-rising) flour, sifted
2 cooking apples, peeled, cored and sliced
50g/2oz/⅓ cup sultanas (golden raisins)

To decorate
1 red dessert apple, cored, thinly sliced and tossed in lemon juice
25g/1oz/2 tbsp caster (superfine) sugar, sifted
pinch of ground cinnamon

1 Preheat the oven to 180°C/350°F/Gas 4. Grease a deep 18cm/7in springform tin (pan), line the base with baking parchment and grease the paper.

2 To make the topping, sift the flour and cinnamon into a mixing bowl. Rub the butter into the flour using your fingertips or a pastry cutter until it resembles breadcrumbs, then stir in the sugar. Set aside.

3 To make the base, put the butter, sugar, egg and flour into a bowl and beat for 1–2 minutes, or until smooth. Spoon into the prepared tin.

4 Mix together the apple slices and sultanas, and spread them evenly over the top. Sprinkle with the topping.

5 Bake for about 1 hour. Cool in the tin for 10 minutes before turning out on to a wire rack and peeling off the lining paper. Serve warm or cool, decorated with slices of red dessert apple and sprinkled with caster sugar and cinnamon.

Energy 211kcal/890kJ; Fat 8.3g, Saturated Fat 4.9g; Carbohydrate 33.7g, Fibre 1.1g

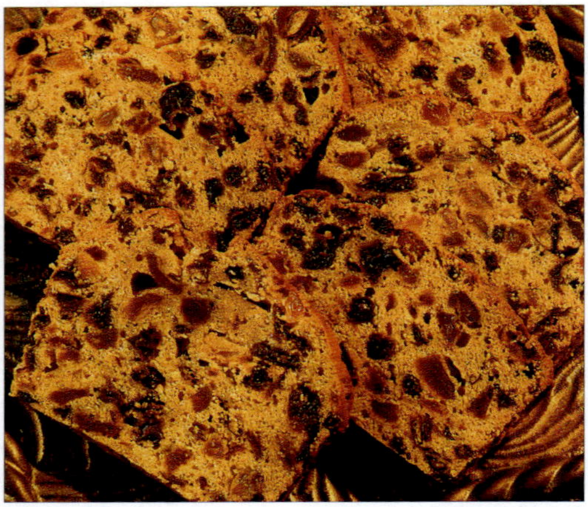

Light Fruit Cake

Dried fruit soaked in wine and rum gives this fruit cake an exquisite flavour. For the best taste, wrap it in foil and store it for a week before cutting.

Makes two 23 x 13cm/ 9 x 5in cakes

225g/8oz/1 cup prunes
225g/8oz/1⅓ cups dates
225g/8oz/1 cup currants
225g/8oz/generous 1¼ cups sultanas (golden raisins)
250ml/8fl oz/1 cup dry white wine
250ml/8fl oz/1 cup rum
350g/12oz/3 cups plain (all-purpose) flour
10ml/2 tsp baking powder
5ml/1 tsp ground cinnamon
2.5ml/½ tsp freshly grated nutmeg
225g/8oz/1 cup butter, at room temperature
225g/8oz/generous 1 cup caster (superfine) sugar
4 eggs, lightly beaten
5ml/1 tsp vanilla extract

1 Stone (pit) the prunes and dates and chop finely. Place in a bowl with the currants and sultanas. Stir in the wine and rum and leave, covered, for 2 days. Stir occasionally.

2 Preheat the oven to 150°C/300°F/Gas 2 with a tray of hot water in the bottom. Line two 23 x 13cm/9 x 5in loaf tins (pans) with baking parchment and grease the paper.

3 Sift together the dry ingredients. Cream the butter and sugar together until light and fluffy. Gradually add the eggs and vanilla extract. Fold in the flour mixture in three batches, and finally fold in the dried fruit mixture and its liquid.

4 Divide the mixture between the prepared tins and bake until a skewer inserted into the centre comes out clean, about 1½ hours. Leave to stand for 20 minutes, then unmould the cake on to a wire rack to cool completely.

Variation
You can use a combination of any dried fruit, such as apricots, figs and cranberries in place of the prunes and/or dates. You could also add glacé (candied) cherries.

Energy 3456kcal/14545kJ; Fat 107.4g, Saturated Fat 62.2g; Carbohydrate 524.1g, Fibre 20.7g

Rich Fruit Cake

Sweet sherry adds to the fruit and spices in this cake.

Makes one 23 x 8cm/ 9 x 3in cake

150g/5oz/generous ½ cup currants
170g/6oz/generous 1 cup raisins
50g/2oz/½ cup sultanas (golden raisins)
50g/2oz/¼ cup glacé (candied) cherries, halved
45ml/3 tbsp sweet sherry
175g/6oz/¾ cup butter
200g/7oz/scant 1 cup soft dark brown sugar
2 eggs, at room temperature
200g/7oz/1¾ cups plain (all-purpose) flour
10ml/2 tsp baking powder
10ml/2 tsp each ground ginger, allspice, and cinnamon
15ml/1 tbsp golden (light corn) syrup
15ml/1 tbsp milk
55g/2oz/⅓ cup cut mixed (candied) peel
115g/4oz/1 cup chopped walnuts

For the decoration
120ml/4fl oz/scant ½ cup orange marmalade
crystallized citrus fruit slices
glacé (candied) cherries

1 A day in advance, combine the dried fruit and cherries in a bowl. Stir in the sherry, cover and soak overnight.

2 Preheat the oven to 150°C/300°F/Gas 2. Line and grease a 23 x 7.5cm/9 x 3in springform tin (pan) with baking parchment. Place a tray of hot water in the bottom of the oven.

3 Cream the butter and sugar. Beat in the eggs, one at a time. Sift the flour, baking powder and spices together three times. Fold into the butter mixture in three batches. Fold in the syrup, milk, dried fruit and liquid, mixed peel and walnuts.

4 Spoon into the prepared tin, spreading the mixture out so that there is a slight depression in the centre. Bake for about 2½–3 hours. Cover with foil when the top is golden to prevent over-browning. Cool in the tin on a rack. To decorate, melt the marmalade over a low heat, then brush over the top of the cake. Decorate the cake with the crystallized citrus fruit slices and glacé cherries.

Energy 4509kcal/18916kJ; Fat 220.7g, Saturated Fat 95.2g; Carbohydrate 629.3g, Fibre 14.6g

Creole Christmas Cake

Makes one 23cm/9in cake

450g/1lb/3 cups raisins
225g/8oz/1 cup currants
115g/4oz/¾ cup sultanas (golden raisins)
115g/4oz/½ cup ready-to-eat prunes, chopped
115g/4oz/⅔ cup candied orange peel, chopped
115g/4oz/1 cup chopped walnuts
60ml/4 tbsp dark brown sugar
5ml/1 tsp vanilla extract
5ml/1 tsp ground cinnamon
1.5ml/¼ tsp each nutmeg and ground cloves
5ml/1 tsp salt
60ml/4 tbsp each rum, brandy and whisky

For the second stage
225g/8oz/2 cups plain (all-purpose) flour
5ml/1 tsp baking powder
225g/8oz/1 cup demerara (raw) sugar
225g/8oz/1 cup butter
4 eggs, beaten

For the topping
225g/8oz/scant ¾ cup apricot jam, sieved
pecan halves and crystallized kumquat slices, to decorate

1 Put the fruit, nuts, sugar, spices, salt and alcohol into a pan, mix well and heat gently. Simmer over low heat for 15 minutes. Remove from the heat and cool. Transfer to a lidded jar and leave in the refrigerator for 7 days, stirring at least once a day.

2 Preheat the oven to 140°C/275°F/Gas 1. Line a 23cm/9in round cake tin (pan) with a double thickness of baking parchment and grease it well. Beat the flour, baking powder, sugar and butter together until smooth, then gradually beat in the eggs until the mixture is well blended and smooth.

3 Fold in the fruit mixture from the jar and stir well to mix. Spoon the mixture into the prepared tin, level the surface and bake in the centre of the oven for 3 hours. Cover with foil and continue baking for 1 hour, or until the cake feels springy. Cool on a wire rack then remove from the tin. Wrap in foil until needed. The cake will keep well for 1 year.

4 To decorate, heat the jam with 30ml/2 tbsp water, and brush half over the cake. Arrange the nuts and fruit over the cake and brush with the remaining apricot glaze.

Energy 8205kcal/34536kJ; Fat 293.5g, Saturated Fat 130.3g, Carbohydrate 1285g, Fibre 38.6g

Light Jewelled Fruit Cake

If you want to cover this cake with marzipan and icing, omit the almond decoration.

Makes one 20cm/8in round or 18cm/7in square cake

115g/4oz/½ cup currants
115g/4oz/⅔ cup sultanas (golden raisins)
225g/8oz/1 cup mixed glacé (candied) cherries, quartered
50g/2oz/⅓ cup mixed (candied) peel, finely chopped
30ml/2 tbsp rum, brandy or sherry
225g/8oz/1 cup butter
225g/8oz/generous 1 cup caster (superfine) sugar
finely grated rind of 1 orange
grated rind of 1 lemon
4 eggs
50g/2oz/½ cup chopped almonds
50g/2oz/5 tbsp ground almonds
225g/8oz/2 cups plain (all-purpose) flour

For the decoration
50g/2oz/⅓ cup whole blanched almonds (optional)
15ml/1 tbsp apricot jam

1 A day in advance, soak the currants, sultanas, glacé cherries and mixed peel in the rum, brandy or sherry, cover and leave to soak overnight.

2 Grease and line a 20cm/8in round cake tin (pan) or an 18cm/7in square cake tin with a double thickness of baking parchment. Preheat the oven to 160°C/325°F/Gas 3. Beat the butter, sugar, and orange and lemon rinds together until light and fluffy. Beat in the eggs, one at a time.

3 Mix in the chopped almonds, ground almonds, soaked fruits (with the liquid) and the flour. Spoon into the cake tin and level the top. Bake for 30 minutes.

4 To decorate, arrange the almonds, if using, on top of the cake (do not press them into the cake or they will sink during cooking). Return the cake to the oven and cook for 1½–2 hours, or until the centre is firm to the touch. Let the cake cool in the tin for 30 minutes, then turn it out in its paper on to a wire rack. When cold, wrap foil over the paper and store in a cool place. To finish, warm the jam, then sieve it and use to glaze the cake.

Energy 5298kcal/22248kJ; Fat 239.3g, Saturated Fat 126.1g, Carbohydrate 751.5g, Fibre 19.6g

Iced Angel Cake

Served with fromage frais or low-fat yogurt and fresh raspberries, this makes a light dessert.

Serves 10

40g/1½oz/scant ½ cup cornflour (cornstarch)
40g/1½oz/scant ½ cup plain (all-purpose) flour
8 egg whites
225g/8oz/generous 1 cup caster (superfine) sugar, plus extra for sprinkling
5ml/1 tsp vanilla extract
icing (confectioners') sugar, for dusting

1 Preheat the oven to 180°C/350°F/Gas 4. Sift both flours into a bowl.

2 Whisk the egg whites in a large grease-free bowl until very stiff, then gradually add the sugar and vanilla extract, a spoonful of sugar at a time, whisking until the mixture is thick and glossy.

3 Fold in the flour mixture with a large metal spoon. Spoon into an ungreased 25cm/10in angel cake tin, smooth the surface and bake for 40–45 minutes.

4 Sprinkle a piece of baking parchment with caster sugar and set an egg cup in the centre. Invert the cake tin over the paper, balancing the cake on the egg cup. When cold, the cake will drop out of the tin. Transfer it to a plate and serve.

Variation
Make a lemon icing by mixing 175g/6oz/1½ cups icing (confectioners') sugar with 15–30ml/1–2 tbsp lemon juice. Drizzle over the cake and decorate with physalis.

Cook's Tip
You can also bake this cake in a 20cm/8in cake tin (pan); it will probably take a little longer to cook. When it is well-risen and springy to the touch it is done.

Energy 1788kcal/7618kJ; Fat 1.9g, Saturated Fat 0.3g; Carbohydrate 426.4g, Fibre 4.1g

Spice Cake with Ginger Frosting

Preserved stem ginger makes the frosting for this cake particularly delicious.

Makes one 20cm/8in round cake

300ml/10fl oz/1¼ cups milk
30ml/2 tbsp golden (light corn) syrup
10ml/2 tsp vanilla extract
75g/3oz/¾ cup chopped walnuts
175g/6oz/¾ cup butter, at room temperature
285g/10½oz/1½ cups caster (superfine) sugar
1 whole egg, plus 3 egg yolks
275g/10oz/2½ cups plain (all-purpose) flour
15ml/1 tbsp baking powder
5ml/1 tsp freshly grated nutmeg
5ml/1 tsp ground cinnamon
2.5ml/½ tsp ground cloves
1.5ml/¼ tsp ground ginger
1.5ml/¼ tsp mixed (apple pie) spice
preserved stem ginger pieces, to decorate

For the frosting
175g/6oz/¾ cup cream cheese
25g/1oz/2 tbsp unsalted (sweet) butter
200g/7oz/1¾ cups icing (confectioners') sugar
30ml/2 tbsp finely chopped preserved stem ginger
30ml/2 tbsp syrup from stem ginger

1 Preheat the oven to 180°C/350°F/Gas 4. Line and grease three 20cm/8in shallow round cake tins (pans) with baking parchment. In a bowl, combine the milk, golden syrup, vanilla extract and chopped walnuts.

2 Cream the butter and caster sugar until light and fluffy. Beat in the egg and egg yolks.

3 Add the milk and syrup mixture, and stir well. Sift together the flour, baking powder and spices three times. Add to the butter mixture in four batches, folding in carefully.

4 Divide the mixture between the tins. Bake for 25 minutes. Leave in the tins for 5 minutes, then cool on a wire rack.

5 For the frosting, combine the cream cheese with the butter, icing sugar, stem ginger and ginger syrup, beating with a wooden spoon until smooth. Spread the frosting between the layers and over the top. Decorate with pieces of stem ginger.

Energy 5257kcal/21970kJ; Fat 326g, Saturated Fat 169.8g; Carbohydrate 572g, Fibre 2.6g

Lemon Coconut Layer Cake

Makes one 20cm/8in round cake

175g/6oz/1½ cups plain (all-purpose) flour, sifted with 1.5ml/¼ tsp salt
7 eggs
350g/12oz/1¾ cups caster (superfine) sugar
15ml/1 tbsp grated orange rind
grated rind of 1½ lemons
juice of 1 lemon
65g/2½oz/scant 1 cup desiccated (dry unsweetened shredded) coconut
15ml/1 tbsp cornflour (cornstarch)
120ml/4fl oz/½ cup water
40g/1½oz/3 tbsp butter

For the icing
75g/3oz/6 tbsp unsalted (sweet) butter
175g/6oz/1½ cups icing (confectioners') sugar
grated rind of 1½ lemons
30ml/2 tbsp lemon juice
200g/7oz/2½ cups desiccated (dry unsweetened shredded) coconut

1 Preheat the oven to 180°C/350°F/Gas 4. Line and grease three 20cm/8in shallow round cake tins (pans) with baking parchment.

2 Place six of the eggs in a bowl set over a pan of hot water and beat until frothy. Beat in 225g/8oz/generous 1 cup sugar until the mixture doubles in volume. Remove from the heat. Fold in the orange rind, half the lemon rind, 15ml/1 tbsp of the lemon juice and the coconut. Sift over the flour mixture and gently fold in.

3 Divide between the cake tins. Bake for 20–25 minutes. Leave in the tins for 5 minutes, then cool on a wire rack.

4 Blend the cornflour with a little cold water to dissolve. Whisk in the remaining egg until blended. In a pan, mix the remaining lemon rind and juice, water, remaining sugar and butter. Bring to the boil. Whisk in the cornflour, return to the boil and whisk until thick. Remove, cover with clear film (plastic wrap) until cool.

5 Cream the butter and icing sugar. Stir in the lemon rind and enough lemon juice to obtain a spreadable consistency. Sandwich the cake layers with the lemon custard. Spread the icing over the top and sides. Cover with the coconut.

Energy 5225kcal/21906kJ; Fat 274g, Saturated Fat 173.1g, Carbohydrate 659.5g, Fibre 20.4g

Lemon Yogurt Ring

The glaze gives this dessert a refreshing finishing touch.

Serves 12
225g/8oz/1 cup butter, at room temperature
285g/10½oz/1½ cups caster (superfine) sugar
4 eggs, separated
10ml/2 tsp grated lemon rind
90ml/6 tbsp lemon juice
250ml/8fl oz/1 cup natural (plain) yogurt
275g/10oz/2½ cups plain (all-purpose) flour
10ml/2 tsp baking powder
5ml/1 tsp bicarbonate of soda (baking soda)
2.5ml/½ tsp salt

For the glaze
115g/4oz/1 cup icing (confectioners') sugar
30ml/2 tbsp lemon juice
45–60ml/3–4 tbsp natural (plain) yogurt

1 Preheat the oven to 180°C/350°F/Gas 4. Grease a 3-litre/5¼-pint/13¼-cup *bundt* or fluted tube tin and dust lightly with flour.

2 Cream the butter and caster sugar in a large bowl until light and fluffy. Add the egg yolks, one at a time, beating well after each addition. Add the lemon rind, juice and yogurt, and stir gently to incorporate.

3 Sift together the flour, baking powder and bicarbonate of soda. In another bowl, beat the egg whites and salt until they hold stiff peaks.

4 Fold the dry ingredients into the butter mixture, then fold in a spoonful of egg whites to lighten the mixture. Fold in the remaining egg whites.

5 Pour into the tin and bake until a skewer inserted in the centre comes out clean, about 50 minutes. Leave in the tin for 15 minutes, then turn out and cool on a wire rack.

6 To make the glaze, sift the icing sugar into a bowl. Stir in the lemon juice and just enough yogurt to make a smooth glaze. Set the cooled cake on the wire rack over a sheet of baking parchment. Pour over the glaze and allow to set.

Energy 387kcal/1626kJ; Fat 17.8g, Saturated Fat 10.5g; Carbohydrate 54.6g, Fibre 0.7g

Carrot Cake with Geranium Cheese

The scented cheese topping makes this carrot cake special.

Makes one 23 x 12cm/ 9 x 5in cake

115g/4oz/1 cup self-raising (self-rising) flour
5ml/1 tsp bicarbonate of soda (baking soda)
2.5ml/½ tsp ground cinnamon
2.5ml/½ tsp ground cloves
200g/7oz/scant 1 cup soft brown sugar
225g/8oz/generous 1½ cups grated carrot
150g/5oz/scant 1 cup sultanas (golden raisins)
150g/5oz/½ cup finely chopped preserved stem ginger
150g/5oz/scant 1 cup pecan nuts
150ml/¼ pint/⅔ cup sunflower oil
2 eggs, lightly beaten

For the topping
2 or 3 lemon-scented geranium leaves
225g/8oz/2 cups icing (confectioners') sugar
60g/2¼oz/generous 4 tbsp cream cheese
30g/1¼oz/generous 2 tbsp softened butter
5ml/1 tsp grated lemon rind

1 For the topping, put the geranium leaves, torn into small pieces, in a small bowl and mix with the icing sugar. Leave in a warm place overnight for the sugar to take up the scent.

2 For the cake, sift the flour, bicarbonate of soda and spices together. Add the sugar, grated carrots, sultanas, stem ginger and pecan nuts. Stir well, then add the oil and beaten eggs. Mix with an electric mixer for 5 minutes.

3 Preheat the oven to 180°C/350°F/Gas 4. Then grease a 23 x 13cm/9 x 5in loaf tin (pan), line the base with baking parchment, and grease the paper. Pour the mixture into the tin and bake for about 1 hour. Remove the cake from the oven, leave to stand for a few minutes, and then cool on a wire rack.

4 Meanwhile, make the cream cheese topping. Remove the pieces of geranium leaf from the icing sugar and discard. Place the cream cheese, butter and lemon rind in a bowl. Using an electric mixer, gradually add the icing sugar, beating well until smooth. Spread over the top of the cooled cake.

Energy 5413kcal/22706kJ; Fat 272.2g, Saturated Fat 57.6g, Carbohydrate 740.3g, Fibre 21.4g

Carrot and Courgette Cake

This unusual sponge has a delicious creamy topping.

Makes one 18cm/7in square cake

1 carrot
1 courgette (zucchini)
3 eggs, separated
115g/4oz/1 cup soft light brown sugar
30ml/2 tbsp ground almonds
finely grated rind of 1 orange
150g/5oz/1¼ cups self-raising (self-rising) wholemeal (whole-wheat) flour
5ml/1 tsp ground cinnamon
5ml/1 tsp icing (confectioners') sugar, for dusting
fondant carrots and courgettes (zucchini), to decorate

For the topping
175g/6oz/¾ cup low-fat soft cheese
5ml/1 tsp clear honey

1 Preheat the oven to 180°C/350°F/Gas 4. Line an 18cm/7in square tin (pan) with baking parchment. Coarsely grate the carrot and courgette.

2 Put the egg yolks, sugar, ground almonds and orange rind into a bowl and whisk until very thick and light. Sift together the flour and cinnamon, and fold into the mixture together with the grated vegetables. Add any bran left in the sieve.

3 Whisk the egg whites until stiff and carefully fold them in, a little at a time. Spoon into the tin. Bake in the oven for 1 hour, covering the top with foil after 40 minutes. Leave to cool in the tin for 5 minutes, then turn out on to a wire rack and remove the lining paper.

4 To make the topping, beat together the cheese and honey, and spread over the cake. Dust with icing sugar and decorate with fondant carrots and courgettes.

Cook's Tip
To make fondant carrots and courgettes, roll tinted sugarpaste into the shapes and paint details using a fine paintbrush. Use thin lengths of green sugarpaste to make the carrot tops.

Energy 1455kcal/6145kJ; Fat 35g, Saturated Fat 14.5g, Carbohydrate 237.8g, Fibre 17.1g

Banana Coconut Cake

Slightly over-ripe bananas are best for this perfect coffee-morning cake topped with honey and coconut.

Makes one 18cm/7in square cake

115g/4oz/½ cup butter, softened
115g/4oz/generous ½ cup caster (superfine) sugar
2 eggs
115g/4oz/1 cup self-raising (self-rising) flour
50g/2oz/½ cup plain (all-purpose) flour
5ml/1 tsp bicarbonate of soda (baking soda)
120ml/4fl oz/½ cup milk
2 large bananas, peeled and mashed
75g/3oz/1 cup desiccated (dry unsweetened shredded) coconut, toasted

For the topping
25g/1oz/2 tbsp butter
30ml/2 tbsp clear honey
115g/4oz/2 cups shredded coconut

1 Preheat the oven to 190°C/375°F/Gas 5. Grease a deep 18cm/7in square cake tin (pan), line with baking parchment and grease the paper.

2 Beat the butter and sugar until smooth and creamy. Beat in the eggs, one at a time. Sift together the flours and bicarbonate of soda, sift half into the butter mixture and stir to mix.

3 Combine the milk and mashed banana, and beat half into the egg mixture. Stir in the remaining flour and banana mixtures and the toasted coconut. Transfer the batter to the cake tin and smooth the surface.

4 Bake for 1 hour, or until a skewer inserted into the centre of the cake comes out clean. Leave in the tin for 5 minutes, then turn out on to a wire rack, peel off the paper and leave to cool completely.

5 To make the topping, gently melt the butter and honey in a small pan. Stir in the shredded coconut and cook, stirring, for 5 minutes or until lightly browned. Remove from the heat and allow to cool slightly. Spoon the topping over the cake and allow to cool.

Energy 3291kcal/13744kJ; Fat 208.5g, Saturated Fat 144.6g, Carbohydrate 332.2g, Fibre 24.4g

St Clement's Cake

A tangy orange-and-lemon cake makes a spectacular centrepiece when decorated with fruits, silver dragées and fresh flowers.

Makes one 23cm/9in ring cake

175g/6oz/¾ cup butter
75g/3oz/scant ⅓ cup soft light brown sugar
3 eggs, separated
grated rind and juice of 1 orange and 1 lemon
150g/5oz/1¼ cups self-raising (self-rising) flour
75g/3oz/6 tbsp caster (superfine) sugar
15g/½oz/1 tbsp ground almonds
350ml/12fl oz/1½ cups double (heavy) cream
15ml/1 tbsp Grand Marnier
16 crystallized orange and lemon slices, silver dragées, sugared almonds and fresh flowers, to decorate

1 Preheat the oven to 180°C/350°F/Gas 4. Grease and flour a 900ml/1½ pint/3¾ cup ring mould.

2 Cream half the butter and all of the brown sugar until pale and light. Beat in the egg yolks, orange rind and juice and fold in 75g/3oz/⅔ cup flour.

3 Cream the remaining butter and the caster sugar in another bowl. Stir in the lemon rind and juice and fold in the remaining flour and the ground almonds. Whisk the egg whites until they form stiff peaks, and fold into the batter.

4 Spoon the two mixtures alternately into the prepared tin. Using a skewer or small spoon, swirl through the mixture to create a marbled effect. Bake for 45–50 minutes, or until risen, and a skewer inserted in the cake comes out clean. Cool in the tin for 10 minutes then transfer to a wire rack to cool.

5 Whip the cream and Grand Marnier together until lightly thickened. Spread over the cake and swirl a pattern over the icing with a metal spatula. Decorate the ring with the crystallized fruits, dragées and sugared almonds to resemble a jewelled crown. Arrange a few fresh flowers with their stems wrapped in foil in the centre.

Energy 4486kcal/18629kJ; Fat 358.8g, Saturated Fat 213.6g, Carbohydrate 281.3g, Fibre 5.8g

Apple Cake

A deliciously moist cake with a silky icing.

Makes one ring cake

675g/1½lb apples, peeled, cored and quartered
500g/1¼lb/generous 4½ cups caster (superfine) sugar
15ml/1 tbsp water
350g/12oz/3 cups plain (all-purpose) flour
9ml/1¾ tsp bicarbonate of soda (baking soda)
5ml/1 tsp ground cinnamon
5ml/1 tsp ground cloves
175g/6oz/generous 1 cup raisins
150g/5oz/1¼ cups chopped walnuts
225g/8oz/1 cup butter or margarine, at room temperature
5ml/1 tsp vanilla extract

For the icing

115g/4oz/1 cup icing (confectioners') sugar
1.5ml/¼ tsp vanilla extract
30–45ml/2–3 tbsp milk

1 Put the apples, 50g/2oz/¼ cup of the sugar and the water in a pan and bring to the boil. Simmer for 25 minutes, stirring occasionally to break up any lumps. Leave to cool. Preheat the oven to 160°C/325°F/Gas 3. Thoroughly butter and flour a 1.75-litre/3-pint/7½-cup tube tin (pan).

2 Sift the flour, bicarbonate of soda and spices into a bowl. Remove 30ml/2 tbsp of the mixture to another bowl and toss with the raisins and 115g/4oz/1 cup of the walnuts.

3 Cream the butter or margarine and remaining sugar together until light and fluffy. Fold in the apple mixture gently. Fold the flour mixture into the apple mixture. Stir in the vanilla extract and the raisin and walnut mixture. Pour into the tube tin. Bake until a skewer inserted in the centre comes out clean, about 1½ hours. Cool completely in the tin on a wire rack, then unmould on to the rack.

4 To make the icing, put the sugar in a bowl and stir in the vanilla extract and 15ml/1 tbsp milk. Add more milk until the icing is smooth and has a thick pouring consistency. Transfer the cake to a serving plate and drizzle the icing over the top. Sprinkle with the remaining nuts. Allow the icing to set.

Energy 7049kcal/29657kJ; Fat 294.1g, Saturated Fat 126.6g; Carbohydrate 1103.7g, Fibre 30.4g

Chocolate Amaretto Marquise

This light-as-air marquise is perfect for a special occasion, served with amaretto cream.

Makes one heart-shaped cake

15ml/1 tbsp sunflower oil
75g/3oz/7–8 amaretti, crushed
25g/1oz/2 tbsp unblanched almonds, toasted and finely chopped
450g/1lb plain (semisweet) chocolate, broken into pieces
75ml/5 tbsp amaretto liqueur
75ml/5 tbsp golden (light corn) syrup
475ml/16fl oz/2 cups double (heavy) cream
cocoa powder, to dust

For the amaretto cream

350ml/12fl oz/1½ cups whipping or double (heavy) cream
30–45ml/2–3 tbsp amaretto liqueur

1 Lightly oil a 23cm/9in heart-shaped or springform cake tin (pan). Line the base with baking parchment and oil the paper. In a small bowl, combine the crushed amaretti and the toasted and chopped almonds. Sprinkle evenly over the base of the tin.

2 Place the chocolate, amaretto liqueur and golden syrup in a pan over very low heat. Stir frequently until the chocolate is melted and the mixture is smooth. Allow to cool for 6–8 minutes, or until the mixture feels just warm.

3 Beat the cream until it just begins to hold its shape. Stir a large spoonful into the chocolate mixture, then quickly add the remaining cream and gently fold into the chocolate mixture. Pour into the prepared tin and tap the tin gently on the work surface to release any large air bubbles. Cover the tin with clear film (plastic wrap) and leave in the refrigerator overnight.

4 To unmould, run a thin-bladed sharp knife under hot water and dry carefully. Run the knife around the edge of the tin to loosen, place a serving plate over the tin, then invert to unmould. Carefully peel off the paper then dust with cocoa. To make the amaretto cream, whip the cream and liqueur together and serve separately.

Energy 7040kcal/29238kJ; Fat 548.8g, Saturated Fat 324.4g; Carbohydrate 448.7g, Fibre 14.2g

Tangy Lemon Cake

The lemon syrup forms a crusty topping when it has completely cooled. Leave the cake in the tin until ready to serve.

Makes one 900g/2lb loaf

175g/6oz/¾ cup butter
175g/6oz/scant 1 cup caster (superfine) sugar
3 eggs, beaten
175g/6oz/1½ cups self-raising (self-rising) flour
grated rind of 1 orange
grated rind of 1 lemon

For the syrup

115g/4oz/generous ½ cup caster (superfine) sugar
juice of 2 lemons

1 Preheat the oven to 180°C/350°F/Gas 4. Grease a 900g/2lb loaf tin (pan).

2 Beat the butter and sugar together until light and fluffy, then gradually beat in the eggs.

3 Fold in the flour and the orange and lemon rinds.

4 Turn the cake mixture into the prepared cake tin and bake for 1¼–1½ hours, or until set in the centre, risen and golden.

5 Remove the cake from the oven, but leave it in the tin rather than turning out on to a wire rack.

6 To make the syrup, gently heat the sugar in a small pan with the lemon juice until the sugar has completely dissolved, then boil for 15 seconds.

7 Pour the syrup over the hot cake in the tin and leave to cool completely.

Cook's Tip

You can use a skewer to pierce holes over the cake's surface so that the syrup will drizzle through and soak into the cake. There will still be a crusty, sugary top, but the cake itself will be moist.

Energy 2849kcal/11927kJ; Fat 162.6g, Saturated Fat 96.2g; Carbohydrate 331.9g, Fibre 5.4g

Pineapple and Apricot Cake

This is not a long-keeping cake, but it does freeze, well wrapped in baking parchment and then foil.

Makes one 18cm/7in square or 20cm/8in round cake

175g/6oz/¾ cup unsalted (sweet) butter
150g/5oz/generous ¾ cup caster (superfine) sugar
3 eggs, beaten
few drops vanilla extract
225g/8oz/2 cups plain all-purpose) flour
1.5ml/¼ tsp salt
7.5ml/1½ tsp baking powder
225g/8oz/1 cup ready-to-eat dried apricots, chopped
115g/4oz/½ cup each chopped crystallized ginger and crystallized pineapple
grated rind and juice of ½ orange
grated rind and juice of ½ lemon
a little milk

1 Preheat the oven to 180°C/350°F/Gas 4. Double line an 18cm/7in square or 20cm/8in round cake tin (pan).

2 Cream the butter and sugar together until light and fluffy.

3 Gradually beat in the eggs with the vanilla extract, beating well after each addition.

4 Sift together the flour, salt and baking powder. Add a little of the flour with the last of the egg, then fold in the remainder.

5 Gently fold in the apricots, ginger and pineapple and the orange and lemon rinds, then add sufficient fruit juice and milk to give the batter a fairly soft dropping consistency.

6 Spoon the batter into the prepared cake tin and smooth the top with a wet spoon.

7 Bake for 20 minutes, then reduce the oven temperature to 160°C/325°F/Gas 3 and bake for a further 1½–2 hours, or until a skewer inserted into the centre comes out clean.

8 Leave the cake to cool completely in the tin. Wrap in fresh paper before storing in an airtight tin.

Energy 3400kcal/14276kJ; Fat 165.6g, Saturated Fat 96.3g; Carbohydrate 455 1g, Fibre 25.9g

Sour Cream Crumble Cake

The consistency of this cake, with its two layers of crumble, is sublime.

Makes one 23cm/9in square cake

115g/4oz/½ cup butter, at room temperature
130g/4½oz/scant ¾ cup caster (superfine) sugar
3 eggs
210g/7½oz/scant 2 cups plain (all-purpose) flour
5ml/1 tsp bicarbonate of soda (baking soda)
5ml/1 tsp baking powder
250ml/8fl oz/1 cup sour cream

For the topping

225g/8oz/1 cup soft dark brown sugar
10ml/2 tsp ground cinnamon
115g/4oz/1 cup finely chopped walnuts
50g/2oz/¼ cup cold butter, diced

1 Preheat the oven to 180°C/350°F/Gas 4. Line the base of a 23cm/9in square cake tin (pan) with baking parchment and grease the paper and sides.

2 To make the topping, place the brown sugar, cinnamon and walnuts in a bowl. Mix, then add the butter and rub in using your fingertips or a pastry cutter until the mixture resembles breadcrumbs.

3 To make the cake, cream the butter until soft. Add the sugar and beat until light and fluffy. Add the eggs, one at a time, beating well after each addition.

4 In another bowl, sift the flour, bicarbonate of soda and baking powder together three times. Fold the dry ingredients into the butter mixture in three batches, alternating with the sour cream. Fold until blended after each addition.

5 Pour half of the batter into the prepared tin and sprinkle over half of the topping. Pour the remaining batter on top and sprinkle over the remaining topping.

6 Bake until browned, 60–70 minutes. Leave in the tin for 5 minutes, then turn out on a wire rack to cool completely.

Energy 4867kcal/20353kJ; Fat 283.5g, Saturated Fat 128.7g; Carbohydrate 548.4g, Fibre 10.5g

Plum Crumble Cake

This cake can also be made with the same quantity of apricots or cherries.

Serves 8–10

675g/1½lb red plums
150g/5oz/10 tbsp butter or margarine, at room temperature
150g/5oz/¾ cup caster (superfine) sugar
4 eggs, at room temperature
7.5ml/1½ tsp vanilla extract
150g/5oz/1¼ cups plain (all-purpose) flour
5ml/1 tsp baking powder

For the topping

115g/4oz/1 cup plain (all-purpose) flour
130g/4½oz/generous 1 cup soft light brown sugar
7.5ml/1½ tsp ground cinnamon
75g/3oz/6 tbsp butter, diced

1 Halve and stone (pit) the plums and set them aside.

2 Preheat the oven to 180°C/350°F/Gas 4. Using baking parchment, line a 25 x 5cm/10 x 2in tin (pan) and grease the paper.

3 To make the topping, combine the flour, light brown sugar and cinnamon in a bowl. Add the butter and rub in well using your fingertips or a pastry cutter until it resembles coarse breadcrumbs.

4 Cream the butter or margarine and sugar until light and fluffy. Beat in the eggs, one at a time. Stir in the vanilla. Sift the flour and baking powder into a bowl then fold into the creamed mixture in three batches.

5 Pour the batter into the prepared tin. Arrange the plums on top and sprinkle with the topping.

6 Bake until a skewer inserted in the centre comes out clean, about 45 minutes. Cool in the tin.

7 To serve, run a knife around the inside edge of the cake and invert on to a plate. Invert again on to a serving plate so that the topping is uppermost.

Energy 426kcal/1787kJ; Fat 21.1g, Saturated Fat 12.4g; Carbohydrate 57g, Fibre 1.9g

Pineapple Upside-down Cake

Canned pineapple rings make this a useful and unusual cake to make with a few ingredients that you might already have in the cupboard.

Makes one 25cm/10in round cake

115g/4oz/½ cup butter
200g/7oz/scant 1 cup soft dark brown sugar
450g/1lb canned pineapple slices, drained
4 eggs, separated
grated rind of 1 lemon
pinch of salt
115g/4oz/generous ½ cup caster (superfine) sugar
75g/3oz/⅔ cup plain (all-purpose) flour
5ml/1 tsp baking powder

1 Preheat the oven to 180°C/350°F/Gas 4. Melt the butter in a 25cm/10in ovenproof cast-iron frying pan. Then reserve 15ml/1 tbsp butter. Add the brown sugar to the pan and stir to blend. Place the pineapple slices on top in one layer. Set aside.

2 Whisk together the egg yolks, reserved butter and lemon rind until well blended. Set aside.

3 Beat the egg whites and salt until they form stiff peaks. Gradually fold in the caster sugar, then the egg yolk mixture.

4 Sift the flour and baking powder together. Carefully fold into the egg mixture in three batches.

5 Pour the mixture over the pineapple. Bake until a skewer inserted in the centre comes out clean, about 30 minutes.

6 While still hot, invert on to a serving plate. Serve hot or cold.

Variation
For an apricot cake, replace the pineapple slices with 225g/8oz/1¾ cups dried ready-to-eat apricots.

Energy 2858kcal/12025kJ; Fat 117.7g, Saturated Fat 66.3g; Carbohydrate 443g, Fibre 4.6g

Upside-down Pear and Ginger Cake

This light spicy sponge, topped with glossy baked fruit and ginger, makes an excellent pudding.

Serves 6–8

900g/2lb can pear halves, drained
120ml/8 tbsp finely chopped preserved stem ginger
120ml/8 tbsp ginger syrup from the jar
175g/6oz/1½ cups self-raising (self-rising) flour
2.5ml/½ tsp baking powder
5ml/1 tsp ground ginger
175g/6oz/¾ cup soft light brown sugar
175g/6oz/¾ cup butter, softened
3 eggs, lightly beaten

1 Preheat the oven to 180°C/350°F/Gas 4. Base-line and grease a deep 20cm/8in round cake tin (pan).

2 Fill the hollow in each pear with half the chopped preserved stem ginger. Arrange, flat sides down, in the base of the cake tin, then spoon over half the ginger syrup.

3 Sift together the flour, baking powder and ground ginger. Stir in the sugar and butter, add the eggs and beat until creamy, about 1–2 minutes.

4 Spoon the mixture into the cake tin. Bake in the oven for 50 minutes, or until a skewer inserted in the centre of the cake comes out clean. Leave the cake in the tin for 5 minutes. Turn out on to a wire rack, peel off the lining paper and leave to cool completely.

5 Add the reserved ginger to the pear halves and drizzle over the remaining syrup.

Cook's Tip
Canned pears are ideal for this cake, but you can also core, peel and halve fresh pears, and then poach them until tender in a little white wine to cover with 50g/2oz/½ cup sugar added.

Energy 433kcal/1818kJ; Fat 20.4g, Saturated Fat 12g; Carbohydrate 61.4g, Fibre 2.3g

Cranberry and Apple Ring

Tangy cranberries add an unusual flavour to this moist cake, which is best eaten very fresh.

Makes one ring cake

225g/8oz/2 cups self-raising (self-rising) flour
5ml/1 tsp ground cinnamon
75g/3oz/scant ½ cup light muscovado (brown) sugar
1 eating apple, cored and diced
75g/3oz/¾ cup fresh or frozen cranberries
60ml/4 tbsp sunflower oil
150ml/¼ pint/⅔ cup apple juice
cranberry jelly and apple slices, to decorate

1 Preheat the oven to 180°C/350°F/Gas 4. Lightly grease a 1-litre/1¾-pint/4-cup ring tin (pan) with oil.

2 Sift together the flour and ground cinnamon in a large bowl, then stir in the light muscovado sugar.

3 Toss together the diced apple and cranberries in a small bowl.

4 Stir the apple mixture into the dry ingredients, then add the oil and apple juice and beat together until everything is thoroughly combined.

5 Spoon the cake mixture into the prepared ring tin and bake for 35–40 minutes, or until the cake is firm to the touch.

6 Leave the cake in the tin for 5 minutes, then turn out on to a wire rack and leave to cool completely.

7 To serve, arrange apple slices over the cake and drizzle warmed cranberry jelly over the top.

Cook's Tip

This moist, tangy ring would be an ideal alternative to Christmas cake for those who do not like such dense, rich cakes. It would also be a good way of using up any left-over cranberries or cranberry jelly.

Energy 1565kcal/6610kJ; Fat 47.2g, Saturated Fat 5.7g; Carbohydrate 280.7g, Fibre 9.2g

Greek Honey and Lemon Cake

A wonderfully moist and tangy cake, you could ice it if you wished.

Makes one 19cm/7½in square cake

40g/1½oz/3 tbsp sunflower margarine
60ml/4 tbsp clear honey
finely grated rind and juice of 1 lemon
150ml/¼ pint/⅔ cup milk
150g/5oz/1¼ cups plain (all-purpose) flour
7.5ml/1½ tsp baking powder
2.5ml/½ tsp freshly grated nutmeg
50g/2oz/⅓ cup semolina
2 egg whites
10ml/2 tsp sesame seeds

1 Preheat the oven to 200°C/400°F/Gas 6. Lightly oil and base-line a 19cm/7½in square deep cake tin (pan).

2 Place the margarine and 45ml/3 tbsp of the honey in a pan and heat gently until melted.

3 Reserve 15ml/1 tbsp lemon juice, then stir in the rest with the lemon rind and milk.

4 Sift together the flour, baking powder and nutmeg, then beat in with the semolina. Whisk the egg whites until they form soft peaks, then fold evenly into the mixture.

5 Spoon into the cake tin and sprinkle with sesame seeds. Bake for 25–30 minutes, or until golden brown. Mix the reserved honey and lemon juice, and drizzle over the cake while warm. Cool in the tin, then cut into fingers to serve.

Cook's Tip

Baking powder is a useful raising agent for making cakes and is used with plain (all-purpose) flour. When mixed with a liquid it forms a gas that causes the cake to rise. It also acts further when the cake is baked. Always check the use-by date on the packet and replace as necessary for successful baking.

Energy 1307kcal/5510kJ; Fat 43.8g, Saturated Fat 9.2g; Carbohydrate 208.7g, Fibre 6.5g

Pear and Cardamom Spice Cake

Fresh pears and cardamoms – a classic combination – are used together in this moist fruit and nut cake.

Makes one 20cm/8in round cake

115g/4oz/½ cup butter
115g/4oz/generous ½ cup caster (superfine) sugar
2 eggs, lightly beaten
225g/8oz/2 cups plain (all-purpose) flour
15ml/1 tbsp baking powder
30ml/2 tbsp milk
crushed seeds from 2 cardamom pods
50g/2oz/½ cup walnuts, finely chopped
15ml/1 tbsp poppy seeds
500g/1¼lb dessert pears, peeled, cored and thinly sliced
3 walnut halves, to decorate
clear honey, to glaze

1 Preheat the oven to 180°C/350°F/Gas 4. Grease and base-line a 20cm/8in round, loose-based cake tin (pan).

2 Cream the butter and sugar in a large bowl until pale and light. Gradually beat in the eggs.

3 Sift over the flour and baking powder, and fold in gently with the milk.

4 Stir in the cardamom seeds, chopped nuts and poppy seeds. Reserve one-third of the pear slices, and chop the remainder. Fold into the creamed mixture.

5 Transfer to the cake tin. Smooth the surface, making a small dip in the centre. Place the walnut halves in the centre of the cake and fan the reserved pear slices around the walnuts, covering the cake mixture.

6 Bake for 1¼–1½ hours, or until a skewer inserted into the centre comes out clean.

7 Remove the cake from the oven and brush with the honey. Leave in the tin for 20 minutes, then transfer to a wire rack to cool completely before serving.

Energy 2781kcal/11648kJ; Fat 143.8g; Saturated Fat 66.6g; Carbohydrate 348.8g; Fibre 19.7g

Spiced Honey Nut Cake

A combination of ground pistachio nuts and breadcrumbs replaces flour in this recipe, resulting in a light, moist sponge cake.

Makes one 20cm/8in square cake

115g/4oz/generous ½ cup caster (superfine) sugar
4 eggs, separated
grated rind and juice of 1 lemon
130g/4½oz/generous 1 cup ground pistachio nuts
50g/2oz/scant 1 cup dried breadcrumbs

For the glaze
1 lemon
90ml/6 tbsp clear honey
1 cinnamon stick
15ml/1 tbsp brandy

1 Preheat the oven to 180°C/350°F/Gas 4. Grease and base-line a 20cm/8in square cake tin (pan).

2 Beat the sugar, egg yolks, lemon rind and juice together in a large bowl until pale and creamy. Fold in 115g/4oz/1 cup of the ground pistachio nuts and the breadcrumbs.

3 Whisk the egg whites until stiff peaks form and fold into the creamed mixture.

4 Transfer to the cake tin and bake for 15 minutes, or until risen and springy to the touch. Cool in the tin for 10 minutes, then transfer to a wire rack.

5 To make the glaze pare thin pieces of lemon rind and then cut them into very thin strips using a sharp knife.

6 Squeeze the lemon juice into a small pan and add the honey and cinnamon stick. Bring the mixture to the boil, add the shredded rind, and simmer fast for 1 minute. Cool slightly and stir in the brandy.

7 Place the cake on a serving plate, prick all over with a skewer so that the syrupy glaze will drain into the cake, and pour over the cooled syrup, lemon shreds and cinnamon stick. Sprinkle over the reserved pistachio nuts.

Energy 1965kcal/8248kJ; Fat 95.2g; Saturated Fat 15.8g; Carbohydrate 238.3g; Fibre 9g

American Carrot Cake

This light and spicy carrot cake has the traditional topping.

Makes one 20cm/8in round cake

250ml/8fl oz/1 cup corn oil
175g/6oz/scant 1 cup caster (superfine) sugar
3 eggs
175g/6oz/1½ cups plain (all-purpose) flour
7.5ml/1½ tsp baking powder
7.5ml/1½ tsp bicarbonate of soda (baking soda)
1.5ml/¼ tsp salt
7.5ml/1½ tsp ground cinnamon
a good pinch of freshly grated nutmeg
1.5ml/¼ tsp ground ginger
115g/4oz/1 cup chopped walnuts
225g/8oz/generous 1½ cups finely grated carrots
5ml/1 tsp vanilla extract
30ml/2 tbsp sour cream
8 tiny marzipan carrots, to decorate

For the frosting

175g/6oz/¾ cup full-fat soft cheese
25g/1oz/2 tbsp butter, softened
225g/8oz/2 cups icing (confectioners') sugar, sifted

1 Preheat the oven to 180°C/350°F/Gas 4. Grease and line two 20cm/8in loose-based round cake tins (pans).

2 Put the corn oil and sugar into a bowl and beat well. Add the eggs, one at a time, and beat thoroughly. Sift the flour, baking powder, bicarbonate of soda, salt, cinnamon, nutmeg and ginger into the bowl and beat well.

3 Fold in the chopped walnuts and grated carrots, and stir in the vanilla extract and sour cream.

4 Divide the mixture between the prepared cake tins and bake in the centre of the oven for about 65 minutes, or until a skewer inserted into the centre of the cakes comes out clean. Leave to cool in the tins on a wire rack. Meanwhile, beat all the frosting ingredients together until smooth.

5 Sandwich the cakes together with a little frosting. Spread the remaining frosting over the top and sides of the cake. Just before serving, decorate with the marzipan carrots.

Energy 5897kcal/24604kJ; Fat 387.8g, Saturated Fat 106.3g, Carbohydrate 576.8g, Fibre 14.9g

Passion Cake

This cake is associated with Passion Sunday. The carrot and banana give it a rich, moist texture.

Makes one 20cm/8in round cake

200g/7oz/1¾ cups self-raising (self-rising) flour
10ml/2 tsp baking powder
5ml/1 tsp cinnamon
2.5ml/½ tsp freshly grated nutmeg
150g/5oz/10 tbsp butter, softened, or sunflower margarine
150g/5oz/generous 1 cup soft light brown sugar
grated rind of 1 lemon
2 eggs, beaten
2 carrots, coarsely grated
1 ripe banana, mashed
115g/4oz/¾ cup raisins
50g/2oz/½ cup chopped walnuts or pecan nuts
30ml/2 tbsp milk
6–8 walnuts, halved, to decorate
coffee crystal sugar, to decorate

For the frosting

200g/7oz/scant 1 cup cream cheese, softened
30g/1½oz/scant ⅓ cup icing (confectioners') sugar
juice of 1 lemon
grated rind of 1 orange

1 Line and grease a deep 20cm/8in round cake tin (pan). Preheat the oven to 180°C/350°F/Gas 4. Sift the flour, baking powder and spices into a bowl.

2 In another bowl, cream the butter or margarine and sugar with the lemon rind until it is light and fluffy, then beat in the eggs. Fold in the flour mixture, then the carrots, banana, raisins, chopped nuts and milk.

3 Spoon the mixture into the prepared cake tin, level the top and bake for about 1 hour, or until risen and the top is springy to the touch. Turn the tin upside down and allow the cake to cool in the tin for 30 minutes. Then turn out on to a wire rack and leave to cool completely. When cold, split the cake in half.

4 To make the frosting, cream the cheese with the icing sugar, lemon juice and orange rind, then sandwich the two halves of the cake together with half of the frosting. Spread the rest of the frosting on top and decorate with walnut halves and sugar.

Energy 4318kcal/18033kJ; Fat 267.4g, Saturated Fat 144.1g, Carbohydrate 456.2g, Fibre 14.7g

Caribbean Fruit and Rum Cake

Definitely a festive treat, this spicy cake contains both rum and sherry.

Makes one 25cm/10in round cake

450g/1lb/2 cups currants
450g/1lb/3¼ cups raisins
225g/8oz/1 cup prunes, pitted
115g/4oz/¾ cup mixed (candied) peel
400g/14oz/1¾ cups soft dark brown sugar
5ml/1 tsp mixed (apple pie) spice
90ml/6 tbsp rum, plus more if needed
300ml/½ pint/1¼ cups sherry, plus more if needed
450g/1lb/4 cups self-raising (self-rising) flour
450g/1lb/2 cups butter, softened
10 eggs, beaten
5ml/1 tsp vanilla extract

1 Finely chop the currants, raisins, prunes and peel in a food processor. Combine them in a bowl with 115g/4oz/generous ½ cup of the sugar, the mixed spice, rum and sherry.

2 Put in a large screwtop jar or in a bowl with a lid, and leave for 2 weeks. Stir daily and add more rum or sherry if you wish.

3 Preheat the oven to 160°C/325°F/Gas 3. Grease and then line a 25cm/10in round cake tin (pan) with a double layer of baking parchment.

4 Sift the flour into a bowl, and set aside. Cream together the butter and remaining sugar, and beat in the eggs until the mixture is smooth and creamy. Add a spoonful of flour halfway through adding the eggs, to stop the mixture curdling.

5 Add the fruit mixture, then gradually stir in the remaining flour and vanilla extract. Mix well, adding more sherry if the mixture is too stiff; it should just fall off the back of the spoon.

6 Spoon the mixture into the prepared tin, cover loosely with foil and bake for about 2½ hours, or until the cake is firm and springy. Leave to cool in the tin overnight.

Energy 10550kcal/44342kJ; Fat 436.8g, Saturated Fat 250.8g, Carbohydrate 1536g, Fibre 49.8g

Thai Rice Cake

This unusual celebration gateau is made from fragrant Thai rice, covered with a tangy cream icing and topped with fresh fruits.

Makes one 25cm/10in round cake

225g/8oz/1¼ cups Thai fragrant rice
1 litre/1¾ pints/4 cups milk
115g/4oz/½ cup caster (superfine) sugar
6 cardamom pods, crushed open
2 bay leaves
300ml/½ pint/1¼ cups whipping cream
6 eggs, separated

For the topping
300ml/½ pint/1¼ cups double (heavy) cream
200g/7oz/scant 1 cup quark
5ml/1 tsp vanilla extract
grated rind of 1 lemon
30g/1½oz/scant ¼ cup caster (superfine) sugar
soft berry fruits and sliced star fruit (carambola) or kiwi fruit, to decorate

1 Grease and line a deep 25cm/10in round cake tin (pan). Boil the rice in unsalted water for 3 minutes, then drain.

2 Return the rice to the pan with the milk, sugar, cardamom pods and bay leaves. Bring to the boil, then simmer for 20 minutes, stirring occasionally.

3 Allow to cool, then remove the bay leaves and any cardamom husks. Turn into a bowl. Beat in the cream and then the egg yolks. Preheat the oven to 180°C/350°F/Gas 4.

4 Whisk the egg whites until they form soft peaks and fold into the rice mixture. Spoon into the cake tin and bake for 45–50 minutes, or until risen and golden brown. The centre should be slightly wobbly – it will firm up as it cools.

5 Chill overnight in the tin. Turn out on to a large serving plate. Whip the double cream until stiff, then mix in the quark, vanilla extract, lemon rind and sugar.

6 Cover the top and sides of the cake with the cream. Decorate with soft berry fruits and sliced star fruit or kiwi fruit.

Energy 5009kcal/20846kJ; Fat 333.6g, Saturated Fat 196.1g, Carbohydrate 400.5g, Fibre 0g

Luxurious Chocolate Cake

This attractive and delicious chocolate cake contains no flour and has a light mousse-like texture.

Makes one 20cm/8in round cake

9 x 25g/1oz squares plain (semisweet) chocolate
175g/6oz/¾ cup butter, softened
130g/3½oz/⅔ cup caster (superfine) sugar
225g/8oz/2 cups ground almonds
4 eggs, separated
4 x 25g/1oz squares white chocolate, melted, to decorate

1 Preheat the oven to 180°C/350°F/Gas 4. Grease and base-line a 20cm/8in springform cake tin (pan).

2 Melt the chocolate in a heatproof bowl over a pan of simmering water. Beat 115g/4oz/½ cup butter and all the sugar until light and fluffy in a large bowl. Add two-thirds of the plain chocolate, the almonds and egg yolks, and beat well.

3 Whisk the egg whites in another clean, dry bowl until stiff peaks form. Fold them into the chocolate mixture, then transfer to the tin and smooth the surface. Bake for 50–55 minutes, or until a skewer inserted into the centre comes out clean.

4 Cool in the tin for 5 minutes, then remove from the tin and transfer to a wire rack. Remove the lining paper and cool completely.

5 Place the remaining butter and remaining melted chocolate in a pan. Heat very gently, stirring constantly, until melted. Place a large sheet of baking parchment under the wire rack to catch any drips. Pour the chocolate topping over the cake, allowing the topping to coat the top and sides. Leave to set for at least 1 hour.

6 To decorate, fill a paper piping (icing) bag with the melted white chocolate and snip the end. Drizzle the white chocolate around the edges. Use any remaining chocolate to pipe leaves on to baking parchment or greaseproof (waxed) paper. Allow to set then place on top of the cake.

Energy 5162kcal/21484kJ; Fat 385.5g, Saturated Fat 163.5g, Carbohydrate 353.6g, Fibre 22.3g

One-stage Chocolate Sponge

For family teas, quick and easy favourites like this chocolate cake are invaluable.

Makes one 18cm/7in round cake

175g/6oz/¾ cup soft margarine, at room temperature
115g/4oz/generous ½ cup caster (superfine) sugar
50g/2oz/4 tbsp golden (light corn) syrup
175g/6oz/1½ cups self-raising (self-rising) flour, sifted
45ml/3 tbsp unsweetened cocoa powder, sifted
2.5ml/½ tsp salt
3 eggs, beaten
a little milk, as required
150ml/¼ pint/⅔ cup whipping cream
15–30ml/1–2 tbsp fine shred marmalade
icing (confectioners') sugar, for dusting

1 Preheat the oven to 180°C/350°F/Gas 4. Lightly grease or line two 18cm/7in shallow round cake tins (pans).

2 Place the margarine, sugar, syrup, flour, cocoa powder, salt and eggs in a large bowl, and cream together until well blended using a wooden spoon or electric whisk. If the mixture seems a little thick, stir in 15–30ml/1–2 tbsp milk, until you have a soft dropping consistency.

3 Spoon the mixture into the prepared tins and bake for about 30 minutes, changing shelves if necessary after 15 minutes, until the tops are just firm and the cakes are springy to the touch.

4 Leave the cakes to cool for 5 minutes, then remove from the tins and leave to cool completely on a wire rack.

5 Whip the cream and fold in the marmalade, then use to sandwich the two cakes together. Sprinkle the top with sifted icing sugar.

Cook's Tip
You could also use butter at room temperature cut into small pieces for this one-stage sponge mixture.

Energy 3476kcal/14495kJ; Fat 234g, Saturated Fat 78.4g, Carbohydrate 315.7g, Fibre 10.9g

One-stage Victoria Sandwich

This recipe can be used as the base for other cakes.

Makes one 18cm/7in round cake

175g/6oz/1½ cups self-raising (self-rising) flour
a pinch of salt
175g/6oz/¾ cup butter, softened
175g/6oz/scant 1 cup caster (superfine) sugar
3 eggs

To finish
60–90ml/4–6 tbsp raspberry jam
caster (superfine) sugar or icing (confectioners') sugar

1 Preheat the oven to 180°C/350°F/Gas 4. Grease two 18cm/7in shallow round cake tins (pans), line the bases with baking parchment and grease the paper.

2 Put the flour, salt, butter, caster sugar and eggs into a large bowl. Whisk the ingredients together until smooth and creamy.

3 Divide the mixture between the prepared cake tins and smooth the surfaces. Bake for 25–30 minutes, or until a skewer inserted into the centre of the cakes comes out clean.

4 Turn out on to a wire rack, peel off the lining paper and leave to cool. Place one of the cakes on a serving plate and spread with the raspberry jam. Place the other cake on top.

5 Cut out paper star shapes, place on the cake and dredge with sugar. Remove the paper to reveal the pattern.

Variation
Sponge Cake with Strawberries and Cream is delicious on a summer's day. Whip 300ml/½ pint/1¼ cups double (heavy) cream with 5ml/1 tsp icing (confectioners') sugar until stiff. Wash and hull 450g/1lb/4 cups strawberries, then cut them in half. Spread one of the cakes with half of the cream and sprinkle over half of the strawberries. Place the other cake on top, spread with the remaining cream and arrange the remaining strawberries.

Energy 2965kcal/12419kJ; Fat 162.8g, Saturated Fat 96.2g; Carbohydrate 361.3g, Fibre 5.4g

Mocha Victoria Sponge

A light coffee- and cocoa-flavoured sponge with a rich buttercream topping.

Makes one 18cm/7in round cake

175g/6oz/¾ cup butter
175g/6oz/generous ¾ cup caster (superfine) sugar
3 eggs
175g/6oz/1½ cups self-raising (self-rising) flour, sifted
15ml/1 tbsp strong black coffee
15ml/1 tbsp unsweetened cocoa powder mixed with 15–30ml/1–2 tbsp boiling water

For the coffee buttercream
150g/5oz/10 tbsp butter
15ml/1 tbsp coffee extract or 10ml/2 tsp instant coffee powder dissolved in 15–30ml/1–2 tbsp warm milk
275g/10oz/2½ cups icing (confectioners') sugar

1 Preheat the oven to 180°C/350°F/Gas 4. Grease and base-line two 18cm/7in shallow round cake tins (pans). Cream the butter and sugar in a large bowl until light and fluffy. Add the eggs, one at a time, beating well after each addition. Fold in the flour.

2 Divide the mixture between two bowls. Fold the coffee into one and the cocoa mixture into the other.

3 Place alternate spoonfuls of each mixture side by side in the cake tins. Bake for 25–30 minutes. Turn out on to a wire rack to cool.

4 For the buttercream, beat the butter until soft. Gradually beat in the remaining ingredients until smooth.

5 Sandwich the cakes, bases together, with a third of the buttercream. Cover the top and side with the remainder.

Cook's Tip
When mixing eggs into creamed sugar and butter, whisk only briefly, and if the mixture begins to curdle add a spoonful of the flour before you add any more of the eggs.

Energy 4668kcal/19505kJ; Fat 289.6g, Saturated Fat 176.4g; Carbohydrate 506.1g, Fibre 7.2g

Lemon and Apricot Cake

This cake is soaked in a tangy lemon syrup after baking to keep it really moist.

Makes one 23 x 13cm/ 9 x 5in loaf

175g/6oz/¾ cup butter, softened
175g/6oz/1½ cups self-raising (self-rising) flour
2.5ml/½ tsp baking powder
175g/6oz/generous ¾ cup caster (superfine) sugar
3 eggs, lightly beaten
finely grated rind of 1 lemon
175g/6oz/1½ cups ready-to-eat dried apricots, finely chopped
75g/3oz/¾ cup ground almonds
40g/1½oz/6 tbsp pistachio nuts, chopped
50g/2oz/½ cup flaked (sliced) almonds
15g/½oz/2 tbsp whole pistachio nuts

For the syrup

45ml/3 tbsp caster (superfine) sugar
freshly squeezed juice of 1 lemon

1 Preheat the oven to 180°C/350°F/Gas 4. Grease and line a 23 x 13cm/9 x 5in loaf tin (pan) with baking parchment and grease the paper.

2 Place the butter in a large bowl. Sift over the flour and baking powder, then add the sugar, eggs and lemon rind.

3 Using an electric whisk or a wooden spoon, beat for 1–2 minutes, or until smooth and glossy, then stir in the apricots, ground almonds and chopped pistachio nuts.

4 Spoon the mixture into the loaf tin and smooth the surface. Sprinkle with the flaked almonds and the whole pistachio nuts.

5 Bake for 1¼ hours, or until a skewer inserted into the centre of the cake comes out clean. Check the cake after 45 minutes and cover with a piece of foil when the top is nicely browned. Leave the cake to cool in the tin.

6 To make the lemon syrup, gently dissolve the sugar in the lemon juice in a small pan over a low heat. Spoon the syrup over the cake. When the cake is completely cooled, turn it carefully out of the tin and peel off the lining paper.

Energy 4358kcal/18221kJ; Fat 264g; Saturated Fat 105.8g; Carbohydrate 443.9g; Fibre 29.1g

Cherry Batter Cake

This colourful tray bake looks pretty cut into neat squares or fingers. Its unusual topping makes it especially tasty.

Makes one 33 x 23cm/ 13 x 9in cake

225g/8oz/2 cups self-raising (self-rising) flour
5ml/1 tsp baking powder
75g/3oz/6 tbsp butter, softened
150g/5oz/scant 1 cup soft light brown sugar
1 egg, lightly beaten
150ml/¼ pint/⅔ cup milk
icing (confectioners') sugar, for dusting
whipped cream, to serve (optional)

For the topping

675g/1½lb jar black cherries or blackcurrants, drained
175g/6oz/¾ cup soft light brown sugar
50g/2oz/½ cup self-raising (self-rising) flour
50g/2oz/¼ cup butter, melted

1 Preheat the oven to 190°C/375°F/Gas 5. Grease and line a 33 x 23cm/13 x 9in Swiss roll tin (jelly roll pan) with baking parchment, and grease the paper.

2 To make the base, sift the flour and baking powder into a large bowl. Add the butter, sugar, egg and milk.

3 Beat until the mixture becomes smooth, then turn into the prepared tin and smooth the surface.

4 To make the topping, sprinkle the drained cherries or blackcurrants evenly over the batter mixture.

5 Mix together the brown sugar, flour and melted butter, and spoon evenly over the fruit.

6 Bake for 40 minutes, or until the top is golden brown and the centre is firm to the touch.

7 Leave to cool for 15 minutes in the tin, then turn out and leave on a wire rack to cool completely. Dust with icing sugar. Serve with whipped cream, if you like.

Energy 3770kcal/15932kJ; Fat 114.4g; Saturated Fat 68.8g; Carbohydrate 686g; Fibre 12.6g

Fruit Salad Cake

You can use any combination of dried fruits in this rich, dark fruit cake.

Makes one 18cm/7in round cake

175g/6oz/1 cup roughly chopped mixed dried fruit, such as apples, apricots, prunes and peaches
250ml/8fl oz/1 cup hot tea
225g/8oz/2 cups self-raising (self-rising) wholemeal (whole-wheat) flour
5ml/1 tsp freshly grated nutmeg
50g/2oz/¼ cup muscovado (molasses) sugar
45ml/3 tbsp sunflower oil
45ml/3 tbsp skimmed milk
demerara (raw) sugar, for sprinkling

1 Soak the dried fruits in the tea for several hours or overnight. Drain and reserve the liquid.

2 Preheat the oven to 180°C/350°F/Gas 4. Grease an 18cm/7in round cake tin (pan) and line the base with baking parchment.

3 Sift the flour into a bowl with the nutmeg. Stir in the muscovado sugar, and the dried fruit and tea. Add the oil and milk, and mix well.

4 Spoon the mixture into the prepared cake tin and sprinkle with demerara sugar.

5 Bake for 50–55 minutes, or until firm. Turn out on to a wire rack to cool.

Cook's Tips

- *For successful baking always level the mixture in the cake tin (pan) before baking.*
- *Test that the cake is cooked before the stated cooking time as oven temperatures can vary and it might take less time. Fan-assisted ovens usually cook foods more quickly.*
- *Check that the oven shelf is level, as an uneven surface will cause the cake to cook lopsidedly.*

Energy 1482kcal/6266kJ; Fat 39.1g, Saturated Fat 4.7g; Carbohydrate 261.9g, Fibre 31.3g

Fairy Cakes with Blueberries

This luxurious treatment of fairy cakes means they will be as popular with adults as with children.

Makes 8–10

115g/4oz/½ cup soft margarine
115g/4oz/½ cup caster (superfine) sugar
5ml/1 tsp grated lemon rind
a pinch of salt
2 eggs, beaten
115g/4oz/1 cup self-raising (self-rising) flour, sifted
120ml/4fl oz/½ cup whipping cream
75–115g/3–4oz/¾–1 cup blueberries
icing (confectioners') sugar, for dusting

1 Preheat the oven to 190°C/375°F/Gas 5. Cream the margarine, sugar, lemon rind and salt in a large bowl until pale and fluffy.

2 Gradually beat in the eggs, then fold in the flour.

3 Spoon the mixture into eight to ten paper cases on baking sheets and bake for 15–20 minutes, or until just golden.

4 Leave the cakes to cool, then scoop out a circle of sponge from the top of each using the point of a small sharp knife, and set them aside.

5 Whip the cream and place a spoonful in each cake, plus a couple of blueberries. Replace the lids at an angle and sift over some icing sugar.

Variation

These fairy cakes are perfect for making into Angel Cakes with butter icing. Slice the domed top from the cake and cut in two. Make some butter icing and flavour it as you like (orange or chocolate are particular favourites with children). Spread some butter icing on the top of each cake and position the cut tops with the cut sides outwards to look like wings.

Energy 231kcal/962kJ; Fat 15.5g, Saturated Fat 3.4g; Carbohydrate 21.5g; Fibre 0.6g

Jewel Cake

This pretty cake is excellent served as a teatime treat.

Makes one 23 x 13cm/ 9 x 5in cake

115g/4oz/½ cup mixed glacé (candied) cherries, halved, washed and dried
50g/2oz/4 tbsp preserved stem ginger in syrup, chopped, washed and dried
50g/2oz/⅓ cup chopped mixed (candied) peel
115g/4oz/1 cup self-raising (self-rising) flour
75g/3oz/⅔ cup plain (all-purpose) flour
25g/1oz/¼ cup cornflour (cornstarch)
175g/6oz/¾ cup butter
175g/6oz/scant 1 cup caster (superfine) sugar
3 eggs
grated rind of 1 orange

To decorate

175g/6oz/1½ cups icing (confectioners') sugar, sifted
30–45ml/2–3 tbsp freshly squeezed orange juice
50g/2oz/¼ cup mixed glacé (candied) cherries, chopped
25g/1oz/2½ tbsp mixed (candied) peel, chopped

1 Preheat the oven to 180°C/350°F/Gas 4. Grease and line a 23 x 13cm/9 x 5in loaf tin (pan) and grease the paper.

2 Place the glacé cherries, stem ginger and mixed peel in a plastic bag with 25g/1oz/¼ cup of the self-raising flour and shake to coat evenly. Sift together the remaining flours and cornflour.

3 In a large bowl, beat together the butter and sugar until light and fluffy. Beat in the eggs, one at a time. Fold in the sifted flours with the orange rind, then stir in the dried fruit.

4 Transfer the mixture to the cake tin and bake for 1¼ hours, or until a skewer inserted into the centre comes out clean. Leave in the tin for 5 minutes, then cool on a wire rack.

5 For the decoration, mix the icing sugar with the orange juice until smooth. Drizzle the icing over the cake.

6 Mix together the glacé cherries and mixed peel, then use to decorate the cake. Allow the icing to set before serving.

Energy 4369kcal/18404kJ; Fat 164.9g, Saturated Fat 96.5g Carbohydrate 726.1g, Fibre 11.5g

Iced Paradise Cake

Serve this rich and creamy delight chilled.

Makes one 23 x 13cm/ 9 x 5in cake

3 eggs
75g/3oz/scant ½ cup caster (superfine) sugar
65g/2½oz/9 tbsp plain (all-purpose) flour, sifted
15g/½oz/2 tbsp cornflour (cornstarch), sifted
90ml/6 tbsp dark rum
250g/9oz/1½ cups plain (semisweet) chocolate chips
30ml/2 tbsp golden (light corn) syrup
30ml/2 tbsp water
400ml/14fl oz/1⅔ cups double (heavy) cream, whipped
115g/4oz/generous 1 cup desiccated (dry unsweetened shredded) coconut, toasted
25g/1oz/2 tbsp unsalted (sweet) butter
30ml/2 tbsp single (light) cream
50g/2oz/⅓ cup white chocolate chips, melted
coconut curls, to decorate
cocoa powder, for dusting

1 Preheat the oven to 200°C/400°F/Gas 6. Grease and flour two baking sheets. Line a 23 x 13cm/9 x 5in loaf tin (pan) with clear film (plastic wrap).

2 Whisk the eggs and sugar together in a heatproof bowl. Place over a pan of simmering water and whisk until pale and thick. Whisk off the heat until cool. Fold in the flour and cornflour. Pipe 30 7.5cm/3in sponge fingers on to the baking sheets. Bake for 8–10 minutes. Cool slightly, then transfer to a wire rack.

3 Line the base and sides of the loaf tin with sponge fingers. Brush with rum. Melt 75g/3oz/½ cup chocolate chips, the syrup, water and 30ml/2 tbsp rum in a bowl over simmering water.

4 Stir the chocolate mixture and coconut into the cream. Pour into the tin and top with the remaining fingers. Brush with the remaining rum. Cover with clear film and freeze until firm.

5 Melt the remaining chocolate with the butter and single cream as before, then cool slightly. Turn the cake out on to a wire rack. Coat with the icing. Chill. Drizzle with white chocolate zigzags. Chill. Sprinkle with coconut curls and dust with cocoa powder.

Energy 5502kcal/22864kJ; Fat 416.4g, Saturated Fat 267.8g Carbohydrate 349.1g, Fibre 26.4g

Pound Cake with Red Fruit

This orange-scented cake is good for tea, or served as a dessert with cream.

Makes one 20 x 10cm/ 8 x 4in cake

450g/1lb/4 cups fresh raspberries, strawberries or pitted cherries, or a combination of any of these
175g/6oz/generous ¾ cup caster (superfine) sugar, plus 15–30ml/ 1–2 tbsp, plus extra for sprinkling
15ml/1 tbsp lemon juice
175g/6oz/1½ cups plain (all-purpose) flour
10ml/2 tsp baking powder
pinch of salt
175g/6oz/¾ cup unsalted (sweet) butter, softened
3 eggs
grated rind of 1 orange
15ml/1 tbsp orange juice

1 Reserve a few whole fruits for decorating. In a blender or food processor, process the fruit until smooth. Add 15–30ml/1–2 tbsp sugar and the lemon juice, and process again. Strain the sauce and chill.

2 Grease the base and sides of a 20 x 10cm/8 x 4in loaf tin (pan) and line the base with baking parchment. Grease the paper. Sprinkle with sugar and tip out any excess. Preheat the oven to 180°C/350°F/Gas 4.

3 Sift together the flour, baking powder and a pinch of salt. In another bowl, beat the butter until creamy. Add the sugar and beat until light and fluffy. Add the eggs, one at a time, beating well after each addition.

4 Beat in the orange rind and juice. Gently fold the flour mixture into the butter mixture in three batches, then spoon the mixture into the loaf tin and tap gently to release any air bubbles.

5 Bake for 35–40 minutes, or until the top is golden and it is springy to the touch. Leave the cake in its tin on a wire rack for 10 minutes, then remove the cake from the tin and cool for 30 minutes. Remove the paper and serve slices of cake with a little of the fruit sauce, decorated with the reserved fruit.

Energy 2927kcal/12264kJ; Fat 164.1g, Saturated Fat 96.6g; Carbohydrate 341.9g, Fibre 16.7g

Madeleines

These little tea cakes, baked in a special tin with shell-shaped cups, are best eaten on the day they are made.

Makes 12

165g/5½oz/generous 1¼ cups plain (all-purpose) flour
5ml/1 tsp baking powder
2 eggs
75g/3oz/¾ cup icing (confectioners') sugar, plus extra for dusting
grated rind of 1 lemon or orange
15ml/1 tbsp lemon or orange juice
75g/3oz/6 tbsp unsalted (sweet) butter, melted and slightly cooled

1 Preheat the oven to 190°C/375°F/Gas 5. Generously grease a 12-cup madeleine tin (pan). Sift together the flour and the baking powder.

2 Beat the eggs and icing sugar in a large bowl until the mixture is thick and creamy and leaves ribbon trails. Gently fold in the lemon or orange rind and juice.

3 Beginning with the flour mixture, alternately fold in the flour and melted butter in four batches. Leave to stand for 10 minutes, then spoon into the tin. Tap gently to release any air bubbles.

4 Bake for 12–15 minutes, rotating the tin halfway through cooking. The cake is cooked when a skewer inserted in the centre comes out clean.

5 Turn out on to a wire rack to cool completely and dust with icing sugar before serving.

Cook's Tip

These cakes look sweet baked in the traditional Madeleine tins (pans), but cooking equipment suppliers now stock all kinds of novelty cake tins, such as flowers, stars and hearts that would be suitable for using with this recipe. You could even drizzle some orange-flavoured glacé icing over the tops.

Energy 130kcal/547kJ; Fat 6.2g, Saturated Fat 3.5g; Carbohydrate 17.3g, Fibre 0.4g

Chocolate Orange Battenburg Cake

A tasty variation on the traditional pink-and-white Battenburg cake. Use good quality marzipan for the best flavour.

Makes one 18cm/7in long rectangular cake

115g/4oz/½ cup soft margarine
115g/4oz/½ cup caster (superfine) sugar
2 eggs, beaten
a few drops ofvanilla extract
15g/½oz/1 tbsp ground almonds
115g/4oz/1 cup self-raising (self-rising) flour, sifted
grated rind and juice of ½ orange
15g/½oz/2 tbsp unsweetened cocoa powder, sifted
30–45ml/2–3 tbsp milk
1 jar chocolate and nut spread
225g/8oz white marzipan

1 Preheat the oven to 180°C/350°F/Gas 4. Grease and line an 18cm/7in square cake tin (pan) with baking parchment. Put a double piece of foil across the middle of the tin, to divide it into two equal oblongs.

2 Cream the margarine and sugar. Beat in the eggs, vanilla extract and almonds. Divide the mixture evenly into two halves.

3 Fold half of the flour into one half, with the orange rind and enough juice to give a soft dropping consistency. Fold the rest of the flour and the cocoa powder into the other half, with enough milk to give a soft dropping consistency. Fill the tin with the two mixes and level the top.

4 Bake for 15 minutes, reduce the heat to 160°C/325°F/Gas 3 and cook for 20–30 minutes, or until the top is just firm. Leave to cool in the tin for a few minutes. Turn out on to a board, cut each cake into two strips and trim evenly. Leave to cool.

5 Using the chocoloate and nut spread, sandwich the cakes together, Battenburg-style.

6 Roll out the marzipan on a board lightly dusted with cornflour to a rectangle 18cm/7in wide and long enough to wrap around the cake. Wrap the paste around the cake, putting the join underneath. Press to seal.

Energy 3916kcal/16370kJ; Fat 234.1g, Saturated Fat 41.6g; Carbohydrate 426.6g, Fibre 9.3g

Best-Ever Chocolate Sandwich

A three-layered cake is ideal for a birthday party.

Makes one 20cm/8in round cake

115g/4oz/1 cup plain (all-purpose) flour
50g/2oz/½ cup unsweetened cocoa powder
5ml/1 tsp baking powder
6 eggs
225g/8oz/generous 1 cup caster (superfine) sugar
10ml/2 tsp vanilla extract
115g/4oz/½ cup unsalted (sweet) butter, melted

For the icing

225g/8oz plain (semisweet) chocolate, chopped
75g/3oz/6 tbsp unsalted (sweet) butter
3 eggs, separated
250ml/8fl oz/1 cup whipping cream
45ml/3 tbsp caster (superfine) sugar

1 Preheat the oven to 180°C/350°F/Gas 4. Line three 20cm/8in round shallow cake tins (pans) with baking parchment, grease the paper and dust with flour. Sift the flour, cocoa powder, baking powder and a pinch of salt together three times.

2 Place the eggs and sugar in the top of a double boiler. Beat until doubled in volume. Add the vanilla extract. Fold in the flour mixture in three batches, then the melted butter. Transfer the mixture into the tins. Bake until the cakes pull away from the tin sides, about 25 minutes. Transfer to a wire rack.

3 To make the icing, melt the chocolate in the top of a double boiler. Off the heat, stir in the butter and egg yolks. Return to the heat and stir until thick. Whip the cream until firm.

4 In another bowl, beat the egg whites until stiff peaks form. Add the sugar and beat until glossy. Fold the cream, then the egg whites, into the chocolate mixture. Chill the cake for 20 minutes, then sandwich together and cover with icing.

Variation
Try coffee butter icing (see p248) instead of chocolate icing.

Energy 5787kcal/24151kJ; Fat 382.2g, Saturated Fat 220.4g; Carbohydrate 528g, Fibre 15.2g

Chocolate Layer Cake

The surprise ingredient – beetroot – makes a beautifully moist cake.

Makes one 23cm/9in cake

unsweetened cocoa powder, for dusting
225g/8oz can cooked whole beetroot, drained and juice reserved
115g/4oz/½ cup unsalted (sweet) butter, softened
550g/1lb 6oz/2¾ cups soft light brown sugar
3 eggs
15ml/1 tbsp vanilla extract
75g/3oz unsweetened chocolate, melted
285g/10oz/2½ cups plain (all-purpose) flour
10ml/2 tsp baking powder
2.5ml/½ tsp salt
120ml/4fl oz/½ cup buttermilk
chocolate curls, to decorate (optional)

For the frosting

4750ml/16fl oz/2 cups double (heavy) cream
500g/1¼lb plain (semisweet) chocolate, chopped
15ml/1 tbsp vanilla extract

1 Preheat the oven to 180°C/350°F/Gas 4. Grease two 23cm/9in cake tins (pans) and dust with cocoa powder. Grate the beetroot and add it to its juice. Beat the butter, brown sugar, eggs and vanilla until pale and fluffy. Beat in the chocolate.

2 Sift together the flour, baking powder and salt. With the mixer on low speed and beginning and ending with flour mixture, alternately beat in flour and buttermilk. Add the beetroot and juice and beat for 1 minute. Transfer to the cake tins.

3 Bake for 30–35 minutes. Cool in the tin for 10 minutes, then unmould and transfer to wire rack to cool.

4 To make the frosting, heat the cream in a pan until it just begins to boil, stirring occasionally to prevent scorching. Remove from the heat and stir in the chocolate, until melted and smooth. Stir in the vanilla extract. Strain into a bowl and chill, stirring every 10 minutes, for 1 hour.

5 Sandwich and cover the cake with the frosting, and top with chocolate curls, if you like. Allow to set for 20–30 minutes, then chill before serving.

Energy 9521kcal/39888kJ; Fat 518.1g, Saturated Fat 312.1g; Carbohydrate 1196.3g, Fibre 27.5g

Marbled Chocolate and Peanut Cake

A deliciously rich treat for a special tea.

Serves 12–14

115g/4oz unsweetened chocolate, chopped
225g/8oz/1 cup unsalted (sweet) butter, softened
225g/8oz/1 cup peanut butter
200g/7oz/1 cup caster (superfine) sugar
225g/8oz/1 cup soft light brown sugar
5 eggs
275g/10oz/2½ cups plain (all-purpose) flour
10ml/2 tsp baking powder
2.5ml/½ tsp salt
125ml/4fl oz/½ cup milk
50g/2oz/⅓ cup chocolate chips

For the chocolate–peanut butter glaze

25g/1oz/2 tbsp butter, diced
25g/1oz/2 tbsp smooth peanut butter
45ml/3 tbsp golden (light corn) syrup
5ml/1 tsp vanilla extract
175g/6oz plain (semisweet) chocolate, broken into pieces

1 Preheat the oven to 180°C/350°F/Gas 4. Grease and flour a 3-litre/5¼-pint/13¼-cup tube tin (pan) or ring mould. Melt the chocolate in a double boiler or in a heatproof bowl over a pan of simmering water.

2 Beat the butter, peanut butter and sugars until light and creamy. Add the eggs, one at a time, beating well after each addition. Sift together the flour, baking powder and salt. Add to the butter mixture alternately with the milk.

3 Pour half the batter into another bowl. Stir the melted chocolate into one half and stir the chocolate chips into the other half. Drop alternate large spoonfuls of the two batters into the tin or mould. Using a knife, pull through the batters to create a swirled marbled effect; do not let the knife touch the side or base of the tin. Bake for 50–60 minutes, or until the top springs back when touched. Cool in the tin on a wire rack for 10 minutes. Then unmould on to the wire rack.

4 Combine the glaze ingredients and 15ml/1 tbsp water in a small pan. Melt over a low heat, stirring. Cool slightly, then drizzle over the cake, allowing it to run down the sides.

Energy 450kcal/1876kJ; Fat 32.3g, Saturated Fat 16g; Carbohydrate 34.4g, Fibre 1.5g

Chocolate Fairy Cakes

Make these delightful butter-iced fairy cakes to serve for a children's party.

Makes 24

115g/4oz good quality plain (semi-sweet) chocolate, cut into small pieces
15ml/1 tbsp water
300g/10oz/2½ cups plain (all-purpose) flour
5ml/1 tsp baking powder
2.5ml/½ tsp bicarbonate of soda (baking soda)
a pinch of salt
300g/11oz/generous 1½ cups caster (superfine) sugar
175g/6oz/¾ cup butter or margarine, at room temperature
150ml/¼ pint/⅔ cup milk
5ml/1 tsp vanilla extract
3 eggs
1 recipe quantity butter icing, flavoured to taste, see p248

1 Preheat the oven to 180°C/350°F/Gas 4. Grease and flour 24 deep bun cups, about 6.5cm/2¾in in diameter, or use paper cases in the tins (pans).

2 Put the chocolate and water in a bowl set over a pan of almost simmering water. Heat until melted and smooth, stirring. Remove from the heat and leave to cool.

3 Sift the flour, baking powder, bicarbonate of soda, salt and sugar into a large bowl. Add the chocolate mixture, butter or margarine, milk and vanilla extract.

4 With an electric mixer on medium-low speed, beat until smoothly blended. Increase the speed to high and beat for 2 minutes. Add the eggs and beat for 2 more minutes.

5 Divide the mixture evenly among the prepared bun tins and bake for 20–25 minutes, or until a skewer inserted into the centre of a cake comes out clean.

6 Cool in the tins for 10 minutes, then turn out to cool completely on a wire rack.

7 Ice the top of each cake with butter icing, swirling it into a peak in the centre.

Energy 228kcal/957kJ; Fat 11.5g, Saturated Fat 3.3g; Carbohydrate 30.6g, Fibre 0.5g

Chocolate Mint-filled Cupcakes

For extra mint flavour, chop eight thin mint cream-filled after-dinner mints and fold into the cake batter.

Makes 12

225g/8oz/2 cups plain (all-purpose) flour
5ml/1 tsp bicarbonate of soda (baking soda)
a pinch of salt
50g/2oz/½ cup unsweetened cocoa powder
150g/5oz/10 tbsp unsalted (sweet) butter, softened
300g/11oz/generous 1½ cups caster (superfine) sugar
3 eggs
5ml/1 tsp peppermint extract
250ml/8fl oz/1 cup milk

For the filling
300ml/½ pint/1¼ cups double (heavy) or whipping cream
5ml/1 tsp peppermint extract

For the glaze
175g/6oz plain (semisweet) chocolate
115g/4oz/½ cup unsalted (sweet) butter
5ml/1 tsp peppermint extract

1 Preheat the oven to 180°C/350°F/Gas 4. Line a 12-cup bun tray with paper cases. Sift together the dry ingredients.

2 In another bowl, beat the butter and sugar until light and creamy. Add the eggs, one at a time, beating well after each addition; beat in the peppermint. On low speed, beat in the flour mixture alternately with the milk, until just blended. Spoon into the paper cases.

3 Bake for 12–15 minutes. Transfer to a wire rack to cool. When cool, remove the paper cases.

4 To make the filling, whip the cream and peppermint extract until stiff. Spoon into a piping (icing) bag fitted with a small plain nozzle. Pipe 15ml/1 tbsp into each cake through the base.

5 To make the glaze, melt the chocolate and butter in a heatproof bowl over a pan of simmering water, stirring until smooth. Remove from the heat and stir in the peppermint extract. Cool, then spread on top of each cake.

Energy 535kcal/2234kJ; Fat 35.1g, Saturated Fat 21.4g; Carbohydrate 52g, Fibre 1.4g

Rich Chocolate Nut Cake

Use walnuts or pecan nuts for the cake sides if you prefer.

Makes one 23cm/9in round cake

225g/8oz/1 cup butter
225g/8oz plain (semisweet) chocolate
115g/4oz/1 cup unsweetened cocoa powder
350g/12oz/1¾ cups caster (superfine) sugar
6 eggs
85ml/3fl oz/5½ tbsp brandy
225g/8oz/2 cups finely chopped hazelnuts

For the glaze

50g/2oz/¼ cup butter
150g/5oz cooking chocolate
30ml/2 tbsp milk
5ml/1 tsp vanilla extract

1 Preheat the oven to 180°C/350°F/Gas 4. Line a 23 x 5cm/9 x 2in round tin (pan) with baking parchment and grease the paper.

2 Melt the butter and chocolate in the top of a double boiler. Leave to cool.

3 Sift the cocoa powder into a bowl. Add the sugar and eggs, and stir until just combined. Pour in the chocolate mixture and brandy.

4 Fold in three-quarters of the hazelnuts, then pour the mixture into the prepared cake tin.

5 Set the tin in a roasting pan and pour 2.5cm/1in hot water into the outer pan. Bake until the cake is firm to the touch, about 45 minutes. Leave for 15 minutes, then unmould on to a wire rack. When cool, wrap in baking parchment and chill for at least 6 hours.

6 To make the glaze, melt the butter and chocolate with the milk and vanilla extract as before.

7 Place the cake on a wire rack over a plate. Drizzle the glaze over, letting it drip down the sides. Cover the cake sides with the remaining nuts. Transfer to a serving plate when set.

Energy 7802kcal/32523kJ; Fat 532.7g, Saturated Fat 241.2g; Carbohydrate 633.7g, Fibre 37.9g

Multi-layer Chocolate Cake

For a change, sandwich the cake layers with softened vanilla ice cream. Freeze before serving.

Makes one 20cm/8in round cake

115g/4oz plain (semisweet) chocolate
175g/6oz/¾ cup butter
450g/1lb/2¼ cups caster (superfine) sugar
3 eggs
5ml/1 tsp vanilla extract
175g/6oz/1½ cups plain (all-purpose) flour
5ml/1 tsp baking powder
115g/4oz/1 cup chopped walnuts

For the filling and topping

350ml/12fl oz/1½ cups whipping cream
225g/8oz plain (semisweet) chocolate
15ml/1 tbsp vegetable oil

1 Preheat the oven to 180°C/350°F/Gas 4. Line two 20cm/8in shallow round cake tins (pans) with baking parchment and grease the paper.

2 Melt the chocolate and butter in the top of a double boiler or in a heatproof bowl over a pan of simmering water. Transfer to a bowl and stir in the sugar. Add the eggs and vanilla and mix well.

3 Sift over the flour and baking powder. Stir in the chopped walnuts.

4 Pour the mixture into the prepared cake tins. Bake until a skewer inserted into the centre comes out clean, about 30 minutes. Leave to stand for 10 minutes, then unmould on to a wire rack to cool completely.

5 To make the filling and topping, whip the cream until firm. Slice the cakes in half horizontally. Sandwich them together with the cream and cover the cake with the remainder. Chill.

6 To make the chocolate curls, melt the chocolate and oil as before. Stir to combine well. Spread on to a non-porous surface. Just before it sets, hold the blade of a knife at an angle to the chocolate and scrape across the surface to make curls. Use to decorate the cake and add tiny curls made with the tip of a rounded knife as well, if you like.

Energy 7850kcal/32796kJ; Fat 488.8g, Saturated Fat 249.3g; Carbohydrate 836.4g, Fibre 17.9g

Chocolate Frosted Layer Cake

The contrast between the frosting and the sponge creates a dramatic effect when the cake is cut.

Makes one 20cm/8in round cake

225g/8oz/1 cup butter or margarine, at room temperature
300g/11oz/scant 1½ cups caster (superfine) sugar
4 eggs, separated
10ml/2 tsp vanilla extract
385g/13½oz/3⅓ cups plain (all-purpose) flour
10ml/2 tsp baking powder
1.5ml/¼ tsp salt
250ml/8fl oz/1 cup milk

For the frosting
150g/5oz plain (semisweet) chocolate
120ml/4fl oz/½ cup sour cream
1.5ml/¼ tsp salt

1 Preheat the oven to 180°C/350°F/Gas 4. Line two 20cm/8in round cake tins (pans) with baking parchment and grease the paper. Dust the tins with flour. Tap to remove any excess.

2 Cream the butter or margarine until soft. Gradually add the sugar and beat until light and fluffy. Beat the egg yolks, then add to the butter mixture with the vanilla extract.

3 Sift the flour with the baking powder three times. Set aside. Beat the egg whites with the salt until they form stiff peaks.

4 Fold the dry ingredients into the butter mixture in three batches, alternating with the milk. Add a dollop of the egg white to the batter and fold in to lighten the mixture. Fold in the remainder until just blended.

5 Spoon into the cake tins and bake until the cakes pull away from the sides, about 30 minutes. Leave in the tins for 5 minutes, then turn out on to a wire rack to cool completely.

6 To make the frosting, melt the chocolate in the top of a double boiler or in a heatproof bowl over a pan of simmering water. When cool, stir in the sour cream and salt. Sandwich the layers with frosting, then spread on the top and side.

Energy 5530kcal/23187kJ; Fat 282.3g, Saturated Fat 167g; Carbohydrate 709.9g, Fibre 15.7g

Devil's Food Cake with Orange

Chocolate and orange always taste great together.

Makes one 23cm/9in round cake

50g/2oz/½ cup unsweetened cocoa powder
175ml/6fl oz/¾ cup boiling water
175g/6oz/¾ cup butter, at room temperature
350g/12oz/2 cups soft dark brown sugar
3 eggs
275g/10oz/2½ cups plain (all-purpose) flour
7.5ml/1½ tsp bicarbonate of soda (baking soda)
1.5ml/¼ tsp baking powder
120ml/4fl oz/½ cup sour cream
blanched orange rind shreds, to decorate

For the frosting
300g/11oz/scant 1½ cups caster (superfine) sugar
2 egg whites
60ml/4 tbsp orange juice concentrate
15ml/1 tbsp lemon juice
grated rind of 1 orange

1 Preheat the oven to 180°C/350°F/Gas 4. Line two 23cm/9in cake tins (pans) with baking parchment and grease the paper. In a bowl, mix the cocoa powder and water until smooth.

2 Cream the butter and sugar until light and fluffy. Add the eggs, one at a time, beating well after each addition. When the cocoa mixture is lukewarm, add to the butter mixture. Sift together the flour, bicarbonate of soda and baking powder twice. Fold into the cocoa mixture in three batches, alternating with the sour cream. Pour into the tins and bake until the cakes pull away from the sides, 30–35 minutes. Leave to cool in the tins for 15 minutes, then turn out on to a wire rack to cool completely.

3 To make the frosting, place all the ingredients in the top of a double boiler or in a heatproof bowl over a pan of simmering water. With an electric mixer, beat until the mixture holds soft peaks. Continue beating off the heat until thick enough to spread.

4 Sandwich the cake layers with frosting, then spread over the top and side. Decorate with orange rind shreds.

Energy 5459kcal/23002kJ; Fat 199g, Saturated Fat 117.8g; Carbohydrate 906.2g, Fibre 14.8g

French Chocolate Cake

This is typical of a French home-made cake – dense, dark and delicious. Serve with cream or a fruit coulis.

Makes one 24cm/9½in round cake

150g/5oz/¾ cup caster (superfine) sugar
275g/10oz plain (semisweet) chocolate, chopped
175g/6oz/¾ cup unsalted (sweet) butter, cut into pieces
10ml/2 tsp vanilla extract
5 eggs, separated
40g/1½oz/¼ cup plain (all-purpose) flour, sifted
a pinch of salt
icing (confectioners') sugar, for dusting

1 Preheat the oven to 160°C/325°F/Gas 3. Butter a 24cm/9½in springform tin (pan), sprinkle with sugar and tap out the excess.

2 Set aside 45ml/3 tbsp of the caster sugar. Place the chopped chocolate, butter and remaining sugar in a heavy pan and cook gently over a low heat until melted, stirring occasionally.

3 Remove the pan from the heat, stir in the vanilla extract and leave to cool slightly.

4 Beat the egg yolks, one at a time, into the chocolate mixture, then stir in the flour.

5 Beat the egg whites with the salt until soft peaks form. Sprinkle over the reserved sugar and beat until stiff and glossy. Beat one-third of the whites into the chocolate mixture to lighten it, then fold in the rest.

6 Pour the mixture into the tin and tap it gently to release any air bubbles.

7 Bake the cake for 35–45 minutes, or until well risen and the top springs back when touched lightly. Transfer to a wire rack, remove the sides of the tin and leave the cake to cool. Remove the tin base, dust the cake with icing sugar and transfer to a serving plate.

Energy 3799kcal/15862kJ; Fat 249.1g, Saturated Fat 145.2g; Carbohydrate 363.5g, Fibre 8.1g

Almond Cake

Serve this wonderfully nutty cake with a cup of coffee, or, for a treat, with a glass of almond liqueur.

Makes one 23cm/9in round cake

225g/8oz/1⅓ cups blanched, toasted whole almonds
75g/3oz/¾ cup icing (confectioners') sugar
3 eggs
25g/1oz/2 tbsp butter, melted
2.5ml/½ tsp almond extract
25g/1oz/4 tbsp plain (all-purpose) flour
3 egg whites
15ml/1 tbsp caster (superfine) sugar
toasted whole almonds, to decorate

1 Preheat the oven to 160°C/325°F/Gas 3. Line a 23cm/9in round cake tin (pan) with baking parchment and grease the paper.

2 Coarsely chop the almonds and grind them with half the icing sugar in a blender or food processor. Transfer to a mixing bowl.

3 Beat in the whole eggs and remaining icing sugar with an electric whisk until the mixture forms ribbon trails when the whisk is lifted out of the batter. Mix in the butter and almond extract. Sift over the flour and fold in.

4 Beat the egg whites until they peak softly. Add the caster sugar and beat until stiff and glossy. Fold into the almond mixture in four batches.

5 Spoon the mixture into the cake tin and bake until golden brown, 15–20 minutes. Leave to cool in the tin for 10 minutes and then turn out on a wire rack to cool completely. Decorate the cake with toasted almonds.

Cook's Tip
Always use pure extracts as flavourings in your baking. Extracts are 100 per cent pure and natural, and their flavour is far superior to that of essences and other flavourings.

Energy 2258kcal/9407kJ; Fat 163.1g, Saturated Fat 27.7g; Carbohydrate 129.2g, Fibre 17.4g

Caramel Layer Cake

Just the ticket for all those with a sweet tooth.

Makes one 20cm/8in round cake

275g/10oz/2½ cups plain (all-purpose) flour
7.5ml/1½ tsp baking powder
175g/6oz/¾ cup butter, at room temperature
165g/5½oz/generous ¾ cup caster (superfine) sugar
4 eggs, beaten
5ml/1 tsp vanilla extract
120ml/4fl oz/½ cup milk
whipped cream, to decorate
caramel threads, to decorate (optional)

For the frosting
285g/10½oz/1⅓ cups soft dark brown sugar
250ml/8fl oz/1 cup milk
25g/1oz/2 tbsp unsalted (sweet) butter
45–75ml/3–5 tbsp whipping cream

1 Preheat the oven to 180°C/350°F/Gas 4. Line two 20cm/8in cake tins (pans) with baking parchment and grease the paper. Sift the flour and baking powder together three times.

2 Cream the butter and caster sugar until light and fluffy. Slowly mix in the beaten eggs. Add the vanilla extract. Fold in the flour mixture, alternating with the milk. Divide the batter between the cake tins and spread evenly. Bake until the cakes pull away from the sides of the tin, about 30 minutes. Cool in the tins for 5 minutes, then turn out and cool on a wire rack.

3 To make the frosting, bring the brown sugar and milk to the boil, cover and cook for 2 minutes. Uncover and continue to boil, without stirring, until the mixture reaches 119°C/238°F (soft ball stage) on a sugar thermometer.

4 Remove the pan from the heat and add the butter, but do not stir it in. Leave to cool until lukewarm, then beat until smooth. Stir in enough cream to obtain a spreadable consistency.

5 Sandwich the cake together with one-third of the frosting and then cover the top and side. Decorate with whipped cream, and caramel threads if you like.

Energy 5236kcal/21969kJ; Fat 260.9g, Saturated Fat 155.2g; Carbohydrate 701.3g, Fibre 8.5g

Marbled Spice Cake

You could bake this cake in a 20cm/8in round tin (pan) if you do not have a *kugelhopf.*

Makes one ring cake

75g/3oz/6 tbsp butter, softened
115g/4oz/generous ½ cup caster (superfine) sugar
2 eggs, lightly beaten
a few drops of vanilla extract
130g/4½oz/generous 1 cup plain (all-purpose) flour
7.5ml/1½ tsp baking powder
45ml/3 tbsp milk
45ml/3 tbsp black treacle (molasses)
5ml/1 tsp mixed (apple pie) spice
2.5ml/½ tsp ground ginger
175g/6oz/1½ cups icing (confectioners') sugar, sifted, to decorate

1 Preheat the oven to 180°C/350°F/Gas 4. Grease and flour a 900g/2lb *kugelhopf* or ring mould.

2 Cream together the butter and sugar until light and fluffy. Beat in the eggs and vanilla extract.

3 Sift together the flour and baking powder, then fold into the butter mixture, alternating with the milk.

4 Add the treacle and spices to one-third of the mixture. Drop alternating spoonfuls of the two mixtures into the tin. Run a knife through them to give a marbled effect.

5 Bake for 50 minutes, or until a skewer inserted into the centre comes out clean. Leave in the tin for 10 minutes, then turn out on to a wire rack to cool.

6 To decorate, make a smooth icing with the icing sugar and some warm water. Drizzle over the cake and leave to set.

Cook's Tip
Cakes baked in ring moulds take a little less time to cook than those baked in a round tin (pan) because the tube in the centre allows the air to circulate. So adjust the time accordingly if you use a round tin instead.

Energy 2427kcal/10247kJ; Fat 75.2g, Saturated Fat 42.9g; Carbohydrate 436.9g, Fibre 4g

Raspberry Meringue Gateau

A rich hazelnut meringue filled with cream and raspberries makes a delicious combination of textures and tastes.

Serves 8

4 egg whites
225g/8oz/generous 1 cup caster (superfine) sugar
a few drops of vanilla extract
5ml/1 tsp malt vinegar
115g/4oz/1⅔ cup toasted chopped hazelnuts, ground
300ml/½ pint/1¼ cups double (heavy) cream
350g/12oz/2 cups raspberries
icing (confectioners') sugar, for dusting
raspberries and mint sprigs, to decorate

For the sauce

225g/8oz/1⅓ cups raspberries
45ml/3 tbsp icing (confectioners') sugar
15ml/1 tbsp orange liqueur

1 Preheat the oven to 180°C/350°F/Gas 4. Grease two 20cm/8in shallow round cake tins (pans) and line the bases with baking parchment.

2 Whisk the egg whites in a large bowl until they hold stiff peaks, then gradually whisk in the caster sugar a tablespoon at a time, whisking well after each addition.

3 Continue whisking the meringue mixture for a minute or two until very stiff, then fold in the vanilla extract, malt vinegar and the ground hazelnuts. Divide the meringue mixture between the prepared tins and spread level. Bake for 50–60 minutes, or until crisp. Remove the meringues from the tins and leave to cool on a wire rack.

4 Meanwhile, make the sauce. Purée the raspberries with the icing sugar and orange liqueur in a blender or food processor, then press the purée through a nylon sieve to remove any pips. Chill the sauce until ready to serve.

5 Whip the cream until just thickened then fold in the raspberries. Sandwich the meringue rounds with the raspberry cream. Dust with icing sugar, and then decorate with fruit and mint. Serve the meringue with the sauce.

Energy 445kcal/1860kJ; Fat 29.5g, Saturated Fat 13.3g; Carbohydrate 40.5g, Fibre 2.7g

Strawberry Mint Sponge

This combination of summer fruit, fresh mint and ice cream will prove popular with everyone.

Makes one 20cm/8in round cake

6–10 fresh mint leaves, plus extra to decorate
175g/6oz/scant 1 cup caster (superfine) sugar
175g/6oz/¾ cup butter
175g/6oz/1½ cups self-raising (self-rising) flour
3 eggs
1.2 litres/2 pints/5 cups strawberry ice cream, softened
600ml/1 pint/2½ cups double (heavy) cream
30ml/2 tbsp mint liqueur
350g/12oz/3 cups fresh strawberries

1 Tear the fresh mint leaves into pieces, mix with the sugar, and leave overnight. Remove the leaves from the sugar the next day.

2 Preheat the oven to 190°C/375°F/Gas 5. Grease and line a 20cm/8in deep springform tin (pan).

3 Cream the butter and mint-flavoured sugar, add the flour, and then the eggs. Pour the mixture into the prepared tin.

4 Bake for 20–25 minutes, or until a skewer inserted in the centre comes out clean. Turn out on to a wire rack to cool completely. When cool, split into two layers.

5 Wash the cake tin and line with clear film (plastic wrap). Put the cake base back in the tin. Spread evenly with the softened ice cream, then cover with the top half of the cake. Freeze for 3–4 hours.

6 Whip the cream with the mint liqueur. Turn the cake out on to a serving plate and quickly spread a layer of whipped cream all over it, leaving a rough finish. Freeze until 10 minutes before serving.

7 Decorate the cake with the strawberries and place fresh mint leaves around it.

Energy 7965kcal/33162kJ; Fat 574.1g, Saturated Fat 340.9g; Carbohydrate 636.8g, Fibre 9.3g

Chestnut Cake

This rich, moist cake can be made up to a week in advance and kept, undecorated and wrapped, in an airtight tin.

Serves 8–10

150g/5oz/1¼ cups plain (all-purpose) flour
a pinch of salt
225g/8oz/1 cup butter, softened
150g/5oz/¾ cup caster (superfine) sugar
425g/15oz can chestnut purée
9 eggs, separated
105ml/7 tbsp dark rum
300ml/½ pint/1¼ cups double (heavy) cream
115g/4oz/1 cup icing (confectioners') sugar
marrons glacés and icing sugar, to decorate

1 Preheat the oven to 180°C/350°F/Gas 4. Grease and line a 20cm/8in springform tin (pan).

2 Sift the flour and salt and set aside. Beat the butter and sugar together until light and fluffy. Fold in two-thirds of the chestnut purée, with the egg yolks. Fold in the flour and salt.

3 Whisk the egg whites in a clean, dry bowl until stiff peaks form. Beat a little of the egg whites into the chestnut and butter mixture, until evenly blended, then fold in the remainder. Transfer the cake mixture to the tin and smooth the surface. Bake in the centre of the oven for about 1¼ hours, or until a skewer comes out clean. Leave in the tin and place on a wire rack.

4 Using a skewer, pierce holes over the cake. Sprinkle with 60ml/4 tbsp rum, then leave to cool. Remove the cake from the tin, peel off the lining paper and cut horizontally into two layers. Place the base layer on a serving plate. Whisk the cream with the remaining rum, icing sugar and chestnut purée until smooth.

5 To assemble, spread two-thirds of the chestnut cream mixture over the bottom layer and place the other layer on top. Spread some chestnut cream over the top and side of the cake. Using a piping (icing) bag and a large star nozzle, pipe the remainder of the chestnut cream in large swirls around the edge of the cake. Decorate with chopped marrons glacés and icing sugar.

Energy 588kcal/2448kJ; Fat 40.9g, Saturated Fat 23.4g; Carbohydrate 43.5g, Fibre 2.2g

Marbled Ring Cake

Glaze this cake with runny glacé icing if you prefer.

Makes one 25cm/10in ring cake

115g/4oz plain (semisweet) chocolate
350g/12oz/3 cups plain (all-purpose) flour
5ml/1 tsp baking powder
450g/1lb/2 cups butter, at room temperature
725g/1lb 10oz/3¾ cups caster (superfine) sugar
15ml/1 tbsp vanilla extract
10 eggs, at room temperature
icing (confectioners') sugar, for dusting

1 Preheat the oven to 180°C/350°F/Gas 4. Line a 25 x 10cm/10 x 4in ring mould with baking parchment and grease the paper. Dust with flour. Melt the chocolate in the top of a double boiler or in a heatproof bowl over a pan of simmering water, stirring occasionally. Set aside.

2 Sift together the flour and baking powder. In another bowl, cream the butter, sugar and vanilla extract until light and fluffy. Add the eggs, two at a time, then gradually blend in the flour mixture.

3 Spoon half the mixture into the ring mould. Stir the melted chocolate into the remaining mixture, then spoon into the tin. With a metal spatula, swirl the mixtures to create a marbled effect.

4 Bake until a skewer inserted in the centre comes out clean, about 1¾ hours. Cover with foil halfway through baking. Leave to cool in the tin for 15 minutes, then unmould and transfer to a wire rack to cool completely. To serve, dust with icing sugar.

Cook's Tip

With marbling cake mixtures, less is definitely more! Three or four wide swirling movements are all you will need to create the effect. If you over-swirl the batter the definition of the marbling will become lost.

Energy 8720kcal/36545kJ; Fat 462.1g, Saturated Fat 269.9g; Carbohydrate 1105.3g, Fibre 13.7g

Chocolate and Nut Gateau

Hazelnuts give an interesting crunchy texture to this delicious iced dessert.

Serves 6–8

75g/3oz/½ cup shelled hazelnuts
about 32 sponge fingers
150ml/¼ pint/⅔ cup cold strong black coffee
30ml/2 tbsp brandy
450ml/¾ pint/scant 2 cups double (heavy) cream
75g/3oz/¾ cup icing (confectioners') sugar, sifted
150g/5oz plain (semisweet) chocolate
icing sugar and unsweetened cocoa powder, for dusting

1 Preheat the oven to 200°C/400°F/Gas 6. Spread out the hazelnuts on a baking sheet and toast them in the oven for 5 minutes until golden.

2 Transfer the nuts to a clean dish towel and rub off the skins while still warm. Cool the nuts and then finely chop them.

3 Line a 1.2 litre/2 pint/5 cup loaf tin (pan) with clear film (plastic wrap) and cut enough sponge fingers to fit the base and sides. Reserve the remaining fingers.

4 Mix the coffee and brandy in a shallow dish. Dip the sponge fingers briefly into the coffee mixture and return to the tin, sugary side down.

5 Whip the cream with the icing sugar until it forms soft peaks. Roughly chop 75g/3oz of the chocolate, and fold into the cream with the hazelnuts.

6 Melt the remaining chocolate in a double boiler or a heatproof bowl over a pan of barely simmering water. Cool, then fold into the cream mixture. Spoon into the tin.

7 Moisten the remaining cookies in the coffee mixture and lay over the filling. Wrap and freeze until firm.

8 Remove from the freezer 30 minutes before serving. Turn out on to a serving plate and dust with icing sugar and cocoa.

Energy 481kcal/1993kJ; Fat 41.4g, Saturated Fat 22.4g; Carbohydrate 23.2g, Fibre 1.1g

Chocolate and Orange Angel Cake

This light-as-air sponge with its fluffy icing is the answer to a cake-lover's prayer.

Makes one 20cm/8in ring cake

25g/1oz/¼ cup plain (all-purpose) flour
15g/½oz/2 tbsp unsweetened cocoa powder
15g/½oz/2 tbsp cornflour (cornstarch)
a pinch of salt
5 egg whites
2.5ml/½ tsp cream of tartar
115g/4oz/generous ½ cup caster (superfine) sugar
blanched and shredded rind of 1 orange, to decorate

For the icing

200g/7oz/1 cup caster (superfine) sugar
1 egg white

1 Preheat the oven to 180°C/350°F/Gas 4. Sift the flour, cocoa powder, cornflour and salt together three times.

2 Beat the egg whites in a large bowl until foamy. Add the cream of tartar, then whisk until soft peaks form.

3 Add the caster sugar to the egg whites a spoonful at a time, whisking after each addition. Sift a third of the flour and cocoa mixture over the meringue and gently fold in. Repeat twice more.

4 Spoon the mixture into a non-stick 20cm/8in ring mould and level the top. Bake for 35 minutes, or until springy when lightly pressed. Turn upside-down on to a wire rack and leave to cool in the tin. Carefully ease out of the tin.

5 To make the icing, put the sugar in a pan with 75ml/5 tbsp cold water. Stir over a low heat until dissolved. Boil until the syrup reaches soft ball stage (119°C/238°F on a sugar thermometer). Remove from the heat.

6 Whisk the egg white until stiff. Add the syrup in a thin stream, whisking all the time, until the mixture is very thick and fluffy.

7 Spread the icing over the top and sides of the cooled cake. Sprinkle the orange rind over the top of the cake and serve.

Energy 1495kcal/6373kJ; Fat 3.7g, Saturated Fat 2g; Carbohydrate 364.1g, Fibre 2.6g

Chocolate Date Cake

A stunning cake that tastes wonderful. Rich and gooey – it's a chocoholic's delight!

Serves 8

4 egg whites
115g/4oz/generous ½ cup caster (superfine) sugar
200g/7oz plain (semisweet) chocolate
175g/6oz/1 cup Medjool dates, stoned (pitted) and chopped
175g/6oz/1½ cups chopped walnuts or pecan nuts
5ml/1 tsp vanilla extract

For the frosting

200g/7oz/scant 1 cup fromage frais or ricotta cheese
200g/7oz/scant 1 cup mascarpone
a few drops of vanilla extract
icing (confectioners') sugar, to taste

1 Preheat the oven to 180°C/350°F/Gas 4. Grease and base-line a 20cm/8in springform tin (pan).

2 To make the frosting, mix together the fromage frais or ricotta and mascarpone, add a few drops of vanilla extract and icing sugar to taste, then set aside.

3 Whisk the egg whites until they form stiff peaks. Whisk in 30ml/2 tbsp of the caster sugar until the meringue is thick and glossy, then fold in the remainder.

4 Chop 175g/6oz of the chocolate. Carefully fold into the meringue with the dates, nuts and 5ml/1 tsp of the vanilla extract. Pour into the prepared tin, spread level and bake for about 45 minutes, or until risen around the edges.

5 Allow to cool in the tin for about 10 minutes, then unmould, peel off the lining paper and leave to cool completely. Swirl the frosting over the top of the cake.

6 Melt the remaining chocolate in a double boiler or in a heatproof bowl over a pan of simmering water. Spoon into a small paper piping (icing) bag and drizzle the chocolate over the cake. Chill before serving.

Energy 441kcal/1841kJ; Fat 27.6g, Saturated Fat 9.1g; Carbohydrate 40.3g, Fibre 1.8g

Warm Lemon Syrup Cake

This delicious cake is perfect as a winter dessert.

Serves 8

3 eggs
175g/6oz/¾ cup butter, softened
175g/6oz/scant 1 cup caster (superfine) sugar
175g/6oz/1½ cups self-raising (self-rising) flour
50g/2oz/½ cup ground almonds
1.25ml/¼ tsp freshly grated nutmeg
50g/2oz/5 tbsp candied lemon peel, finely chopped
grated rind of 1 lemon
30ml/2 tbsp lemon juice
poached pears, to serve

For the syrup

175g/6oz/scant 1 cup caster sugar
juice of 3 lemons

1 Preheat the oven to 180°C/350°F/Gas 4. Grease and base-line a deep, round 20cm/8in cake tin (pan).

2 Place the butter, sugar, flour and ground almonds in a large bowl. Add the nutmeg, chopped candied lemon peel and the lemon rind and juice. Beat for 2–3 minutes, until light and fluffy.

3 Tip the mixture into the prepared tin, spread level and bake for 1 hour, or until golden and firm to the touch.

4 To make the syrup, put the sugar, lemon juice and 75ml/5 tbsp water in a pan. Heat gently, stirring, until the sugar has dissolved, then boil, without stirring, for a further 1–2 minutes.

5 Turn out the cake on to a plate with a rim. Prick the surface of the cake all over with a fork, then pour over the hot syrup. Leave to soak for about 30 minutes. Serve the cake warm with thin wedges of poached pears.

Cook's Tip

To poach the pears, peel, core and quarter 450g/1lb pears. Place in a pan with 300ml/½ pint/1¼ cups water, 75g/3oz/6 tbsp sugar and a cinnamon stick. Simmer gently until just tender. Cool in the syrup.

Energy 490kcal/2056kJ; Fat 23.9g, Saturated Fat 12.3g; Carbohydrate 67g, Fibre 1.4g

Strawberry Shortcake Gateau

A light cookie-textured sponge forms the base of this summertime dessert.

Makes one 20cm/8in round cake

225g/8oz/2 cups fresh strawberries, hulled
30ml/2 tbsp ruby port
225g/8oz/2 cups self-raising (self-rising) flour
10ml/2 tsp baking powder
75g/3oz/6 tbsp unsalted (sweet) butter, diced
40g/1½oz/3 tbsp caster (superfine) sugar
1 egg, lightly beaten
15–30ml/1–2 tbsp milk
melted butter, for brushing
250ml/8fl oz/1 cup double (heavy) cream
icing (confectioners') sugar, for dusting

1 Preheat the oven to 220°C/425°F/Gas 7. Grease and base-line two 20cm/8in shallow, round, loose-based cake tins (pans).

2 Reserve 5 strawberries, slice the remainder and marinate in the port for about 1–2 hours. Strain, reserving the port.

3 Sift the flour and baking powder into a bowl. Rub in the butter until the mixture resembles fine breadcrumbs and stir in the sugar. Work in the egg and 15ml/1 tbsp of the milk to form a soft dough, adding more milk if needed.

4 Knead briefly on a lightly floured surface and divide into two pieces. Roll out each piece, mark one into eight wedges, and transfer both to the prepared cake tins. Brush with a little melted butter and bake for 15 minutes. Cool in the tins for 10 minutes, then transfer to a wire rack to cool completely.

5 Cut the marked cake into wedges. Reserving a little cream for decoration, whip the remainder until it holds its shape, and fold in the reserved port and marinated strawberry slices. Spread over the round cake. Place the wedges on top tilting them at a slight angle, and dust with icing sugar.

6 Whip the remaining cream and use to pipe swirls on each wedge. Halve the reserved strawberries and decorate the cake.

Energy 2911kcal/12118kJ; Fat 204.9g, Saturated Fat 124.7g; Carbohydrate 239.1g, Fibre 9.4g

Almond and Raspberry Roll

A light and airy sponge cake is rolled up with a fresh cream and raspberry filling for a decadent tea-time treat.

Makes one 23cm/9in long roll

3 eggs
75g/3oz/6 tbsp caster (superfine) sugar
50g/2oz/½ cup plain (all-purpose) flour
30ml/2 tbsp ground almonds
caster (superfine) sugar, for dusting
250ml/8fl oz/1 cup double (heavy) cream
225g/8oz/1⅓ cups fresh raspberries
16 flaked almonds, toasted, to decorate

1 Preheat the oven to 200°C/400°F/Gas 6. Grease a 33 x 23cm/13 x 9in Swiss roll tin (jelly roll pan) and line with baking parchment. Grease the paper.

2 Whisk the eggs and sugar in a heatproof bowl until blended. Place the bowl over a pan of simmering water and whisk until thick and pale.

3 Whisk off the heat until cool. Sift over the flour and almonds, and fold in gently.

4 Transfer to the prepared tin and bake for 10–12 minutes, until risen and springy to the touch.

5 Invert the cake in its tin on to baking parchment dusted with caster sugar. Leave to cool, then remove the tin and lining paper.

6 Reserve a little cream, then whip the remainder until it holds its shape. Fold in all but 8 raspberries and spread the mixture over the cooled cake, leaving a narrow border. Roll the cake up and sprinkle with caster sugar.

7 Whip the reserved cream until it just holds its shape, and spoon or pipe a line along the top of the roll in the centre. Decorate the cream with the reserved raspberries and toasted flaked almonds.

Energy 2166kcal/9012kJ; Fat 169g, Saturated Fat 89.8g; Carbohydrate 133.9g, Fibre 9.4g

Orange and Walnut Swiss Roll

This unusual cake is tasty enough to serve alone, but you could also pour over some single (light) cream.

Makes one 23cm/9in long roll

4 eggs, separated
115g/4oz/generous ½ cup caster (superfine) sugar
115g/4oz/1 cup very finely chopped walnuts
a pinch of cream of tartar
a pinch of salt
icing (confectioners') sugar, for dusting

For the filling

300ml/½ pint/1¼ cups whipping cream
15ml/1 tbsp caster (superfine) sugar
grated rind of 1 orange
15ml/1 tbsp orange-flavoured liqueur

1 Preheat the oven to 180°C/350°F/Gas 4. Line a 30 x 23cm/12 x 9in Swiss roll tin (jelly roll pan) with baking parchment and grease the paper.

2 Beat the egg yolks and sugar until thick. Stir in the walnuts. In another bowl beat the egg whites with the cream of tartar and salt until stiffly peaking. Fold into the walnut mixture.

3 Pour the mixture into the prepared tin and level the top. Bake for 15 minutes. Invert the cake on to baking parchment dusted with icing sugar. Peel off the lining paper. Roll up the cake with the sugared paper. Leave to cool.

4 For the filling, whip the cream until softly peaking. Fold in the caster sugar, orange rind and liqueur.

5 Unroll the cake. Spread with the filling, then re-roll. Chill. To serve, dust with icing sugar.

Cook's Tip
Rolling up the Swiss roll (jelly roll) while still warm ensures that it will re-roll around its cream filling when it is cold without cracking.

Energy 2788kcal/11573kJ; Fat 221.9g, Saturated Fat 88.3g; Carbohydrate 151.4g, Fibre 4g

Chocolate Roll

Fresh cream in a chocolate roll is always popular.

Makes one 33cm/13in long roll

225g/8oz plain (semisweet) chocolate
45ml/3 tbsp water
30ml/2 tbsp rum, brandy or strong coffee
7 eggs, separated
175g/6oz/scant 1 cup caster (superfine) sugar
1.5ml/¼ tsp salt
icing (confectioners') sugar, for dusting
350ml/12fl oz/1½ cups whipping cream

1 Preheat the oven to 180°C/350°F/Gas 4. Line and grease a 38 x 33cm/15 x 13in Swiss roll tin (jelly roll pan) with baking parchment. Combine the chocolate, water and rum or other flavouring in the top of a double boiler or in a heatproof bowl over a pan of simmering water. Heat until melted. Set aside.

2 With an electric mixer, beat the egg yolks and sugar until thick. Stir in the melted chocolate. In another bowl, beat the egg whites and salt until they hold stiff peaks. Fold a large dollop of egg whites into the yolk mixture to lighten it, then carefully fold in the rest of the egg whites.

3 Pour the mixture into the tin and smooth evenly with a metal spatula. Bake for 15 minutes. Remove from the oven, cover with baking parchment and a damp cloth. Leave to stand for 1–2 hours. With an electric mixer, whip the cream until stiff. Set aside.

4 Run a knife along the inside edge of the tin to loosen the cake, then invert the cake on to a sheet of baking parchment that has been dusted with icing sugar.

5 Whip the cream until it holds its shape. Peel off the lining paper. Spread with an even layer of whipped cream, then roll up the cake using the sugared paper. Chill for several hours. Before serving, dust with an even layer of icing sugar.

Energy 3732kcal/15572kJ; Fat 242.9g, Saturated Fat 137g; Carbohydrate 330g, Fibre 5.6g

Apricot Brandy-Snap Roulade

A magnificent combination of soft and crisp textures, this cake looks impressive and is easy to prepare.

Makes one 33cm/13in long roll

4 eggs, separated
7.5ml/1½ tsp fresh orange juice
115g/4oz/generous ½ cup caster (superfine) sugar
175g/6oz/1½ cups ground almonds
4 brandy snaps, crushed, to decorate

For the filling

150g/5oz canned apricots, drained
300ml/½ pint/1¼ cups double (heavy) cream
25g/1oz/¼ cup icing (confectioners') sugar

1 Preheat the oven to 190°C/375°F/Gas 5. Base-line and grease a 33 x 23cm/13 x 9in Swiss roll tin (jelly roll pan).

2 Beat together the egg yolks, orange juice and sugar until thick and pale, about 10 minutes. Fold in the ground almonds.

3 Whisk the egg whites until they hold stiff peaks. Fold into the almond mixture, then transfer to the Swiss roll tin and smooth the surface.

4 Bake for 20 minutes, or until a skewer inserted into the centre comes out clean. Leave to cool in the tin, covered with a just-damp dish towel.

5 To make the filling, process the apricots in a blender or food processor until smooth. Whip the cream and icing sugar until it holds soft peaks. Fold in the apricot purée.

6 Spread the crushed brandy snaps over a sheet of baking parchment. Spread one-third of the cream mixture over the cake, then carefully invert it on to the brandy snaps. Peel off the lining paper.

7 Use the remaining cream mixture to cover the whole cake, then roll up the roulade from a short end, being careful not to disturb the brandy snap coating. Transfer the roulade to a serving dish.

Energy 3674kcal/15272kJ; Fat 291.3g, Saturated Fat 114.1g; Carbohydrate 208.1g, Fibre 14.7g

Apricot and Orange Roulade

This sophisticated dessert is very good served with a spoonful of thick yogurt or crème fraîche.

Makes one 33cm/13in long roll

4 egg whites
115g/4oz/generous ½ cup golden caster (superfine) sugar
50g/2oz/½ cup plain (all-purpose) flour
finely grated rind of 1 orange
45ml/3 tbsp orange juice

For the filling

115g/4oz/½ cup ready-to-eat dried apricots
150ml/¼ pint/⅔ cup orange juice

For the decoration

10ml/2 tsp icing (confectioners') sugar
shredded orange rind

1 Preheat the oven to 200°C/400°F/Gas 6. Base-line and grease a 33 x 23cm/13 x 9in Swiss roll tin (jelly roll pan).

2 Place the egg whites in a large bowl and whisk until they hold soft peaks. Gradually add the sugar, whisking well between each addition, until all of the sugar has been incorporated.

3 Fold in the flour, orange rind and juice. Spoon the mixture into the prepared tin and spread it evenly.

4 Bake the cake for 15–18 minutes, or until the sponge is firm and light golden in colour. Turn out on to a sheet of baking parchment and roll it up loosely from one short side. Leave to cool completely.

5 Roughly chop the apricots and place them in a pan with the orange juice. Cover and leave to simmer until most of the liquid has been absorbed. Purée the apricots in a food processor or blender until smooth.

6 Unroll the roulade and spread with the apricot mixture. Roll up. To decorate, arrange strips of paper diagonally across the roll, sprinkle lightly with icing sugar and then remove the paper. Sprinkle the top with orange rind.

Energy 1145kcal/4878kJ; Fat 1.5g, Saturated Fat 0.1g; Carbohydrate 270.4g, Fibre 9g

Classic Cheesecake

Dust the top of the cheesecake with icing (confectioners') sugar to decorate, if you wish.

Serves 8

50g/2oz/⅔ cup crushed digestive cookies (graham crackers)
900g/2lb/4 cups cream cheese, at room temperature
245g/8¾oz/ generous 1¼ cups sugar
grated rind of 1 lemon
45ml/3 tbsp lemon juice
5ml/1 tsp vanilla extract
4 eggs

1 Preheat the oven to 160°C/325°F/Gas 3. Grease a 20cm/8in springform tin (pan).

2 Place on a 30cm/12in circle of foil. Press it up the sides to seal tightly. Press the crushed cookies into the base of the tin.

3 Beat the cream cheese until smooth. Add the sugar, lemon rind and juice. Add the vanilla extract, and beat until blended. Beat in the eggs, one at a time.

4 Pour into the prepared tin. Set the tin in a larger baking tray and place in the oven. Pour enough hot water into the outer tray to come 2.5cm/1in up the side of the tin.

5 Bake until the top is golden brown, about 1½ hours. Cool in the tin.

6 Run a knife around the edge to loosen, then remove the rim of the tin. Chill for at least 4 hours before serving.

Cook's Tips
- *For a perfect cheesecake bring all the ingredients to room temperature first.*
- *Use a springform tin (pan) if possible.*
- *Don't open the oven door during baking.*
- *Cool slowly away from draughts.*
- *Chill the cake before removing the base of the pan.*

Energy 680kcal/2823kJ; Fat 57.5g, Saturated Fat 34.8g; Carbohydrate 36.3g, Fibre 0.1g

Chocolate Cheesecake

Substitute digestive cookies (graham crackers) for the base for a change.

Serves 10–12

275g/10oz plain (semisweet) chocolate
1.1kg/2½lb/5 cups cream cheese, at room temperature
200g/7oz/1 cup caster (superfine) sugar
10ml/2 tsp vanilla extract
4 eggs
15ml/1 tbsp unsweetened cocoa powder
175ml/6fl oz/¾ cup sour cream

For the base
200g/7oz/2⅓ cups crushed chocolate cookies
75g/3oz/6 tbsp butter, melted
2.5ml/½ tsp ground cinnamon

1 Preheat the oven to 180°C/350°F/Gas 4. Grease the base and sides of a 23 x 7.5cm/9 x 3in springform tin (pan).

2 For the base, thoroughly mix the crushed cookies with the butter and cinnamon in a large bowl. Press the mixture into the base of the prepared tin.

3 Melt the chocolate in the top of a double boiler or in a heatproof bowl over a pan of simmering water. Set aside to cool slightly.

4 Beat the cream cheese until smooth. Add the sugar and vanilla extract and beat until blended. Beat in the eggs one at a time, mixing well after each addition.

5 Stir the cocoa powder into the sour cream. Add to the cream cheese mixture. Stir in the melted chocolate.

6 Pour the cream cheese mixture over the crust. Bake for 1 hour. Cool in the tin, then remove the rim. Chill before serving.

Variation
For a sweeter, less intense flavour, use milk chocolate instead of plain (semisweet) chocolate.

Energy 772kcal/3204kJ; Fat 64.1g, Saturated Fat 38.9g; Carbohydrate 43.8g, Fibre 1.1g

Marbled Cheesecake

A cheesecake with a difference: marbled chocolate and vanilla.

Serves 10

900g/2lb/4 cups cream cheese, at room temperature
200g/7oz/1 cup caster (superfine) sugar
4 eggs
5ml/1 tsp vanilla extract
50g/2oz/½ cup unsweetened cocoa powder, dissolved in 75ml/5 tbsp hot water
65g/2½oz/1 cup crushed digestive cookies (graham crackers)

1 Preheat the oven to 180°C/350°F/Gas 4. Grease and base-line a 20 x 7.5cm/8 x 3in cake tin (pan).

2 With an electric mixer, beat the cheese until smooth and creamy. Add the sugar and beat to incorporate. Beat in the eggs, one at a time. Do not overmix.

3 Divide the mixture between two bowls. Stir the vanilla extract into one, then add the chocolate mixture to the other.

4 Pour a cupful of the vanilla mixture into the centre of the tin to make an even layer. Slowly pour over a cupful of chocolate mixture in the centre. Repeat, alternating cupfuls of the batter in a circular pattern until both are used up.

5 Set the tin in a larger baking tray and pour in hot water to come 4cm/1½in up the sides of the cake tin. Bake until the top of the cake is golden, about 1½ hours. It will rise during baking but will sink later. Leave to cool in the tin on a rack.

6 To turn out, run a knife around the inside edge. Place a flat plate, bottom-side up, over the tin and invert on to the plate.

7 Sprinkle the crushed cookies evenly over the base, gently place another plate over them, and invert again.

8 Cover and chill for at least 3 hours, or overnight. To serve, cut slices with a sharp knife dipped in hot water.

Energy 552kcal/2287kJ; Fat 47.5g, Saturated Fat 28.6g; Carbohydrate 26.3g, Fibre 0.8g

Baked Cheesecake with Fresh Fruits

Vary the fruit decoration to suit the season for this rich, creamy dessert.

Serves 12

175g/6oz/2 cups crushed digestive cookies (graham crackers)
50g/2oz/¼ cup unsalted (sweet) butter, melted
450g/1lb/2 cups curd (farmer's) cheese
150ml/¼ pint/⅔ cup sour cream
115g/4oz/generous ½ cup caster (superfine) sugar
3 eggs, separated
grated rind of 1 lemon
30ml/2 tbsp Marsala
2.5ml/½ tsp almond extract
50g/2oz/½ cup ground almonds
50g/2oz/⅓ cup sultanas (golden raisins)
450g/1lb prepared mixed fruits, such as figs, cherries, peaches and strawberries, to decorate

1 Preheat the oven to 180°C/350°F/Gas 4. Grease and line the sides of a 25cm/10in round springform tin (pan) with baking parchment. Combine the cookies and butter, and press into the base of the tin. Chill for 20 minutes.

2 For the cake mixture, beat together the cheese, cream, sugar, egg yolks, lemon rind, Marsala and almond extract until smooth and creamy.

3 Whisk the egg whites until stiff and fold into the cheese mixture with the almonds and sultanas until evenly combined. Pour over the cookie base and bake for 45 minutes, until risen and just set in the centre.

4 Leave in the tin until completely cold. Carefully remove the tin and peel away the lining paper.

5 Chill the cheesecake for at least 1 hour before decorating with the prepared fruits, just before serving.

Cook's Tip
Don't add the fruit topping in advance or it will make the cake soggy.

Energy 296kcal/1238kJ; Fat 18g, Saturated Fat 9g; Carbohydrate 27.1g, Fibre 1.1g

Tofu Berry "Cheesecake"

Strictly speaking, this summery "cheesecake" is not a cheesecake at all, as it's based on tofu – but who would guess?

Serves 6

50g/2oz/¼ cup margarine
30ml/2 tbsp apple juice
115g/4oz/5¾ cups bran flakes

For the filling

275g/10oz/1½ cups silken tofu or low-fat soft cheese
200g/7oz/scant 1 cup natural (plain) yogurt
15ml/1 tbsp/1 sachet powdered gelatine
60ml/4 tbsp apple juice

For the topping

175g/6oz/1½ cups mixed summer soft fruits, such as strawberries, raspberries, redcurrants, blackberries
30ml/2 tbsp redcurrant jelly
30ml/2 tbsp hot water

1 Place the margarine and apple juice in a pan and heat gently until melted. Crush the cereal and stir it into the pan. Spoon into a 23cm/9in round flan tin (tart pan) and press down firmly. Leave to set.

2 For the filling, place the tofu or low-fat soft cheese and yogurt in a food processor or blender and process until smooth. Dissolve the gelatine in the apple juice and stir into the tofu mixture.

3 Spread the tofu mixture over the chilled base, smoothing it evenly. Chill until set.

4 Remove the flan tin and place the "cheesecake" on a serving plate. Arrange the soft fruits over the top. Melt the redcurrant jelly with the hot water. Leave it to cool, and then spoon it over the fruit to serve.

Cook's Tip
For a vegetarian version use vegetarian gelatine.

Energy 204kcal/854kJ; Fat 9.5g, Saturated Fat 0.5g; Carbohydrate 23.2g, Fibre 2.8g

Baked Blackberry Cheesecake

The first scented blackberries of the season make this cheesecake truly scrumptious. Serve with a dollop of cream if you like.

Serves 6

175g/6oz/¾ cup cottage cheese
150g/5oz/scant ¾ cup natural (plain) yogurt
15ml/1 tbsp plain (all-purpose) wholemeal (whole-wheat) flour
25g/1oz/2 tbsp golden caster (superfine) sugar
1 egg
1 egg white
finely grated rind and juice of ½ lemon
200g/7oz/scant 2 cups fresh or frozen and thawed blackberries

1 Preheat the oven to 180°C/350°F/Gas 4. Lightly grease and base-line an 18cm/7in shallow round cake tin (pan) with baking parchment.

2 Place the cottage cheese in a food processor or blender and process until smooth. Place in a bowl, then add the yogurt, flour, sugar, egg and egg white, and mix. Add the lemon rind, juice and blackberries, reserving a few.

3 Transfer the mixture to the prepared tin and bake for 30–35 minutes, or until just set. Turn off the oven and leave the cake in it for a further 30 minutes.

4 Run a knife around the edge of the cheesecake and turn it out. Remove the lining paper and place the cheesecake on a warm serving plate.

5 Decorate the cheesecake with the reserved blackberries and serve warm.

Cook's Tip
Wild blackberries are the best for this cheesecake, but if you are unable to gather any, use cultivated or frozen ones instead.

Energy 88kcal/368kJ; Fat 2.4g, Saturated Fat 1.1g; Carbohydrate 9.9g, Fibre 1.1g

Coffee, Peach and Almond Daquoise

Makes one 23cm/9in gateau
5 eggs, separated
425g/15oz/generous 2 cups caster (superfine) sugar
15ml/1 tbsp cornflour (cornstarch)
175g/6oz/1½ cups ground almonds, toasted
135ml/4½fl oz/ generous ½ cup milk
275g/10oz/1¼ cups unsalted (sweet) butter, diced
45–60ml/3–4 tbsp coffee extract
2 x 400g/14oz cans peach halves in juice, drained
65g/2½oz/generous ½ cup flaked (sliced) almonds, toasted
icing (confectioners') sugar, for dusting
a few fresh mint leaves, to decorate

1 Preheat the oven to 150°C/300°F/Gas 2. Draw three 23cm/9in circles on to baking parchment and invert on to baking sheets.

2 Whisk the egg whites until stiff. Gradually whisk in 275g/10oz/scant 1½ cups of the sugar until thick and glossy. Fold in the cornflour and almonds. Using a 1cm/½in plain icing nozzle, pipe the meringue to cover the circles drawn on the paper. Bake for 2 hours. Turn on to wire racks to cool.

3 For the pastry cream, beat together the egg yolks and remaining sugar until thick and pale. Heat the milk in a small pan to boiling point and beat into the egg mixture. Return to the pan and heat until the mixture coats the back of a spoon. Strain into a large bowl and beat until lukewarm. Gradually beat in the butter until glossy. Beat in the coffee extract.

4 Trim the meringues and crush the trimmings. Reserve 3 peach halves, chop the rest. Divide the pastry cream between two bowls, and fold the peaches into one bowl with the crushed meringue. Use to sandwich the meringues together and place on a serving plate.

5 Ice the cake with the plain pastry cream. Cover the top with flaked almonds and dust generously with icing sugar. Thinly slice the reserved peaches and use to decorate the cake edge. Add some mint leaves.

Energy 5984kcal/24978kJ; Fat 390.1g, Saturated Fat 163.1g; Carbohydrate 560.1g, Fibre 24.2g

Mocha Brazil Layer Torte

Makes one 20cm/8in round cake
3 egg whites
115g/4oz/generous ½ cup caster (superfine) sugar
15ml/1 tbsp coffee extract
75g/3oz/¾ cup brazil nuts, toasted and finely ground
20cm/8in chocolate sponge cake

For the icing
175g/6oz/1 cup plain (semisweet) chocolate chips
30ml/2 tbsp coffee extract
30ml/2 tbsp water
600ml/1 pint/2½ cups double (heavy) cream, whipped

For the decoration
12 chocolate triangles
12 chocolate-coated coffee beans

1 Preheat the oven to 150°C/300°F/Gas 2. Draw two 20cm/8in circles on baking parchment and place on a baking sheet. Grease, base-line and flour a 20cm/8in round springform tin (pan).

2 Whisk the egg whites until stiff. Whisk in the sugar until glossy. Fold in the coffee extract and nuts. Using a 1cm/½in plain nozzle, pipe to cover circles drawn on the paper.

3 Bake the meringues for 2 hours, then remove from the oven and leave to cool. Increase the oven temperature to 180°C/350°F/Gas 4.

4 To make the icing, melt the chocolate chips, coffee extract and water in a bowl over a pan of simmering water. Remove from the heat and fold in the whipped cream.

5 Cut the cake into three equal layers. Trim the meringue discs to the same size and assemble the cake with a layer of sponge, a little icing and a meringue disc, ending with sponge.

6 Reserve a little of the remaining icing; use the rest to cover the cake completely, forming a swirling pattern over the top.

7 Using the reserved icing, and a piping (icing) bag with a star nozzle, pipe 24 small rosettes on top of the cake. Top alternately with the coffee beans and the chocolate triangles.

Energy 6236kcal/25900kJ; Fat 501.5g, Saturated Fat 242g; Carbohydrate 395g, Fibre 7.6g

Fresh Fruit Genoese

This Italian classic can be made with any selection of seasonal fruits.

Serves 8–10

For the sponge

175g/6oz/1 ½ cups plain (all-purpose) flour
a pinch of salt
4 eggs
115g/4oz/generous ½ cup caster (superfine) sugar
90ml/6 tbsp orange-flavoured liqueur

For the filling and topping

60ml/4 tbsp vanilla sugar
600ml/1 pint/2 ½ cups double (heavy) cream
450g/1lb mixed fresh fruits
150g/5oz/1 ¼ cups chopped pistachio nuts
60ml/4 tbsp apricot jam, warmed and sieved

1 Preheat the oven to 180°C/350°F/Gas 4. Grease and line the base of a 20cm/8in springform cake tin (pan) with baking parchment.

2 Sift the flour and salt together three times, then set aside. Using an electric mixer, beat the eggs and sugar together for 10 minutes until thick and pale.

3 Fold the flour mixture gently into the egg and sugar mixture. Transfer the cake mixture to the prepared tin and bake for 30–35 minutes. Leave the cake in the tin for about 5 minutes, and then transfer to a wire rack, remove the paper and cool completely.

4 Cut the cake horizontally into two layers, and place one layer on a plate. Sprinkle both layers with liqueur.

5 To make the filling and topping, add the vanilla sugar to the cream and whisk until the cream holds soft peaks. Spread two-thirds of the cream over the cake base layer and top with half the fruit.

6 Top with the second layer and spread the top and sides with the remaining cream. Press the nuts around the sides, arrange the remaining fruit on top. Brush the fruit with the warmed apricot jam.

Energy 815kcal/3411kJ; Fat 43g, Saturated Fat 21.8g; Carbohydrate 99.6g, Fibre 2g

Fruit Gateau with Heartsease

This strawberry gateau would be lovely to serve as a dessert at a summer lunch party in the garden.

Makes one ring cake

90g/3 ½oz/scant ½ cup soft margarine
90g/3 ½oz/½ cup caster (superfine) sugar
10ml/2 tsp clear honey
150g/5oz/1 ¼ cups self-raising (self-rising) flour
2.5ml/½ tsp baking powder
30ml/2 tbsp milk
2 eggs
15ml/1 tbsp rose water
15ml/1 tbsp Cointreau

To decorate

16 heartsease pansy flowers
1 egg white, lightly beaten
caster (superfine) sugar
icing (confectioners') sugar
450g/1lb/4 cups strawberries
strawberry leaves

1 Preheat the oven to 190°C/375°F/Gas 5. Grease and lightly flour a ring mould. Put the soft margarine, sugar, honey, flour, baking powder, milk and eggs into a mixing bowl and beat well for 1 minute. Add the rose water and the Cointreau, and mix well.

2 Pour the mixture into the mould and bake for 40 minutes. Allow to stand for a few minutes, and then turn out on to a serving plate.

3 Crystallize the heartsease pansies by painting them with the lightly beaten egg white and sprinkling with caster sugar. Leave to dry thoroughly.

4 Sift icing sugar over the cake. Fill the centre of the ring with strawberries – if they will not all fit, place some around the edge. Decorate with the crystallized heartsease flowers and some strawberry leaves.

Cook's Tip

Rose water is distilled from rose petals and water, and it is not only useful for cakes but can also be added to ice creams and sorbets, jams, jellies, milk puddings and fruit salads.

Energy 1586kcal/6630kJ; Fat 86.1g, Saturated Fat 3.5g;Carbohydrate 180.3g, Fibre 6.5g

Nut and Apple Gateau

Pecan nuts and apples give this gateau a beautiful texture and flavour.

Makes one 23cm/9in round cake

115g/4oz/⅔ cup pecan nuts or walnuts, toasted
50g/2oz/½ cup plain (all-purpose) flour
10ml/2 tsp baking powder
1.5ml/¼ tsp salt
2 large cooking apples
3 eggs
225g/8oz/generous 1 cup caster (superfine) sugar
5ml/1 tsp vanilla extract
175ml/6fl oz/¾ cup whipping cream

1 Preheat the oven to 160°C/325°F/Gas 3. Line two 23cm/9in cake tins (pans) with baking parchment and grease the paper.

2 Finely chop the nuts. Reserve 25ml/1½ tbsp and place the remainder in a mixing bowl. Sift over the flour, baking powder and salt, and stir well.

3 Peel and core the apples. Cut into 3mm/⅛in dice, then stir into the flour mixture. Beat the eggs until frothy. Gradually add the sugar and vanilla extract, and beat until ribbon trails form when you lift the whisk out of the mixture, about 8 minutes. Fold in the flour mixture.

4 Pour the mixture into the prepared cake tins and bake until a skewer inserted into the centre comes out clean, about 35 minutes. Leave to stand in the tin for 10 minutes, then turn out on to a wire rack to cool.

5 Whip the cream until firm. Use half for the filling. Using a large star nozzle, pipe rosettes on the top and then sprinkle over the reserved nuts to finish.

Cook's Tip
Toast the nuts on a foil-covered grill (broiling) pan under a hot grill (broiler) or in the oven until golden brown.

Energy 2807kcal/11741kJ; Fat 168.6g, Saturated Fat 55.5g; Carbohydrate 303.2g, Fibre 10.2g

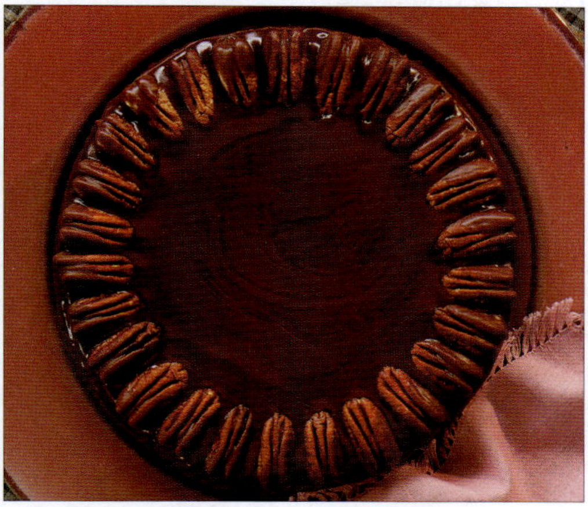

Chocolate Pecan Nut Torte

This torte uses finely ground nuts instead of flour. Toast and cool the nuts before grinding finely in a processor.

Makes one 20cm/8in round cake

200g/7oz plain (semisweet) chocolate, chopped
150g/5oz/10 tbsp unsalted (sweet) butter, diced
4 eggs
100g/3½oz/½ cup caster (superfine) sugar
10ml/2 tsp vanilla extract
115g/4oz/1 cup ground pecan nuts
10ml/2 tsp ground cinnamon
24 toasted pecan nut halves, to decorate (optional)

For the chocolate honey glaze
115g/4oz plain (semisweet) chocolate, chopped
60g/2oz/¼ cup unsalted (sweet) butter, cut into pieces
30ml/2 tbsp honey
a pinch of ground cinnamon

1 Preheat the oven to 180°C/350°F/Gas 4. Grease a 20cm/8in springform tin (pan), line with baking parchment, then grease the paper. Wrap the tin with foil.

2 Melt the chocolate and butter in a double boiler or in a heatproof bowl over a pan of simmering water, stirring until smooth. Set aside. Beat the eggs, sugar and vanilla extract until frothy. Stir in the melted chocolate and butter, ground nuts and cinnamon.

3 Pour into the tin. Place in a large roasting pan and pour boiling water into the roasting pan, to come 2cm/¾in up the side of the springform tin. Bake for 25–30 minutes, or until the edge of the cake is set, but the centre soft. Remove the foil and set on a wire rack.

4 To make the glaze, melt the chocolate, butter, honey and cinnamon as before, stirring until smooth. Remove from the heat. Dip the toasted pecan halves halfway into the glaze and place on baking parchment to set. Remove the cake from its tin and invert on to a wire rack. Remove the paper. Pour the glaze over the cake, tilting the rack to spread it. Use a metal spatula to smooth the sides. Arrange the nuts on top.

Energy 4744kcal/19729kJ; Fat 363.6g, Saturated Fat 175.2g; Carbohydrate 335.4g, Fibre 13.3g

Coconut Lime Gateau

Fresh lime and coconut give this gateau a fabulous flavour.

Makes one 23cm/9in round cake

225g/8oz/2 cups plain (all-purpose) flour
12.5ml/2½ tsp baking powder
1.5ml/¼ tsp salt
225g/8oz/1 cup butter, at room temperature
225g/8oz/generous 1 cup caster (superfine) sugar
grated rind of 2 limes
4 eggs
60ml/4 tbsp fresh lime juice
75g/3oz/1 cup desiccated (dry unsweetened shredded) coconut

For the frosting

450g/1lb/generous 2 cups granulated sugar
60ml/4 tbsp water
a pinch of cream of tartar
1 egg white, whisked until stiff

1 Preheat the oven to 180°C/350°F/Gas 4. Grease and base-line two 23cm/9in shallow round cake tins (pans). Sift together the flour, baking powder and salt.

2 Beat the butter until soft. Add the sugar and lime rind, and beat until pale and fluffy. Beat in the eggs, one at a time.

3 Gradually fold in the dry ingredients, alternating with the lime juice, then stir in two-thirds of the coconut.

4 Divide the mixture between the cake tins, level the tops and bake for 30–35 minutes. Cool in the tins on a wire rack for 10 minutes, then turn out and peel off the lining paper.

5 Bake the remaining coconut on a baking sheet until golden brown, stirring occasionally.

6 To make the frosting, heat the sugar, water and cream of tartar until dissolved, stirring. Boil to reach 120°C/250°F on a sugar thermometer. Remove from the heat and, when the bubbles subside, whisk in the egg white until thick.

7 Sandwich and cover the cake with the frosting. Sprinkle over the toasted coconut. Leave to set before serving.

Energy 5859kcal/24634kJ; Fat 256.6g, Saturated Fat 163.9g; Carbohydrate 886.4g, Fibre 17.3g

Exotic Celebration Gateau

Use any tropical fruits you can find to make a spectacular display of colours and tastes for this cream-covered confection.

Makes one 20cm/8in ring gateau

175g/6oz/¾ cup butter, softened
175g/6oz/scant 1 cup caster (superfine) sugar
3 eggs, beaten
250g/9oz/2¼ cups self-raising (self-rising) flour
30–45ml/2–3 tbsp milk
90–120ml/6–8 tbsp light rum

For the decoration

400ml/14fl oz/1⅔ cups double (heavy) cream
25g/1oz/¼ cup icing (confectioners') sugar, sifted
450g/1lb mixed fresh exotic and soft fruits, such as figs, redcurrants, star fruit (carambola) and kiwi fruit
90ml/6 tbsp apricot jam, warmed and sieved
30ml/2 tbsp warm water
icing (confectioners') sugar

1 Preheat the oven to 190°C/375°F/Gas 5. Grease and flour a deep 20cm/8in ring mould.

2 Beat together the butter and sugar until light and fluffy. Gradually beat in the eggs, then fold in the sifted flour and the milk.

3 Spoon the mixture into the ring mould. Level the top. Bake the cake for 45 minutes, or until a skewer inserted into the centre comes out clean. Turn out on to a wire rack and leave to cool completely.

4 Place the cake on a serving plate. Make holes randomly over the cake with a skewer. Drizzle over the rum and allow it to soak in.

5 To decorate, beat together the cream and icing sugar until the mixture holds soft peaks. Spread all over the cake. Arrange the fruits in the hollow centre of the cake. Mix the apricot jam and warm water together, then brush over the fruit. Sift over some icing sugar to finish.

Energy 5783kcal/24084kJ; Fat 394.7g, Saturated Fat 238.5g; Carbohydrate 481.4g, Fibre 16.3g

Chocolate and Fresh Cherry Gateau

Make this sophisticated cake for a special occasion.

Makes one 20cm/8in round cake

115g/4oz/½ cup butter
150g/5oz/¾ cup caster (superfine) sugar
3 eggs, lightly beaten
175g/6oz/1 cup plain (semisweet) chocolate chips, melted
60ml/4 tbsp Kirsch
150g/5oz/1¼ cups self-raising (self-rising) flour
5ml/1 tsp ground cinnamon
2.5ml/½ tsp ground cloves
350g/12oz fresh cherries, pitted and halved
45ml/3 tbsp morello cherry jam, warmed
5ml/1 tsp lemon juice

For the frosting
115g/4oz/⅔ cup plain chocolate chips
50g/2oz/¼ cup unsalted (sweet) butter
60ml/4 tbsp double (heavy) cream

To decorate
18 fresh cherries dipped in 75g/3oz/½ cup white chocolate chips, melted, and a few rose leaves, washed and dried

1 Preheat the oven to 160°C/325°F/Gas 3. Grease, base-line and flour a 20cm/8in round springform tin (pan).

2 Cream the butter and 115g/4oz/½ cup of the sugar until pale. Beat in the eggs. Stir in the chocolate and half the Kirsch. Fold in the flour and spices. Transfer to the tin and bake for 55–60 minutes. Cool for 10 minutes, then transfer to a wire rack.

3 For the filling, bring the cherries, the remaining kirsch and sugar to the boil, cover, and simmer for 10 minutes. Uncover for a further 10 minutes until syrupy. Leave to cool.

4 Halve the cake horizontally. Cut a 1cm/½in deep circle from the middle of the base, leaving a 1cm/½in edge. Crumble this cake into the filling mixture and fill the cut-away depression.

5 Sieve the jam and lemon juice. Brush all over the cake. For the frosting, melt all the ingredients. Cool, pour over the cake. Decorate with chocolate-dipped cherries and leaves.

Energy 5172kcal/21630kJ; Fat 287.9g, Saturated Fat 171.5g, Carbohydrate 587.6g, Fibre 16.6g

Coffee Almond Flower Gateau

This delicious cake can be made quite quickly. Ring the changes by using a coffee-flavoured sponge.

Makes one 20cm/8in round cake

475g/1lb 2oz/2¼ cups coffee-flavour butter icing
2 x 20cm/8in round sponge cakes with chopped nuts
75g/3oz plain (semisweet) chocolate
20 blanched almonds
4 chocolate-coated coffee beans

1 Reserve 60ml/4 tbsp of the butter icing for piping and use the rest to sandwich the sponge cakes together and cover the top and side of the cake. Smooth the top with a metal spatula and serrate the side with a scraper to give a ridged effect.

2 Melt the chocolate in a double boiler or in a heatproof bowl over a pan of simmering water. Remove the pan from the heat.

3 Dip half of each almond in the chocolate at a slight angle. Leave to dry on baking parchment. Leave the bowl of chocolate over the pan of hot water so it does not set.

4 Arrange the almonds on top of the cake to represent flowers. Place a chocolate-coated coffee bean for the flower centres. Spoon the remaining melted chocolate into a baking parchment piping (icing) bag. Cut a small piece off the end in a straight line. Pipe the chocolate in wavy lines over the top of the cake and in small beads around the top edge.

5 Transfer the cake to a serving plate. Place the reserved butter icing in a fresh piping bag fitted with a fine writing nozzle. Pipe beads of icing all around the bottom of the cake, then top with small beads of chocolate.

Cook's Tip
Either the quick mix sponge or the Genoese sponge cake recipes would be suitable for this cake.

Energy 5901kcal/24633kJ; Fat 377.2g, Saturated Fat 150.2g, Carbohydrate 605.1g, Fibre 13.8g

Vegan Chocolate Gateau

Containing no dairy or other animal produce, this gateau is a rare treat for vegans and tastes really delicious.

Makes one 20cm/8in gateau

275g/10oz/2½ cups self-raising (self-rising) wholemeal (whole-wheat) flour
50g/2oz/½ cup unsweetened cocoa powder
15ml/1 tbsp baking powder
250g/9oz/1¼ cups caster (superfine) sugar
a few drops of vanilla extract
135ml/9 tbsp sunflower oil
350ml/12fl oz/1½ cups water
sifted unsweetened cocoa powder and 25g/1oz/¼ cup chopped nuts, to decorate

For the chocolate fudge

50g/2oz/¼ cup soya margarine
45ml/3 tbsp water
250g/9oz/2¼ cups icing (confectioners') sugar
30ml/2 tbsp unsweetened cocoa powder

1 Preheat the oven to 160°C/325°F/Gas 3. Grease and line a deep 20cm/8in round cake tin (pan) with baking parchment, and grease the paper.

2 Sift the flour, cocoa and baking powder into a large mixing bowl. Add the sugar and vanilla extract, then gradually beat in the oil and water to make a smooth batter. Pour the mixture into the cake tin and smooth the surface.

3 Bake for 45 minutes. Leave in the tin for 5 minutes, then turn out on to a wire rack to cool completely. Cut the cake in half.

4 To make the chocolate fudge, gently melt the margarine with the water. Remove from the heat, add the icing sugar and cocoa powder, and beat until smooth and shiny. Allow to cool until firm enough to spread and pipe.

5 Place a layer of cake on a serving plate and spread over two-thirds of the chocolate fudge. Top with the other layer of cake. Fill a piping (icing) bag with the remaining chocolate fudge. Using a large star nozzle, pipe chocolate fudge stars over the top of the cake. Sprinkle with cocoa powder and chopped nuts.

Energy 4418kcal/18619kJ; Fat 158.8g; Saturated Fat 21.8g; Carbohydrate 746.7g; Fibre 10.1g

Black Forest Gateau

A perfect gateau for a special tea party, or for serving as a sumptuous dinner-party dessert.

Makes one 20cm/8in gateau

5 eggs
175g/6oz/scant 1 cup caster (superfine) sugar
50g/2oz/½ cup plain (all-purpose) flour
50g/2oz/½ cup unsweetened cocoa powder
75g/3oz/6 tbsp butter, melted

For the filling

75–90ml/5–6 tbsp Kirsch
600ml/1 pint/2½ cups double (heavy) cream
425g/15oz can black cherries, drained, pitted and chopped

To decorate

chocolate curls
15–20 fresh cherries, preferably with stems
icing (confectioners') sugar

1 Preheat the oven to 180°C/350°F/Gas 4. Base-line and grease two deep 20cm/8in round cake tins (pans).

2 Beat together the eggs and sugar for 10 minutes, or until thick and pale. Sift over the flour and cocoa powder, and fold in gently. Trickle in the melted butter and fold in gently.

3 Transfer the mixture to the cake tins. Bake for 30 minutes, or until springy to the touch.

4 Leave in the tins for 5 minutes, then turn out on to a wire rack, peel off the lining paper and leave to cool. Cut each cake in half horizontally and sprinkle with the Kirsch.

5 Whip the cream until softly peaking. Combine two-thirds of the cream with the chopped cherries. Place a layer of cake on a serving plate and spread with one-third of the filling. Repeat twice, and top with a layer of cake. Use the reserved cream to cover the top and side of the gateau.

6 Decorate the side of the gateau with chocolate curls, and place more in the centre of the top of the cake. Arrange fresh cherries around the edge and finally dredge the top with icing sugar.

Energy 5386kcal/22373kJ; Fat 423.1g; Saturated Fat 253.7g; Carbohydrate 316.8g; Fibre 10.1g

Walnut Coffee Gateau

Serves 8–10
150g/5oz/scant 1 cup walnuts
150g/5oz/¾ cup caster (superfine) sugar
5 eggs, separated
50g/2oz/scant 1 cup dry breadcrumbs
15ml/1 tbsp unsweetened cocoa powder
15ml/1 tbsp instant coffee
30ml/2 tbsp rum or lemon juice
1.5ml/¼ tsp salt
90ml/6 tbsp redcurrant jelly, warmed
chopped walnuts, for decorating

For the frosting
225g/8oz plain (semisweet) chocolate
750ml/1¼ pint/3 cups whipping cream

1 To make the frosting combine the chocolate and cream in the top of a double boiler until the chocolate melts. Cool, then cover and chill overnight, or until the mixture is firm.

2 Preheat the oven to 180°C/350°F/Gas 4. Line and grease a 23 x 5cm/9 x 2in cake tin (pan). Grind the nuts with 45ml/3 tbsp of the sugar in a food processor, blender or coffee grinder.

3 With an electric mixer, beat the egg yolks and remaining sugar until thick and pale. Fold in the walnuts. Stir in the breadcrumbs, cocoa, coffee and rum or lemon juice.

4 In another bowl, beat the egg whites with the salt until they hold stiff peaks. Fold carefully into the walnut mixture. Pour the meringue batter into the prepared tin and bake until the top of the cake springs back when touched, about 45 minutes. Allow the cake to stand for 5 minutes, then turn out and cool, before slicing the cake in half horizontally.

5 With an electric mixer, beat the chocolate frosting mixture on low speed until it becomes lighter, about 30 seconds. Brush some of the redcurrant jelly over the cut cake layer. Spread with some of the chocolate frosting, then sandwich with the remaining cake layer. Brush the top of the cake with some more jelly, then cover the side and top with the remaining frosting. Make a starburst pattern with a knife and sprinkle chopped walnuts around the edge.

Energy 651kcal/2707kJ; Fat 50.1g; Saturated Fat 24.9g; Carbohydrate 43.5g; Fibre 1.8g

Sachertorte

A rich cake, ideal for a self-confessed chocoholic.

Makes one 23cm/9in round cake
115g/4oz plain (semisweet) chocolate
90g/3oz/6 tbsp unsalted (sweet) butter, at room temperature
50g/2oz/¼ cup caster (superfine) sugar
4 eggs, separated, plus 1 egg white
1.5ml/¼ tsp salt
65g/2½oz/9 tbsp plain (all-purpose) flour, sifted

For the topping
75ml/5 tbsp apricot jam
250ml/8fl oz/1 cup plus 15ml/1 tbsp water
15g/½ oz/1 tbsp unsalted (sweet) butter
175g/6oz plain chocolate
75g/3oz/scant ½ cup caster (superfine) sugar
ready-made chocolate decorating icing

1 Preheat the oven to 160°C/325°F/Gas 3. Line and grease a 23cm/9in cake tin (pan). Melt the chocolate in a heatproof bowl over a pan of simmering water and set aside.

2 Cream the butter and sugar until light and fluffy. Stir in the chocolate, then beat in the egg yolks, one at a time.

3 Beat the egg whites with the salt until stiff. Fold a dollop of whites into the chocolate mixture to lighten it. Fold in the remaining whites in three batches, alternating with the sifted flour. Pour into the tin and bake until a skewer comes out clean, about 45 minutes. Turn out on to a wire rack.

4 To make the topping, melt the jam with 15ml/1 tbsp of the water, then strain for a smooth consistency. For the frosting, melt the butter and chocolate as before. In a heavy pan, dissolve the sugar in the remaining water, then boil until it reaches 107°C/225°F (thread stage) on a sugar thermometer. Plunge the base of the pan into cold water for 1 minute. Stir into the chocolate. Cool for a few minutes.

5 Brush the jam over the cake, then spread the frosting over the top and sides. Leave overnight. Decorate with chocolate icing.

Energy 3484kcal/14593kJ; Fat 190.6g; Saturated Fat 109.8g; Carbohydrate 417.9g; Fibre 9.3g

Dundee Cake

This is the perfect recipe for a festive occasion when a lighter fruit cake is required.

Makes one 20cm/8in round cake

175g/6oz/¾ cup butter
175g/6oz/¾ cup soft light brown sugar
3 eggs
225g/8oz/2 cups plain (all-purpose) flour
10ml/2 tsp baking powder
5ml/1 tsp ground cinnamon
2.5ml/½ tsp ground cloves
1.5ml/¼ tsp freshly grated nutmeg
225g/8oz/generous 1½ cups sultanas (golden raisins)
175g/6oz/generous 1 cup raisins
175g/6oz/¾ cup glacé (candied) cherries, halved
115g/4oz/¾ cup chopped mixed (candied) peel
50g/2oz/½ cup chopped blanched almonds
grated rind of 1 lemon
30ml/2 tbsp brandy
115g/4oz/1 cup whole blanched almonds, to decorate

1 Preheat the oven to 160°C/325°F/Gas 3. Grease a 20cm/8in round deep cake tin (pan) and line with baking parchment.

2 Cream the butter and sugar until pale and light. Add the eggs, one at a time, beating well after each addition.

3 Sift together the flour, baking powder and spices. Put the nutmeg, sultanas, raisins, glacé cherries, mixed peel, almonds, lemon rind and brandy into a bowl.

4 Fold the flour mixture into the egg mixture alternately with the fruit mixture until evenly combined. Transfer to the cake tin. Smooth the surface, then make a small dip in the centre so that the cake will not rise to a point.

5 Decorate the top of the cake by pressing the blanched almonds in decreasing circles over the entire surface. Bake for 2–2¼ hours, or until a skewer inserted in the centre of the cake comes out clean.

6 Leave to cool in the tin for 30 minutes then transfer the cake to a wire rack to cool completely.

Energy 5855kcal/24598kJ; Fat 258.1g, Saturated Fat 103.6g, Carbohydrate 831.7g, Fibre 34.3g

Vegan Dundee Cake

As it contains neither eggs nor dairy products, this cake is suitable for vegans.

Makes one 20cm/8in square cake

350g/12oz/3 cups plain (all-purpose) wholemeal (whole-wheat) flour
5ml/1 tsp mixed (apple pie) spice
175g/6oz/¾ cup soya margarine
175g/6oz/¾ cup muscovado (molasses) sugar, plus 30ml/2 tbsp
175g/6oz/generous 1 cup sultanas (golden raisins)
175g/6oz/¾ cup currants
175g/6oz/generous 1 cup raisins
75g/3oz/½ cup chopped mixed (candied) peel
150g/5oz/generous ½ cup glacé (candied) cherries, halved
finely grated rind of 1 orange
30ml/2 tbsp ground almonds
25g/1oz/¼ cup chopped blanched almonds
5ml/1 tsp bicarbonate of soda (baking soda)
120ml/4fl oz/½ cup soya milk
75ml/2½fl oz/⅓ cup sunflower oil
30ml/2 tbsp malt vinegar

To decorate

mixed nuts, such as pistachio nuts, pecan nuts and macadamia nuts
glacé (candied) cherries
angelica
60ml/4 tbsp clear honey, warmed

1 Preheat the oven to 150°C/300°F/Gas 2. Grease a deep 20cm/8in square loose-based cake tin (pan) and double-line with baking parchment.

2 Sift together the flour and mixed spice in a large bowl. Rub in the soya margarine. Stir in the sugar, sultanas, currants and raisins, mixed peel, cherries, orange rind, ground almonds and blanched almonds.

3 Dissolve the bicarbonate of soda in a little of the milk. Warm the remaining milk with the oil and vinegar, and add the bicarbonate of soda mixture. Stir into the flour mixture.

4 Spoon into the tin and smooth the surface. Bake for 2½ hours. Leave in the tin for 5 minutes, then cool on a rack. Decorate with the nuts, cherries and angelica, and brush with the warmed honey to glaze the cake.

Energy 6098kcal/25669kJ; Fat 236.7g, Saturated Fat 38.2g, Carbohydrate 977.4g, Fibre 55.6g

Panforte

This rich, spicy nougat-type cake is a Christmas speciality of Siena in Italy. Choose the best-quality exotic peel you can find as it really makes a difference to the flavour.

Makes one 20cm/8in round cake

275g/10oz/1⅔ cups mixed chopped exotic (candied) peel, to include lemon orange, citron, papaya and pineapple
115g/4oz/⅔ cup unblanched almonds
50g/2oz/½ cup walnut halves
50g/2oz/½ cup plain (all-purpose) flour
5ml/1 tsp ground cinnamon
1.5ml/¼ tsp each freshly grated nutmeg, ground cloves and ground coriander
175g/6oz/scant 1 cup caster (superfine) sugar
60ml/4 tbsp water
icing (confectioners') sugar, for dusting

1 Preheat the oven to 180°C/350°F/Gas 4. Grease and base-line a 20cm/8in round loose-based cake tin (pan) with rice paper.

2 Put the mixed peel and nuts in a bowl. Sift in the flour and spices, and mix well.

3 Dissolve the caster (superfine) sugar and water in a small pan, then boil until the mixture reaches thread stage (107°C/225°F on a sugar thermometer). Pour on to the fruit mixture, stirring to coat well.

4 Transfer the cake mixture to the cake tin, pressing into the sides with a metal spoon.

5 Bake for 25–30 minutes, or until the mixture is bubbling. Cool in the tin for 5 minutes.

6 Use a lightly oiled metal spatula to work around the edges of the cake to loosen it. Remove the cake from the tin, leaving the base in place.

7 Leave to cool completely, then remove the base and dust the cake generously with icing sugar.

Energy 3233kcal/13647kJ; Fat 101.5g, Saturated Fat 8g; Carbohydrate 576.7g, Fibre 25g

Kulich

This rich Russian yeast cake is traditionally made at Eastertime.

Makes two cakes

15ml/1 tbsp active dried yeast
90ml/6 tbsp lukewarm milk
75g/3oz/6 tbsp caster (superfine) sugar
500g/1¼ lb/5 cups plain (all-purpose) flour
a pinch of saffron threads
30ml/2 tbsp dark rum
2.5ml/½ tsp ground cardamom seeds
2.5ml/½ tsp ground cumin
50g/2oz/¼ cup unsalted (sweet) butter
2 eggs plus 2 egg yolks
½ vanilla pod (bean), finely chopped
25g/1oz/2 tbsp each crystallized ginger, mixed (candied) peel, almonds and currants, chopped

For the decoration

75g/3oz/¾ cup icing (confectioners') sugar, sifted
7.5–10ml/1½–2 tsp warm water
a drop of almond extract
2 candles
blanched almonds
mixed (candied) peel

1 Blend together the yeast, milk, 25g/1oz/¼ cup sugar and 50g/2oz/½ cup flour. Leave in a warm place for 15 minutes, or until frothy. Soak the saffron in the rum for 15 minutes.

2 Sift together the remaining flour and spices and rub in the butter. Stir in the rest of the sugar. Add the yeast mixture, saffron liquid and remaining ingredients. Knead the dough until smooth. Put in an oiled bowl, cover with clear film (plastic wrap) and leave until doubled in size.

3 Preheat the oven to 190°C/375°F/Gas 5. Grease, line and flour two 500g/1¼lb coffee tins or 15cm/6in clay flowerpots.

4 Knock back (punch down) the dough and form into two rounds. Press into the tins or pots, cover and leave to rise for 30 minutes. Bake for 35 minutes for the pots or 50 minutes for the tins. Remove from the tins or pots and cool.

5 To decorate, mix together the icing sugar, water and almond extract. Pour over the cakes. Decorate with the candles, nuts and peel.

Energy 1521kcal/6432kJ; Fat 33g, Saturated Fat 16.4g; Carbohydrate 282.3g, Fibre 8.4g

Yule Log

This rich seasonal treat could provide an economical alternative to a traditional iced fruit cake.

Makes one 28cm/11in long roll

4 eggs, separated
150g/5oz/¾ cup caster (superfine) sugar
5ml/1 tsp vanilla extract
a pinch of cream of tartar
115g/4oz/1 cup plain (all-purpose) flour, sifted
250ml/8fl oz/1 cup whipping cream
300g/11oz plain (semisweet) chocolate, chopped
30ml/2 tbsp rum or Cognac
icing (confectioners') sugar, for dusting

1 Preheat the oven to 190°C/375°F/Gas 5. Grease, line and flour a 40 x 28cm/16 x 11in Swiss roll tin (jelly roll pan).

2 Whisk the egg yolks with all but 25g/1oz/¼ cup of the sugar until pale and thick. Add the vanilla extract.

3 Whisk the egg whites with the cream of tartar until they form soft peaks. Add the reserved sugar and continue whisking until the mixture is stiff and glossy.

4 Fold half the flour into the yolk mixture. Add a quarter of the egg whites and fold in to lighten the mixture. Fold in the remaining flour, then the remaining egg whites.

5 Spread the mixture in the tin. Bake for 15 minutes. Turn on to paper sprinkled with caster sugar. Roll up and leave to cool.

6 Put the cream into a small pan and bring it to the boil. Put the chocolate in a bowl and add the cream. Stir until the chocolate has melted, then beat until it is fluffy and has thickened to a spreading consistency. Mix one-third of the chocolate cream with the rum or Cognac.

7 Unroll the cake and spread with the rum mixture. Re-roll and cut off about a quarter, at an angle. Arrange to form a branch. Spread the chocolate cream over the cake. Mark with a fork, add Christmas decorations and dust with icing sugar.

Energy 3826kcal/16020kJ; Fat 208.4g, Saturated Fat 119.9g; Carbohydrate 443.4g, Fibre 11.1g

Chocolate Chestnut Roulade

A traditional version of Bûche de Nöel, the delicious French Christmas gateau.

Makes one 33cm/13in long roll

225g/8oz plain (semisweet) chocolate
50g/2oz white chocolate
4 eggs, separated
115g/4oz/generous ½ cup caster (superfine) sugar

For the chestnut filling

150ml/¼ pint/⅔ cup double (heavy) cream
225g/8oz can chestnut purée
50–65g/2–2½oz/ 4–5 tbsp icing (confectioners') sugar, plus extra for dusting
15–30ml/1–2 tbsp brandy

1 Preheat the oven to 180°C/350°F/Gas 4. Line and grease a 23 x 33cm/9 x 13in Swiss roll tin (jelly roll pan).

2 For the chocolate curls, melt 50g/2oz of the plain and all of the white chocolate in separate bowls set over pans of simmering water. When melted, spread on a non-porous surface and leave to set. Hold a long sharp knife at a 45-degree angle to the chocolate and push it along the chocolate, using a sawing motion. Put the curls on baking parchment.

3 Melt the remaining plain chocolate. Beat the egg yolks and caster (superfine) sugar until thick and pale. Stir in the chocolate.

4 Whisk the egg whites until they form stiff peaks, then fold into the chocolate mixture. Turn into the prepared tin and bake for 15–20 minutes. Cool, covered with a just-damp dish towel, on a wire rack.

5 Sprinkle a sheet of baking parchment with caster (superfine) sugar. Turn the roulade out on to it. Peel off the lining paper and trim the edges of the roulade. Cover with the dish towel.

6 To make the filling, whip the cream until softly peaking. Beat together the chestnut purée, icing sugar and brandy until smooth, then fold in the cream. Spread over the roulade and roll it up. Top with chocolate curls and dust with icing sugar.

Energy 3496kcal/14645kJ; Fat 187.3g, Saturated Fat 104.4g; Carbohydrate 424.1g, Fibre 14.9g

Chocolate Christmas Cups

These fabulous little confections would be perfect to serve during the Christmas festivities. You will need about 70–80 foil or paper sweet cases to make and serve them.

Makes about 35 cups

275g/10oz plain (semisweet) chocolate, broken into pieces
175g/6oz cooked, cold Christmas pudding
75ml/2½fl oz/⅓ cup brandy or whisky
chocolate leaves and a few crystallized cranberries, to decorate

1 Place the chocolate in a double boiler or in a bowl over a pan of hot water. Heat gently until the chocolate is melted, stirring until the chocolate is smooth.

2 Using a pastry brush, brush or coat the base and sides of about 35 paper or foil sweet cases. Allow to set, then repeat, reheating the melted chocolate if necessary, and apply a second coat. Leave to cool and set completely, 4–5 hours or overnight. Reserve the remaining chocolate.

3 Crumble the Christmas pudding in a small bowl, sprinkle with the brandy or whisky and allow to stand for 30–40 minutes, until the spirit is absorbed.

4 Spoon a little of the pudding mixture into each cup, smoothing the top. Reheat the remaining chocolate and spoon over the top of each cup to cover the surface of each cup to the edge. Leave to set.

5 When completely set, peel off the cases and place in clean foil cases. Decorate with chocolate leaves and crystallized cranberries.

Cook's Tip

To crystallize cranberries for decoration, beat an egg white until frothy. Dip each berry in egg white then in sugar. Leave to dry.

Energy 59kcal/249kJ; Fat 2.7g, Saturated Fat 1.3g; Carbohydrate 7.5g, Fibre 0.3g

Eggless Christmas Cake

This simple cake contains a wealth of fruit and nuts to give it that traditional Christmas flavour. It is decorated with large pieces of glacé (candied) fruits.

Makes one 18cm/7in square cake

75g/3oz/½ cup sultanas (golden raisins)
75g/3oz/scant ½ cup raisins
75g/3oz/scant ½ cup currants
75g/3oz/scant ½ cup glacé (candied) cherries, halved
50g/2oz/⅓ cup mixed (candied) peel
250ml/8fl oz/1 cup apple juice
25g/1oz/2 tbsp toasted hazelnuts
30ml/2 tbsp pumpkin seeds
2 pieces preserved stem ginger in syrup, chopped
finely grated rind of 1 lemon
120ml/4fl oz/½ cup milk
50ml/2fl oz/¼ cup sunflower oil
225g/8oz/2 cups self-raising (self-rising) wholemeal (whole-wheat) flour
10ml/2 tsp mixed (apple pie) spice
45ml/3 tbsp brandy or dark rum
apricot jam, for brushing
glacé (candied) fruits, to decorate

1 Soak the sultanas, raisins, currants, cherries and mixed peel in the apple juice overnight.

2 Preheat the oven to 150°C/300°F/Gas 2. Grease and line an 18cm/7in square cake tin (pan).

3 Transfer the soaked fruit to a large bowl. Add the hazelnuts, pumpkin seeds, ginger and lemon rind to the fruit.

4 Stir in the milk and oil. Sift the flour and spice into another bowl, then add to the fruit mixture with the brandy or rum. Combine thoroughly.

5 Spoon the mixture into the prepared cake tin and bake for about 1½ hours, or until the cake is golden brown and firm to the touch.

6 Turn out and cool on a wire rack. Warm the apricot jam and sieve it. Brush over the cake to glaze it and decorate with glacé fruits.

Energy 2366kcal/9987kJ; Fat 68.1g, Saturated Fat 8.6g; Carbohydrate 393.4g, Fibre 30.3g

Flourless Fruit Cake

This makes the perfect base for a birthday cake for anyone who needs to avoid eating flour.

Makes one 25cm/10in round cake

450g/1lb/1⅓ cups mincemeat
350g/12oz/2 cups dried mixed fruit
115g/4oz/½ cup ready-to eat dried apricots, chopped
115g/4oz/⅔ cup ready-to-eat dried figs, chopped
115g/4oz/½ cup glacé (candied) cherries, halved
115g/4oz/1 cup walnut pieces
225g/8oz/8–10 cups cornflakes, crushed
4 eggs, lightly beaten
410g/14½oz can evaporated milk
5ml/1 tsp mixed (apple pie) spice
5ml/1 tsp baking powder
mixed glacé (candied) fruits, chopped, to decorate (optional)

1 Preheat the oven to 150°C/300°F/Gas 2.

2 Grease a 25cm/10in round cake tin (pan), line the base and sides with a double thickness of baking parchment and grease the paper.

3 Put the mincemeat, dried mixed fruit, figs and glacé cherries into a large bowl. Beat together until well combined.

4 Add the walnut pieces and cornflakes. Stir in the eggs, evaporated milk, mixed spice and baking powder.

5 Turn into the cake tin and smooth the surface.

6 Bake for about 1¾ hours, or until a skewer inserted in the centre of the cake comes out clean.

7 Allow the cake to cool in the tin for 10 minutes, then turn out on to a wire rack, peel off the lining paper and leave to cool completely.

8 Once the cake has cooled, decorate with the chopped glacé fruits, if you like.

Energy 5252kcal/22194kJ; Fat 142.5g, Saturated Fat 23.3g; Carbohydrate 939.6g, Fibre 35.8g

Glazed Christmas Ring

Whole brazil nuts decorate this fabulous fruit-packed cake.

Makes one 25cm/10in ring cake

225g/8oz/generous 1⅓ cups sultanas (golden raisins)
175g/6oz/¾ cup raisins
175g/6oz/generous 1 cup currants
175g/6oz/1 cup dried figs, chopped
90ml/6 tbsp whisky
45ml/3 tbsp orange juice
225g/8oz/1 cup butter
225g/8oz/1cup dark soft brown sugar
5 eggs
250g/9oz/2¼ cups plain (all-purpose) flour
15ml/1 tbsp baking powder
15ml/1 tbsp mixed (apple pie) spice
115g/4oz/½ cup glacé (candied) cherries, chopped
115g/4oz/1 cup chopped brazil nuts
50g/2oz/⅓ cup chopped mixed (candied) peel
50g/2oz/½ cup ground almonds
grated rind and juice 1 orange
30ml/2 tbsp thick-cut orange marmalade

To decorate

150ml/¼ pint/⅔ cup thick-cut orange marmalade
15ml/1 tbsp orange juice
175g/6oz/¾ cup glacé (candied) cherries
115g/4oz/⅔ cup dried figs, halved
75g/3oz/½ cup whole brazil nuts

1 Put the dried fruits in a bowl, pour over 60ml/4 tbsp of the whisky and all the orange juice, and marinate overnight.

2 Preheat the oven to 160°C/325°F/Gas 3. Grease and line a 25cm/10in ring mould. Cream the butter and sugar. Beat in the eggs. Sift together the flour, baking powder and mixed spice. Fold into the egg mixture, alternating with the remaining ingredients, except the whisky. Transfer to the tin.

3 Bake for 1 hour, then reduce the oven temperature to 150°C/300°F/Gas 2 and bake for a further 1¾–2 hours.

4 Prick the cake all over and pour over the reserved whisky. Cool in the tin for 30 minutes, then transfer to a wire rack. Boil the marmalade and orange juice for 3 minutes. Stir in the fruit and nuts. Cool, then spoon over the cake and leave to set.

Energy 9132kcal/38385kJ; Fat 380.9g, Saturated Fat 158.8g; Carbohydrate 1340.7g, Fibre 58.7g

Noel Cake

If you like a traditional royal-iced Christmas cake, this is a simple design using only one icing and easy-to-pipe decorations.

Makes one 20cm/8in round cake
20cm/8in round rich fruit cake
30ml/2 tbsp apricot jam, warmed and sieved
750g/1lb 10oz marzipan
900g/2lb/6 cups royal icing
green and red food colouring

Materials/equipment
23cm/9in round silver cake board
3 baking parchment piping (icing) bags
44 large gold dragées
fine writing nozzles
2 very fine writing nozzles
2.5m/2½ yd gold ribbon, 2cm/¾in wide
2.5m/2½ yd red ribbon, 5mm/¼in wide

1 Brush the fruit cake with apricot jam, cover with the marzipan and place on the cake board.

2 Using a metal spatula flat-ice the top of the cake with two layers of royal icing and leave to dry. Ice the sides of the cake and then peak the royal icing using the metal spatula, leaving a space around the centre for the ribbon. Leave to dry. Reserve the remaining royal icing.

3 Pipe tiny beads of icing around the top edge of the cake and place a gold dragée on alternate beads.

4 Using the fine writing nozzle, write "NOEL" across the cake and pipe holly leaves, stems and berries around the top.

5 Secure the ribbons around the side of the cake. Tie a red bow and attach to the front of the cake. Use the remaining ribbon for the board. Leave to dry overnight.

6 Tint 30ml/2 tbsp of the royal icing bright green and 15ml/1 tbsp bright red. Using a very fine writing nozzle, over-pipe "NOEL" in red, then the edging beads and berries. Overpipe the holly in green with the other very fine nozzle. Leave to dry.

Energy 10111kcal/42759kJ; Fat 218.3g, Saturated Fat 43.7g, Carbohydrate 1948.7g, Fibre 36.8g

Christmas Tree Cake

No piping is involved in this bright and colourful cake, making it an easy choice.

Makes one 20cm/8in round cake
45ml/3 tbsp apricot jam
20cm/8in round rich fruit cake
900g/2lb marzipan
green, red, yellow and purple food colouring
225g/8oz/1½ cups royal icing
edible silver balls

Materials/equipment
25cm/10in round cake board

1 Warm, then sieve the apricot jam and brush the cake with it. Colour 675g/1½lb/4½ cups of the marzipan green. Use to cover the cake. Leave to dry overnight.

2 Secure the cake to the cake board with a thin layer of royal icing. Spread the icing halfway up the cake side. Press the flat side of a metal spatula into the icing, then pull away sharply to form peaks.

3 Make three different-size Christmas tree templates. Tint half the remaining marzipan a deeper green than marzipan used for the cake. Using the templates, cut out three tree shapes and arrange them on the cake.

4 Divide the remaining marzipan into three and then colour red, yellow and purple. Use a little of each marzipan to make five 9cm/3in rolls. Loop them alternately around the top edge of the cake. Make small red balls and press on to the loop ends.

5 Use the remaining marzipan to make the tree decorations. Arrange on the trees, securing with water, if necessary. Finish the cake by adding silver balls to the Christmas trees.

Cook's Tip
A rich fruit cake suitable for a Christmas cake improves with storage so remember to make yours at least 3 weeks before you begin decorating and icing.

Energy 9354kcal/39507kJ; Fat 237.3g, Saturated Fat 45.3g, Carbohydrate 1694.8g, Fibre 39.6g

Christmas Stocking Cake

A bright and happy cake that is sure to delight children at Christmas time. The stocking, packed with toys, is simple to make.

Makes one 20cm/8in square cake

20cm/8in square rich fruit cake
45ml/3 tbsp apricot jam, warmed and sieved
900g/2lb marzipan
1.2kg/2½lb/7½ cups sugarpaste icing
15ml/1 tbsp royal icing
red and green food colouring

Materials/equipment

25cm/10in square silver cake board
1.5m/1½ yd red ribbon, 2cm/¾in wide
1m/1yd green ribbon, 2cm/¾in wide

1 Brush the cake with the apricot jam and place on the cake board. Cover with marzipan.

2 Set aside 225g/8oz/1½ cups of the sugarpaste icing. Cover the cake with the remainder. Leave to dry.

3 Secure the red ribbon around the board and the green ribbon around the cake with royal icing.

4 Divide the sugarpaste in half and roll out one half. Using a template, cut out two sugarpaste stockings, one 5mm/¼in larger all round. Put the smaller one on top of the larger one.

5 Divide the other half of the sugarpaste into two and tint one red and the other green. Roll out and cut each colour into seven 1cm/½in strips. Alternate the strips on top of the stocking. Roll lightly to fuse and press the edges together. Leave to dry.

6 Shape the remaining white sugarpaste into four parcels. Trim each with red and green sugarpaste ribbons. Use the remaining red and green sugarpaste to make thin strips to decorate the cake sides. Secure in place with royal icing and stick small sugarpaste balls to cover the joins. Arrange the stocking and parcels on the cake top.

Energy 11915kcal/50432kJ; Fat 237.3g, Saturated Fat 45.3g; Carbohydrate 2373.9g, Fibre 39.6g

Marbled Cracker Cake

Here is a Christmas cake that is decorated in a most untraditional way! Sugarpaste is easy to make yourself but if you are in a hurry you can buy it.

Makes one 20cm/8in round cake

20cm/8in round rich fruit cake
45ml/3 tbsp apricot jam, warmed and sieved
675g/1½lb marzipan
750g/1¾ lb/5¼ cups sugarpaste icing
red and green food colouring
edible gold balls

Materials /equipment

wooden cocktail sticks (toothpicks)
25cm/10in round cake board
red, green and gold thin gift-wrapping ribbon
3 red and 3 green ribbon bows

1 Brush the cake with the jam. Roll out the marzipan and use to cover the cake. Leave to dry overnight.

2 Form a roll with 500g/1¼lb/3¾ cups of the sugarpaste icing. With a cocktail stick, dab a few drops of red colouring on to the icing. Repeat with the green. Knead lightly.

3 Roll out the icing until it has marbled. Brush the marzipan with water and cover with the icing. Position the cake on the cake board.

4 Colour half of the remaining sugarpaste icing red and the remainder green. Use half of each colour to make five crackers, about 6cm/2½ in long. Decorate each with a gold ball. Leave to dry on baking parchment.

5 Roll out the remaining red and green icings, and cut into 1cm/½ in wide strips. Cut into 12 red and 12 green diamonds. Attach them alternately around the top and base of the cake with water.

6 Cut the ribbons into 10cm/4in lengths. Arrange them with the crackers on top of the cake. Attach the bows with softened sugarpaste icing, positioning them between the diamonds at the top cake edge.

Energy 9858kcal/41695kJ; Fat 208.7g, Saturated Fat 43g; Carbohydrate 1908.3g, Fibre 35.3g

Greek New Year Cake

A "good luck", foil-wrapped gold coin is traditionally baked into this cake.

Makes one 23cm/9in square cake

275g/10oz/2½ cups plain (all-purpose) flour
10ml/2 tsp baking powder
50g/2oz/½ cup ground almonds
225g/8oz/1 cup butter, softened
175g/6oz/generous ¾ cup caster (superfine) sugar, plus extra for sprinkling
4 eggs
150ml/¼ pint/⅔ cup fresh orange juice
50g/2oz/⅓ cup blanched almonds
15g/½ oz/1 tbsp sesame seeds

1 Preheat the oven to 180°C/350°F/Gas 4. Grease a 23cm/9in square cake tin (pan), line with baking parchment and grease the paper.

2 Sift together the flour and baking powder and stir in the ground almonds.

3 Cream the butter and sugar until light and fluffy. Beat in the eggs, one at a time. Fold in the flour mixture, alternating with the orange juice.

4 Spoon the mixture into the prepared cake tin. Arrange the blanched almonds on top, then sprinkle over the sesame seeds. Bake for 50 minutes, or until a skewer inserted in the centre comes out clean.

5 Leave in the tin for 5 minutes, then turn out on to a wire rack and peel off the lining paper. Sprinkle with caster sugar before serving.

Cook's Tip
Be careful not to overbeat the mixture if you are using an electric whisk, as this will cause the cooked cake to sag in the middle. Scrape the mixture from the sides of the bowl as you mix so that all the ingredients are well incorporated.

Energy 4261kcal/17800kJ; Fat 266.7g, Saturated Fat 128.4g; Carbohydrate 418g, Fibre 16.1g

Starry New Year Cake

Makes one 23cm/9in round cake

23cm/9in round Madeira cake
675g/1½lb/3 cups butter icing
750g/1lb 10oz/5½ cups sugarpaste icing
grape violet and mulberry food colouring
gold, lilac shimmer and primrose sparkle powdered food colouring

Materials/equipment
fine paintbrush
star-shaped cutter
florist's wire, cut into short lengths
28cm/11in round cake board
purple ribbon with gold stars

1 Cut the cake into three layers. Sandwich together with three-quarters of the butter icing. Spread the rest thinly over the top and side of the cake.

2 Tint 500g/1¼lb/3¾ cups of the sugarpaste icing purple with the grape violet and mulberry food colouring. Roll out and use to cover the cake. Leave to dry overnight.

3 Place the cake on a sheet of baking parchment. Water down some gold and lilac food colouring. Use a paintbrush to flick each colour in turn over the cake. Leave to dry.

4 For the stars, divide the remaining sugarpaste icing into three pieces. Tint one portion purple with the grape violet food colouring, one with the lilac shimmer and one with the primrose sparkle.

5 Roll out each colour to 3mm/⅛in thick. Cut out ten stars in each colour and highlight the stars by flicking on the watered-down gold and lilac colours.

6 While the icing is soft, push the florist's wire through the middle of 15 of the stars. Leave to dry overnight. Put the cake on the board.

7 Arrange the stars on top of the cake. Secure the unwired ones with water. Secure the ribbon around the base.

Energy 6452kcal/27052kJ; Fat 326.3g, Saturated Fat 197.7g; Carbohydrate 886.7g, Fibre 7.2g

Simnel Cake

This is a traditional marzipan and fruit cake to celebrate Easter, but it is delicious at any time of the year.

Makes one 20cm/8in round cake

225g/8oz/1 cup butter, softened
225g/8oz/generous 1 cup caster (superfine) sugar
4 eggs, beaten
500g/1¼lb/3⅓ cups mixed dried fruit
115g/4oz/½ cup glacé (candied) cherries
45ml/3 tbsp sherry (optional)
275g/10oz/2½ cups plain (all-purpose) flour
15ml/1 tbsp mixed (apple pie) spice
5ml/1 tsp baking powder
675g/1½lb yellow marzipan
1 egg yolk, beaten
ribbons, sugared eggs and sugarpaste animals, to decorate

1 Preheat the oven to 160°C/325°F/Gas 3. Grease a deep 20cm/8in round cake tin (pan), line with a double thickness of baking parchment and grease the paper.

2 Beat together the butter and sugar until light and fluffy. Gradually beat in the eggs. Stir in the dried fruit, glacé cherries and sherry, if using. Sift over the flour, mixed spice and baking powder, then fold in.

3 Roll out half the marzipan to a 20cm/8in round. Spoon half of the cake mixture into the cake tin and place the round of marzipan on top. Add the other half of the cake mixture and smooth the surface.

4 Bake for 2½ hours, or until golden and springy to the touch. Leave in the tin for 15 minutes, then turn out on to a wire rack, peel off the lining paper and leave to cool.

5 Roll out the reserved marzipan to fit the cake. Brush the cake top with egg yolk and place the marzipan on top. Flute the edges and make a pattern on top with a fork. Brush with more egg yolk. Put the cake on a baking sheet and grill (broil) for 5 minutes to brown the top lightly. Cool before decorating with sugared eggs and little animals made with sugarpaste.

Energy 8108kcal/34162kJ; Fat 303.9g, Saturated Fat 132.5g; Carbohydrate 1323.3g, Fibre 33.4g

Easter Sponge Cake

This light lemon quick-mix sponge cake is decorated with lemon butter icing and cut-out marzipan flowers.

Makes one 20cm/8in round cake

3-egg quantity lemon-flavour quick-mix sponge cake
675g/1½lb/3 cups lemon-flavour butter icing
50g/2oz/½ cup flaked (sliced) almonds, toasted

To decorate

50g/2oz home-made or commercial white marzipan
green, orange and yellow food colouring

1 Preheat the oven to 160°C/325°F/Gas 3. Bake the cakes in two lined and greased 20cm/8in shallow round cake tins (pans) for 35–40 minutes, or until they are golden brown and spring back when lightly pressed in the centre.

2 Loosen the edges of the cakes with a metal spatula, turn out, remove the lining paper and cool on a wire rack.

3 Sandwich the cakes together with one-quarter of the butter icing. Spread the side of the cake evenly with one-third of the remaining butter icing.

4 Press the almonds on to the sides to cover evenly. Spread the top of the cake evenly with half the remaining icing.

5 Finish with a metal spatula dipped in hot water, spreading backwards and forwards to give an even lined effect.

6 Place the remaining icing into a nylon piping (icing) bag fitted with a medium-size gateau nozzle, and pipe a scroll edging.

7 Using the marzipan and food colouring, make six cut-out daffodils, and then ten green and eight orange cut-out marzipan flowers.

8 Arrange the flowers on the cake and leave the icing to set.

Energy 4115kcal/17189kJ; Fat 251.2g, Saturated Fat 0.5g; Carbohydrate 453g, Fibre 5.8g

Easter Egg Nest Cake

Celebrate Easter with this colourfully adorned, fresh-tasting lemon sponge cake. The marzipan nests are easy to make and could be made with sugarpaste if you prefer.

Makes one 20cm/8in ring cake

20cm/8in lemon sponge ring cake
350g/12oz/1½ cups lemon-flavour butter icing
225g/8oz marzipan
pink, green and purple food colouring
small foil-wrapped chocolate eggs

Materials/equipment
25cm/10in cake board

1 Cut the cake in half horizontally and sandwich together with one-third of the butter icing. Place on the cake board.

2 Use the remaining icing to cover the cake. Smooth the top and swirl the side with a metal spatula.

3 For the marzipan braids, divide the marzipan into three and tint the pieces pink, green and purple.

4 Cut each portion in half. Using half of each colour, roll thin sausages long enough to go around the base of the cake. Pinch the ends together, then twist the strands into a rope. Pinch the other ends to seal.

5 Place the coloured marzipan rope on the cake board around the base of the cake.

6 For the nests, take the remaining portions of coloured marzipan and divide each into five pieces. Roll each piece into a 16cm/6¼in rope.

7 Take a rope of each colour and pinch the ends together. Twist the strands to form a multicoloured rope and pinch the other ends to secure. Form into a circle. Repeat to make five nests.

8 Space the nests evenly on the cake. Place small chocolate eggs in the nests.

Energy 5187kcal/21670kJ; Fat 315.1g, Saturated Fat 115.3g; Carbohydrate 571.9g, Fibre 9.7g

Mother's Day Bouquet

A piped bouquet of flowers can bring as much pleasure as a fresh one for a Mother's Day treat.

Makes one 18cm/7in round cake

675g/1½lb/3 cups butter icing
2 x 18cm/7in round sponge cakes
green, blue, yellow and pink food colouring

Materials/equipment
serrated scraper
medium writing and petal nozzles
5 baking parchment piping bags

1 Reserve one-third of the butter icing for decorating. Sandwich together the two sponges with one-third of the remaining butter icing and place on a serving plate.

2 Cover the top and side with the remaining butter icing, smoothing the top with a metal spatula and serrating the side using a scraper.

3 Divide the reserved butter icing into four bowls. Tint the portions green, blue, yellow and pink.

4 Decorate the top of the cake first. Use medium writing nozzles for the blue and green icing and medium petal nozzles for the yellow and pink. Pipe on the vase and flowers.

5 For the side decoration, spoon the remaining yellow icing into a fresh piping bag fitted with a medium writing nozzle. Pipe the stems, then the flowers and flower centres.

6 Finish by piping green beads at the top and base edges of the cake.

Cook's Tips
- *Use paste colours rather than liquid colours when colouring icing. They are available from sugarcraft suppliers and there is a wide range of shades available.*
- *If piping your own flowers seems a little too advanced, you can use sugar flowers instead.*

Energy 7340kcal/30671kJ; Fat 436.4g, Saturated Fat 162.2g; Carbohydrate 838.7g, Fibre 9g

Mother's Day Basket

Any Mum would be thrilled to receive this delightful cake.

Makes one 15cm/6in cake

175g/6oz/1½ cups self-raising (self-rising) flour, sifted
175g/6oz/scant 1 cup caster (superfine) sugar
175g/6oz/¾ cup soft margarine
3 eggs
900g/2lb/4 cups orange-flavour butter icing

Materials/equipment

thin 15cm/6in round silver cake board
baking parchment piping (icing) bag
basketweave nozzle
foil
1m/1yd mauve ribbon, 1cm/½in wide
fresh flowers
50cm/20in spotted mauve ribbon, 3mm/⅛in wide

1 Preheat the oven to 160°C/325°F/Gas 3. Lightly grease and base-line a 15cm/6in brioche mould.

2 Place the self-raising flour, sugar, margarine and eggs in a bowl, mix together then beat for 1–2 minutes, or until smooth.

3 Transfer to the prepared mould and bake for about 1¼ hours, or until risen and golden. Leave to cool in the tin for 15 minutes and then remove from the tin and leave to cool completely.

4 Place the cooled cake upside-down on the cake board. Cover the sides with one-third of the butter icing. Using a basketweave nozzle, pipe the sides with a basketweave pattern.

5 Carefully invert the cake on to the board and spread the top with butter icing. Pipe a shell edging with the basketweave nozzle. Pipe the basketweave pattern over the cake top, starting at the edge. Leave to set.

6 Fold a strip of foil several layers thick. Wrap the plain ribbon around the strip and bend up the ends to secure the ribbon. Form the foil into a handle and press into the icing.

7 Finish by tying a posy of fresh flowers with the spotted ribbon and making a mixed ribbon bow for the handle.

Energy 8096kcal/33735kJ; Fat 572.7g, Saturated Fat 265.4g; Carbohydrate 741.6g, Fibre 5.4g

Basket Cake

This is a perfect cake for a retirement gathering or other special occasion.

Makes one basket-shaped cake

20cm/8in round Madeira cake
225g/8oz pastillage
450g/1lb/2 cups coloured butter icing
chocolates or sweets (candies) and ribbon for decoration

Materials/equipment

2 baking parchment piping (icing) bags, fitted with a plain nozzle and a basketweave nozzle

1 Cut a template from card to the same size as the top of the cake, fold it in half and cut along the fold. Roll out the pastillage fairly thinly and cut out two pieces for the lid, using the templates as a guide. Leave to dry thoroughly in a warm, dry place.

2 Coat the top of the cake with butter icing. Fill both piping bags with butter icing and pipe a plain vertical line on the side of the cake, and another about 2.5cm/1in inside the top of the cake. Pipe short lengths of basketweave across each line.

3 Pipe another plain line along the ends of the basketweave strips. Pipe the next row of basketweave strips in the spaces left between the existing strips and over the new plain line. Continue until the side of the cake and the area on the top is completely covered.

4 Brush the underside of the pastillage lid with powder food colour, then pipe a basketweave on top of the lid.

5 Divide the top of the cake in half and pipe a line of basketweave along this central line. Use two or three pieces of pastillage to support each lid half in an open position on the cake.

6 Fill the area under each lid half with chocolates or sweets, and decorate with ribbon.

Energy 5292kcal/22160kJ; Fat 285.2g, Saturated Fat 171.6g; Carbohydrate 677.4g, Fibre 7.2g

Valentine's Heart Cake

Cut-out hearts make a simple but effective decoration for a special cake. This cake could also be used to celebrate a special birthday or anniversary.

Makes one 20cm/8in square cake

20cm/8in square light fruit cake
45ml/3 tbsp apricot jam, warmed and sieved
900g/2lb marzipan
1.3kg/3lb/9 cups royal icing
115g/4oz/¾ cup sugarpaste icing
red food colouring

Materials/equipment
25cm/10in square cake board
5cm/2in heart-shaped cutter
2.5cm/1in heart-shaped cutter
4 baking parchment piping (icing) bags
1 very fine writing nozzle, 1 fine writing nozzle and 1 medium star nozzle

1 Brush the cake with the apricot jam. Roll out the marzipan and use to cover the cake. Leave to dry overnight.

2 Secure the cake on the cake board with a little royal icing. Flat-ice the cake with three or four layers of smooth icing using a metal spatula or smoother. Set aside some royal icing in an airtight container for piping.

3 Tint the sugarpaste icing red. Roll it out and cut 12 hearts with the larger cutter. Stamp out the middles with the smaller cutter. Cut four more small hearts. Dry on baking parchment.

4 Using the very fine writing nozzle, pipe wavy lines in royal icing around the four small hearts. Leave to dry.

5 Using a fresh piping bag and the star nozzle, pipe swirls around the top and base of the cake.

6 Colour 15ml/1 tbsp of the remaining royal icing red and pipe red dots on top of each white swirl with the very fine nozzle.

7 Secure the ribbon in place. Using the fine writing nozzle, pipe beads down each corner, avoiding the ribbon. Decorate the cake with the hearts, using royal icing to secure them.

Energy 13123kcal/55505kJ; Fat 336.3g, Saturated Fat 112.6g; Carbohydrate 2553.1g, Fibre 17.1g

Valentine's Box of Chocolates Cake

This cake would also make a wonderful surprise for Mother's Day.

Makes one 20cm/8in heart-shaped cake

20cm/8in heart-shaped chocolate sponge cake
275g/10oz marzipan
120ml/8 tbsp apricot jam, warmed and sieved
900g/2lb/6 cups sugarpaste icing
red food colouring
225g/8oz/about 16–20 hand-made chocolates

Materials/equipment
23cm/9in square piece of stiff card
23cm/9in square cake board
piece of string
small heart-shaped cutter
length of ribbon
small paper sweet (candy) cases

1 Place the cake on the card, draw around it and cut out the heart shape. It will be used to support the box lid. Cut through the cake horizontally just below the dome. Place the top section on the card and the base on the cake board.

2 Use the string to measure around the outside of the base. Roll the marzipan into a long sausage to the measured length. Place on the cake around the outside edge.

3 Brush both sections of the cake with apricot jam. Tint the sugarpaste icing red and cut off one-third. Cut another 50g/2oz/8 tbsp portion from the larger piece. Set aside. Use the large piece to cover the base section of cake. Use your hand to smooth the sugarpaste around the curves.

4 Stand the lid on a raised surface. Use the reserved one-third of sugarpaste icing to cover the lid. Roll out the remaining piece of icing and stamp out small hearts with the cutter. Stick them around the edge of the lid with water. Tie the ribbon in a bow and secure on top of the lid with some diluted sugarpaste.

5 Place the chocolates in the paper cases and arrange in the cake base. Position the lid slightly off-centre, to reveal the chocolates. Remove the ribbon before serving.

Energy 9848kcal/41510kJ; Fat 361.9g, Saturated Fat 40.6g; Carbohydrate 1647.4g, Fibre 10.9g

Double Heart Engagement Cake

For a celebratory engagement party, these sumptuous cakes make the perfect centrepiece.

Makes two 20cm/8in heart-shaped cakes

350g/12oz plain (semisweet) chocolate
2 x 20cm/8in heart-shaped chocolate sponge cakes
675g/1½lb/3 cups coffee-flavour butter icing
icing (confectioners') sugar, for dusting
fresh raspberries, to decorate

Materials/equipment
2 x 23cm/9in heart-shaped cake boards

1 Melt the chocolate in a double boiler or in a heatproof bowl over a pan of simmering water. Pour the chocolate on to a smooth, non-porous surface and spread it out with a metal spatula. Leave to cool until just set, but not hard.

2 To make the chocolate curls, hold a large sharp knife at a 45-degree angle to the chocolate and push it along the chocolate in short sawing movements. Leave to set on baking parchment.

3 Cut each cake in half horizontally. Use one-third of the butter icing to sandwich the cakes together. Use the remaining icing to coat the tops and sides of the cakes.

4 Place the cakes on the cake boards. Generously cover the tops and sides of the cakes with the chocolate curls, pressing them gently into the butter icing.

5 Sift a little icing sugar over the top of each cake and decorate with raspberries. Chill until ready to serve.

Variation
If you are making this cake when fresh raspberries are not available, try glacé-icing-coated physalis, crystallized fruits or tiny chocolate flowers instead.

Energy 4694kcal/19625kJ; Fat 283.8g, Saturated Fat 94.5g; Carbohydrate 520.7g, Fibre 4.4g

Sweetheart Cake

Sugarpaste is a super icing for covering a cake neatly.

Makes one 20cm/8in heart-shaped cake

20cm/8in heart-shaped light fruit cake
30ml/2 tbsp apricot jam warmed and sieved
900g/2lb marzipan
900g/2lb/6 cups sugarpaste icing
red food colouring
225g/8oz/1½ cups royal icing

Materials/equipment
25cm/10in silver heart-shaped cake board
large and medium heart-shaped plunger cutters
1m/1yd red ribbon, 2.5cm/1in wide
1m/1yd looped red ribbon, 1cm/½ in wide
50cm/20in red ribbon, 5mm/¼in wide
baking parchment piping (pastry) bag
small star nozzle
fresh red rosebud

1 Brush the cake with apricot jam, place on the cake board and cover with marzipan.

2 Cover the cake and board with sugarpaste icing. Use your hand to remove any joins. Leave to dry overnight.

3 Tint the sugarpaste icing red. Cut out 18 large and 21 medium hearts. Leave to dry on baking parchment.

4 Secure the wide ribbon around the cake board. Secure a band of the looped ribbon around the side of the cake with a bead of icing.

5 Tie a bow with long tails and attach to the side of the cake with a bead of icing.

6 Using the star nozzle, pipe a row of royal icing stars around the base of the cake and attach a medium heart to every third star. Pipe stars around the cake top, and arrange large red hearts on each one.

7 Tie a bow on to the rosebud stem and place on the cake top just before serving.

Energy 10835kcal/45851kJ; Fat 262.3g, Saturated Fat 78.2g; Carbohydrate 2148.6g, Fibre 17.1g

Cloth-of-Roses Cake

This lovely cake simply says "congratulations". It is a very pretty cake that is bound to impress your guests.

Makes one 20cm/8in round cake

20cm/8in round light fruit cake
45ml/3 tbsp apricot jam, warmed and sieved
675g/1½lb marzipan
900g/2lb/6 cups sugarpaste icing
yellow, orange and green food colouring
115g/4oz/¾ cup royal icing

Materials/equipment

25cm/10in cake board
5.5cm/2¼in plain cutter
petal cutter
thin yellow ribbon

1 Brush the cake with apricot jam. Cover with marzipan and leave to dry overnight.

2 Cut off 675g/1½lb/4½ cups of the sugarpaste icing and divide in half. Colour pale yellow and pale orange.

3 Make a baking parchment template for the orange icing by drawing a 25cm/10in circle round the cake board then, using the plain cutter, draw scallops around the outside of the circle.

4 Cover the side of the cake with yellow sugarpaste icing. Place the cake on the board. Using the template, cut out the orange sugarpaste icing. Place on the cake and bend the scallops slightly. Leave to dry overnight.

5 For the roses and leaves, cut off three-quarters of the remaining sugarpaste icing and divide into four. Tint pale yellow, deep yellow, orange, and marbled yellow and orange.

6 Make 18 roses by making a small cone of sugarpaste and then flattening five small balls of paste and attaching them to the cone. Arrange the petals. Tint the remaining icing green.

7 Cut out 24 leaves with a petal cutter. Dry on baking parchment. Secure the leaves and roses with royal icing. Decorate the cake with the ribbon.

Energy 8469kcal/35840kJ; Fat 204.1g, Saturated Fat 62.1g; Carbohydrate 1682.1g, Fibre 12.8g

Rose Blossom Wedding Cake

Serves 80

23cm/9in square rich fruit cake
15cm/6in square rich fruit cake
75ml/5 tbsp apricot jam, warmed and sieved
1.6kg/3½lb marzipan
1.6kg/3½lb/10½ cups royal icing, to coat
675g/1½lb/4½ cups royal icing, to pipe
pink and green food colouring

Materials/equipment

28cm/11in square cake board
20cm/8in square cake board
very fine writing and small star nozzles
baking parchment piping (icing) bags
thin pink ribbon
8 pink bows
3 or 4 cake pillars
12 miniature roses
a few fern sprigs

1 Brush the cakes with the jam and cover with marzipan. Leave to dry overnight, then secure to their boards with icing. Flat-ice with four layers, drying each layer overnight, then for several days.

2 Use the very fine writing nozzle to pipe double triangles in white icing on baking parchment. You will need at least 40 pieces. Tint some icing pale pink and some pale green. Using very fine writing nozzles, pipe pink dots on the corners of the top triangles and green on the corners of the lower triangles.

3 Use a pin to mark out the triangles on the tops and sides of each cake. Using a very fine writing nozzle, pipe double white lines over the pin marks, then pipe cornelli inside all the triangles. With a small star nozzle, pipe white shells around the top and base edges of each cake, between the triangles.

4 Using the very fine writing nozzles, pipe pink and green dots on the cake corners. Secure the sugar pieces to the cakes and boards with icing. Attach the ribbons and bows. Assemble the cake on the pillars and decorate with roses and fern sprigs.

Cook's Tip
Cornelli work is a series of continuous 'm' shapes piped horizontally across an area in separate horizontal lines.

Energy 253kcal/1071kJ; Fat 5.5g, Saturated Fat 1.1g; Carbohydrate 48.8g, Fibre 0.9g

Basketweave Wedding Cake

Flavour the buttercream to your preference.

Serves 150
25cm/10in, 20cm/8in and 15cm/6in square Madeira cakes
2.75kg/6lb/12 cups butter icing

Materials/equipment
30cm/12in square silver cake board
20cm/8in and 15cm/6in thin silver cake board
smooth scraper
12 small greaseproof piping (icing) bags
medium writing and basketweave nozzles
1.5m/1½yd pale lilac ribbon, 2.5cm/1in wide
2.5m/2½yd deep lilac ribbon, 5mm/¼in wide
30 fresh lilac-coloured freesias

1 Level the cake tops, then invert the cakes on to the boards and cover with butter icing. Use a smooth scraper on the sides and a metal spatula to smooth the top. Leave to set for 1 hour.

2 Pipe a line of icing with the medium writing nozzle on to the corner of the large cake, from the base to the top.

3 Using the basketweave nozzle, pipe a basketweave pattern. Pipe all around the side of the cake and neaten the top edge with a shell border, using the basketweave nozzle. Repeat for the second cake.

4 To decorate the top of the small cake, start at the edge with a straight plain line, then pipe across with the basketweave nozzle, spacing the lines equally apart.

5 When the top is complete, work the design around the sides, making sure the top and side designs align. Leave the cakes overnight to set.

6 Fit the wide and narrow lilac ribbons around the board. Use the remaining narrow ribbon to tie eight small bows with long tails. Trim off the flower stems.

7 Assemble the cakes. Decorate with the bows and flowers.

Energy 180kcal/754kJ; Fat 8.4g, Saturated Fat 5g; Carbohydrate 26.1g, Fibre 0.2g

Chocolate-iced Anniversary Cake

This attractive cake is special enough to celebrate any wedding anniversary. The unusual glossy chocolate icing looks delicious contrasted with the exotic fruits.

Makes one 20cm/8in round cake
20cm/8in round Madeira cake
475g/1lb 2oz/2¼ cups chocolate-flavour butter icing

For the chocolate icing
175g/6oz plain chocolate
150ml/¼ pint/⅔ cup single (light) cream
2.5ml/½ tsp instant coffee powder

To decorate
chocolate buttons, quartered
selection of fresh fruits, such as kiwi fruit, nectarines, peaches, apricots and physalis, peeled and sliced as necessary

Materials/equipment
medium star nozzle
baking parchment piping (icing) bag
gold ribbon, about 5mm/¼ in wide
florist's wire

1 Cut the cake horizontally into three and sandwich together with three-quarters of the butter icing. Place on a wire rack over a baking sheet.

2 To make the satin chocolate icing, put all the ingredients in a pan and melt over a very low heat until smooth. Immediately pour over the cake to coat completely. Use a metal spatula, if necessary. Allow to set.

3 Transfer the cake to a serving plate. Using a medium star nozzle, pipe butter icing scrolls around the top edge. Decorate with chocolate button pieces and fruit.

4 Make seven ribbon decorations. For each one, make two small loops from ribbon and secure the ends with a twist of florist's wire.

5 Cut the wire to the length you want and use to position the decoration in the fruit. Remove before serving.

Energy 6708kcal/28073kJ; Fat 379.1g, Saturated Fat 228.8g; Carbohydrate 800.4g, Fibre 20.6g

Silver Wedding Cake

This pretty cake is perfect for this special occasion.

Makes one 25cm/10in round cake

25cm/10in round rich or light fruit cake
60ml/4 tbsp apricot jam, warmed and sieved
1.2kg/2½lb marzipan
1.5kg/3lb/9 cups royal icing

For the petal paste

10ml/2 tsp powdered gelatine
75ml/5 tbsp cold water
10ml/2 tsp liquid glucose
10ml/2 tsp white vegetable fat
450g/1lb/4 cups icing (confectioners') sugar, sifted
5ml/1 tsp gum tragacanth, sifted
1 egg white

Materials/equipment

30cm/12in round silver cake board
1.5m/1½ yd white ribbon, 2.5cm/1in wide
2m/2yd silver ribbon, 2.5cm/1in wide
club cocktail cutter
tiny round cutter
baking parchment piping (icing) bag
very fine writing nozzle
50 large silver dragées
1.5m/1½yd silver ribbon, 5mm/¼in wide
7 silver leaves
"25" silver cake decoration

1 Brush the cake with apricot jam and cover with marzipan. Place on the board. Flat-ice the top and side of the cake with three or four layers of royal icing. Leave to dry overnight, then ice the board. Reserve the remaining royal icing. Secure the wider ribbons around the board and cake with icing.

2 For the petal paste, melt the first four ingredients in a pan set over a bowl of hot water. Mix the sugar, gum tragacanth, egg white and gelatine mixture to a paste and knead until smooth. Leave for 2 hours, then re-knead. Make 65 cut-outs using the two cutters. Leave to dry overnight.

3 Arrange 25 cut-outs around the top of the cake and secure with icing beads piped with a very fine writing nozzle. Repeat at the base. Pipe icing beads between and press a silver dragée in each. Leave to dry. Thread the thin ribbon through the cutouts. Arrange seven cut-outs and seven dragées in the centre. Position the leaves and the number "25".

Energy 14213kcal/60177kJ; Fat 322.6g, Saturated Fat 91.6g, Carbohydrate 2876.9g, Fibre 22.8g

Golden Wedding Heart Cake

You can buy specialist cake-decorating equipment from sugarcraft suppliers to help you achieve these professional effects.

Makes one 23cm/9in round cake

60ml/4 tbsp apricot jam
23cm/9in round rich fruit cake
900g/2lb marzipan
900g/2lb/6 cups sugarpaste icing
cream food colouring
115g/4oz/¾ cup royal icing

Materials/equipment

28cm/11in round cake board
crimping tool
pins
small heart-shaped plunger tool
7.5cm/3in plain cutter
dual large and small blossom cutter
stamens
frill cutter
wooden cocktail stick (toothpick)
foil-wrapped chocolate hearts

1 Warm, then sieve the apricot jam and brush over the cake. Cover with marzipan and leave to dry overnight.

2 Tint 675g/1½lb/4½ cups of the sugarpaste icing very pale cream and cover the cake. Put on the board. Crimp the top edge using the crimping tool. With pins, mark eight equidistant points around the top edge. Crimp slanting lines to the base. Emboss the base edge with the heart-shaped plunger. Use the plain cutter to emboss a circle on top.

3 Divide the remaining sugarpaste icing in two and tint one cream and the other pale cream. Using half of each colour, make flowers with the blossom cutter. Make pinholes in the large flowers. Leave to dry then secure the stamens in the holes with royal icing.

4 Make eight frills with the remainder of the sugarpaste icing using the frill cutter, and a cocktail stick to trim and fill the edges. Attach the frills with water next to the crimped lines on the cake side. Crimp the edges of the deeper coloured frills.

5 Secure the flowers on the top and side of the cake with royal icing. Place the chocolate hearts in the centre.

Energy 9846kcal/41683kJ; Fat 196.3g, Saturated Fat 33.3g, Carbohydrate 1980.3g, Fibre 32.1g

Marzipan Bell Cake

This cake can be easily adapted to make a christening cake if you leave out the holly decorations.

Makes one 18cm/7in round cake
18cm/7in round rich or light fruit cake
30ml/2 tbsp apricot jam, warmed and sieved
900g/2lb marzipan
green, yellow and red food colouring

Materials/equipment
20cm/8in round silver cake board
crimping tool
bell and holly leaf cutter
1m/1yd red ribbon, 2cm/¾in wide
1m/1yd green ribbon, 5mm/¼in wide
25cm/10in red ribbon, 5mm/¼ in wide

1 Brush the cake with apricot jam and place on the cake board.

2 Tint two-thirds of the marzipan pale green. Use to cover the cake. Crimp the top edge of the cake with a crimping tool to make a scalloped pattern.

3 Tint a small piece of remaining marzipan bright yellow, another bright red and the rest bright green. Make two yellow bells using the bell cutter and clappers by rolling out a small ball of marzipan.

4 Cut out 11 green holly leaves and mark the veins with the back of a knife.

5 Make two green bell ropes, 16 red holly berries and two bell-rope ends. Leave all the decorations to dry.

6 Secure the wide red and fine green ribbons around the side of the cake with a pin. Tie a double bow from red and green fine ribbon and attach to the side with a pin.

7 Arrange the bells, clappers, bell ropes, holly leaves and berries on top of the cake and secure with apricot jam.

Energy 6323kcal/26653kJ; Fat 225.3g, Saturated Fat 60.9g; Carbohydrate 1053g, Fibre 17.1g

Christening Sampler

Be creative for this delightful Christening sampler.

Serves 30
20cm/8in square rich fruit cake
45ml/3 tbsp apricot jam, warmed and sieved
450g/1lb marzipan
675g/1½lb/4½ cups sugarpaste icing
brown, yellow, orange, purple, cream, blue, green and pink food colouring

Materials/equipment
25cm/10in square cake board
fine paintbrush
small heart-shaped cutter

1 Brush the cake with apricot jam. Roll out the marzipan, cover the cake and leave to dry overnight. Roll out 150g/5oz/1 cup of the sugarpaste icing to fit the cake top. Brush the top with water and cover with the icing.

2 Colour 300g/10oz/2 cups of the icing brown and roll out four pieces measuring the length and about 1cm/½ in wider than the cake sides. Brush the cake sides with water and cover with the brown paste, folding over the extra width at the top and cutting the corners at an angle to make the picture frame.

3 Place on a cake board. With a fine paintbrush, paint over the sides with watered-down brown food colouring to represent wood grain.

4 Take the remaining icing and colour small amounts yellow, orange, brown, purple and cream and two shades of blue, green and pink. Leave a little white. Use these colours to shape the ducks, teddy bear, bulrushes, water, branch and leaves. Cut out a pink heart and make the baby's initial from white icing.

5 Mix the white and pink icings together for the apple blossom flowers. Make the shapes for the border. Attach the decorations to the cake with a little water.

6 Use the leftover colours to make "threads". Arrange in loops around the base of the cake on the board.

Energy 299kcal/1267kJ; Fat 6g, Saturated Fat 1.4g; Carbohydrate 58.5g, Fibre 1g

Teddy Bear Christening Cake

To personalize the cake, make a simple plaque for the top and pipe on the name of the new baby.

Makes one 20cm/8in square cake

20cm/8in square light fruit cake
45ml/3 tbsp apricot jam, warmed and sieved
900g/2lb marzipan
800g/1¾lb/5¼ cups sugarpaste icing
cornflour (cornstarch), for dipping
peach, yellow, blue and brown food colouring
115g/4oz/¾ cup royal icing

Materials/equipment

25cm/10in square cake board
crimping tool
fine paintbrush
wooden cocktail stick (toothpick)
peach ribbon
small blue ribbon bow

1 Brush the cake with the apricot jam. Roll out the marzipan and use to cover the cake. Leave to dry overnight.

2 Colour 500g/1¼lb/3¾ cups of the sugarpaste icing peach, then roll it out. Brush the marzipan with water and cover the cake with the sugarpaste.

3 Place the cake on the board. Using a crimping tool dipped in cornflour, crimp the top and base edges of the cake.

4 Divide the remaining sugarpaste into three. Leave one-third white and tint one-third yellow. Divide the last third in two, tint one half peach and the other blue.

5 Make flowers from the peach and blue sugarpaste. Leave to dry. Reserve the blue trimmings. Make a yellow teddy bear and paint on its features with brown food colouring. Give it a blue button. Leave to dry. Make a blue blanket and frill the white edge with a cocktail stick. Secure the frill to the blanket with water.

6 Decorate the cake with the ribbon, place the bear on top under its blanket, securing with royal icing. Secure the flowers and the bear's bow-tie in the same way.

Energy 9344kcal/39534kJ; Fat 232.7g, Saturated Fat 64.4g; Carbohydrate 1834.2g, Fibre 17.1g

Daisy Christening Cake

A ring of daisies sets off this pretty pink christening cake.

Makes one 20cm/8in round cake

20cm/8in round rich fruit cake
45ml/3 tbsp apricot jam, warmed and sieved
675g/1½lb marzipan
900g/2lb/6 cups royal icing
pink and yellow food colouring
115g/4oz/¾ cup sugarpaste icing

Materials/equipment

25cm/10in round cake board
fine paintbrush
5cm/2in fluted cutter
wooden cocktail stick (toothpick)
2 baking parchment piping (icing) bags
small star nozzle
pink and white ribbon

1 Brush the cake with the apricot jam. Roll out the marzipan and use to cover the cake. Leave to dry overnight.

2 Use a little royal icing to secure the cake to the board. Tint three-quarters of the royal icing pink. Flat-ice the cake with three or four layers, using white for the top and pink for the side. Allow each layer to dry overnight before applying the next. Set aside a little of both icings in airtight containers.

3 Make 28 daisies. For each daisy, shape a small piece of sugarpaste icing to look like a golf tee. Snip the edges and curl them slightly. Dry on baking parchment. Trim the stems and paint the edges pink and the centres yellow.

4 To make the plaque, roll out the remaining sugarpaste icing and cut out a circle with the fluted cutter. Roll a cocktail stick around the edge until it frills. Dry on baking parchment, then paint the name and the edges with pink food colouring.

5 Pipe twisted ropes (see p253) around the top and base of the cake with the reserved white royal icing. Then pipe a row of stars around the top of the cake with the star nozzle.

6 Stick the plaque in the centre with royal icing. Stick on the daisies and decorate with the ribbons.

Energy 10646kcal/45057kJ; Fat 208.7g, Saturated Fat 43g; Carbohydrate 2117.3g, Fibre 35.3g

Birthday Parcel

Use any combination of colours you fancy for the icing.

Serves 10

15cm/6in square Madeira cake
275g/10oz/1 1/3 cup orange-flavour butter icing
45ml/3 tbsp apricot jam, warmed and sieved
450g/1lb/3 cups sugarpaste icing
blue, orange and green food colouring
icing (confectioners') sugar, for dusting

Materials/equipment
15–18cm/7–8in square cake board
small triangular and round cocktail cutters

1 Cut the cake in half horizontally and sandwich together with the butter icing. Brush the cake with apricot jam. Colour three-quarters of the sugarpaste icing blue. Divide the remaining sugarpaste icing in half and colour one half orange and the other half green. Wrap the orange and green sugarpaste separately in clear film (plastic wrap) and set aside. Roll out the blue icing on a work surface lightly dusted with icing sugar and use it to cover the cake. Position on the cake board.

2 While the sugarpaste covering is still soft, use the cocktail cutters to cut out triangles and circles from the blue icing, lifting out the shapes to expose the cake.

3 Roll out the orange and green icings and cut out circles and triangles to fill the exposed holes in the blue icing. Roll out the trimmings and cut three orange strips, 2cm/¾in wide and long enough to go over the corner of the cake, and 3 very thin green strips the same length as the orange ones. Place the strips next to each other to make three striped ribbons, and secure the pieces together with a little water.

4 Place one striped ribbon over one corner of the cake, securing with a little water. Place a second strip over the opposite corner. Cut the remaining ribbon in half. Bend each half to make loops and attach both to one corner of the cake with water to form a loose bow.

Energy 358kcal/1515kJ; Fat 7.6g, Saturated Fat 4.2g; Carbohydrate 74.1g, Fibre 0.5g

Chocolate Fruit Birthday Cake

The modelled marzipan fruits on this moist chocolate Madeira cake make an eye-catching decoration.

Makes one 18cm/7in square cake

18cm/7in square deep chocolate Madeira cake
45ml/3 tbsp apricot jam, warmed and sieved
450g/1lb marzipan
450g/1lb/2 cups chocolate fudge icing
red, yellow, orange, green and purple food colouring
whole cloves
angelica strips

Materials/equipment
20cm/8in square silver cake board
medium gateau nozzle
nylon piping (icing) bag
75cm/2 1/2ft yellow ribbon, 1cm/1/2in wide

1 Level the cake top and invert. Brush over the top and sides of the cake with apricot jam.

2 Use two-thirds of the marzipan to cover the cake. Reserve the trimmings.

3 Place the cake on a wire rack over a tray and pour three-quarters of the chocolate fudge icing over the top, spreading it evenly over the top and sides with a metal spatula.

4 Leave for 10 minutes, then place on the cake board.

5 Using the reserved icing and a medium gateau nozzle, pipe large stars around the top edge and base of the cake. Leave to set.

6 Colour small quantities of the reserved marzipan for the fruits and use it to model bananas, peaches, pears, cherries and grapes. Use the angelica strips and cloves to make stalks for those fruits which require them.

7 Secure the ribbon around the sides of the cake. Decorate the top with the marzipan fruits.

Energy 6127kcal/25877kJ; Fat 176.5g, Saturated Fat 72.3g; Carbohydrate 1138g, Fibre 14.9g

Eighteenth Birthday Cake

A really striking cake for an eighteenth birthday. Change the shape if you don't have the diamond-shaped tin. If you don't have an "18" template you can easily make one out of paper, using a computer or photocopier to enlarge the number.

Serves 80

33.5 x 20cm/13 x 8in diamond-shaped deep rich or light fruit cake
45ml/3 tbsp apricot jam, warmed and sieved
1.2kg/2½lb marzipan
1.6kg/3½lb/10½ cups sugarpaste
black food colouring
30ml/2 tbsp royal icing

Materials/equipment

38 x 23cm/15 x 9in diamond-shaped cake board
"18" template
small baking parchment piping (icing) bag
fine writing nozzle
2m/2yd white ribbon, 2.5cm/1in wide
2m/2yd black ribbon, 3mm/⅛in wide

1 Make the cake using quantities for a 23cm/9in round cake. Brush the top and sides with apricot jam and cover in marzipan.

2 Place on the cake board. Cover the cake using 1.2kg/2½lb/7½ cups sugarpaste icing. Knead the trimmings into the remaining sugarpaste and tint black.

3 Use two-thirds of the black sugarpaste to cover the board.

4 Use a quarter of the remaining sugarpaste to cut out a number "18" using a template.

5 Use the remainder to cut out a variety of bow ties, wine glasses and music notes. Leave to dry on baking parchment.

6 Tint the royal icing black. Using the fine writing nozzle, attach the cut-outs to the cake top and sides.

7 Tie four small bows with the black ribbon. Secure with royal icing to the top corners. Position and secure black ribbon around the cake base and white ribbon around the board.

Energy 169kcal/713kJ; Fat 3.3g, Saturated Fat 0.6g; Carbohydrate 34g, Fibre 0.5g

Flickering Birthday Candle Cake

Flickering stripy candles are ready to blow out on this birthday cake for all ages.

Makes one 20cm/8in square cake

20cm/8in square Madeira cake
350g/12oz/1½ cups butter icing
45ml/3 tbsp apricot jam, warmed and sieved
800g/1¾lb/5¼ cups sugarpaste icing
pink, yellow, purple and jade food colouring
edible silver balls

Materials/equipment

23cm/9in square cake board
small round cutter
pink and purple food colouring pens
5mm/¼ in-wide jade-coloured ribbon

1 Cut the cake into three layers. Sandwich the layers together with the butter icing and brush the cake with the apricot jam.

2 Roll out 500g/1¼lb/3¾ cups of the sugarpaste icing and use to cover the cake. Position on the cake board.

3 Divide the remaining sugarpaste into four pieces and tint them pink, yellow, pale purple and jade.

4 Make the candles from jade and the flames from yellow icing. Press a silver ball into their bases. Position the candles and flames on the cake with a little water. Mould strips in yellow and purple icing to go around the candles. Secure with water.

5 Cut small wavy pieces from the pink and purple icing for smoke, and arrange them, using water, above the candles.

6 Cut out yellow circles with the cutter for the side decorations. Mould small pink balls and press a silver ball into their centres. Attach using water.

7 Using food colouring pens, draw wavy lines and dots coming from the purple and pink wavy icings. Decorate the sides of the cake board with the ribbon, securing at the back with a little softened sugarpaste.

Energy 6841kcal/28896kJ; Fat 195.4g, Saturated Fat 115.3g; Carbohydrate 1305.7g, Fibre 6.8g

Flower Birthday Cake

A simple birthday cake decorated with piped yellow and white flowers and ribbons will be received with delight whatever the recipient's age.

Makes one 18cm/7in round cake

18cm/7in round light fruit cake
30ml/2 tbsp apricot jam, warmed and sieved
675g/1½lb marzipan
1.2kg/2½lb/7½ cups royal icing
yellow and orange food colouring

Materials/equipment

23cm/9in round silver cake board
petal nozzle, very fine and fine writing nozzles, and medium star nozzle
baking parchment piping (icing) bags
1m/1yd white ribbon, 2cm/¾in wide
2m/2yd coral ribbon, 1cm/½in wide
25cm/10in coral ribbon, 5mm/¼in wide

1 Brush the cake with apricot jam and cover with marzipan. Place on the board.

2 Flat-ice the top and side of the cake with three layers of royal icing smoothed using a metal spatula.

3 Leave the icing to dry, then ice the board. Reserve the remaining royal icing.

4 Tint one-third of the reserved royal icing yellow and 15ml/1 tbsp of it orange.

5 Using the petal nozzle for the petals and the very fine writing nozzle for the centres, make four white narcissi with yellow centres and nine yellow narcissi with orange centres.

6 Use the star nozzle to pipe shell edgings to the cake top and base. Pipe "Happy Birthday" using the fine writing nozzle. Overlay in orange using the very fine writing nozzle.

7 Secure the ribbons around the board and cake side. Finish with a coral bow.

Energy 8600kcal/36442kJ; Fat 151.3g, Saturated Fat 26.2g; Carbohydrate 1792.2g, Fibre 24.8g

Jazzy Chocolate Gateau

This cake is made with Father's Day in mind, although you can make it for anyone who loves chocolate.

Serves 12–15

2 x quantity chocolate-flavour quick-mix sponge cake mix
75g/3oz plain (semisweet) chocolate
75g/3oz white chocolate
175g/6oz fudge frosting
115g/4oz/1 cup glacé icing
5ml/1 tsp weak coffee
8 tbsp chocolate nut spread

Materials/equipment

2 x 20cm/8in round cake tins
baking parchment piping (icing) bag
fine writing nozzle

1 Preheat the oven to 160°C/325°F/Gas 3. Grease two 20cm/8in cake tins (pans), line the bases with baking parchment and grease the paper. Divide the cake mixture evenly between the tins and smooth the surfaces.

2 Bake in the centre of the oven for about 20–30 minutes, or until firm to the touch. Turn out on to a wire rack, peel off the lining paper and leave to cool.

3 Melt the chocolates in two separate bowls over pans of simmering water, pour on to baking parchment and spread evenly. As it begins to set, place another sheet of baking paper on top and turn the chocolate "sandwich" over. When set, peel off the paper and turn the chocolate sheets over. Cut out haphazard triangular shapes of chocolate and set aside.

4 Sandwich the two cakes together using the fudge frosting. Place the cake on a stand or plate. Colour the glacé icing using the weak coffee and add enough water to form a spreading consistency. Spread the icing on top of the cake almost to the edges. Cover the side of the cake with chocolate nut spread.

5 Press the chocolate pieces around the side of the cake and, using a piping bag fitted with the fine nozzle, decorate the top of the cake with "jazzy" lines over the glacé icing.

Energy 444kcal/1862kJ; Fat 22.5g, Saturated Fat 2.6g; Carbohydrate 58g, Fibre 0.2g

Petal Retirement Cake

A sugar gift card is a delightful touch for this cake.

Makes one 20cm/8in petal-shaped cake

20cm/8in petal-shaped deep light fruit cake
45ml/3 tbsp apricot jam, warmed and sieved
900g/2lb marzipan
mulberry and pink food colouring
900g/2lb/6 cups sugarpaste icing
275g/10oz petal paste
15ml/1 tbsp royal icing

Materials/equipment

23cm/9in petal-shaped silver cake board
foam sponge
large and small blossom plunger cutters
very fine writing nozzle
2m/2yd white ribbon, 2cm/¾in wide
2m/2yd fuchsia ribbon, 1cm/½in wide
2m/2yd fuchsia ribbon, 3mm/⅛in wide
baking parchment piping (icing) bag
pink food colouring pen
fresh flowers

1 Brush the cake with jam and put on the board. Cover with marzipan. Knead mulberry colouring into the sugarpaste icing. Use to cover the cake and board. Dry overnight.

2 Tint the petal paste with pink colouring. Roll and cut out a 5 x 2.5cm/2 x 1in rectangle. Fold in half and make holes in the top edges of the fold for the ribbon. Dry over a foam sponge to make the card. Cut out 30 large and four small plunger blossom flowers. Leave to dry.

3 Using the royal icing and the very fine writing nozzle, secure the white and narrow fuchsia ribbons around the board and the medium ribbon around the cake base. Tie six small bows from the narrow ribbon for the base.

4 Attach the large flowers to the side of the cake with icing. Secure the small flowers to the board. Draw a design and write a message inside the card with the pen. Thread ribbon through the holes and tie a bow. Place the card on the cake top with the fresh flowers.

Energy 10015kcal/42406kJ; Fat 196.3g, Saturated Fat 33.3g; Carbohydrate 2022.2g, Fibre 32.1g

Pansy Retirement Cake

You can use other edible flowers such as nasturtiums, roses or tiny primroses for this cake, if you prefer.

Makes one 20cm/8in round cake

20cm/8in round light fruit cake
45ml/3 tbsp apricot jam, warmed and sieved
675g/1½lb marzipan
1.2kg/2½lb/7½ cups royal icing
orange food colouring
about 7 sugar-frosted pansies (orange and purple)

Materials/equipment

25cm/10in round cake board
2 baking parchment piping (icing) bags
medium star and very fine writing nozzles
2cm/¾in wide purple ribbon
3mm/⅛in wide dark purple ribbon

1 Brush the cake with the apricot jam. Roll out the marzipan and use to cover the cake. Leave to dry overnight.

2 Secure the cake to the cake board with a little royal icing. Tint a quarter of the royal icing pale orange. Flat-ice the cake with three layers of smooth icing using a metal spatula.

3 Use the orange icing for the top and the white for the side. Set aside a little of both icings in airtight containers for decoration.

4 Spoon the reserved white royal icing into a baking parchment piping bag fitted with a medium star nozzle. Pipe a row of scrolls around the cake top. Pipe a second row directly underneath the first row in the reverse direction. Pipe another row of scrolls around the base of the cake.

5 Spoon the reserved orange icing into a fresh piping bag fitted with a very fine writing nozzle. Pipe around the outline of the top of each scroll. Pipe a row of single orange dots below the lower row of reverse scrolls at the top and a double row of dots above the base row of scrolls.

6 Arrange the sugar-frosted pansies on top of the cake. Decorate the side with the ribbons.

Energy 8982kcal/38056kJ; Fat 159.5g, Saturated Fat 28.6g; Carbohydrate 1862.4g, Fibre 26.3g

Hallowe'en Pumpkin Patch Cake

Celebrate Hallowe'en with this autumn-coloured cake, colourfully decorated with sugarpaste pumpkins.

Makes one 20cm/8in round cake

175g/6oz/generous 1 cup sugarpaste icing
brown and orange food colouring
2 x 20cm/8in round chocolate sponge cakes
675g/1 ½lb/3 cups orange-flavour butter icing
chocolate chips
angelica

Materials/equipment

wooden cocktail stick (toothpick)
fine paintbrush
23cm/9in round cake board
serrated scraper
thick writing nozzle
baking parchment piping (icing) bag

1 For the pumpkins, tint a very small piece of the sugarpaste icing brown, and the rest orange.

2 Shape some balls of the orange icing the size of walnuts and some a bit smaller.

3 Make ridges with a cocktail stick. Make stems from the brown icing and secure with water. Paint highlights on the pumpkins in orange. Leave to dry on baking parchment.

4 Cut both cakes in half horizontally. Use one-quarter of the butter icing to sandwich the cakes together.

5 Place the cake on the board. Use two-thirds of the remaining icing to cover the cake. Texture the icing using a serrated scraper.

6 Using a thick writing nozzle, pipe a twisted rope pattern around the top and base edges of the cake with the remaining butter icing. Decorate with chocolate chips.

7 Cut the angelica into diamond shapes and arrange on the cake with the pumpkins.

Energy 6909kcal/28947kJ; Fat 375.6g, Saturated Fat 104.2g, Carbohydrate 874.6g, Fibre 0g

Fudge-frosted Starry Roll

Whether it's for a birthday or another occasion, this sumptuous-looking cake is sure to please.

Makes one 23cm/9in long roll

23 x 33cm/9 x 13in sponge roll
175g/6oz/¾ cup chocolate butter icing
50g/2oz white chocolate
50g/2oz plain (semisweet) chocolate

For the fudge frosting

75g/3oz plain (semisweet) chocolate, broken into pieces
350g/12oz/3 cups icing (confectioners') sugar, sifted
75g/3oz/6 tbsp butter or margarine
65ml/4½ tbsp milk or single (light) cream
7.5ml/1½ tsp vanilla extract

Materials/equipment

small star cutter
several baking parchment piping (icing) bags
big star nozzle

1 Unroll the sponge roll and spread with the butter icing. Re-roll and set aside.

2 For the decorations, melt the white chocolate in a bowl set over a pan of simmering water and spread on to a non-porous surface. Leave to firm up slightly, then cut out stars with the star cutter. Leave to set on baking parchment. To make lace curls, melt the plain chocolate as before and then cool slightly. Cover a rolling pin with baking parchment. Pipe zigzags on the paper and leave on the rolling pin until cool.

3 To make the frosting, stir all the ingredients over a low heat until melted. Remove from the heat and beat frequently until cool and thick. Cover the cake with two-thirds of the frosting, swirling with a metal spatula.

4 With a big star nozzle, use the remaining frosting to pipe diagonal lines on to the cake.

5 Position the lace curls and stars. Transfer the cake to a serving plate and decorate with more stars.

Energy 5460kcal/23020kJ; Fat 198g, Saturated Fat 70.5g, Carbohydrate 916.8g, Fibre 13.2g

Lucky Horseshoe Cake

This horseshoe-shaped cake, is made from a round cake and the shape is then cut out using a template.

Makes one 25cm/10in horseshoe cake

25cm/10in rich fruit cake
60ml/4 tbsp apricot jam, warmed and sieved
800g/1¾lb marzipan
1kg/2¼lb/6¾ cups sugarpaste icing
peach and blue food colouring
edible silver balls
115g/4oz/¾ cup royal icing

Materials/equipment

30cm/12in round cake board
crimping tool
pale blue ribbon, 3mm/⅛in wide
craft (utility) knife
modelling tool
large and small blossom cutters

1 Make a horseshoe template and use to shape the cake. Brush the cake with the apricot jam. Roll out 350g/12oz/2¼ cups of the marzipan to a 25cm/10in circle. Using the template, cut out the shape and place on the cake.

2 Measure the inside and outside of the cake. Cover with the remaining marzipan. Place the cake on the board and leave overnight. Tint 800g/1¾lb/5¼ cups of the sugarpaste icing peach. Cover the cake as before. Crimp the top edge.

3 Draw and measure the ribbon insertion on the template. Cut 13 pieces of ribbon fractionally longer than each slit. Make the slits through the template with a scalpel. Insert the ribbon with a modelling tool. Leave to dry overnight.

4 Make a tiny horseshoe template. Tint half the remaining sugarpaste icing pale blue. Using the template, cut out nine blue shapes. Mark each horseshoe with a sharp knife.

5 Cut out 12 large and 15 small flowers with the blossom cutters. Press a silver ball into the centres of the larger blossoms. Leave to dry. Repeat with the white icing. Decorate the cake and board with the ribbon, horseshoes and blossoms, securing with royal icing.

Energy 8428kcal/35700kJ; Fat 159g, Saturated Fat 25g; Carbohydrate 1733g, Fibre 25.7g

Bluebird Bon-voyage Cake

This delightful cake is a special way to see someone off on an exciting journey.

Makes one 20cm/8in round cake

450g/1lb/3 cups royal icing
blue food colouring
800g/1¾lb/5¼ cups sugarpaste icing
20cm/8in round Madeira cake
350g/12oz/1½ cups butter icing
45ml/3 tbsp apricot jam, warmed and sieved
edible silver balls

Materials/equipment

very fine writing nozzle
baking parchment piping (icing) bags
25cm/10in round cake board
thin pale blue ribbon

1 Soften two-thirds of the royal icing by adding a few drops of water. Make the rest stiffer by adding a little icing (confectioners') sugar. Tint the softer icing bright blue. Cover and leave overnight.

2 Draw two different-size bird templates on a piece of paper. Lay a sheet of baking parchment over the templates and trace the outline of the birds using the stiffer royal icing and a very fine writing nozzle. Fill in the run-outs with the stiffer icing. Repeat until you have four large and five small birds. Leave to dry for at least 2 days.

3 Tint two-thirds of the sugarpaste icing blue. Form all the sugarpaste into small rolls and place them alternately together on a work surface. Form into a round and lightly knead to marble.

4 Cut the cake horizontally into three and sandwich together with the butter icing. Place the cake on the board, flush with an edge, and brush with apricot jam. Roll out the marbled icing and use to cover the cake and board.

5 Using the very fine writing nozzle and the stiffer royal icing, pipe a wavy line around the edge of the board. Position the balls evenly in the icing. Secure the birds to the cake with royal icing. Pipe beads of white icing for eyes and stick on a ball. Drape the ribbon between the beaks, securing with icing.

Energy 8614kcal/36357kJ; Fat 270.1g, Saturated Fat 163.2g; Carbohydrate 1600g, Fibre 6.3g

Ghost Cake

This children's cake is really simple to make yet very effective. It is ideal for a Hallowe'en party.

Serves 15–20

900g/2lb/6 cups white sugarpaste icing
black food colouring
2 Madeira cakes, baked in an 18cm/7in square cake tin and a 300ml/½ pint/1¼ cup pudding bowl
350g/12oz/1½ cups butter icing

Materials/equipment

23cm/9in round cake board
fine paintbrush

1 Tint 115g/4oz/¾ cup of the sugarpaste icing dark grey and use to cover the cake board.

2 Cut two small corners off the large cake. Cut two larger wedges off the other two corners, then stand the cake on the board. Divide the larger trimmings in half and wedge around the base of the cake.

3 Secure the small cake to the top of the larger cake with butter icing. Completely cover both of the cakes with the remaining butter icing.

4 Roll out the remaining sugarpaste icing to an oval shape 50 x 30cm/20 x 12in. Lay it over the cake, letting the icing fall into folds around the sides.

5 Gently smooth the icing over the top half of the cake using your hands, and trim off any excess sugarpaste.

6 Using black food colouring and a fine paintbrush, paint two oval eyes on to the head.

Cook's Tip

Instead of painting on the eyes you could colour some sugarpaste trimmings black and cut out two ovals using a small oval cutter, if you like.

Energy 344kcal/1447kJ; Fat 13g, Saturated Fat 7.7g; Carbohydrate 57.7g, Fibre 0.4g

Cat-in-a-Basket Cake

This adorable cat, asleep in its basket, will appeal to all children.

Makes one 15cm/6in round cake

800g/1¾lb marzipan
red, green, yellow and brown food colouring
15cm/6in round deep sponge cake
30ml/2 tbsp apricot jam, warmed and sieved
50g/2oz/4 tbsp white sugarpaste icing

Materials/equipment

20cm/8in round cake board
fine paintbrush

1 Tint 350g/12oz/2¼ cups of the marzipan pink. Divide the rest in half and tint one half green and the other yellow. Brush the cake with the apricot jam and place it on the board.

2 Roll out the pink marzipan to a rectangle measuring 15 x 25cm/6 x 10in. Cut five 1cm/½in wide strips, about 24cm/9½in long, keeping them attached to the rectangle at one end.

3 Roll out the green marzipan and cut it into 7.5cm/3in lengths of the same width. Fold back alternate pink strips and lay a green strip across widthways. Bring the pink strips over the green strip to form the weave. Keep repeating the process until the entire length is woven. Press lightly to join. Repeat with the rest of the rectangle and more strips of green marzipan.

4 Press the two pieces of basketweave on to the side of the cake, joining them neatly. Model a yellow marzipan cat about 7.5cm/3in across. Leave to dry overnight.

5 Roll out the sugarpaste icing and place on the centre of the cake. Put the cat on top and arrange the icing in folds around it. Trim the edges neatly.

6 Make long ropes from any leftover pink and green marzipan. Twist together and press on to the top edge of the cake. Paint the cat's features in brown food colouring.

Energy 6094kcal/25595kJ; Fat 278.7g, Saturated Fat 63.3g; Carbohydrate 876g, Fibre 19.7g

Fish-shaped Cake

A very easy and colourful cake, this fun little fish is perfect for a small child's birthday party.

Makes one cake

450g/1lb/3 cups sugarpaste icing
blue, orange, red, mauve and green food colouring
sponge cake, baked in a 3.5 litre/6 pint/15 cup ovenproof mixing bowl
350g/12oz/1½ cups butter icing
1 blue sweet (candy)

Materials/equipment

large oval cake board
2.5cm/1in plain cutter
baking parchment piping (icing) bag

1 Tint two-thirds of the sugarpaste icing blue, roll out very thinly and use to cover the dampened cake board.

2 Make a template of a fish out of paper. Invert the cake, place the template on top and trim into the fish shape. Slope the sides. Place on the cake board.

3 Tint all but 15ml/1 tbsp of the butter icing orange. Use to cover the cake, smoothing with a metal spatula. Score curved lines for scales, starting from the tail end.

4 Tint half the remaining sugarpaste icing red. Shape and position two lips.

5 Cut out the tail and fins. Mark with lines using a knife and position on the fish. Make the eye from white sugarpaste and the blue sweet.

6 Tint a little sugarpaste mauve, cut out crescent-shaped scales using a biscuit cutter and place on the fish. Tint the remaining sugarpaste green and cut into long thin strips. Twist each strip and arrange around the board.

7 To make the bubbles around the fish, place the reserved butter icing in a piping bag, snip off the end and pipe small circles on to the board.

Pink Monkey Cake

This cheeky little monkey could be made in any colour icing you wish.

Makes one 20cm/8in cake

20cm/8in round sponge cake
115g/4oz/½ cup butter icing
45ml/3 tbsp apricot jam, warmed and sieved
450g/1lb marzipan
500g/1¼lb/3¾ cups sugarpaste icing
red, blue and black food colouring

Materials/equipment

25cm/10in round cake board
2 candles and holders

1 Trace the outline and paws of the monkey from the photograph. Using a photocopier or a computer enlarge to fit the cake and then cut out a template.

2 Split the cake and fill with butter icing. Place on the cake board and use the template to cut out the basic shape of the monkey. Use the trimmings to shape the nose and tummy. Brush with apricot jam and cover with a layer of marzipan.

3 Tint 450g/1lb/3 cups of the sugarpaste icing pale pink and use to cover the cake. Leave to dry overnight.

4 Mark the position of the face and paws. Tint a little of the sugarpaste icing blue and use for the eyes. Tint a little icing black and cut out the pupils and tie.

5 Tint the remaining sugarpaste icing dark pink and cut out the nose, mouth, ears and paws. Stick all the features in place with water. Roll the trimmings into balls and place on the board to hold the candles.

Variation

You could adapt this circular cake to make a cat or an elephant, perhaps side on with his trunk curling upwards. Try some different shapes on paper then transfer your finished idea on to baking parchment to use as a template.

Porcupine Cake

Melt-in-the-mouth pieces of flaked chocolate give this porcupine its spiky coating.

Serves 15–20

2 chocolate sponge cakes, baked in a 1.2 litre/2 pint/5 cup and a 600ml/1 pint/2½ cup pudding bowl
500g/1¼lb/2½ cups chocolate-flavour butter icing
cream, black, green, brown and red food colouring
5–6 flaked chocolate bars
50g/2oz/⅓ cup white marzipan

Materials/equipment
35cm/14in long rectangular cake board
wooden cocktail stick (toothpick)
fine paintbrush

1 Use the smaller cake for the head and shape a pointed nose at one end. Reserve the trimmed wedges.

2 Place the cakes side-by-side on the cake board, inverted, and use the trimmings to fill in the sides and top where they meet. Secure with butter icing.

3 Cover the cake with the remaining butter icing and mark the nose with a cocktail stick.

4 Make the spikes by breaking the flaked chocolate into thin strips and sticking them into the butter icing all over the body section of the porcupine.

5 Reserve a small portion of marzipan. Divide the remainder into three and tint cream, black and green.

6 Tint a tiny portion of the reserved marzipan brown.

7 Shape cream ears and feet, black-and-white eyes, and black claws and nose. Arrange all the features on the cake and press them into the buttercream.

8 Make green apples and highlight in red with a fine paintbrush. Make the stalks from the brown marzipan and push them in to the apples.

Energy 364kcal/1523kJ; Fat 22.4g, Saturated Fat 5.7g; Carbohydrate 39g, Fibre 0.1g

Mouse-in-Bed Cake

This cake is suitable for both girls and boys. Make the mouse well in advance to give it time to dry.

Makes one 20 x 15cm/8 x 6in cake

20cm/8in square sponge cake
115g/4oz/½ cup butter icing
45ml/3 tbsp apricot jam, warmed and sieved
450g/1lb marzipan
675g/1½lb/4½ cups sugarpaste icing
blue and red food colouring

Materials/equipment
25cm/10in square cake board
flower cutter
blue and red food colouring pens

1 Cut 5cm/2in off one side of the cake. Split and fill the main cake with butter icing. Place on the cake board, brush with apricot jam and cover with a layer of marzipan.

2 With the cake off-cut, shape a pillow with a hollow for the mouse's head, and the torso and the legs of the mouse. Cover with marzipan and leave to dry overnight.

3 Cover the cake and pillow with white sugarpaste icing. Lightly frill the edge of the pillow with a fork. To make the valance, roll out 350g/12oz/2¼ cups of sugarpaste icing and cut into four 7.5cm/3in wide strips. Attach to the bed with water. Arrange the pillow and mouse body on the cake.

4 For the quilt, tint 75g/3oz/½ cup of sugarpaste icing blue and roll out to an 18cm/7in square. Mark with a diamond pattern and the flower cutter. Cover the mouse with the quilt.

5 Cut a 2.5 x 19cm/1 x 7½in white sugarpaste icing strip for the sheet, mark the edge and place over the quilt, tucking it under at the top edge.

6 Tint 25g/1oz/2 tbsp of marzipan pink and make the head and paws of the mouse. Put the head on the pillow, tucked under the sheet, and the paws over the edge of the sheet. Use food colouring pens to draw on the face of the mouse.

Energy 7749kcal/32592kJ; Fat 315.8g, Saturated Fat 77.1g; Carbohydrate 1225g, Fibre 15.8g

Teddy's Birthday

After the sugarpaste pieces have been assembled and stuck into the cake, an icing smoother is useful to flatten the design.

Makes one 20cm/8in round cake

20cm/8in round cake
115g/4oz/½ cup butter icing
45ml/3 tbsp apricot jam, warmed and sieved
350g/12oz marzipan
450g/1lb/3 cups sugarpaste icing
brown, red, blue and black food colouring
115g/4oz/¾ cup royal icing
edible silver balls

Materials/equipment

25cm/10in round cake board
small baking parchment piping (icing) bags
medium shell and star nozzles
1.5m/1½yd red ribbon
2 candles and holders

1 Copy the teddy design on to a piece of paper that will fit the top of the cake.

2 Split the cake and fill with butter icing. Place on the cake board and brush with apricot jam. Cover with a layer of marzipan then a layer of sugarpaste icing.

3 Using the paper template, mark the design on top of the cake.

4 Colour one-third of the remaining sugarpaste icing pale brown. Colour a piece pink, a piece red, some blue and a tiny piece black. Using the template, cut out the pieces and place in position on the cake. Stick down by lifting the edges carefully and brushing the undersides with a little water.

5 Roll small ovals for the eyes and stick in place with the nose and eyebrows. Cut out a mouth and press flat.

6 Tie the ribbon around the cake. Colour the royal icing blue and pipe the border around the base of the cake with the shell nozzle. Pipe tiny stars around the small cake with the star nozzle. Insert silver balls on the piped stars. Put the candles on the cake.

Energy 6210kcal/26127kJ; Fat 248.8g, Saturated Fat 64.5g; Carbohydrate 995.4g, Fibre 12.1g

Party Teddy Bear Cake

The cuddly teddy on this cake is built up with royal icing and coloured coconut and is a very simple effect to achieve.

Makes one 20cm/8in square cake

20cm/8in square sponge cake
115g/4oz/½ cup butter icing
45ml/3 tbsp apricot jam, warmed and sieved
450g/1lb marzipan
350g/12oz/2¼ cups white sugarpaste icing
25g/1oz/⅓ cup desiccated (dry unsweetened shredded) coconut
blue and black food colouring
115g/4oz/¾ cup royal icing

Materials/equipment

25cm/10in square cake board
2 small baking parchment piping (icing) bags
small red bow
no.7 shell nozzle
1.5m/1½yd red ribbon
6 candles and holders

1 Make a paper template of the teddy so that it will fit the top of the cake.

2 Cut the cake in half and sandwich together with butter icing. Place on the cake board and brush with apricot jam. Cover with a thin layer of marzipan and then white sugarpaste icing. Leave to dry overnight.

3 Using the template, carefully mark the position of the teddy on to the cake.

4 Put the coconut into a bowl and mix in a drop of blue colouring to colour it pale blue. Spread a thin layer of royal icing on to the cake within the outline of the teddy. Before the icing dries, sprinkle on some pale blue coconut and press it down lightly.

5 Roll out the sugarpaste trimmings and cut out a nose, ears and paws. Stick in place with a little royal icing. Tint some royal icing black and pipe on the eyes, nose and mouth. Use the red bow as a tie and attach in place with royal icing. Pipe a white royal icing border around the base of the cake, tie the ribbon around the cake and position the candles on top.

Energy 7900kcal/33215kJ; Fat 331.4g, Saturated Fat 90.4g; Carbohydrate 1226.6g, Fibre 19.2g

Iced Fancies

These cakes are ideal for a children's tea-party. Ready-made cake decorating products may be used instead, if you like.

Makes 16

115g/4oz/½ cup butter, at room temperature
225g/8oz/generous 1 cup caster (superfine) sugar
2 eggs, at room temperature
175g/6oz/1½ cups plain (all-purpose) flour
1.5ml/¼ tsp salt
7.5ml/1½ tsp baking powder
120ml/4fl oz/½ cup milk
5ml/1 tsp vanilla extract

For the icing

2 large egg whites
400g/14oz/3½ cups sifted icing (confectioners') sugar
1–2 drops glycerine
juice of 1 lemon
food colourings of your choice
coloured vermicelli, and crystallized lemon and orange slices, to decorate

1 Preheat the oven to 190°C/375°F/Gas 5. Line a 16-cup bun tray with paper cases.

2 Cream the butter and sugar until light and fluffy. Add the eggs, one at a time, beating well after each addition.

3 Sift over and stir in the flour, salt and baking powder, alternating with the milk. Add the vanilla extract.

4 Half-fill the cups and bake for about 20 minutes, or until the tops spring back when touched. Stand in the tray to cool for 5 minutes, then unmould on to a wire rack.

5 To make the icing, beat the egg whites until stiff. Gradually add the sugar, glycerine and lemon juice, and beat for 1 minute.

6 Tint the icing with the different food colourings, and use to ice the tops of the cakes.

7 Decorate the cakes with coloured vermicelli and crystallized lemon and orange slices. You can also make freehand decorations such as animal faces using a paper piping (icing) bag.

Energy 259kcal/1094kJ; Fat 6.9g, Saturated Fat 4g; Carbohydrate 49.7g, Fibre 0.3g

Fairy Castle Cake

If the icing on this cake dries too quickly, dip a metal spatula into hot water to help smooth the surface.

Makes one cake

20cm/8in round sponge cake
115g/4oz/½ cup butter icing
45ml/3 tbsp apricot jam, warmed and sieved
675g/1½lb/4½ cups marzipan
8 mini Swiss rolls (jelly rolls)
675g/1½lb/4½ cups royal icing
red, blue and green food colouring
jelly diamonds
4 ice cream cones
2 ice cream wafers
50g/2oz/⅔ cup desiccated (dry unsweetened shredded) coconut
8 marshmallows

Materials/equipment

30cm/12in square cake board
wooden cocktail stick (toothpick)

1 Split the cake and fill with butter icing, place in the centre of the board and brush with apricot jam. Cover with a layer of marzipan.

2 Cover each of the Swiss rolls (jelly rolls) with marzipan. Stick four of them around the cake and cut the other four in half.

3 Tint two-thirds of the royal icing pale pink and cover the cake. Ice the extra pieces of Swiss roll and stick them around the top of the cake.

4 Use a cocktail stick to score the walls with a brick pattern. Make windows on the corner towers from jelly diamonds. Cut the ice cream cones to make the tower spires and stick them in place. Leave to dry overnight.

5 Tint half the remaining royal icing pale blue and cover the cones. Use a fork to pattern the icing. Shape the wafers for the gates, stick to the cake and cover with blue icing. Use the back of a knife to mark planks.

6 Tint the coconut with a few drops of green colouring. Spread the board with the remaining royal icing and sprinkle over the coconut. Stick on the marshmallows with a little royal icing to make the small turrets.

Energy 9249kcal/38959kJ; Fat 342.6g, Saturated Fat 82.4g; Carbohydrate 1545.3g, Fibre 19.1g

Sailing Boat

For chocoholics, make this cake using chocolate sponge.

Makes one cake
20cm/8in square sponge cake
225g/8oz/1 cup butter icing
15ml/1 tbsp unsweetened cocoa powder
4 large flaked chocolate bars
blue and red powder tints
115g/4oz/¾ cup royal icing
blue food colouring

Materials/equipment
25cm/10in square cake board
rice paper
paintbrush
plastic drinking straw
wooden cocktail stick (toothpick)
2 small cake ornaments

1 Split the cake and fill with half of the butter icing. Cut 7cm/2¾in from one side of the cake. Shape the larger piece to resemble the hull of a boat. Place diagonally across the cake board.

2 Mix the cocoa powder into the remaining butter icing and spread evenly over the top and sides of the boat.

3 Make the rudder and tiller from short lengths of flaked chocolate bars and place them at the stern of the boat. Split the rest of the flaked chocolate bars lengthways and press on to the sides of the boat, horizontally, to resemble planks of wood. Sprinkle the crumbs over the top.

4 Cut two rice paper rectangles, one 14 x 16cm/5¾ x 6½in and the other 15 x 7.5cm/6 x 3in. Cut the bigger one in a gentle curve to make the large sail and the smaller one into a triangle. Brush a circle of blue powder tint on to the large sail.

5 Wet the edges of the sails and stick on to the straw. Make a hole for the straw 7.5cm/3in from the bow of the boat and push into the cake.

6 Cut a rice paper flag and brush with red powder tint. Stick the flag on to a cocktail stick and insert into the top of the straw. Tint the royal icing blue and spread on the board in waves. Place the small ornaments on the boat.

Energy 5147kcal/21498kJ; Fat 310.1g, Saturated Fat 104.6g; Carbohydrate 568g, Fibre 9.6g

Spiders' Web Cake

A delightfully spooky cake for any occasion, fancy dress or otherwise.

Makes one 900g/2lb cake
900g/2lb dome-shaped lemon sponge cake
225g/8oz/¾ cup lemon-flavour glacé icing
black and yellow food colouring

For the spiders
115g/4oz plain chocolate, broken into pieces
150ml/¼ pint/⅔ cup double (heavy) cream
45ml/3 tbsp ground almonds
unsweetened cocoa powder, for dusting
chocolate vermicelli
2–3 liquorice wheels, sweet centres removed
15g/½oz/2 tbsp sugarpaste icing

Materials/equipment
small baking parchment piping (icing) bag
wooden skewer
20cm/8in cake board

1 Place the cake on baking parchment. Tint 45ml/3 tbsp of the glacé icing black. Tint the rest yellow and pour it over the cake, letting it run down the side.

2 Fill a piping bag with the black icing and, starting at the centre top, drizzle it round the cake in an evenly-spaced spiral. Finish the web by drawing downwards through the icing with a skewer. When set, place on the cake board.

3 To make the spiders, gently melt the chocolate with the cream, stirring frequently. Transfer to a bowl, allow to cool, then beat the mixture for 10 minutes, or until thick and pale. Stir in the ground almonds, then chill until firm enough to handle. Dust your hands with a little cocoa, then make walnut-size balls with the mixture. Roll the balls in chocolate vermicelli.

4 For the legs, cut the liquorice into 4cm/1½in lengths. Make holes in the sides of the spiders and insert the legs. For the spiders' eyes, tint a piece of sugarpaste icing black and form into tiny balls. Make larger balls with white icing. Stick on using water. Arrange the spiders on and around the cake.

Energy 6266kcal/26208kJ; Fat 358.4g, Saturated Fat 119.8g; Carbohydrate 734.2g, Fibre 14.5g

Toy Telephone Cake

Very small children love to chat on the phone so this cake would be sure to appeal. The child's name could be piped in a contrasting colour of icing, if you wish.

Makes one cake

15cm/6in square sponge cake
50g/2oz/¼ cup butter icing
30ml/2 tbsp apricot jam, warmed and sieve
275g/10oz marzipan
350g/12oz/2¼ cups sugarpaste icing
yellow, blue, red and black food colouring
liquorice strips
115g/4oz/¾ cup royal icing

Materials/equipment

20cm/8in square cake board
piping nozzle
small baking parchment piping (icing) bag
very fine writing nozzle

1 Split the cake and fill with butter icing. Trim to the shape of a telephone. Round off the edges and cut a shallow groove where the receiver rests on the telephone. Place the cake on the cake board and brush with apricot jam.

2 Cover the cake with marzipan and then cover with the sugarpaste icing. Tint half the remaining sugarpaste icing yellow, a small piece blue and the rest of the icing red.

3 To make the dial, cut out an 8cm/3½in diameter circle in yellow and a 4cm/1½in diameter circle in blue. Stamp out 12 red discs for the numbers with the end of a piping nozzle and cut out a red receiver. Position on the cake with water.

4 Twist the liquorice around to form a curly cord and use royal icing to stick one end to the telephone and the other end to the receiver. Tint the royal icing black and pipe the numbers on the discs and the child's name on the telephone.

Variation
If you like, you could cut the cake into two rectangles and make a modern push-button phone with its receiver lying beside it.

Energy 6250kcal/26250kJ; Fat 277.2g, Saturated Fat 64.9g; Carbohydrate 929g, Fibre 12.4g

Bumble Bee Cake

The edible sugar flowers that are used to decorate this cake were bought ready-made but you can make your own if you like.

Makes one cake

20cm/8in round sponge cake
115g/4oz/½ cup butter icing
45ml/3 tbsp apricot jam, warmed and sieved
350g/12oz marzipan
500g/1¼lb/3¾ cups sugarpaste icing
yellow, black, blue and red food colouring
115g/4oz/¾ cup royal icing
50g/2oz/⅔ cup desiccated (dry unsweetened shredded) coconut
6 sugarpaste daisies

Materials/equipment

25cm/10in square cake board
1 paper doily
adhesive tape
1 pipe cleaner

1 Split the cake and fill with butter icing. Cut in half to make semicircles, sandwich the halves together and stand upright on the cake board. Trim the ends to shape the head and tail.

2 Brush with apricot jam and cover with a layer of marzipan. Tint 350g/12oz/2¼ cups of the sugarpaste icing yellow and use to cover the cake.

3 Tint 115g/4oz/¾ cup of the sugarpaste icing black. Roll out and cut three stripes, each 2.5 x 25cm/1 x 10in. Space evenly on the cake and stick on with water.

4 Use the remaining icing to make the eyes and mouth, tinting the icing blue for the pupils and pink for the mouth. Stick on with water.

5 Tint the coconut with a drop of yellow colouring. Cover the cake board with royal icing then sprinkle with coconut. Place the daisies on the board.

6 To make the wings, cut the doily in half, wrap each half into a cone shape and stick together with adhesive tape. Cut the pipe cleaner in half and stick the pieces into the cake, just behind the head. Place the wings over the pipe cleaners.

Energy 7859kcal/33037kJ; Fat 334.1g, Saturated Fat 102.8g; Carbohydrate 1212.8g, Fibre 20.7g

Toy Car Cake

You can add a personalized number plate with the child's name and age to the back of this bright yellow car, if you like.

Makes one car-shaped cake
20cm/8in round sponge cake
115g/4oz/½ cup butter icing
45ml/3 tbsp apricot jam, warmed and sieved
450g/1lb marzipan
500g/1¼lb/3¾ cups sugarpaste icing
yellow, red and black food colouring
30ml/2 tbsp royal icing
red and green sweets (candies)

Materials/equipment
25cm/10in round cake board
wooden cocktail stick (toothpick)
cutters, 4cm/1½in and 2.5cm/1in
small baking parchment piping (icing) bag
very fine writing nozzle
candles and holders

1 Split the cake and fill with the butter icing. Cut in half and sandwich the halves together. Stand upright and slice off pieces to create the windscreen and bonnet. Place on the cake board and brush with apricot jam.

2 Cut a strip of marzipan to cover the top of the cake to level the joins. Then cover the cake all over with marzipan.

3 Tint 450g/1lb/3 cups of the sugarpaste icing yellow and use to cover the cake. Leave to dry overnight.

4 Mark the outlines of the doors and windows on to the car with a cocktail stick.

5 Tint the remaining sugarpaste icing red. Cut out four wheels with the larger cutter. Stick in place with water. Mark the hubs in the centre of each wheel with the smaller cutter.

6 Tint the royal icing black and pipe over the outline marks of the doors and windows.

7 Stick on sweets for headlights with royal icing. Press the candles into sweets and stick to the board with royal icing.

Energy 7749kcal/32592kJ; Fat 315.8g, Saturated Fat 77.1g; Carbohydrate 1225g, Fibre 15.8g

Fire Engine Cake

This bright and jolly fire engine is simplicity itself as the decorations are mainly bought sweets and novelties.

Makes one 20 x 10cm/8 x 4in cake
20cm/8in square sponge cake
115g/4oz/½ cup butter icing
45ml/3 tbsp apricot jam, warmed and sieved
350g/12oz marzipan
450g/1lb/3 cups sugarpaste icing
red, black and green food colouring
liquorice strips
115g/4oz/4 tbsp royal icing
sweets (candies)
50g/2oz/1⅔ cup desiccated (dry unsweetened shredded) coconut

Materials/equipment
25cm/10in round cake board
small baking parchment piping (icing) bag
fine plain nozzle
2 silver bells
candles and holders

1 Split the cake and fill with the butter icing. Cut in half and sandwich one half on top of the other. Place on the cake board and brush with apricot jam.

2 Trim a thin wedge off the front edge to make a sloping windscreen. Cover with marzipan. Tint 350g/12oz/2¼ cups of the sugarpaste icing red and use to cover the cake.

3 For the ladder, cut the liquorice into two strips and some short pieces for the rungs. Tint half the royal icing black and use some to stick the ladder to the top of the cake.

4 Roll out the remaining sugarpaste icing, cut out windows and stick them on to the cake with a little water.

5 Pipe around the windows in black royal icing using the fine plain nozzle. Stick sweets in place for headlights, lamps and wheels and stick the silver bells on the roof.

6 Tint the coconut green, spread a little royal icing over the cake board and sprinkle with the coconut so that it resembles grass. Stick sweets to the board with royal icing and press the candles into the sweets.

Energy 7662kcal/32196kJ; Fat 334.1g, Saturated Fat 102.8g; Carbohydrate 1160.6g, Fibre 20.7g

Sandcastle Cake

Crushed digestive cookies (graham crackers) make realistic-looking sand when used to cover this cake.

Makes one 15cm/6in round cake
2 x 15cm/6in round sponge cakes
115g/4oz/½ cup butter icing
45ml/3 tbsp apricot jam, warmed and sieved
115g/4oz digestive cookies (graham crackers)
115g/4oz/¾ cup royal icing
blue food colouring
shrimp-shaped sweets (candies)

Materials/equipment
25cm/10in square cake board
rice paper
plastic drinking straw
4 candles and holders

1 Split both of the cakes, then sandwich all the layers together with the butter icing. Place in the centre of the cake board.

2 Cut 3cm/1¼in off the top just above the filling and set aside. Shape the rest of the cake with slightly sloping sides.

3 Cut four 3cm/1¼in cubes from the reserved piece of cake. Stick on the cubes for the turrets and brush with apricot jam.

4 Crush the digestive cookies and press through a sieve to make the "sand". Press some crushed cookies on to the cake, using a metal spatula to get a smooth finish.

5 Colour some royal icing blue and spread on the board around the sandcastle to make a moat.

6 Spread a little royal icing on to the board around the outside edge of the moat and sprinkle on some crushed cookie.

7 To make the flag, cut a small rectangle of rice paper and stick on to half a straw with water. Push the end of the straw into the cake.

8 Stick candles into each turret and arrange the shrimp-shaped sweets on the board.

Energy 5154kcal/21569kJ; Fat 282g, Saturated Fat 82.8g; Carbohydrate 633.9g, Fibre 9.7g

Clown Face Cake

Children will love this clown whose bright, frilly collar is surprisingly simple to make.

Makes one 20cm/8in cake
20cm/8in round sponge cake
115g/4oz/½ cup butter icing
45ml/3 tbsp apricot jam, warmed and sieved
450g/1lb marzipan
450g/1lb/3 cups sugarpaste icing
115g/4oz/¾ cup royal icing
edible silver balls
red, green, blue and black food colouring

Materials/equipment
25cm/10in round cake board
small baking parchment piping (icing) bag
medium star nozzle
wooden cocktail stick (toothpick)
cotton wool (balls)
candles and holders

1 Split the cake and fill with butter icing. Place on the cake board and brush with apricot jam. Cover with a thin layer of marzipan then with white sugarpaste icing. Mark the position of the features. Using the star nozzle, pipe stars around the base of the cake with some royal icing, placing silver balls on some of the stars as you work, and leave to dry overnight.

2 Make a paper template for the face and features. Tint half the remaining sugarpaste icing pink and cut out the face base. Tint and cut out all the features, rolling a thin sausage to make the mouth. Cut thin strands for the hair. Stick all the features and hair in place with a little water.

3 Tint the remaining sugarpaste icing green. Cut three strips 4cm/1½in wide. Give each a scalloped edge and stretch by rolling a cocktail stick along it to make the frill. Stick the frills on with water and arrange, holding them in place with cotton wool (cotton balls) until dry. Put the candles at the top of the head.

Cook's Tip
For colouring sugarpaste always use paste colours, as liquid colours will make the sugarpaste too wet; this is especially important when you are making a strong or dark colour.

Energy 7422kcal/31187kJ; Fat 323.2g, Saturated Fat 81.8g; Carbohydrate 1120.6g, Fibre 15.8g

Pinball Machine

Make this brightly coloured cake for the pinball wizard in your life.

Serves 8–10

25cm/10in square sponge cake
225g/8oz/1½ cups butter icing
45ml/3 tbsp apricot jam, warmed and sieved
450g/1lb marzipan
115g/4oz/¾ cup royal icing
450g/1lb/3 cups sugarpaste icing
yellow, blue, green and red food colouring
sweets (candies)
2 ice cream fan wafers

Materials/equipment

20cm/8in round cake tin (pan)
30cm/12in square cake board
small baking parchment piping (icing) bag
no.1 writing nozzle

1 Split the sponge cake and fill with butter icing. Cut off a 5cm/2in strip from one side and reserve. Cut a thin wedge off the top of the cake, diagonally along its length, to end just above the halfway mark. This will give a sloping table.

2 Using the round cake tin (pan) as a guide, cut the reserved strip of cake to make a rounded back for the pinball table. Brush the back and table with apricot jam, then cover separately with marzipan and place on the board. Stick them together with royal icing. Leave to dry overnight.

3 Cover with a layer of sugarpaste icing and leave to dry. Use a template to mark out the pinball design on the top of the cake. Colour the remaining sugarpaste icing yellow, blue, green and pink. Roll out the colours and cut to fit the design. Stick on the pieces with water and smooth the joins carefully.

4 Using royal icing, stick sweets on the cake as buffers, flippers, lights and knobs. Roll some blue sugarpaste icing into a long sausage and use to add an edge to the pinball table and divider.

5 Cut zigzags for the sides and a screen for the back. Stick on with water. Stick the ice cream fans at the back of the screen. Load the pinball sweets. Add the child's name on the screen with iced letters or piping.

Energy 792kcal/3320kJ; Fat 40.5g, Saturated Fat 15.7g; Carbohydrate 106.9g, Fibre 1.4g

Pirate's Hat

If you prefer, buy ready-made black sugarpaste icing for the hat rather than tinting it yourself.

Serves 8–10

25cm/10in round sponge cake
225g/8oz/1 cup butter icing
45ml/3 tbsp apricot jam, warmed and sieved
450g/1lb marzipan
500g/1¼lb/3¾ cups sugarpaste icing
black and gold food colouring
chocolate money
jewel sweets (candies)

Materials/equipment

30cm/12in square cake board
fine paintbrush

1 Split the cake and fill with butter icing. Cut in half and sandwich the halves together. Stand upright diagonally across the cake board and cut shallow dips from each end to create the brim of the hat. Brush with apricot jam.

2 Cut a strip of marzipan to lay over the top of the cake. Then cover the whole of the cake with a layer of marzipan. Tint 450g/1lb/3 cups of the sugarpaste icing black. Use to cover the cake.

3 Roll out the remaining sugarpaste icing and cut some 1cm/½in strips. Stick the strips in place with a little water around the brim of the pirate's hat and mark with the prongs of a fork to make a braid.

4 Make a skull and crossbones template and mark on to the hat. Cut the shapes out of the white sugarpaste icing and stick in place with water. Paint the braid strip gold and arrange the chocolate money and jewel sweets on the board.

Variation
To make a sandy board for your pirate's hat to rest on, simply cover the board with a thin layer of butter icing and sprinkle finely crushed cookies over.

Energy 699kcal/2938kJ; Fat 30.3g, Saturated Fat 9.2g; Carbohydrate 106.8g, Fibre 1.4g

Noah's Ark Cake

This charming cake is decorated with small animals, about 4cm/1½in high, available from cake decorating stores.

Makes one 20 x 13cm/ 8 x 5in cake

20cm/8in square sponge cake
115g/4oz/½ cup butter icing
45ml/3 tbsp apricot jam, warmed and sieved
450g/1lb marzipan
450g/1lb/3 cups sugarpaste icing
brown, yellow and blue food colouring
115g/4oz/¾ cup royal icing
chocolate mint stick

Materials/equipment

25cm/10in square cake board
skewer
rice paper
small animal cake ornaments

1 Split the cake and fill with butter icing. Cut off and set aside a 7.5cm/3in strip. Shape the remaining piece of cake to form the hull of the boat. Place diagonally on the cake board.

2 Use the set-aside piece of cake to cut a rectangle 10 x 6cm/ 4 x 2½in for the cabin and a triangular piece for the roof. Sandwich the roof and the cabin with butter icing or apricot jam.

3 Cover the three pieces with a layer of marzipan. Tint the sugarpaste icing brown and use most of it to cover the hull and cabin.

4 Use the remaining brown icing to make a long sausage. Stick around the edge of the hull with water. Mark planks with the back of a knife. Leave to dry overnight.

5 Tint one-third of the royal icing yellow and spread it over the cabin roof with a metal spatula. Roughen it with a skewer to create a thatch effect.

6 Tint the remaining royal icing blue and spread over the cake board, making rough waves. Cut a small triangle out of rice paper to make a flag. Stick the flag on to the chocolate mint stick and press on the back of the boat. Stick the small animals on to the boat with a dab of icing.

Energy 6888kcal/28960kJ; Fat 288.6g, Saturated Fat 71.3g; Carbohydrate 1068.1g, Fibre 14.9g

Balloons Cake

This is a simple yet effective cake design that can be adapted to suit any age.

Makes one 20cm/8in round cake

20cm/8in round cake
115g/4oz/½ cup butter icing
45ml/3 tbsp apricot jam, warmed and sieved
450g/1lb marzipan
450g/1lb/3 cups sugarpaste icing
red, blue, green and yellow food colouring
115g/4oz/¾ cup royal icing

Materials/equipment

25cm/10in round cake board
2 small baking parchment piping (icing) bags
fine plain and medium star nozzles
1.5m/1½yd blue ribbon
candles and holders

1 Split the cake and fill with butter icing. Place on the cake board and brush with apricot jam. Cover with a layer of marzipan then sugarpaste icing.

2 Divide the remaining sugarpaste icing into three pieces and tint pink, blue and green. Make a balloon template, roll out the coloured sugarpaste and cut out one balloon from each colour. Stick on to the cake with water and rub the edges gently to round them off.

3 Tint the royal icing yellow. With a plain nozzle, pipe on the balloon strings and then pipe a number on to each balloon. Using the star nozzle, pipe a border around the base of the cake.

4 Tie the ribbon around the cake and place the candles in their holders on top.

Cook's Tip

If you are not a fan of marzipan, it is not necessary to cover any sponge cake with marzipan that you will be covering with sugarpaste. Simply spread a thin layer of butter icing over the cake first to stick the sugarpaste.

Energy 6888kcal/28960kJ; Fat 288.6g, Saturated Fat 71.3g; Carbohydrate 1068.1g, Fibre 14.9g

Horse Stencil Cake

Make this cake for a horse lover. You can find stencils at art stores or sugarcraft suppliers. Use a fairly dry brush when painting the design on this cake and allow each colour to dry before adding the next.

Makes one 20cm/8in round cake

20cm/8in round sponge cake
115g/4oz/½ cup butter icing
45ml/3 tbsp apricot jam, warmed and sieved
450g/1lb marzipan
450g/1lb/3 cups sugarpaste icing
yellow, brown, black, red, orange and blue food colouring

Materials/equipment
25cm/10in round cake board
fine paintbrush
spoon with decorative handle
horse and letter stencils
1.5m/1½yd blue ribbon
candles and holders

1 Split the cake and fill with butter icing. Place on the cake board and brush with apricot jam. Cover with a layer of marzipan.

2 Tint the sugarpaste icing yellow, roll out and use to cover the cake. Roll the trimmings into two thin ropes, long enough to go halfway round the cake. Brush water in a thin band around the base of the cake, lay on the ropes and press together. Pattern the border with the decorative spoon handle. Leave to dry overnight.

3 If you do not have a stencil, make one by tracing a simple design on to a piece of thin card (stock) and cutting out the shape with a craft (utility) knife.

4 Place the horse stencil in the centre of the cake. With a fairly dry brush, gently paint over the parts you want to colour first. Allow these to dry completely before adding another colour, otherwise the colours will run into each other. Clean the stencil between colours.

5 When the horse picture is finished carefully paint on the lettering. Tie the ribbon around the side of the cake and place the candles in their holders on top.

Energy 6691kcal/28120kJ; Fat 288.6g, Saturated Fat 71.3g; Carbohydrate 1015.9g, Fibre 14.9g

Dolls' House Cake

This is a very straightforward cake to make and is decorated with store-bought flowers, or you can make your own if you like.

Serves 8–10

25cm/10in square sponge cake
225g/8oz/1 cup butter icing
45ml/3 tbsp apricot jam, warmed and sieved
450g/1lb marzipan
450g/1lb/3 cups sugarpaste icing
red, yellow, blue, black, green and gold food colouring
115g/4oz/¾ cup royal icing

Materials/equipment
30cm/12in square cake board
pastry wheel
large and fine paintbrushes
wooden cocktail stick (toothpick)
small baking parchment piping (icing) bags
fine writing nozzle
flower decorations

1 Split the cake and fill with butter icing. Cut triangles off two corners and use the pieces to make a chimney. Place on the cake board and brush with apricot jam. Cover with a layer of marzipan then sugarpaste icing.

2 Mark the roof with a pastry wheel and the chimney with the back of a knife. Paint the chimney red and the roof yellow.

3 Tint 25g/1oz/2 tbsp of sugarpaste icing red and cut out a 7.5 x 12cm/3 x 4½in door. Tint enough sugarpaste icing blue to make a fanlight. Stick to the cake with water.

4 Mark windows, 6cm/2½in square, with a cocktail stick. Paint on curtains with blue food colouring. Tint half the royal icing black and pipe around the windows and the door.

5 Tint the remaining royal icing green. Pipe the flower stems and leaves under the windows with the fine writing nozzle and the climber up on to the roof. Stick the flowers in place with a little icing and pipe green flower centres.

6 Pipe the house number or child's age on the door and add a knocker and handle. Leave to dry for 1 hour, then paint with gold food colouring.

Energy 832kcal/3496kJ; Fat 35.7g, Saturated Fat 10.3g; Carbohydrate 127.8g, Fibre 1.6g

Treasure Chest Cake

Allow yourself a few days before the party to make this cake as the lock and handles need to dry for 48 hours.

Makes one 20 x 10cm/ 8 x 4in cake

20cm/8in square sponge cake
115g/4oz/½ cup butter icing
45ml/3 tbsp apricot jam, warmed and sieved
350g/12oz marzipan
400g/14oz/generous 2½ cups sugarpaste icing
brown and green food colouring
50g/2oz/⅔ cup desiccated (dry unsweetened shredded) coconut
115g/4oz/¾ cup royal icing
edible gold dusting powder
edible silver balls
chocolate money

Materials/equipment
30cm/12in round cake board
fine paintbrush

1 Split the cake and fill with butter icing. Cut the cake in half and sandwich the halves on top of each other with butter icing. Place on the cake board.

2 Shape the top of the cake into a rounded lid (you could make a paper template to use on the ends if you like) and brush with apricot jam. Cover with a layer of marzipan. Tint 350g/12oz/2¼ cups of the sugarpaste icing brown and use to cover the cake.

3 Use the brown sugarpaste trimmings to make strips. Stick on to the chest with water. Mark the lid with a sharp knife. Tint the coconut with a few drops of green colouring. Spread a little royal icing over the cake board and press the green coconut lightly into it to make the grass.

4 From the remaining sugarpaste icing, cut out the padlock and two handles. Cut a keyhole shape from the padlock and shape the handles over a small box. Leave to dry for 48 hours. Stick the padlock and handles in place with royal icing and paint them with the gold dusting powder. Stick silver balls on to look like nails. Arrange the chocolate money around the chest on the board.

Energy 6600kcal/27758kJ; Fat 269.6g, Saturated Fat 69.7g; Carbohydrate 1045.1g, Fibre 12g

Lion Cake

For an animal lover or a celebration cake for a Leo horoscope sign, this cake is ideal. The shaggy mane is simply made with grated marzipan.

Makes one 28 x 23cm/ 11 x 9in oval cake

25 x 30cm/10 x 12in sponge cake
350g/12oz/1½ cups orange-flavour butter icing
orange and red food colouring
675g/1½lb yellow marzipan
50g/2oz/generous 4 tbsp sugarpaste icing
red and orange liquorice bootlaces
long and round marshmallows

Materials/equipment
30cm/12in square cake board
small heart-shaped cutter

1 With the flat side of the cake uppermost, cut it to make an oval shape with an uneven scallop design around the edge. Turn the cake over and trim the top level.

2 Place the cake on the cake board. Tint the butter icing orange and use it to cover the cake.

3 Roll 115g/4oz/¾ cup of marzipan to a 15cm/6in square. Place in the centre of the cake for the lion's face.

4 Grate the remaining marzipan and use to cover the sides and the top of the cake up to the face panel.

5 Tint the sugarpaste icing red. Use the heart-shaped cutter to stamp out the lion's nose and position on the cake with water.

6 Roll the remaining red icing into two thin, short strands to make the lion's mouth, and stick on with water.

7 Cut the liquorice into graduated lengths, and place on the cake for the whiskers.

8 Use two flattened round marshmallows for the eyes and two snipped long ones for the eyebrows and place in position on the cake.

Energy 8108kcal/33970kJ; Fat 426.6g, Saturated Fat 131.5g; Carbohydrate 1043.6g, Fibre 20g

Train Cake

This cake is made in a train-shaped tin, so all you need to do is decorate it.

Makes one train-shaped cake

train-shaped sponge cake, about 35cm/14in long
675g/1½lb/3 cups butter icing
yellow food colouring
red liquorice bootlaces
90–120ml/6–8 tbsp coloured vermicelli
4 liquorice wheels

Materials/equipment

25 x 38cm/10 x 15in cake board
2 fabric piping bags
fine round and small star nozzles
pink and white cotton wool (cotton balls)

1 Slice off the top surface of the cake to make it flat. Place diagonally on the cake board.

2 Tint the butter icing yellow. Use half of it to cover the cake.

3 Using a round piping nozzle and a quarter of the remaining butter icing, pipe a straight double border around the top edge of the cake.

4 Place the red liquorice bootlaces on the piped border. Snip the bootlaces around the curves on the train.

5 Using a small star nozzle and the remaining butter icing, pipe small stars over the top of the cake. Add extra liquorice and piping, if you like. Use a metal spatula to press on the coloured vermicelli all around the sides of the cake.

6 Pull a couple of balls of cotton wool apart for the steam and stick on to the cake board with butter icing. Press the liquorice wheels in place for the wheels.

Cook's Tip

You can buy novelty cake tins (pans) in all kinds of shapes or hire them from specialist cake suppliers if you are not confident that you could shape your cake well.

Energy 8457kcal/35303kJ; Fat 521.7g, Saturated Fat 216.3g; Carbohydrate 921.4g, Fibre 10.1g

Number 7 Cake

Any combination of colours will work well for this cake with its marbled effect.

Makes one 30cm/12in long cake

23 x 30cm/9 x 12in sponge cake
350g/12oz/1½ cups orange-flavour butter icing
60ml/4 tbsp apricot jam, warmed and sieved
675g/1½lb/4½ cups sugarpaste icing
blue and green food colouring
rice paper sweets

Materials/equipment

25 x 33cm/10 x 13in cake board
small "7" cutter

1 Place the cake flat side up and cut out the number seven. Slice the cake horizontally, sandwich together with the butter icing and place on the board.

2 Brush the cake evenly with apricot jam. Divide the sugarpaste icing into three and tint one of the pieces blue and another green. Set aside 50g/2oz/scant ½ cup from each of the coloured icings. Knead together the large pieces of blue and green icing with the third piece of white icing to marble. Use to cover the cake.

3 Immediately after covering, use the "7" cutter to remove several sugarpaste shapes in a random pattern from the covered cake.

4 Roll out the reserved blue and green sugarpaste icing and stamp out shapes with the same cutter. Use these to fill the stamped-out shapes from the cake. Decorate the board with some rice paper sweets.

Cook's Tip

You could make any number out of sponge cake using round and/or rectangular cakes (or you could hire a purpose-made tin (pan) instead). Use two cakes for numbers in their teens and over.

Energy 8883kcal/37220kJ; Fat 464.2g, Saturated Fat 202.7g; Carbohydrate 1193.9g, Fibre 7.2g

Musical Cake

Creating a sheet of music requires delicate piping work, so it is best to practise first.

Makes one 20 x 25cm/8 x 10in cake

25cm/10in square sponge cake
225g/8oz/1 cup butter icing
45ml/3 tbsp apricot jam, warmed and sieved
450g/1lb marzipan
450g/1lb/3 cups sugarpaste icing
115g/4oz/¾ cup royal icing
black food colouring

Materials/equipment

25 x 30cm/10 x 12in cake board
wooden cocktail stick (toothpick)
2 small baking parchment piping (icing) bags
very fine writing and fine shell nozzles
1.5m/1½yd red ribbon

1 Split the cake and fill with a little butter icing. Cut a 5cm/2in strip off one side of the cake. Place the cake on the cake board and brush with apricot jam. Cover with a layer of marzipan then sugarpaste icing. Leave to dry overnight.

2 Make a template for the sheet of music and the child's name. L ay the template on the cake and trace over the music and name with a cocktail stick. Using white royal icing and a very fine writing nozzle, begin by piping the lines and bars. Leave to dry.

3 Tint the remaining icing black and pipe the clefs, name and notes. With the shell nozzle, pipe a royal icing border around the base of the cake. Finally, tie a ribbon around the side.

Cook's Tip

Find a sheet of simple music to copy for the cake – a beginner's piano book would be ideal. Practise writing the treble clef on paper first, and always start at the centre of the symbol: make a dot and then curl round to the right; curl to the left and then up and out to the right to make the loop at the top; finish with the downward line that ends with a curl to the left at the base of the symbol.

Energy 7924kcal/33281kJ; Fat 356.9g, Saturated Fat 103.1g; Carbohydrate 1173.1g, Fibre 15.8g

Magic Rabbit Cake

Delight a child with this cute rabbit bursting out of a hat.

Makes one 15cm/6in tall round cake

2 x 15cm/6in round cakes
225g/8oz/1 cup butter icing
115g/4oz/¾ cup royal icing
45ml/3 tbsp apricot jam, warmed and sieved
675g/1½lb marzipan
675g/1½lb/4½ cups sugarpaste icing
black and pink food colouring
edible silver balls

Materials/equipment

25cm/10in square cake board
2 small baking parchment piping (icing) bags
medium star nozzle
1.5m/1½yd pink ribbon

1 Split the cakes and fill with butter icing, then sandwich them one on top of the other. Stick on the centre of the cake board with a little royal icing. Brush with apricot jam. Use 450g/1lb/3 cups of the marzipan to cover the cake.

2 Tint the sugarpaste icing grey. Use about two-thirds of it to cover the cake. For the hat's brim roll out the remaining grey sugarpaste to a 20cm/8in round. Cut a 15cm/6in circle from its centre. Lower the brim over the cake. Shape the brim sides over wooden spoon handles until dry.

3 Cut a cross in the 15cm/6in grey circle and place on the hat. Curl the triangles over a wooden spoon handle to shape. Smooth the join at the top and sides of the hat using the warmth of your hand

4 Tint the remaining marzipan pink and make the rabbit's head, about 5cm/2in wide with a pointed face. Mark the position of the eyes, nose and mouth. Leave to dry overnight.

5 Stick the rabbit in the centre of the hat with a little royal icing. Pipe a border of royal icing around the top and base of the hat and decorate with silver balls while still wet. Tint the remaining royal icing black and pipe the rabbit's eyes and mouth. Tie the ribbon around the hat.

Energy 10054kcal/42289kJ; Fat 412.7g, Saturated Fat 111.2g; Carbohydrate 1586.6g, Fibre 20.9g

Nurse's Kit Cake

The box is easy to make and is simply filled with toys from a nurse's or doctor's set. It's sure to delight any budding medical professionals.

Makes one 20 x 17cm/ 8 x 6½in cake

35 x 20cm/14 x 8in chocolate sponge cake
120ml/4fl oz/½ cup apricot jam, warmed and sieved
675g/1½lb/4½ cups sugarpaste icing
red food colouring

Materials/equipment

25cm/10in square cake board
selection of toy medical equipment

1 Place the cake dome-side down and cut in half widthways.

2 To make the base of the nurse's box, turn one cake half, dome-side up, and hollow out the centre to a depth of 1cm/½in, leaving a 1cm/½in border on the three uncut edges. Brush the tops and sides of both cake halves with jam.

3 Tint 150g/5oz/scant 1 cup sugarpaste icing deep pink. Use a little to make a small handle for the box. Wrap in clear film (plastic wrap) and set aside. Cover the cake board with the remainder of the pink icing. Tint 25g/1oz/2 tbsp of the sugarpaste icing red. Cover with clear film and set aside.

4 Tint the remaining icing light pink and divide into two portions, one slightly bigger than the other. Roll out the bigger portion and use to cover the base of the box, easing it into the hollow and along the edges. Trim, then position the base on the cake board.

5 Roll out the other portion and use to cover the lid of the box. Trim, then place on top of the base at a slight angle.

6 Stick the handle to the base of the box using water. Cut a small cross out of red icing and stick it on the lid. Place a few toy items of medical equipment under the lid, protruding slightly. Arrange some more items around the board and cake.

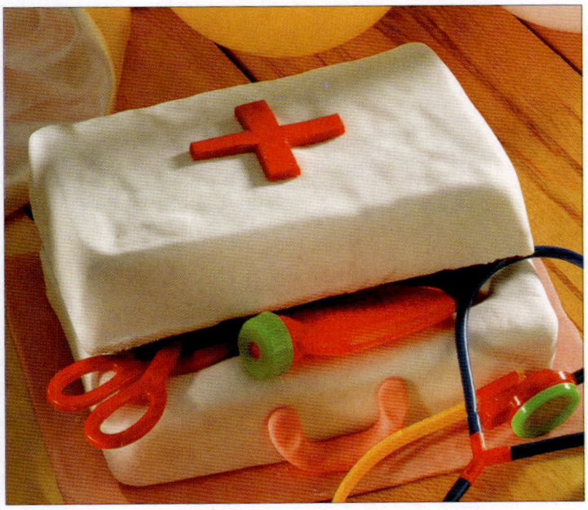

Energy 5993kcal/25233kJ; Fat 237.6g, Saturated Fat 0g; Carbohydrate 954.4g, Fibre 0g

Ballerina Cake

Use flower cutters with ejectors to make the tiny flowers for this cake.

Makes one 20cm/8in round cake

20cm/8in round sponge cake
115g/4oz/½ cup butter icing
45ml/3 tbsp apricot jam, warmed and sieved
450g/1lb marzipan
450g/1lb/3 cups sugarpaste icing
pink, yellow, blue and green food colouring
115g/4oz/¾ cup royal icing

Materials/equipment

25cm/10in round cake board
small flower cutter
small circle cutter
wooden cocktail stick (toothpick)
cotton wool (cotton balls)
fine paintbrush
3 small baking parchment piping (icing) bags
fine shell nozzle
1.5m/1½yd pink ribbon

1 Split the cake and fill with butter icing. Place on the board and brush with apricot jam. Cover with marzipan then sugarpaste icing. Leave to dry overnight. Divide the rest of the sugarpaste into three. Tint flesh tone, light pink and dark pink. Stamp out 15 pale pink flowers. Leave to dry.

2 Make a template of the ballerina. Mark her position on the cake. Cut out a flesh-tone body and dark pink bodice. Stick on with water, rounding off the edges.

3 Cut two dark pink underskirts, a pale pink top skirt and a dark pink bodice extension to make the tutu. Stamp out hollow, fluted circles, divide the circles into four and frill the fluted edges with a cocktail stick. Stick the tutu in place, supported with cotton wool. Cut out and stick on pale pink shoes. Leave to dry overnight.

4 Paint the ballerina's face and hair. Position 12 hoop and three headdress flowers. Tint some royal icing green and dark pink to complete the flowers and ballet shoes. Pipe a border around the base with the shell nozzle. Tie the pink ribbon around the outside of the cake.

Energy 6771kcal/28459kJ; Fat 288.6g, Saturated Fat 71.3g; Carbohydrate 1037.1g, Fibre 14.9g

Monsters on the Moon

A great cake for little monsters! This cake is covered with a sugar frosting and is best eaten on the day of making.

Serves 12–15
1 quantity quick-mix sponge cake
500g/1¼lb/3¾ cups sugarpaste icing
black food colouring
225g/8oz marzipan
edible silver glitter powder (optional)
375g/12oz/1¾ cups caster (superfine) sugar
2 egg whites
60ml/4 tbsp water

Materials/equipment
ovenproof wok
various sizes of plain round and star cutters
30cm/12in round cake board
small monster toys

1 Preheat the oven to 180°C/350°F/Gas 4. Grease the wok and line with baking parchment. Spoon in the cake mixture and smooth the surface.

2 Bake in the centre of the oven for 35–40 minutes. Leave for 5 minutes, then turn out on to a rack and peel off the paper. Leave to cool completely.

3 With the cake dome-side up, use the round cutters to cut out craters. Press in the cutters to about 2.5cm/1in deep, then remove and cut the craters out of the cake with a knife.

4 Use 115g/4oz/¾ cup of the sugarpaste icing to cover the cake, pulling off small pieces and pressing them in uneven strips around the edges of the craters.

5 Tint the remaining sugarpaste icing black. Roll out and cover the board. Stamp out stars and replace with marzipan stars of the same size. Dust with glitter powder, if using, and place on the board.

6 Put the sugar, egg whites and water in a heatproof bowl over a pan of simmering water. Beat until thick and peaky. Spoon the icing over the cake, swirling it into the craters and peaking it unevenly. Sprinkle over the silver glitter powder, if using, then position the monsters on the cake.

Energy 438kcal/1850kJ; Fat 12.8g, Saturated Fat 2.5g; Carbohydrate 81.9g, Fibre 0.6g

Circus Cake

This colourful design is easy to achieve and is sure to delight young children.

Makes one 20cm/8in cake
20cm/8in round sponge cake
115g/4oz/½ cup butter icing
45ml/3 tbsp apricot jam, warmed and sieved
450g/1lb marzipan
450g/1lb/3 cups sugarpaste icing
red and blue food colouring
115g/4oz/¾ cup royal icing
edible silver balls
3 digestive cookies (graham crackers)

Materials/equipment
25cm/10in round cake board
small baking parchment piping (icing) bag
small star nozzle
5cm/2in plastic circus ornaments

1 Split the cake and fill with butter icing. Place on the cake board and brush with apricot jam. Cover with a layer of marzipan then sugarpaste icing.

2 Tint 115g/4oz/¾ cup sugarpaste icing pink, then roll into a rope and stick around the top edge of the cake with a little water.

3 Tint half the remaining sugarpaste icing red and half blue. Roll out each colour and cut into twelve 2.5cm/1in squares. Stick the squares alternately at an angle around the side of the cake with a little water. Using the star nozzle, pipe stars around the base of the cake with royal icing and stick in the edible silver balls.

4 Crush the digestive cookies by pressing through a sieve to make the "sand" for the circus ring. Sprinkle the "sand" over the top of the cake and place small circus ornaments on top.

Variation
Instead of a circus you could make the cake into an ice rink. Cover the top of the cake with very pale blue marbled sugarpaste (by colouring two or three balls of sugarpaste different shades of pale blue and then rolling them out with the white to get a marbled effect). Then buy some ice skaters to go on the top.

Energy 6888kcal/28960kJ; Fat 288.6g, Saturated Fat 71.3g; Carbohydrate 1068.1g, Fibre 14.9g

Frog Prince Cake

Our happy frog will bring a smile to any young child's face – and will probably even get a kiss!

Serves 8–10

20cm/8in round sponge cake
115g/4oz/½ cup butter icing
45ml/3 tbsp apricot jam, warmed and sieved
450g/1lb marzipan
cornflour (cornstarch), for dusting
500g/1¼lb/3¾ cups sugarpaste icing
115g/4oz/¾ cup royal icing
green, red, black and gold food colouring

Materials/equipment

25cm/10in square cake board
glass
fine paintbrush

1 Split the cake and fill with butter icing. Cut in half and sandwich the halves together with apricot jam. Stand upright diagonally across the cake board. Brush the cake with apricot jam and cover with marzipan.

2 Tint 450g/1lb/3 cups of the sugarpaste icing green and cover the cake. Roll the remaining green sugarpaste icing into 1cm/½in diameter sausages. You will need two folded 20cm/8in lengths for the back legs and 14 10cm/4in lengths for the front legs and feet. Stick in place with a little royal icing. Roll balls for the eyes and stick in place.

3 Roll out the reserved sugarpaste icing and cut a 5 x 19cm/2 x 7½in strip. Cut out triangles along one edge to make the crown shape. Wrap around a glass dusted with cornflour and moisten the edges to join. Leave to dry.

4 Cut a 10cm/4in circle for the white shirt. Stick in place and trim the base edge. Cut white circles and stick to the eyes.

5 Tint a little sugarpaste pink, roll into a sausage and stick on for the mouth. Tint the rest black and use for the pupils and the bow tie. Stick in place.

6 Paint the crown with gold food colouring, leave to dry, then stick into position with royal icing.

Energy 681kcal/2862kJ; Fat 28.9g, Saturated Fat 7.1g; Carbohydrate 104.7g, Fibre 1.5g

Ladybird Cake

Children will love this colourful and appealing ladybird, and it is very simple to make.

Serves 10–12

3-egg quantity quick-mix sponge cake
175g/6oz butter icing
60ml/4 tbsp lemon curd, warmed
icing (confectioners') sugar, for dusting
1kg/2¼lb/6¾ cups sugarpaste icing
red, black and green food colourings
5 marshmallows
50g/2oz marzipan
2 pipe cleaners

1 Preheat the oven to 180°C/350°F/Gas 4. Grease and line the base of a 1.2 litre/2 pint/5 cup ovenproof bowl. Spoon in the cake mixture and smooth the surface. Bake for 55–60 minutes, or until a skewer inserted into the centre comes out clean. Cool.

2 Cut the cake in half crossways and sandwich together with the butter icing. Cut vertically through the cake, about a third of the way in. Brush both pieces with the lemon curd.

3 Colour 450g/1lb/3 cups of the sugarpaste icing red. Dust a work surface with icing sugar and roll out the icing to about 5mm/¼in thick. Use to cover the larger piece of cake to make the body. Using a wooden skewer, make an indentation down the centre for the wings. Colour 350g/12oz of the sugarpaste icing black, roll out three-quarters and use to cover the smaller piece of cake for the head. Place both cakes on a cake board, press together.

4 Roll out 50g/2oz/4 tbsp icing and cut out two 5cm/2in circles for the eyes, stick to the head with water. Roll out the remaining black icing and cut out eight 4cm/1½in circles. Use two of these for the eyes and stick the others on to the body.

5 Colour some icing green and squeeze through a garlic press to make grass. Flatten the marshmallows and stick a marzipan round in the centre of each. Colour the pipe cleaners black and press a ball of black icing on to the end of each for the feelers. Arrange grass on the board, with the decorations.

Energy 539kcal/2270kJ; Fat 19.5g, Saturated Fat 6.3g; Carbohydrate 92.7g, Fibre 0.5g

Spaceship Cake

The perfect cake for all would-be astronauts.

Serves 10–12

25cm/10in square sponge cake
225g/8oz/1 cup butter icing
60ml/4 tbsp apricot jam, warmed and sieved
350g/12oz marzipan
450g/1lb/3 cups sugarpaste icing
blue, red and black food colouring

Materials/equipment

30cm/12in square cake board
silver candles and holders
gold paper stars

1 Split the sponge cake and fill with butter icing. Cut a 10cm/4in wide piece diagonally across the middle of the cake, about 25cm/10in long. Shape the nose end and straighten the other end.

2 From the off-cuts make three 7.5cm/3in triangles for the wings and top of the ship. Cut two smaller triangles for the booster jets.

3 Position the main body, wings and top of the cake diagonally across the cake board. Add extra pieces of cake in front of the triangle on top of the cake to shape it as shown in the picture.

4 Brush the cake and booster jets with apricot jam, then cover with a layer of marzipan and sugarpaste icing.

5 Divide the remaining sugarpaste icing into three. Tint blue, pink and black. Roll out the blue icing and cut it into 1cm/½in strips. Stick around the base of the cake with water and outline the boosters. Cut a 2.5cm/1in strip and stick down the centre of the spaceship.

6 Roll out the pink and black sugarpaste icing separately and cut shapes, numbers and the child's name to finish the design. When complete, position the boosters.

7 Make small cubes with the off-cuts of sugarpaste icing and use to stick the candles to the cake board. Decorate the board with gold stars.

Energy 320kcal/1350kJ; Fat 10.6g, Saturated Fat 4.6g; Carbohydrate 58.1g, Fibre 0.6g

Racing Track Cake

This simple cake will delight eight-year-old racing car enthusiasts.

Serves 10–12

2 x 15cm/6in round sponge cakes
115g/4oz/½ cup butter icing
60ml/4 tbsp apricot jam, warmed and sieved
450g/1lb marzipan
500g/1¼lb/3¾ cups sugarpaste icing
blue and red food colouring
115g/4oz/¾ cup royal icing

Materials/equipment

25 x 35cm/10 x 14in cake board
5cm/2in fluted cutter
2 small baking parchment piping (icing) bags
medium star and medium plain nozzles
8 candles and holders
2 small toy racing cars

1 Split the cakes and fill with a little butter icing. Cut off a 1cm/½in piece from the side of each cake and place the cakes on the cake board, cut edges together.

2 Brush the cake with apricot jam and cover with a layer of marzipan. Tint 450g/1lb/3 cups of the sugarpaste icing pale blue and use to cover the cake.

3 Mark a 5cm/2in circle in the centre of each cake. Roll out the remaining white sugarpaste icing, cut out two fluted 5cm/2in circles and stick them in the marked spaces.

4 Tint the royal icing red. Pipe a shell border around the base of the cake using the star nozzle.

5 Pipe a track for the cars using the plain nozzle and stick the candles into the two white circles. Place the cars on the track.

Variation

You can adapt this cake by changing the colours or decorating with other shapes, such as colouring the sugarpaste green and adding some toy horses; perhaps add some cut-out flowers to make it look like a meadow.

Energy 624kcal/2624kJ; Fat 26.6g, Saturated Fat 6.4g; Carbohydrate 95.7g, Fibre 1.4g

Floating Balloons Cake

Make brightly coloured balloons to float above the cake from eggshells covered in sugarpaste.

Makes one 20cm/8in round cake

20cm/8in round sponge or fruit cake, covered with 800g/1¾lb marzipan if you like
900g/2lb/6 cups sugarpaste icing
red, green and yellow food colouring
3 eggs
2 egg whites
450g/1lb/4 cups icing (confectioners') sugar

Materials/equipment

25cm/10in round cake board
3 bamboo skewers, 25cm/10in, 24cm/9½in and 23cm/9in long
small star cutter
baking parchment piping bags
fine writing nozzle
1m/1yd fine coloured ribbon
candles

1 Using a skewer, pierce the eggs and carefully empty the contents. Wash and dry the shells.

2 Place the cake on the board. Tint 50g/2oz/scant ½ cup of the sugarpaste icing red, 50g/2oz/scant ½ cup green and 115g/4oz/1 cup yellow. Cover the cake with the remaining icing. Use just under half the yellow icing to cover the board.

3 Cover the eggshells carefully with the tinted sugarpaste and insert a bamboo skewer in each. Use the trimmings to stamp out a star shape of each colour. Thread on to the skewers for the balloon knots.

4 Trace 16 balloon shapes on to baking paper. Beat the egg whites with the icing sugar until smooth, and divide between four bowls. Leave one white and tint the others red, green and yellow. With the fine writing nozzle and white icing, trace around the balloon shapes. Thin the tinted icings with water. Fill the balloon shapes using snipped piping bags. Dry overnight.

5 Stick the balloon shapes around the side of the cake with icing. Pipe white balloon strings. Push the large balloons into the centre and decorate with the ribbon. Push the candles into the icing around the edge.

Energy 10835kcal/45729kJ; Fat 335.8g, Saturated Fat 59.3g; Carbohydrate 1952.8g, Fibre 22.4g

Number 6 Cake

Boys and girls will love this delightful cake.

Serves 10–12

15cm/6in round and 15cm/6in square sponge cakes
115g/4oz/½ cup butter icing
60ml/4 tbsp apricot jam, warmed and sieved
450g/1lb marzipan
500g/1¼lb/3¾ cups sugarpaste icing
yellow and green food colouring
115g/4oz/¾ cup royal icing

Materials/equipment

25 x 35cm/10 x 14in cake board
2 small baking parchment piping (icing) bags
7.5cm/3in fluted cutter
fine plain and medium star nozzles
plastic train set and 6 candles

1 Split the cakes and fill with butter icing. Cut the square cake in half and cut, using the round cake tin as a guide, a rounded end from one rectangle to fit around the round cake. Trim the cakes to the same depth and assemble the number 6 on the cake board. Brush with apricot jam and cover with a thin layer of marzipan.

2 Tint 450g/1lb/3 cups of the sugarpaste icing yellow and the rest green. Cover the cake with the yellow icing.

3 With the cutter, mark a circle in the centre of the round cake. Cut out a green sugarpaste icing circle. Stick in place with water and leave to dry overnight.

4 Mark a track the width of the train on the top of the cake. Tint the royal icing yellow and pipe the track with the plain nozzle. Use the star nozzle to pipe a border around the base and top of the cake. Pipe the name on the green circle and attach the train and candles with royal icing.

Variation
You could add a dancer or fairy in the centre and decorate the cake with sugarpaste or commercially made flowers.

Energy 667kcal/2801kJ; Fat 28.9g, Saturated Fat 6.9g; Carbohydrate 100.9g, Fibre 1.4g

Spider's Web Cake

Make the marzipan spider several days before you need the cake, to give it time to dry.

Makes one 20cm/8in round cake

20cm/8in round deep sponge cake
225g/8oz/1 cup butter icing
45ml/3 tbsp apricot jam, warmed and sieved
30ml/2 tbsp unsweetened cocoa powder
chocolate vermicelli
40g/1½oz marzipan
yellow, red, black and brown food colouring
225g/8oz/1½ cups icing (confectioners') sugar
15–30ml/1–2 tbsp water

Materials/equipment

25cm/10in round cake board
2 small baking parchment piping (icing) bags
wooden cocktail stick (toothpick)
medium star nozzle
candles and holders

1 Split the cake and fill with half the butter icing. Brush the sides with apricot jam, add the cocoa to the remaining butter icing then smooth a little over the sides of the cake. Roll the sides of the cake in chocolate vermicelli. Place on the board.

2 For the spider, tint the marzipan yellow. Roll half of it into two balls of equal size for the head and body. Tint a small piece of marzipan red and make a mouth, and three balls to stick on the spider's body. Tint a tiny piece of marzipan black for the eyes. Roll the rest of the yellow marzipan into eight legs and two smaller feelers. Stick together.

3 Gently heat the icing sugar and water over a pan of hot water. Use two-thirds of the glacé icing to cover the cake top.

4 Tint the remaining glacé icing brown and use it to pipe concentric circles on to the cake. Divide the web into eighths by drawing lines across with a cocktail stick. Leave to set.

5 Put the rest of the chocolate butter icing into a piping bag fitted with a star nozzle and pipe a border around the web. Put candles around the border and the spider in the centre.

Energy 5660kcal/23728kJ; Fat 284.2g, Saturated Fat 96.9g; Carbohydrate 768.6g, Fibre 10.7g

Dart Board Cake

This cake is very striking.

Makes one 25cm/10in round cake

25cm/10in round sponge cake
175g/6oz/¾ cup butter icing
5ml/3 tbsp apricot jam, warmed and sieved
450g/1lb marzipan
450g/1lb/3 cups sugarpaste icing
black, red, yellow and silver food colouring
115g/4oz/¾ cup royal icing

Materials/equipment

30cm/12in round cake board
icing smoother
1cm/½in plain circle cutter
small baking parchment piping (icing) bag
fine writing nozzle
3 candles and holders

1 Split the cake and fill with butter icing and put on to the board. Brush with jam and cover with marzipan. Colour some of the sugarpaste icing black, a small piece red and the remainder yellow. Cover the cake with black sugarpaste icing. Cut a 20cm/8in circular template out of baking parchment. Fold it in quarters, then divide each quarter into fifths.

2 Using the template, mark the centre and wedges on the top of the cake with a sharp knife. Cut out ten wedges from the yellow sugarpaste, using the template as a guide. Lay alternate sections on the cake, but do not stick in place yet. Repeat the process with the black sugarpaste. Cut 3mm/⅛in strips off the end of each wedge and swap the colour. Mark a 13cm/5in circle in the centre of the board and cut out 3mm/⅛in strips from each colour to swap with adjoining colours. Stick in place and use an icing smoother to flatten.

3 Use the cutter to remove the centre for the bull's eye. Replace with a circle of red sugarpaste, cut with the same cutter. Surround it with a strip of black sugarpaste. Roll the remaining black sugarpaste into a long sausage to fit round the base of the cake and stick in place with a little water. Mark numbers on the board and pipe on with royal icing using the fine writing nozzle. Leave to dry then paint with silver food colouring. Stick candles in at an angle to resemble darts.

Energy 8090kcal/34014kJ; Fat 340.5g, Saturated Fat 92.7g; Carbohydrate 1256.5g, Fibre 15.8g

Camping Tent Cake

Dream of the outdoor life with this fun cake.

Makes one 20 x 10cm/ 8 x 4in cake

20cm/8in square sponge cake
115g/4oz/½ cup butter icing
45ml/3 tbsp apricot jam, warmed and sieved
450g/1lb marzipan
500g/1¼lb/3¾ cups sugarpaste icing
brown, orange, green, red and blue food colouring
50g/2oz/⅓ cup desiccated (dry unsweetened shredded) coconut
115g/4oz/¾ cup royal icing
chocolate mint sticks

Materials/equipment

25cm/10in square cake board
wooden cocktail sticks (toothpicks)
fine paintbrush
4 small baking parchment piping (icing) bags
very fine basketweave and plain nozzles
toy ball

1 Split the cake and fill with butter icing. Cut the cake in half. Cut one half in two diagonally from the top right edge to the bottom left edge to form the roof of the tent. Stick the two wedges, back-to-back, on top of the rectangle with jam. Trim to 10cm/4in high and use the trimmings on the base. Place the cake diagonally on the board and brush with jam.

2 Cover the entire cake with marzipan, reserving some for modelling. Tint 50g/2oz/scant ½ cup of the sugarpaste icing brown and cover one end of the tent. Tint the rest orange and cover the rest of the cake. Cut a semicircle for the tent opening and a central 7.5cm/3in slit. Lay over the brown end. Secure the flaps with royal icing. Put halved cocktail sticks in the corners and ridge.

3 Tint the coconut green. Spread the board with a thin layer of royal icing and sprinkle with the coconut.

4 Tint the reserved marzipan flesh-colour and use to make a model of a child. Paint on a blue T-shirt and leave to dry. Tint some royal icing brown and pipe on the hair with a basketweave nozzle. Tint the icing and pipe on the mouth and eyes. Make a bonfire with broken chocolate mint sticks.

Energy 5636kcal/23658kJ; Fat 262.5g, Saturated Fat 93.3g; Carbohydrate 819.4g, Fibre 13.1g

Army Tank Cake

Create an authentic camouflaged tank by combining green and brown sugarpaste icing.

Makes one 25 x 15cm/ 10 x 6in cake

25cm/10in square sponge cake
225g/8oz/1 cup butter icing
45ml/3 tbsp apricot jam, warmed and sieved
450g/1lb marzipan
450g/1lb/3 cups sugarpaste icing
brown, green and black food colouring
1 flaked chocolate bar
liquorice strips
60ml/4 tbsp royal icing
round cookies (cookies)
sweets (candies)

Materials/equipment

25 x 35cm/10 x 14in cake board

1 Split the sponge cake and fill with butter icing. Cut off a 10cm/4in strip from one side of the cake. Use the off-cut to make a 15 x 7.5cm/6 x 3in rectangle, and stick on the top.

2 Shape the sloping top and cut a 2.5cm/1in piece from both ends to form the tracks. Shape the rounded ends for the wheels and tracks. Place on the cake board and brush with apricot jam. Cover with a layer of marzipan.

3 Tint a quarter of the sugarpaste icing brown and the rest green. Roll out the green to a 25cm/10in square. Break small pieces of brown icing and place all over the green. Flatten and roll out together to give a camouflage effect. Turn the icing over and repeat.

4 Continue to roll out until the icing is 3mm/⅛in thick. Lay it over the cake and gently press to fit. Using your hand smooth the sugarpaste around all the curves of the tank. Cut away the excess.

5 From the trimmings cut a piece into a 6cm/2½in disc and stick on the top with a little water. Cut a small hole in the front of the tank for the gun and insert the flaked chocolate. Stick liquorice on for the tracks, using a little black royal icing. Stick on cookies for the wheels and sweets for the lights and portholes.

Energy 8226kcal/34566kJ; Fat 360.1g, Saturated Fat 103.4g; Carbohydrate 1244.3g, Fibre 16.2g

Computer Game Cake

Making a cake look like a computer is easier than you think. This cake is ideal for a computer-game fanatic.

Makes one 14 x 13cm/ 5½ x 5in cake

15cm/6in square sponge cake
115g/4oz/½ cup butter icing
45ml/3 tbsp apricot jam, warmed and sieved
225g/8oz marzipan
275g/10oz/scant 2 cups sugarpaste icing
black, blue, red and yellow food colouring
royal icing, to decorate

Materials/equipment

20cm/8in square cake board
wooden cocktail stick (toothpick)
fine paintbrush
small baking parchment piping (icing) bag

1 Split the cake and fill with a little butter icing. Cut 2.5cm/1in off one side of the cake and 1cm/½in off the other side. Round the corners slightly.

2 Place the cake on the cake board and brush with apricot jam. Roll out the marzipan into a thin layer and use to cover the cake.

3 Tint 225g/8oz/1½ cups of the sugarpaste black. Use to cover the cake. Reserve the trimmings. With a cocktail stick, mark the speaker holes and position of the screen and knobs.

4 Tint half the remaining sugarpaste pale blue, roll out and cut out a 6cm/2½in square for the screen. Stick in the centre of the game with a little water.

5 Tint a small piece of sugarpaste red and the rest yellow. Use to cut out the switch and controls. Stick in position with water.

6 Roll the reserved black sugarpaste icing into a long, thin sausage and edge the screen and base of the cake.

7 With a fine paintbrush, draw the game on to the screen with a little blue colouring (choose the child's favourite game, if you like). Pipe letters on to the buttons with royal icing.

Energy 4558kcal/19093kJ; Fat 239.2g, Saturated Fat 63.7g, Carbohydrate 583.9g, Fibre 10.6g

Chessboard Cake

To make this cake look most effective, ensure that the squares have very sharp and clear edges.

Makes one 25cm/10in square cake

25cm/10in square sponge cake
225g/8oz/1 cup butter icing
60ml/4 tbsp apricot jam, warmed and sieved
800g/1¾lb marzipan
500g/1¼lb/3¾ cups sugarpaste icing
black and red food colouring
edible silver balls
115g/4oz/¾ cup royal icing

Materials/equipment

30cm/12in square cake board
small baking parchment piping (icing) bag
medium star nozzle

1 Split the cake and fill with butter icing. Place on the cake board and brush with jam.

2 Roll out 450g/1lb/3 cups marzipan and use to cover the cake.

3 Once the marzipan has dried, cover with 450g/1lb/3 cups of the sugarpaste icing. Leave to dry overnight.

4 Divide the remaining marzipan into two, and tint black and red. To shape the chess pieces, roll 50g/2oz/4 tbsp of each colour into a sausage and cut into eight equal pieces. Shape into pawns.

5 Divide 75g/3oz/generous 4 tbsp of each colour into six equal pieces and use to shape into two castles, two knights and two bishops. (When shaping the chess pieces have a chess set to refer to so that the shapes are correct.)

6 Divide 25g/1oz/2 tbsp of each colour marzipan in half and shape a queen and a king. Decorate with silver balls. Leave to dry overnight.

7 Cut 1cm/½in black strips of marzipan to edge the board and stick in place with water. Pipe a border around the base of the cake with royal icing. Place the chess pieces in position.

Energy 9755kcal/41011kJ; Fat 415g, Saturated Fat 109.6g, Carbohydrate 1498.4g, Fibre 22.9g

Kite Cake

The happy face on this cheerful kite is a great favourite with children of all ages.

Serves 10–12

25cm/10in square sponge cake
225g/8oz/1 cup butter icing
45ml/3 tbsp apricot jam, warmed and sieved
450g/1lb marzipan
675g/1½lb/4½ cups sugarpaste icing
yellow, red, green, blue and black food colouring
115g/4oz/¾ cup royal icing

Materials/equipment

30cm/12in square cake board
wooden cocktail stick (toothpick)
small baking parchment piping (icing) bag
medium star nozzle
candles and holders

1 Trim the cake into a kite shape, then split and fill with butter icing. Place diagonally on the cake board and brush with apricot jam. Cover with a layer of marzipan.

2 Tint 225g/8oz/1½ cups of the sugarpaste icing pale yellow and cover the cake.

3 Make a template of the face, tie and buttons from baking parchment, and mark on to the cake with a cocktail stick. Divide the remainder of the sugarpaste icing into four and tint red, green, blue and black. Cut out the features and stick on with water.

4 Pipe a royal icing border around the base of the cake.

5 For the ribbons on the kite's tail, roll out each colour separately and cut two 4 x 1cm/1½ x ½in lengths in blue, red and green. Pinch each length to shape into a bow.

6 Roll the yellow sugarpaste into a long rope and lay it on the board in a wavy line from the narrow end of the kite. Stick the bows in place with water. To make the candleholders, roll balls of yellow sugarpaste, stick on the board with a little royal icing and press in the candles.

Energy 726kcal/3054kJ; Fat 29.7g, Saturated Fat 8.6g; Carbohydrate 115.2g, Fibre 1.3g

Hotdog Cake

This realistic hotdog cake is sure to be popular at a party.

Makes one 23cm/9in long cake

23 x 33cm/9 x 13in sponge roll
175g/6oz/¾ cup coffee flavour butter icing
90ml/6 tbsp apricot jam, warmed and sieved
450g/1lb/3 cups sugarpaste icing
brown and red food colouring
115g/4oz/¾ cup glacé icing
15–30ml/1–2 tbsp toasted sesame seeds

Filling

175g/6oz sponge cake pieces
50g/2oz/¼ cup soft dark brown sugar
45ml/3 tbsp orange juice
75ml/5 tbsp honey

Materials/equipment

fine paintbrush
2 small baking parchment piping (icing) bags
napkin, plate, knife and fork

1 Unroll the sponge roll, spread with butter icing, then roll up again. Slice the sponge roll along the centre lengthways, almost to the base, and ease the two halves apart.

2 Mix all the filling ingredients in a food processor or blender until smooth. Shape the mixture with your hands to a 23cm/9in sausage shape.

3 Tint all the sugarpaste icing brown. Set aside 50g/2oz/4 tbsp and use the rest to cover the cake.

4 Paint the top of the "bun" with diluted brown food colouring to give a toasted effect. Position the "sausage".

5 Divide the glacé icing in half. Tint one half brown and the other red. Pipe red icing along the sausage, then overlay with brown icing. Sprinkle the sesame seeds over the "bun".

6 Cut the reserved brown sugarpaste icing into thin strips. Place on the cake with the joins under the "sausage".

7 Place on a napkin on a serving plate, with a knife and fork.

Energy 4251kcal/18030kJ; Fat 73.9g, Saturated Fat 11.4g; Carbohydrate 907.4g, Fibre 6g

Drum Cake

This is a colourful cake for very young children. It even comes complete with bright drumsticks.

Makes one 15cm/6in round cake

15cm/6in round sponge cake
50g/2oz/4 tbsp butter icing
45ml/3 tbsp apricot jam, warmed and sieved
350g/12oz marzipan
450g/1lb/3 cups sugarpaste icing
red, blue and yellow food colouring
royal icing, for sticking

Materials/equipment
20cm/8in round cake board

1 Split the cake and fill with a little butter icing. Place on the cake board and brush with apricot jam. Cover with a layer of marzipan and leave to dry overnight.

2 Tint half of the sugarpaste icing red and roll it out to 25 x 30cm/10 x 12in. Cut in half and stick to the side of the cake with water.

3 Roll out a circle of white sugarpaste icing to fit the top of the cake and divide the remainder in half. Tint one half blue and the other yellow.

4 Divide the blue into four pieces and roll each into a sausage long enough to go halfway round the cake. Stick around the base and top of the cake with a little water.

5 To make the drum strings, mark the cake into six around the top and base. Roll the yellow sugarpaste icing into 12 strands long enough to cross diagonally from top to base to form the drum strings. Roll the rest of the yellow icing into 12 small balls and stick at the top and base of the zigzags where the strings join the drum.

6 Knead together the red and white sugarpaste icing until streaky, then roll two balls and sticks 15cm/6in long. Leave to dry thoroughly, ideally overnight in a warm, dry place such as an airing cupboard. Stick together with royal icing to make the drumsticks and place on top of the cake.

Energy 5353kcal/22501kJ; Fat 228.2g, Saturated Fat 51.4g; Carbohydrate 817.3g; Fibre 12.1g

Ice Cream Cones

Individual cakes make a change for a party. Put a candle in the special person's one.

Makes 9

115g/4oz/¾ cup marzipan
9 ice cream cones
9 sponge fairy cakes
350g/12oz/1½ cups butter icing
red, green and brown food colouring
coloured and chocolate vermicelli, wafers and flaked chocolate bars
sweets (candies)

Materials/equipment
3 x 12-egg egg boxes
foil

1 Make the stands for the cakes by turning the egg boxes upside down and pressing three balls of marzipan into evenly spaced holes in each box. Wrap the boxes in foil.

2 Pierce the foil above the marzipan balls and insert the cones, being careful to press them in gently so that you do not crush the bottom of the cones.

3 Gently push a fairy cake into each cone. If the bases of the cakes are too large, trim them down with a small, sharp knife. The cakes should be quite secure in the cones.

4 Divide the butter icing between three bowls and tint them pale red, green and brown.

5 Using a small metal spatula, spread each cake with some of the pink icing, making sure that the finish on the icing is a little textured so that it looks like ice cream. Use the other coloured icings in the same way for all the ice cream cones.

6 To insert a wafer or chocolate stick into an ice cream, use a small, sharp knife to make a hole through the icing and into the cake, then insert the wafer or stick.

7 Add the finishing touches to the cakes by sprinkling over some coloured and chocolate vermicelli. Arrange sweets around the cones.

Energy 576kcal/2416kJ; Fat 28.8g, Saturated Fat 10.5g; Carbohydrate 78.6g, Fibre 1.1g

Treasure Map

Perhaps you could combine this map with a treasure hunt at the party.

Makes one 20 x 25cm/ 8 x 10in cake

25cm/10in square sponge cake
225g/8oz/1½ cups butter icing
45ml/3 tbsp apricot jam, warmed and sieved
450g/1lb/3 cups marzipan
675g/1½lb/4½ cups sugarpaste icing
yellow, brown, paprika, green, black and red food colouring
115g/4oz/¾ cup royal icing

Materials/equipment

25 x 35cm/10 x 14in cake board
fine paintbrush
kitchen paper
4 small baking parchment piping (icing) bags
medium shell and fine writing nozzles
candles and holders

1 Split the cake and fill with butter icing, cut it into a 20 x 25cm/8 x 10in rectangle and place on the cake board. Brush with apricot jam. Cover with a layer of marzipan then with 450g/1lb/3 cups sugarpaste icing.

2 Colour the remaining sugarpaste icing yellow and cut out with an uneven outline. Stick on to the cake with water and leave to dry overnight. Mark the island, river, lake, mountains and trees on the map.

3 With brown and paprika colours and a fine paintbrush, paint the edges of the map to look old, smudging the colours together with kitchen paper.

4 Paint the island pale green and the water around the island, the river and the lake pale blue. Dry overnight before painting on the other details, otherwise the colours will run.

5 Pipe a border of royal icing around the base of the cake with the shell nozzle. Colour a little royal icing red and pipe the path to the treasure, marked with an "X", with the writing nozzle.

6 Colour some icing green and pipe on grass and trees. Colour some icing black and pipe on a north sign with the writing nozzle.

Energy 8201kcal/34461kJ; Fat 356.9g, Saturated Fat 103.1g; Carbohydrate 1246.5g, Fibre 15.8g

Royal Crown Cake

This bejewelled regal cake is sure to delight any prince or princess.

Serves 16–20

20cm/8in and 15cm/6in round sponge cake
175g/6oz/¾ cup butter icing
45ml/3 tbsp apricot jam, warmed and sieved
450g/1lb marzipan
500g/1¼lb/3¾ cups sugarpaste icing
red food colouring
450g/1lb/3 cups royal icing
small black jelly sweets (candies)
4 ice cream fan wafers
edible silver balls
jewel sweets (candies)

Materials/equipment

30cm/12in square cake board
wooden cocktail sticks (toothpicks)

1 Split the cakes and fill with butter icing. Sandwich one on top of the other and place on the cake board. Shape the top cake into a dome.

2 Brush the cake with apricot jam. Roll out the marzipan thinly and use to cover the cake. Set aside 115g/4oz/¾ cup of the sugarpaste icing and use the remainder to cover the cake.

3 Tint the reserved sugarpaste icing red, and use to cover the dome of the cake. Trim away the excess.

4 Spoon rough mounds of royal icing around the base of the cake and stick a black jelly sweet on each mound.

5 Cut the ice cream wafers diagonally in half. Spread both sides of the wafers with royal icing and stick to the cake to form the points of the crown, smoothing the icing level with the sides of the cake.

6 Use cocktail sticks to support the wafers until they are dry.

7 Position silver balls on top of each point and stick jewel sweets around the side of the crown using a little royal icing to stick them securely.

Energy 427kcal/1798kJ; Fat 16.5g, Saturated Fat 4.9g; Carbohydrate 70.4g, Fibre 0.7g

Box of Chocolates Cake

This sophisticated cake is perfect for an adult's birthday and will delight chocolate lovers.

Makes one 15cm/6in square cake

15cm/6in square sponge cake
50g/2oz/4 tbsp butter icing
30ml/2 tbsp apricot jam, warmed and sieved
350g/12oz marzipan
350g/12oz/2¼ cups sugarpaste icing
red food colouring
wrapped chocolates

Materials/equipment

20cm/8in square cake board
small paper sweet (candy) cases
1.35m/1½yd x 4cm/1½in-wide gold and red ribbon

1 Split the cake in half and sandwich together with butter icing. Cut a shallow square from the top of the cake, leaving a 1cm/½in border around the edge.

2 Place on the cake board and brush with apricot jam. Cover with a layer of marzipan.

3 Roll out the sugarpaste icing and cut an 18cm/7in square. Ease it into the hollow dip and trim. Tint the remaining sugarpaste icing red and use to cover the sides.

4 Put the chocolates into paper cases and arrange in the box. Tie the ribbon around the sides with a big bow.

Cook's Tip

If you often make cakes using sugarpaste it is worth investing in a smoother. This is a flat plastic tool with a handle, and it is useful for achieving a professional finish. Use the smoother to smooth the sugarpaste over the top of the cake, using your hand to finish rounded edges. Then push the smoother down the sides of the cake and press the edge along the base where the sugarpaste meets the board. This will give a neat edge for you to cut away with a knife.

Energy 4150kcal/17538kJ; Fat 123g, Saturated Fat 46.5g; Carbohydrate 762.1g, Fibre 6.7g

Strawberry Cake

Use a heart-shaped mould or cut a round cake to shape using a template for this cake.

Makes one 900g/2lb cake

650g/1lb 7oz/scant 4½ cups marzipan
green, red and yellow food colouring
30ml/2 tbsp apricot jam, warmed and sieved
900g/2lb heart-shaped sponge cake
caster (superfine) sugar, for dusting

Materials/equipment

30cm/12in round cake board
icing smoother

1 Tint 175g/6oz/generous 1 cup of the marzipan green. Brush the cake board with apricot jam, roll out the green marzipan and use to cover the board. Trim the edges. Use an icing smoother to flatten and smooth the marzipan.

2 Brush the remaining apricot jam over the top and sides of the cake. Position the cake on the cake board. Tint 275g/10oz/scant 2 cups of the remaining marzipan red. Roll it out to 5mm/¼in thick and use to cover the cake, smoothing down the sides. Trim the edges. Use the handle of a teaspoon to indent the "strawberry" evenly and lightly all over.

3 For the stalk, tint 175g/6oz/generous 1 cup of the marzipan bright green. Cut it in half and roll out one portion into a 10 x 15cm/4 x 6in rectangle. Cut "V" shapes out of the rectangle, leaving a 2.5cm/1in border across the top, to form the calyx. Position on the cake, curling the "V" shapes to make them look realistic.

4 Roll the rest of the green marzipan into a sausage shape 13cm/5in long. Bend it slightly, then position it on the board to form the stalk.

5 For the strawberry pips, tint the remaining marzipan yellow. Pull off tiny pieces and roll them into tear-shaped pips. Place them in the indentations all over the strawberry. Dust the cake and board with sifted caster sugar.

Energy 6810kcal/28566kJ; Fat 327.4g, Saturated Fat 58.9g; Carbohydrate 931.7g, Fibre 20.4g

Gift-wrapped Parcel

If you don't have a tiny flower cutter for the "wrapping paper" design, then press a small decorative button into the icing while still soft to create a pattern.

Makes one 15cm/6in square cake

15cm/6in square cake
50g/2oz/4 tbsp butter icing
45ml/3 tbsp apricot jam, warmed and sieved
450g/1lb marzipan
350g/12oz/2¼ cups pale lemon yellow sugarpaste icing
red and green food colouring
30ml/2 tbsp royal icing

Materials/equipment
20cm/8in square cake board
small flower cutter (optional)

1 Split the cake and fill with butter icing. Place on the cake board and brush with the warmed apricot jam. Cover with half the marzipan, then with the yellow sugarpaste icing, and mark with a small flower cutter.

2 To make the ribbons divide the remaining marzipan in half, and colour one half pink and the other pale green. Roll out the pink marzipan and cut into four 2.5 x 18cm/1 x 7in strips. Roll out the green marzipan and cut into four 1cm/½in strips the same length.

3 Centre the green strips on top of the pink strips and stick on to the cake with a little water. Cut two 5cm/2in strips from each colour and cut a "V" from the ends to form the ends of the ribbon. Stick in place and leave to dry overnight.

4 Cut the rest of the green into four 2.5 x 7.5cm/1 x 3in lengths and the pink into four 1 x 7.5cm/½ x 3in lengths. Centre the pink on top of the green, fold in half, stick the ends together and slip over the handle of a wooden spoon, dusted with cornflour. Leave to dry overnight.

5 Cut the ends into "V" shapes to fit neatly together on the cake. Cut two pieces for the join in the centre. Remove the bows from the spoon and stick in position with royal icing.

Energy 5031kcal/21295kJ; Fat 116.3g, Saturated Fat 36g; Carbohydrate 992g, Fibre 8.6g

Sweetheart Cake

The heart-shaped run-outs can be made a week before the cake is made to ensure that they are completely dry.

Makes one 20cm/8in round cake

20cm/8in round sponge cake
115g/4oz/½ cup butter icing
45ml/3 tbsp apricot jam, warmed and served
450g/1lb marzipan
675g/1½lb/4½ cups sugarpaste icing
red food colouring
115g/4oz/¾ cup royal icing

Materials/equipment
25cm/10in round cake board
spoon with decorative handle
small baking parchment piping (icing) bag
no.1 writing nozzle
candles and holders
1.5m/1½yd x 2.5cm/1in wide ribbon

1 Split the cake and fill with butter icing. Place on the cake board and brush with apricot jam. Cover with a layer of marzipan. Tint the sugarpaste icing pale pink and cover the cake and board. Mark the edge of the icing with the decorative handle of a spoon.

2 Tint the royal icing dark pink. Make a heart-shaped template and draw round this several times on a sheet of baking parchment. Using a no.1 writing nozzle, pipe the outlines for the hearts in a continuous line. Then fill in until the hearts are rounded. You will need eight for the cake top. Make some extra in case of mistakes. Leave to dry for at least 2 days.

3 Arrange the hearts on top of the cake and place the candles in the centre. Tie the ribbon around the cake.

Cook's Tip
When using royal icing to create shapes such as these hearts, make sure that it is the correct consistency. If it is too thin the icing will overflow the edge of the shape; if it is too thick it will form a lumpy surface. Always make several more shapes than you need in case any are damaged when you transfer them from the paper to the cake.

Energy 7060kcal/29760kJ; Fat 245g, Saturated Fat 55.1g; Carbohydrate 1224.6g, Fibre 14g

Rosette Cake

This impressive cake could be used for a Christening or anniversary cake.

Makes one 20cm/8in square cake

20cm/8in square sponge cake
450g/1lb/2 cups butter icing
60ml/4 tbsp apricot jam, warmed and sieved
mulberry-red food colouring
crystallized violets

Materials/equipment
25cm/10in square cake board
serrated scraper
piping (icing) bag
large star nozzle
candles and holders

1 Split the cake and fill with a little butter icing. Place in the centre of the cake board and brush with apricot jam. Tint the remaining butter icing dark pink using the mulberry-red food colouring. Spread the top and sides with butter icing.

2 Using the serrated scraper, hold it against the cake and move it from side to side across the top to make waves. Hold the scraper against the side of the cake, resting the flat edge on the board, and draw it along to give straight ridges along each side.

3 Put the rest of the butter icing into a piping bag fitted with a large star nozzle. Mark a 15cm/6in circle on the top of the cake and pipe stars around it and around the base of the cake. Place the candles and violets in the corners.

Cook's Tip
So that you have perfect little stars for your cake, practise piping icing on to a plate beforehand. Make sure there is no air in the icing by twisting the top of the bag and then squeezing a little icing out before you start. Hold the twist between the joint of the thumb and first finger and hold the bag in the palm of your hand. Hold the piping (icing) bag with the star nozzle directly over and close to the surface to be iced. Squeeze out some icing while gently pushing downwards and then move the icing bag upwards without squeezing to form a point.

Energy 5702kcal/23805kJ; Fat 354.8g, Saturated Fat 144.8g; Carbohydrate 618.4g, Fibre 6.3g

Number 10 Cake

Ideal as a birthday or anniversary cake, this is a very simple cake to decorate. If you can't master the shell edge, pipe stars instead.

Makes one 20cm/8in tall round cake

20cm/8in and 15cm/6in round sponge cakes
450g/1lb/2 cups butter icing
75ml/5 tbsp apricot jam, warmed and sieved
coloured vermicelli
cream food colouring

Materials/equipment
25cm/10in round cake board
wooden cocktail stick (toothpick)
plastic "10" cake decoration
small baking parchment piping (icing) bag
thick shell and star nozzles
10 candles and holders

1 Split both cakes and fill with a little butter icing. Brush the sides with the warmed apricot jam.

2 When the jam is cold, spread a layer of butter icing over the sides and then roll in coloured vermicelli to cover evenly.

3 Tint the rest of the icing cream, and spread over the top of each cake. Place the small cake on top of the large cake. Using a cocktail stick, make a pattern in the icing on top of the cake.

4 Using the remaining icing, pipe around the base of the cakes and around the edge. Stick the "10" decoration in the centre of the top tier and two candles on either side. Arrange the other candles evenly around the base cake.

Cook's Tip
To pipe shells, hold the piping bag at an angle and close to the surface to be iced and gently squeeze out some of the icing while you move the bag gently slightly upwards and away from you then towards you to make a tiny loop. Let the icing touch the surface a fraction behind the loop and continue as before. Practise on a plate before you ice the cake.

Energy 7142kcal/29826kJ; Fat 436.4g, Saturated Fat 162.2g; Carbohydrate 786g, Fibre 9g

Shirt and Tie Cake

Makes one 19 x 26.5cm/ 7½ x 10½in cake

coffee sponge cake, baked in a 19 x 26.5cm/ 7½ x 5in loaf tin
350g/12oz/1½ cups coffee-flavour butter icing
90ml/6 tbsp apricot jam, warmed and sieved
about 1kg/2¼lb/6¾ cups sugarpaste icing
blue food colouring
125g/4oz/1 cup icing (confectioners') sugar, sifted
45–60ml/3–4 tbsp water

Materials/equipment

30 x 39cm/12 x 15½in cake board
steel ruler
small baking parchment piping (icing) bag
small round nozzle
card (stock) collar template
"Happy Birthday" decoration
tissue paper (optional)

1 Cut the cake in half horizontally and sandwich together with the butter icing. Brush the cake with apricot jam. Colour 675g/1½lb/4½ cups sugarpaste icing light blue and roll out to about 5mm/¼in thick. Use to cover the whole cake. Trim away any excess icing. Place the cake on the cake board.

2 Using a steel ruler, make grooves down the length and sides of the cake, about 2.5cm/1in apart. Mix the icing sugar and water to make a glacé icing to pipe into the grooves.

3 To make the collar, roll out 225g/8oz/1½ cups sugarpaste icing to a 40.5 x 10cm/16½ x 4in rectangle. Lay the piece of card for the collar on top. Brush water around the edges, then carefully lift one edge over the card to encase it completely. Trim the two short ends to match the angles of the card. Lift the collar and gently bend it round, and position on the cake.

4 Colour 175g/6oz/1 cup sugarpaste icing dark blue. Cut off one-third and shape into a tie knot. Position the knot. Roll out the rest to about 5mm/½in thick. Cut out a tie piece to fit under the knot and long enough to hang over the edge of the cake. Position the tie piece, tucking it under the knot and securing in place with a little water. Finish the cake with the "Happy Birthday" decoration, and tissue paper, if you like.

Energy 9078kcal/38128kJ; Fat 409.2g, Saturated Fat 156.4g, Carbohydrate 1370.9g, Fibre 8.1g

Mobile Phone Cake

Copy your phone to make the latest model.

Makes one 23 x 13cm/ 9 x 5in cake

sponge cake, baked in a 23 x 13cm/ 9 x 5in loaf tin (pan)
30ml/2 tbsp apricot jam, warmed and sieved
375g/13oz/2¼ cups sugarpaste icing
black food colouring
10 small square sweets (candies)
2 striped liquorice sweets (candies)
30–45ml/2–3 tbsp icing (confectioners') sugar
2.5–5ml/½–1 tsp water

Materials/equipment

25 x 18cm/10 x 7in cake board
diamond-shaped cutter
small piece of foil
small baking parchment piping (icing) bag
small round nozzle

1 Turn the cake upside-down. Make a 2.5cm/1in diagonal cut 2.5cm/1in from one end. Cut down vertically to remove the wedge. Remove the middle of the cake to the wedge depth up to 4cm/1½in from the other end.

2 Place the cake on the board and brush with the warmed apricot jam. Tint 275g/10oz/1¾ cups of the sugarpaste icing black. Use to cover the cake, smoothing it over the carved shape with your hand. Reserve the trimmings.

3 Tint 75g/3oz/½ cup of the sugarpaste icing grey. Cut a piece to fit the hollowed centre, leaving a 1cm/½in border, and another piece 2.5cm/1in square. Stamp out the centre of the square with the diamond cutter. Secure all the pieces on the cake with water.

4 Position the sweets and the foil for the display pad. For the glacé icing, mix the icing sugar with the water and tint black.

5 With the small round nozzle, pipe border lines around the edges of the phone, including the grey pieces of sugarpaste. Pipe the numbers on the keys. Roll a sausage shape from the reserved black sugarpaste for the aerial. Indent one side of the top with a knife and secure the aerial with water.

Energy 5134kcal/21571kJ; Fat 220.5g, Saturated Fat 48.4g, Carbohydrate 781.2g, Fibre 8.3g

Heart Cake

For Valentine's Day, an engagement or just to say "I love you".

Makes one 20cm/8in heart-shaped cake

3 egg whites
350g/12oz/1¾ cups caster (superfine) sugar
30ml/2 tbsp cold water
30ml/2 tbsp fresh lemon juice
1.5ml/¼ tsp cream of tartar
red food colouring
20cm/8in heart-shaped sponge cake
75–115g/3–4oz/¾–1 cup icing (confectioners') sugar

Materials/equipment
30cm/12in square cake board
small greaseproof piping (icing) bag
small nozzle

1 Make the icing by combining 2 of the egg whites, the caster sugar, water, lemon juice and cream of tartar in the top of a double boiler or in a bowl set over a pan of simmering water. With an electric mixer, beat until thick and holding soft peaks, about 7 minutes. Remove from the heat and continue beating until the mixture is thick enough to spread. Colour the icing pale pink.

2 Put the cake on the cake board and spread the icing evenly on the cake. Smooth the top and sides. Leave to set for 3–4 hours, or overnight.

3 Place 15ml/1 tbsp of the remaining egg white in a bowl and whisk until frothy. Gradually beat in enough icing sugar to make a stiff mixture suitable for piping.

4 Spoon the white icing into a piping bag and pipe the decorations on the top and sides of the cake as shown in the photograph above.

Cook's Tip
This simple and attractive frosting develops a thin sugar crust as it dries.

Energy 3638kcal/15233kJ; Fat 190.4g, Saturated Fat 40.6g; Carbohydrate 455.6g, Fibre 6.3g

Bowl-of-Strawberries Cake

The strawberry theme of the painting is carried on into the moulded decorations on this summery birthday cake.

Makes one 20cm/8in petal-shaped cake

350g/12oz/1½ cups butter icing
red, yellow, green and claret food colouring
20cm/8in petal-shaped Madeira cake
45ml/3 tbsp apricot jam, warmed and sieved
675g/1½lb/4½ cups sugarpaste icing
yellow powder tint

Materials/equipment
25cm/10in petal-shaped cake board
paint palette or small saucers
fine paintbrushes
thin red and green ribbons

1 Tint the butter icing pink. Cut the cake horizontally into three. Sandwich together with the butter icing. Brush the cake with apricot jam.

2 Use 500g/1¼lb/3¾ cups of the sugarpaste icing to cover the cake. Place on the cake board and leave to dry overnight.

3 For the strawberries, tint three-quarters of the remaining sugarpaste icing red, and equal portions of the rest yellow and green. Make the strawberries by rolling small balls of red sugarpaste then making them slightly elongated. Roll out tiny dots of yellow sugarpaste and add as seeds to the strawberries.

4 Cut out a green star shape for a calyx and stick to the top, then add a green stalk. Secure with water if necessary. Leave the strawberries to dry on baking parchment.

5 Put the red, green, yellow and claret food colouring in a palette and water them down slightly. Paint the bowl and strawberries, using yellow powder tint to highlight the bowl.

6 Decorate the cake with the ribbons. Secure two of the strawberries to the top of the cake, and arrange the others around the base.

Energy 5837kcal/24534kJ; Fat 255g, Saturated Fat 154.8g; Carbohydrate 905.1g, Fibre 5.4g

Barley Twist Cake

This makes a lovely Christening cake.

Makes one 20cm/8in round cake
20cm/8in round sponge cake
115g/4oz/½ cup butter icing
45ml/3 tbsp apricot jam, warmed and sieved
450/1lb marzipan
450g/1lb/3 cups pale yellow sugarpaste icing
115g/4oz/¾ cup white sugarpaste icing
115g/4oz/¾ cup royal icing
blue food colouring
edible pink dusting powder

Materials/equipment
25cm/10in round cake board
wooden cocktail stick (toothpick)
fine paintbrush
very fine plain nozzle
small baking parchment piping (icing) bags
6 small blue bows

1 Split the cake and fill with butter icing. Place on the board and brush with jam. Cover with marzipan, then yellow sugarpaste icing, extending it over the board. Mark six equidistant points around the cake with a cocktail stick.

2 Colour 40g/½oz/1 tbsp of the white sugarpaste icing pale blue and roll out thinly. Moisten a paintbrush with water and brush lightly over it. Roll out the same quantity of white icing, lay on top and press together. Roll out to a 20cm/8in square.

3 Cut 5mm/¼in strips, carefully twist each one, moisten the six marked points around the cake with water and drape each barley twist into place, pressing lightly to stick to the cake.

4 Cut out a jersey shape from white icing and stick on to the top of the cake with water. Roll some icing into a ball and colour a small amount dark blue. Roll into two tapering 7.5cm/3in long needles with a small ball at the end. Dry overnight. Stick the needles and ball in position. Using royal icing and the very fine nozzle, pipe the stitches and wool in position. Pipe a white border around the base of the cake. Stick small bows around the edge of the cake with a little royal icing and carefully brush the knitting with pink powder tint.

Energy 7304kcal/30793kJ; Fat 247.6g, Saturated Fat 45.2g; Carbohydrate 1276.8g, Fibre 14.9g

Tablecloth Cake

This draped "tablecloth" makes a most unusual effect for a cake.

Makes one 20cm/8in round cake
20cm/8in round sponge cake
115g/4oz/½ cup butter icing
45ml/3 tbsp apricot jam, warmed and sieved
450g/1lb marzipan
675g/1½lb/4½ cups sugarpaste icing
red food colouring
115g/4oz/¾ cup royal icing

Materials/equipment
25cm/10in round cake board
spoon with decorative handle
8 wooden cocktail sticks (toothpicks)
sharp needle
skewer
8 red ribbon bows
small baking parchment piping (icing) bags
very fine and fine plain nozzles

1 Split the cake and fill with butter icing. Place on the board and brush with apricot jam. Cover with a layer of marzipan.

2 Tint 450g/1lb/3 cups of the sugarpaste icing red and cover the cake and board. Roll the rest of the red sugarpaste into a thin rope long enough to go around the cake. Stick around the base of the cake with water. Mark with the decorative handle of a spoon. Leave to dry overnight.

3 Roll out the remaining icing to a 25cm/10in circle and trim. Lay this icing over the cake and drape the "cloth" over the wooden cocktail sticks set at equidistant points.

4 Mark a 10cm/4in circle in the centre of the cake. Make a template of the flower design and transfer to the cake with a needle. Use a skewer to make the flowers; the red colour should show through.

5 Remove the cocktail sticks and stick on the bows with royal icing. With a fine plain nozzle and white royal icing pipe around the circle in the centre. With a very fine plain nozzle, pipe small dots around the edge of the cloth. Colour some royal icing red and pipe a name in the centre.

Energy 7673kcal/32303kJ; Fat 295g, Saturated Fat 71.8g; Carbohydrate 1258.6g, Fibre 15.8g

Pizza Cake

Quick and easy, this really is a definite winner for pizza fanatics everywhere.

Makes one 23cm/9in round cake

23cm/9in shallow sponge cake
350g/12oz/1½ cups butter icing
red and green food colouring
175g/6oz yellow marzipan
25g/1oz/4 tbsp sugarpaste icing
15ml/1 tbsp desiccated (dry unsweetened shredded) coconut

Materials/equipment
25cm/10in pizza plate
leaf cutter

1 Place the cake on the pizza plate. Tint the butter icing red and spread evenly over the cake, leaving a 1cm/½in border.

2 Knead the marzipan for a few minutes, to soften slightly, then grate it like cheese, and sprinkle all over the red butter icing.

3 Tint the sugarpaste icing green. Use the leaf cutter to cut out two leaf shapes to look like basil leaves.

4 Mark the veins with the back of a knife and place on the pizza cake.

5 For the chopped herbs, tint the desiccated coconut dark green. Then sprinkle over the pizza cake.

Variation
Go to town with the topping for this pizza, if you like. For a seafood lover you could make tiny prawns (shrimp) or clams out of sugarpaste or buy prawn-shaped sweets (candies) or chocolate shells. You could also make slices of ham, mushrooms, sausage, or red or green (bell) pepper, as well as whole black or green olives - all from coloured sugarpaste. Or you could cut up cubes of marzipan to look like cubes of cheese and sprinkle them over the top.

Energy 6488kcal/27075kJ; Fat 413.5g, Saturated Fat 160.4g; Carbohydrate 670.3g, Fibre 12.6g

Flowerpot Cake

The perfect gift for a gardening enthusiast or plant lover.

Makes one round cake

Madeira cake, baked in a 1.2-litre/2-pint/5-cup pudding bowl
175g/6oz/generous ½ cup jam
175g/6oz/¾ cup butter icing
30ml/2 tbsp apricot jam, warmed and sieved
575g/1lb 6oz/4¼ cups sugarpaste icing
dark orange-red, red, silver, green, purple and yellow food colouring
125g/4oz/¾ cup royal icing
2 flaked chocolate bars, coarsely crushed

Materials/equipment
fine paintbrush

1 Slice the cake into three layers and stick together again with jam and butter icing. Cut out a shallow circle from the cake top, leaving a 1cm/½in rim.

2 Brush the outside of the cake and rim with apricot jam. Tint 400g/14oz/2¼ cups of the sugarpaste orange-red and cover the cake, moulding it over the rim. Reserve the trimmings. Leave to dry.

3 Use the trimmings to make decorations and handles for the flowerpot. Leave to dry on baking parchment. Sprinkle the chocolate flakes into the pot for soil.

4 Tint a small piece of sugarpaste very pale orange-red. Use to make a seed bag. When dry, paint on a pattern in food colouring. Tint two small pieces of icing red and silver. Make a trowel and dry over a wooden spoon handle.

5 Tint the remaining icing green, purple and a small piece yellow. Use to make the flowers and leaves, attaching together with royal icing. Score leaf veins with the back of a knife. Leave to dry on baking parchment.

6 Attach all the decorations to the flowerpot and arrange the plant, seed bag and trowel with soil, seeds and grass made from leftover tinted sugarpaste.

Energy 6068kcal/25587kJ; Fat 203g, Saturated Fat 119.5g; Carbohydrate 1079.5g, Fibre 7.2g

Glittering Star Cake

With a quick flick of a paintbrush you can give a sparkling effect to this glittering cake. Sparkle and glitter food colours make a cake very special.

Makes one 20cm/8in round cake

20cm/8in round rich fruit cake
40ml/2½ tbsp apricot jam, warmed and sieved
675g/1½lb/4½ cups marzipan
450g/1lb/3 cups sugarpaste icing
115g/4oz/¾ cup royal icing
silver, gold, lilac shimmer, red sparkle, glitter green and primrose sparkle food colouring and powder tints

Materials/equipment

paintbrush
25cm/10in round cake board

1 Brush the cake with the apricot jam. Use two-thirds of the marzipan to cover the cake. Leave to dry overnight.

2 Cover the cake with the sugarpaste icing. Leave to dry.

3 Place the cake on a large sheet of baking parchment. Dilute a little powdered silver food colouring and, using a loaded paintbrush, flick it all over the cake to give a spattered effect. Allow to dry.

4 Make templates of two different-size moon shapes and three irregular star shapes.

5 Divide the remaining marzipan into six pieces and tint them silver, gold, lilac, pink, green and yellow. Cut the coloured sugarpaste into stars and moons using the templates as a guide, cutting some of the stars in half.

6 Place the cut-outs on baking parchment and brush each with its own colour powder tint. Allow to dry.

7 Secure the cake on the board with royal icing. Arrange the marzipan stars and moons at different angles all over the cake, attaching with royal icing, and position the halved stars upright as though coming out of the cake. Allow to set.

Energy 7800kcal/33013kJ; Fat 159.5g; Saturated Fat 28.6g; Carbohydrate 1548.9g; Fibre 26.3g

Racing Ring Cake

Liquorice makes simple but effective tracks for brightly coloured cars.

Serves 12

ring mould sponge cake
350g/12oz/1½ cups butter icing
500g/1¼lb/3¾ cups sugarpaste icing
125g/4oz/¾ cup royal icing, for fixing
black, blue, yellow, green, orange, red, purple food colouring
selection of liquorice sweets (candies), dolly mixtures and teddy bears
113g/4½oz packet liquorice Catherine wheels

Materials/equipment

25cm/10in round cake board
wooden kebab skewer
fine paintbrush

1 Cut the cake in half horizontally and fill with some butter icing. Cover the outside with the remaining butter icing.

2 Use 350g/12oz/2¼ cups of sugarpaste icing to coat the top and inside of the cake. Use the trimmings to roll an oblong for the flag. Cut the skewer to 13cm/5in and fold one end of the flag around it, securing with water. Paint on the pattern with black food colouring. Colour a ball of icing black, and stick on top of the skewer. Make a few folds in the flag and leave to dry.

3 Colour the remaining sugarpaste icing blue, yellow, green, orange, red and a very small amount purple. Shape each car in two pieces, attaching in the centre with royal icing where the seat joins the body of the car. Add decorations and headlights and attach dolly mixture wheels with royal icing. Place a teddy bear in each car and leave to set.

4 Unwind the Catherine wheels and remove the centre sweets. Fix them to the top of the cake with royal icing. Secure one strip around the bottom. Cut some of the liquorice into small strips and attach around the middle of the outside of the cake with royal icing. Arrange small liquorice sweets around the bottom of the cake. Position the cars on top of the cake on the tracks and attach the flag to the outside with royal icing.

Energy 622kcal/2603kJ; Fat 34.3g; Saturated Fat 13.2g; Carbohydrate 77.8g; Fibre 0.8g

Artist's Cake

Making cakes is an art in itself, and this cake proves it! Take your time to model the handle and catches for the box for the best effect.

Makes one 20cm/8in square cake

20cm/8in square rich fruit cake
45ml/3 tbsp apricot jam, warmed and sieved
450g/1lb marzipan
800g/1¾lb/5¼ cups sugarpaste icing
chestnut, yellow, blue, black, silver, paprika, green and mulberry food colouring
115g/4oz/¾ cup royal icing

Materials/equipment

25cm/10in square cake board
fine paintbrush

1 Brush the cake with the apricot jam. Cover in marzipan and leave to dry overnight.

2 Make a template of a painter's palette that will fit the cake top. Tint 175g/6oz/generous 1 cup of the sugarpaste very pale chestnut. Cut out the palette shape, place on baking parchment and leave to dry overnight.

3 Tint 450g/1lb/3 cups of the sugarpaste icing dark chestnut. Use to cover the cake. Secure the cake on the board with royal icing. Leave to dry.

4 Divide half the remaining sugarpaste icing into seven equal parts and tint yellow, blue, black, silver, paprika, green and mulberry.

5 Make all the decorative pieces for the box and palette, using the remaining white sugarpaste for the paint tubes.

6 Leave all the decorative pieces to dry on baking parchment.

7 Paint black markings on the paint tubes and chestnut wood markings on the box.

8 Position all the sugarpaste pieces on the cake and board using royal icing. Leave to dry.

Energy 7370kcal/31233kJ; Fat 122.8g, Saturated Fat 23.8g; Carbohydrate 1546g, Fibre 20.6g

"Liquorice" Cake

Scaled-up versions of favourite sweets (candies) make a great decoration for a cake.

Makes one 20cm/8in square cake

20cm/8in and 15cm/6in square Madeira cakes
675g/1½lb/3 cups butter icing
45ml/3 tbsp apricot jam, warmed and sieved
350g/12oz marzipan
800g/1¾lb/5¼ cups sugarpaste icing
egg-yellow, black, blue and mulberry food colouring

Materials/equipment

25cm/10in square cake board
4.5cm/1¾in round cutter

1 Cut both cakes horizontally into three. Fill with butter icing, reserving a little to coat the smaller cake. Wrap and set aside the smaller cake. Brush the larger cake with apricot jam. Cover with marzipan and secure on the cake board with butter icing. Leave to dry overnight.

2 Tint 350g/12oz/2¼ cups of the sugarpaste icing yellow. Take 115g/4oz/¾ cup of the remaining sugarpaste icing and tint half black and leave the other half white. Cover the top and one-third of the sides of the cake with yellow sugarpaste icing.

3 Use the white icing to cover the lower third of the sides of the cake. Use the black icing to fill the central third.

4 Cut the smaller cake into three equal strips. Divide two of the strips into three squares each. Cut out two circles from the third strip, using a cutter as a guide.

5 Tint 115g/4oz/¾ cup of the remaining sugarpaste black. Divide the rest into four equal portions; leave one white and tint the others blue, pink and yellow.

6 Coat the outsides of the cake cut-outs with the reserved butter icing. Use the tinted and white sugarpaste to cover the pieces to resemble liquorice sweets (candies). Make small rolls from the trimmings. Arrange on and around the cake.

Energy 9108kcal/38287kJ; Fat 396.8g, Saturated Fat 218.9g; Carbohydrate 1409.7g, Fibre 12.9g

Sun Cake

This smiling sun is very easy to make from two round cakes with a quickly piped icing design.

Makes one 20cm/8in star-shaped cake

2 sponge cakes, 20 x 5cm/8 x 2in each
25g/1oz/2 tbsp unsalted (sweet) butter
450g/1lb/4 cups sifted icing (confectioners') sugar
120ml/4fl oz/½ cup apricot jam
30ml/2 tbsp water
2 large (US extra large) egg whites
1–2 drops glycerine
juice of 1 lemon
yellow and orange food colouring

Materials/equipment

40cm/16in square cake board
fabric piping (icing) bag
small star nozzle

1 Cut one of the cakes into eight wedges. Trim the outsides to fit around the other cake.

2 To make the butter icing, combine the butter with 25g/1oz/2 tbsp of the icing sugar.

3 Place the whole cake on a 40cm/16in board and attach the sunbeams with the butter icing.

4 Warm the jam with the water in a small bowl set over a pan of simmering water. Brush the jam all over the cake.

5 For the icing, beat the egg whites until they are stiff. Gradually add the icing sugar, glycerine and lemon juice, and beat together for 1 minute.

6 Tint three-quarters of the icing yellow and spread it all over the cake.

7 Tint the remaining icing bright yellow and orange.

8 Pipe the details on to the cake with the small star nozzle.

Energy 7899kcal/33176kJ; Fat 346.9g, Saturated Fat 82.6g; Carbohydrate 1182g, Fibre 10.8g

Strawberry Basket Cake

For a summer birthday what could be nicer than a basket full of strawberries?

Makes one small rectangular cake

sponge cake baked in a 450g/1lb/3 cup loaf tin (pan)
45ml/3 tbsp apricot jam, warmed and sieved
675g/1½lb marzipan
350g/12oz/1½ cups chocolate-flavour butter icing
red food colouring
50g/2oz/¼ cup caster (superfine) sugar

Materials/equipment

small star nozzle
small baking parchment piping (icing) bag
10 plastic strawberry stalks
30 x 7.5cm/12 x 3in strip foil
30cm/12in thin red ribbon

1 Level the top of the cake and make it perfectly flat. Score a 5mm/¼in border around the edge and scoop out the inside to make a shallow hollow.

2 Brush the sides and border edges of the cake with apricot jam. Roll out 275g/10oz/scant 2 cups of the marzipan, cut into rectangles and use to cover the sides of the cake, overlapping the borders. Press the edges together to seal.

3 Using the star nozzle and the butter icing, pipe vertical lines 2.5cm/1in apart all around the sides of the cake. Pipe short horizontal lines of butter icing alternately crossing over and then stopping at the vertical lines to give a basketweave effect. Pipe a decorative line of icing around the top edge of the basket to finish.

4 Tint the remaining marzipan red and mould it into ten strawberry shapes. Roll in the caster sugar and press a plastic strawberry calyx into each top. Arrange in the "basket".

5 For the basket handle, fold the foil into a thin strip and wind the ribbon around it to cover. Bend up the ends and then bend into a curve. Push the ends into the sides of the cake. Decorate with bows made from the ribbon.

Energy 6807kcal/28601kJ; Fat 303.9g, Saturated Fat 88g; Carbohydrate 1011.2g, Fibre 17.3g

Coffee Sponge Drops

These light cookies are delicious on their own, but taste even better with a filling made by mixing low-fat soft cheese with chopped stem ginger.

Makes about 24

50g/2oz/½ cup plain (all-purpose) flour
15ml/1 tbsp instant coffee powder
2 eggs
75g/3oz/6 tbsp caster (superfine) sugar

For the filling (optional)

115g/4oz/½ cup low-fat soft cheese
40g/1½oz/¼ cup chopped preserved stem ginger

1 Preheat the oven to 190°C/375°F/Gas 5. Line two baking sheets with baking parchment. Sift the flour and coffee powder together.

2 Combine the eggs and caster sugar in a heatproof bowl. Place over a pan of simmering water. Beat with a hand-held electric whisk until thick and mousse-like: when the whisk is lifted a trail should remain on the surface of the mixture for at least 30 seconds.

3 Carefully fold in the sifted flour mixture with a large metal spoon, being careful not to knock out any air.

4 Spoon the mixture into a piping (pastry) bag fitted with a 1cm/½in plain nozzle and pipe 4cm/1½in rounds on to the prepared baking sheets. Bake for 12 minutes. Cool on a wire rack.

5 Sandwich the sponge drops together in pairs with the filling or use a coffee icing, if you like.

Variation

To make Chocolate Sponge Drops, replace the coffee with 30ml/2 tbsp reduced-fat (unsweetened) cocoa powder.

Energy 33kcal/138kJ; Fat 0.9g, Saturated Fat 0.4g; Carbohydrate 5.2g, Fibre 0.1g

Oaty Crisps

These high-fibre oat biscuits are quick and very easy to make. They are extremely crisp and crunchy – ideal to serve with morning coffee or as a tasty mid-afternoon snack.

Makes 18

175g/6oz/1¾ cups rolled oats
75g/3oz/6 tbsp soft light brown sugar
1 egg
60ml/4 tbsp sunflower oil
30ml/2 tbsp malt extract

1 Preheat the oven to 190°C/375°F/Gas 5. Grease two baking sheets. Mix the oats and brown sugar in a bowl, breaking up any lumps in the sugar.

2 Add the egg, oil and malt extract, mix well, then leave to soak for 15 minutes.

3 Using a teaspoon, place small heaps of the mixture on the prepared baking sheets, leaving room for spreading. Press into 7.5cm/3in rounds with a dampened fork.

4 Bake the biscuits for 10–15 minutes, or until golden brown. Leave to cool for 1 minute, then remove with a metal spatula and cool on a wire rack.

Variation

Add 50g/2oz/½ cup chopped almonds or hazelnuts to the mixture. You could also add some jumbo oats to give a coarser texture.

Cook's Tip

As well as being low in fat these oaty cookies are healthy in other ways: oats are a healthy grain that contains soluble fibre, which is helpful in lowering blood cholesterol levels. As the grain does not contain gluten, oats are suitable for people who are gluten intolerant.

Energy 86kcal/364kJ; Fat 3.6g, of Saturated Fat 0.4g; Carbohydrate 12.8g, Fibre 0.7g

Snowballs

These light and airy morsels make a crisp and sweet accompaniment to low-fat frozen yogurt.

Makes about 20

2 egg whites

115g/4oz/½ cup caster (superfine) sugar

15ml/1 tbsp cornflour (cornstarch), sifted

5ml/1 tsp white wine vinegar

1.5ml/¼ tsp vanilla extract

1 Preheat the oven to 150°C/300°F/Gas 2 and line two baking sheets with baking parchment.

2 Whisk the egg whites in a grease-free bowl, using a hand-held electric whisk, until very stiff.

3 Add the caster sugar, a little at a time, whisking after each addition until the meringue is very stiff and glossy. Whisk in the cornflour, vinegar and vanilla extract.

4 Using a teaspoon, mound the mixture into snowballs on the prepared baking sheets. Bake for 30 minutes.

5 Cool on the baking sheets, then remove the snowballs from the paper with a metal spatula.

Variation

Make Pineapple Snowballs by lightly folding about 50g/2oz/⅓ cup finely chopped semi-dried pineapple into the meringue.

Cook's Tip

These meringues contain the magic ingredients that give them a chewy centre rather than being crisp throughout. You can mix the cornflour, white wine vinegar and vanilla extract together in a small bowl and sprinkle it over the mixture before finally folding it in if you like.

Energy 26kcal/113kJ; Fat 0g, Saturated Fat 0g; Carbohydrate 6.7g, Fibre 0g

Caramel Meringues

Muscovado sugar gives these almost fat-free meringues a lovely caramel flavour. Take care not to overcook them, so that they stay chewy in the middle.

Makes about 20

115g/4oz/½ cup light muscovado (brown) sugar

2 egg whites

5ml/1 tsp finely chopped walnuts (optional)

1 Preheat the oven to 160°C/325°F/Gas 3. Line two baking sheets with baking parchment.

2 Press the muscovado sugar through a metal sieve into a large bowl positioned below.

3 Whisk the egg whites in a separate, grease-free bowl until they are very stiff and dry.

4 Add the sieved brown sugar to the stiff egg white, about 15ml/1 tbsp at a time, whisking well between each addition, until the meringue is thick and glossy.

5 Spoon small mounds of the meringue mixture on to the prepared baking sheets.

6 Sprinkle each mound of meringue mixture with chopped walnuts, if you like.

7 Bake the meringues for 30 minutes, then leave them to cool for 5 minutes on the baking sheets.

8 Transfer the meringues to a wire rack to cool completely.

Cook's Tip

For an easy, sophisticated filling, mix 115g/4oz/½ cup low-fat soft cheese with 15ml/1 tbsp icing sugar. Chop 2 slices of fresh pineapple and add to the mixture. Sandwich the meringues together in pairs.

Energy 26kcal/109kJ; Fat 0.2g, Saturated Fat 0g; Carbohydrate 6g, Fibre 0g

Banana Gingerbread Slices

Bananas make this spicy bake delightfully moist and add a natural sweetness. The flavour develops on keeping, so store for a few days before cutting.

Makes 20 slices

275g/10oz/2½ cups plain (all-purpose) flour
20ml/4 tsp ground ginger
10ml/2 tsp mixed (apple pie) spice
5ml/1 tsp bicarbonate of soda (baking soda)
115g/4oz/½ cup soft light brown sugar
60ml/4 tbsp corn oil
30ml/2 tbsp molasses or black treacle
30ml/2 tbsp malt extract
2 eggs, beaten
60ml/4 tbsp orange juice
3 ripe bananas
115g/4oz/scant 1 cup raisins or sultanas (golden raisins)

1 Preheat the oven to 180°C/350°F/Gas 4. Line and grease a 28 x 18cm/11 x 7in baking tin (pan).

2 Sift the flour, ground ginger and mixed spice and the bicarbonate of soda into a mixing bowl. Spoon some of the mixture back into the sieve, add the brown sugar and sift the mixture back into the bowl.

3 Make a well in the centre of the dry ingredients and add the oil, molasses or treacle, malt extract, eggs, and orange juice. Gradually stir the dry ingredients into the liquid working from the centre outwards. Mix thoroughly.

4 Peel the bananas and mash them in a bowl. Add to the gingerbread mixture with the raisins or sultanas. Mix the ingredients thoroughly to combine well.

5 Scrape the mixture into the prepared tin. Bake for 35–40 minutes, or until the centre springs back when the surface of the cake is lightly pressed.

6 Leave the gingerbread in the tin to cool for 5 minutes, then turn on to a wire rack, remove the lining paper and leave to cool completely. Serve spread with butter, if you like.

Energy 132kcal/556kJ; Fat 3g, Saturated Fat 0.5g; Carbohydrate 25.4g, Fibre 0.7g

Banana and Apricot Chelsea Buns

Old favourites get a new twist with a delectable fruity filling.

Serves 9

225g/8oz/2 cups strong plain (all-purpose) flour
10ml/2 tsp mixed (apple pie) spice
2.5ml/½ tsp salt
25g/1oz/2 tbsp soft margarine
7.5ml/1½ tsp easy-blend (rapid-rise) dried yeast
50g/2oz/¼ cup caster (superfine) sugar
90ml/6 tbsp hand-hot milk
1 egg, beaten

For the filling

1 large ripe banana
175g/6oz/1 cup ready-to-eat dried apricots
30ml/2 tbsp soft light brown sugar

For the glaze

30ml/2 tbsp caster (superfine) sugar
30ml/2 tbsp water

1 Grease an 18cm/7in square cake tin (pan). To prepare the filling, mash the banana in a bowl. Using kitchen scissors, cut up the apricots, and add to the bowl, then stir in the brown sugar. Mix together well.

2 Sift the flour, spice and salt into a large bowl. Rub in the margarine, then stir in the yeast and sugar. Make a well in the centre and pour in the milk and the egg. Mix to a soft dough, adding a little extra milk if necessary.

3 Turn the dough on to a floured surface and knead for 5 minutes until smooth and elastic. Roll out to a 30 x 23cm/12 x 9in rectangle. Spread the filling over the dough and roll up lengthways like a Swiss roll (jelly roll), with the join underneath. Cut into 9 pieces and place cut side downwards in the prepared tin. Cover and leave in a warm place until doubled in size, about 1½ hours.

4 Preheat the oven to 200°C/400°F/Gas 6. Bake the buns for 20–25 minutes, or until golden brown. Meanwhile make the glaze: mix the caster sugar and water in a small pan. Heat, stirring, until dissolved, then boil the mixture for 2 minutes. Brush the glaze over the buns while still hot, then remove from the tin and cool on a wire rack.

Energy 193kcal/817kJ; Fat 3.5g, Saturated Fat 0.3g; Carbohydrate 38.4g, Fibre 2.1g

Lemon Sponge Fingers

These dainty sponge fingers are perfect for serving with fruit salads or light, low-fat creamy desserts.

Makes about 20

2 eggs
75g/3oz/6 tbsp caster (superfine) sugar
grated rind of 1 lemon
50g/2oz/½ cup plain (all-purpose) flour, sifted
caster (superfine) sugar, for sprinkling

1 Preheat the oven to 190°C/375°F/Gas 5. Line two baking sheets with baking parchment.

2 Whisk the eggs, sugar and lemon rind together with a hand-held electric whisk until thick and mousse-like: when the whisk is lifted, a trail should remain on the surface of the mixture for at least 30 seconds.

3 Carefully fold in the flour with a large metal spoon using a figure-of-eight action.

4 Place the mixture in a piping (pastry) bag fitted with a 1cm/½in plain nozzle. Pipe into finger lengths on the prepared baking sheets, leaving room for spreading.

5 Sprinkle the fingers with caster sugar. Bake for 6–8 minutes until golden brown, then remove to a wire rack to cool.

Variation
To make Hazelnut Fingers, omit the lemon rind and fold in 25g/1oz/¼ cup toasted ground hazelnuts and 5ml/1 tsp mixed (apple pie) spice with the flour.

Cook's Tip
These delicate sponge fingers also make a good base for a rich sherry trifle if you are not watching your fat intake.

Energy 31kcal/131kJ; Fat 0.6g, Saturated Fat 0.2g; Carbohydrate 5.9g, Fibre 0.1g

Apricot and Almond Fingers

These delicious high-fibre almond fingers will stay moist for several days, thanks to the addition of the apricots.

Makes 18

225g/8oz/2 cups self-raising (self-rising) flour
115g/4oz/½ cup soft light brown sugar
50g/2oz/⅓ cup semolina
175g/6oz/1 cup ready-to-eat dried apricots, chopped
30ml/2 tbsp clear honey
30ml/2 tbsp malt extract
2 eggs, beaten
60ml/4 tbsp skimmed milk
60ml/4 tbsp sunflower oil
a few drops of almond extract
30ml/2 tbsp flaked (sliced) almonds

1 Preheat the oven to 160°C/325°F/Gas 3. Grease and line a 28 x 18cm/11 x 7in baking tin (pan).

2 Sift the flour into a large bowl and stir in the sugar, semolina and apricots. Make a well in the centre and add the honey, malt extract, eggs, milk, oil and almond extract. Mix well until combined.

3 Turn the mixture into the prepared tin, spread to the edges and sprinkle with the flaked almonds.

4 Bake for 30–35 minutes, or until the centre springs back when lightly pressed. Invert the cake on a wire rack to cool. Remove the lining paper if necessary and cut into 18 slices with a sharp knife.

Cook's Tips
- *If you cannot find ready-to-eat dried apricots, soak chopped dried apricots in boiling water for 1 hour, then drain them and add to the mixture. This works well with other dried fruit too. Try ready-to-eat dried pears or peaches for a change.*
- *As well as going extremely well with coffee these fingers will also make a tasty low-fat dessert served with a low-fat ice cream or frozen yogurt.*

Energy 140kcal/589kJ; Fat 4.3g, Saturated Fat 0.6g; Carbohydrate 23.6g, Fibre 1.2g

Raspberry Muffins

Unlike English muffins, which are contain yeast and are cooked on a griddle, these American muffins are baked, giving them a deliciously light texture.

Makes 10–12

275g/10oz/2½ cups plain (all-purpose) flour
15ml/1 tbsp baking powder
115g/4oz/½ cup caster (superfine) sugar
1 egg
250ml/8fl oz/1 cup buttermilk
60ml/4 tbsp sunflower oil
150g/5oz/scant 1 cup fresh raspberries

1 Preheat the oven to 200°C/400°F/Gas 6. Arrange 12 paper cases in a deep muffin tin (pan). Sift the flour and baking powder into a mixing bowl, stir in the sugar, then make a well in the centre.

2 Mix the egg, buttermilk and oil together in a jug (pitcher), pour into the bowl and mix quickly until just combined.

3 Add the raspberries and lightly fold in with a metal spoon. Spoon into the paper cases to within a third of the top.

4 Bake the muffins for 20–25 minutes, or until golden brown and firm in the middle. Remove to a wire rack and serve while it is still warm.

Variation
Use blackberries, blueberries or blackcurrants instead of raspberries if you prefer.

Cook's Tips
- *To keep muffins as low fat as possible, paper cases are used for this recipe rather than greasing a muffin pan.*
- *This is a fairly moist batter which should only be lightly mixed. Over-mixing toughens the muffins and breaks up the fruit.*

Energy 165kcal/696kJ; Fat 4.5g, Saturated Fat 0.7g; Carbohydrate 29.3g, Fibre 1g

Date and Apple Muffins

These healthy muffins are delicious with morning coffee or breakfast. You will only need one or two per person as they are very filling.

Makes 12

150g/5oz/1¼ cups self-raising (self-rising) wholemeal (whole-wheat) flour
150g/5oz/1¼ cups self-raising (self-rising) white flour
5ml/1 tsp ground cinnamon
5ml/1 tsp baking powder
25g/1oz/2 tbsp soft margarine
75g/3oz/6 tbsp soft light brown sugar
250ml/8fl oz/1 cup apple juice
30ml/2 tbsp pear and apple spread
1 egg, lightly beaten
1 eating apple
75g/3oz/½ cup chopped dates
15ml/1 tbsp chopped pecan nuts

1 Preheat the oven to 200°C/400°F/Gas 6. Arrange 12 paper cases in a deep muffin tin.

2 Put the wholemeal flour in a mixing bowl. Sift in the white flour with the cinnamon and baking powder.

3 Rub in the margarine until the mixture resembles breadcrumbs, then stir in the brown sugar.

4 In a bowl, stir a little of the apple juice with the pear and apple spread until smooth.

5 Add the remaining juice, mix well, then add to the rubbed-in mixture with the egg.

6 Peel and core the apple, chop the flesh finely and add it to the bowl with the dates. Mix quickly until just combined.

7 Divide the mixture between the muffin cases. Sprinkle with the chopped pecan nuts.

8 Bake the muffins for 20–25 minutes, or until golden brown and firm in the middle. Turn on to a wire rack and cool a little. Serve while still warm.

Energy 158kcal/670kJ; Fat 3.4g, Saturated Fat 0.3g; Carbohydrate 30.7g, Fibre 1g

Filo and Apricot Purses

Light filo pastry is very easy to use and is low in fat. Always keep a packet in the freezer ready for rustling up a speedy teatime treat.

Makes 12

115g/4oz/1 cup ready-to-eat dried apricots
45ml/3 tbsp apricot compôte
3 amaretti, crushed
3 sheets filo pastry, thawed if frozen
20ml/4 tsp soft margarine, melted
icing (confectioners') sugar, for dusting

1 Preheat the oven to 180°C/350°F/Gas 4, and grease two baking sheets.

2 Chop the apricots, put them in a bowl and stir in the apricot compôte. Mix in the amaretti.

3 Cut the filo pastry into 24 13cm/5in squares, pile the squares on top of each other and cover with a clean, damp dish towel to prevent the pastry from drying out.

4 Lay one pastry square on a flat surface, brush lightly with melted margarine and lay another square diagonally on top. Brush the top square with melted margarine.

5 Spoon a small mound of apricot mixture in the centre of the pastry, bring up the edges and pinch together in a money-bag shape. The margarine will help to make the pastry stick.

6 Repeat with the remaining filo squares and filling to make 12 purses in all. Arrange on the prepared baking sheets and bake for 5–8 minutes, or until golden brown. Dust with icing sugar and serve warm.

Cook's Tip
The easiest way to crush the amaretti is to put them in a plastic bag and roll with a rolling pin.

Energy 62kcal/264kJ; Fat 1.8g, Saturated Fat 0.2g; Carbohydrate 11.3g, Fibre 0.8g

Filo Scrunchies

Quick and easy to make, these fruit scrunchies are ideal to serve at teatime and contain little added sugar. They are best eaten warm.

Makes 6

5 apricots or plums
4 sheets of filo pastry, thawed if frozen
20ml/4 tsp soft margarine, melted
50g/2oz/¼ cup demerara (raw) sugar
30ml/2 tbsp flaked (sliced) almonds
icing (confectioners') sugar, for dusting

1 Preheat the oven to 190°C/375°F/Gas 5. Cut the apricots or plums in half, remove the stones (pits) and slice the fruit thinly.

2 Cut the filo pastry into 12 18cm/7in squares. Pile the squares on top of each other and cover with a clean, damp dish towel to prevent the pastry from drying out.

3 Remove one square and brush it with melted margarine. Lay a second filo square on top, then, using your fingers, mould the pastry into neat folds.

4 Lay the scrunched filo square on a baking sheet. Make five more scrunchies in the same way, working quickly so that the pastry does not dry out.

5 Arrange a few slices of fruit in the folds of each scrunchie, then sprinkle generously with demerara sugar and almonds.

6 Bake the scrunchies for 8–10 minutes, or until golden brown, then loosen from the baking sheet with a metal spatula. Place on a platter, dust with icing sugar and serve immediately.

Cook's Tip
Filo pastry is the most healthy of all the pastries, as it contains very little fat. As long as you are sparing with the amount of fat you brush on to the layers, filo is a useful and tasty pastry to use in a variety of low-fat recipes, both sweet and savoury.

Energy 127kcal/534kJ; Fat 5.7g, Saturated Fat 0.2g; Carbohydrate 18g, Fibre 1.2g

Curry Crackers

These spicy, crisp little crackers are much lower in fat than other snacks.

Makes 12

50g/2oz/½ cup plain (all-purpose) flour
5ml/1 tsp curry powder
1.5ml/¼ tsp chilli powder
1.5ml/¼ tsp salt
15ml/1 tbsp chopped fresh coriander (cilantro)
30ml/2 tbsp water

1 Preheat the oven to 180°C/350°F/Gas 4. Sift the flour, curry powder, chilli powder and salt into a large bowl and make a well in the centre. Add the chopped coriander and water.

2 Stir from the centre outwards, gradually incorporating the flour and mixing to a fine dough.

3 Turn on to a lightly floured surface, and knead until smooth, then leave to rest for 5 minutes.

4 Cut the dough into 12 pieces and knead into small balls. Roll each ball out very thinly to a 10cm/4in round.

5 Arrange the rounds on two ungreased baking sheets. Bake for 15 minutes, turning over once during cooking.

Variations
These can be flavoured in many different ways. Omit the curry and chilli powders and add 15ml/1 tbsp caraway, fennel or mustard seeds. Any of the stronger spices such as nutmeg, cloves or ginger will give a good flavour but you will only need to add 5ml/1 tsp.

Cook's Tip
As this dough does not include yeast it only needs to be lightly kneaded; heavy handling is only suitable for yeast breads.

Energy 14kcal/60kJ; Fat 0.1g, Saturated Fat 0g; Carbohydrate 3.2g, Fibre 0.1g

Oatcakes

Oatmeal not only tastes delicious, but it is also a good source of water-soluble fibre, is low in fat, and is thought to lower cholesterol levels. Try these delicious cakes spread with honey for a great start to the day.

Makes 8

175g/6oz/1½ cups medium oatmeal, plus extra for sprinkling
a pinch of bicarbonate of soda (baking soda)
2.5ml/½ tsp salt
15g/½oz/1 tbsp butter
75ml/5 tbsp water

1 Preheat the oven to 150°C/300°F/Gas 2. Grease a baking sheet. Put the oatmeal, bicarbonate of soda and salt in a large bowl and mix well.

2 Melt the butter with the water in a small pan. Bring to the boil, then add to the oatmeal and mix to a moist dough.

3 Turn the dough on to a surface sprinkled with oatmeal and knead to a smooth ball. Turn a large baking sheet upside down, sprinkle it lightly with oatmeal and place the ball of dough on top. Dust the top of the ball with oatmeal, then roll out thinly to a 25cm/10in round.

4 Stamp out rounds with a 5cm/2in scone (cookie) cutter, or cut the round into eight sections, ease apart slightly and bake for 50–60 minutes, or until crisp. Leave to cool on the baking sheet, then remove the oatcakes with a metal spatula.

Cook's Tips
- *To get a neat circle, place a 25cm/10in cake board or plate on top of the oatcake. Cut away any excess dough with a palette knife, then remove the board or plate.*
- *Oatmeal is ground from the whole kernel of the cereal and is graded according to how finely it is ground, with the coarsest type known as pinhead. Medium oatmeal is widely available but fine is also suitable for oatcakes.*

Energy 102kcal/429kJ; Fat 3.5g, Saturated Fat 1g; Carbohydrate 15.9g, Fibre 1.5g

Chive and Potato Scones

These little cakes should be fairly thin, soft and crisp. They are delicious served warm with cottage cheese as a filling yet low-fat snack at any time of the day.

Makes 20
450g/1lb potatoes
115g/4oz/1 cup plain (all-purpose) flour, sifted
30ml/2 tbsp olive oil
30ml/2 tbsp chopped chives
salt and ground black pepper
low-fat spread, for topping

1 Cook the potatoes in a pan of boiling salted water for 20 minutes, then drain thoroughly. Return the potatoes to the clean pan and mash them.

2 Preheat a griddle or heavy frying pan over low heat. Tip the hot mashed potatoes into a bowl. Add the flour, olive oil and chopped chives, with a little salt and ground black pepper. Mix to a soft dough.

3 Roll out the dough on a well-floured surface to a thickness of 5mm/¼in. Stamp out rounds with a 5cm/2in scone (cookie) cutter, re-rolling and cutting the trimmings, or cut into squares with a sharp floured knife.

4 Cook the scones, in batches, on the hot griddle or frying pan for about 10 minutes, or until they are golden brown. Keep the heat low and turn the scones once.

5 Remove from the griddle or pan, top with a little low-fat spread and serve immediately.

Cook's Tips
- *Use floury potatoes such as King Edwards.*
- *The potatoes must be freshly cooked and mashed and should not be allowed to cool before mixing.*
- *Cook the scones over low heat so that the outside does not burn before the inside is cooked.*

Energy 46kcal/193kJ; Fat 1.3g, Saturated Fat 0.2g; Carbohydrate 8.1g, Fibre 0.5g

Ham and Tomato Scones

These make an ideal accompaniment for soup. If you have any left over the next day, halve them, toast under the grill (broiler) and top with low-fat spread.

Makes 12
225g/8oz/2 cups self-raising (self-rising) flour
5ml/1 tsp mustard powder
5ml/1 tsp paprika, plus extra for topping
2.5ml/½ tsp salt
25g/1oz/2 tbsp soft margarine
50g/2oz Black Forest ham, chopped
15ml/1 tbsp chopped fresh basil
50g/2oz/½ cup drained sun-dried tomatoes in oil, chopped
90–120ml/3–4fl oz/⅓–½ cup skimmed milk, plus extra for brushing

1 Preheat the oven to 200°C/400°F/Gas 6. Flour a large baking sheet.

2 Sift the flour, mustard, paprika and salt into a bowl. Rub in the margarine, using your fingertips or a pastry cutter until the mixture resembles breadcrumbs.

3 Stir in the ham, basil and sun-dried tomatoes; mix lightly. Pour in enough milk to mix to a soft dough.

4 Turn the dough on to a lightly floured surface, knead lightly and roll out to a 20 × 15cm (8 × 6in) rectangle.

5 Cut into 5cm/2in squares and arrange on the baking sheet.

6 Brush sparingly with milk, sprinkle with paprika and bake for 12–15 minutes. Transfer to a wire rack to cool.

Cook's Tip
Scone dough should be soft and moist and mixed for just long enough to bind the ingredients together. Too much kneading makes the scones tough.

Energy 89kcal/378kJ; Fat 2.1g, Saturated Fat 0.1g; Carbohydrate 15.6g, Fibre 0.7g

Low-Fat Drop Scones

These little scones are quick easy to make and contain very little fat.

Makes 18

225g/8oz/2 cups self-raising (self-rising) flour
2.5ml/½ tsp salt
15ml/1 tbsp caster (superfine) sugar
1 egg, beaten
300ml/½ pint/1¼ cups skimmed milk
oil, for brushing

1 Preheat a griddle, heavy frying pan or electric frying pan. Sift the flour and salt into a mixing bowl. Stir in the sugar and make a well in the centre.

2 Add the egg and half the milk. Stir from the centre to the outside, gradually incorporating the surrounding flour to make a smooth batter. Beat in the remaining milk.

3 Lightly grease the griddle or pan. Drop tablespoons of the batter on to the surface, making sure they are spaced well apart. Leave them to cook until they bubble and the bubbles begin to burst.

4 Turn the drop scones with a metal spatula and cook until the undersides are golden brown.

5 Keep the cooked drop scones warm and moist by wrapping them in a clean napkin while cooking successive batches. Serve with jam.

Variations

• For Banana and Raisin Drop Scones mash two ripe bananas and add to the egg and half the milk before adding to the dry ingredients at step 2. Add 25g/1oz/¼ cup of raisins to the banana mixture and then stir in from the centre as before.
• For a savoury version of these tasty scones, add 2 chopped spring onions (scallions) and 15ml/1 tbsp freshly grated Parmesan cheese to the batter. Serve with cottage cheese.

Energy 55kcal/235kJ; Fat 0.5g, Saturated Fat 0.1g; Carbohydrate 11.3g, Fibre 0.4g

Pineapple and Spice Drop Scones

Making the batter with pineapple or orange juice instead of milk cuts down on fat and adds to the taste. Semi-dried pineapple has an intense flavour that makes it ideal to use in baking.

Makes 24

115g/4oz/1 cup self-raising (self-rising) wholemeal (whole-wheat) flour
115g/4oz/1 cup self-raising (self-rising) white flour
5ml/1 tsp ground cinnamon
15ml/1 tbsp caster (superfine) sugar
1 egg, beaten
300ml/½ pint/1¼ cups pineapple juice
75g/3oz/½ cup semi-dried pineapple, chopped
oil, for brushing

1 Preheat a griddle, heavy frying pan or electric frying pan. Put the wholemeal flour in a mixing bowl. Sift in the white flour, ground cinnamon and sugar, and make a well in the centre of the dry ingredients.

2 Add the egg with half the pineapple juice. Stir from the centre to the outside, gradually incorporating the surrounding flour to make a smooth batter. Beat in the remaining juice with the chopped pineapple.

3 Lightly grease the griddle or pan. Drop tablespoons of the batter on to the surface, making sure they are spaced well apart. Leave them to cook until they bubble and the bubbles begin to burst.

4 Turn the drop scones with a metal spatula and cook until the underside is golden brown. Keep the cooked scones warm and moist by wrapping them in a clean napkin while cooking successive batches.

Cook's Tip

Drop scones do not keep well – they are best eaten freshly cooked and taste especially good hot from the pan. These taste good with cottage cheese.

Energy 45kcal/193kJ; Fat 0.4g, Saturated Fat 0.1g; Carbohydrate 9.9g, Fibre 0.4g

Pear and Sultana Teabread

This is an ideal teabread to make when pears are plentiful. There's no better use for autumn windfalls.

Serves 6 – 8

25g/1oz/3 cups rolled oats
50g/2oz/¼ cup soft light brown sugar
30ml/2 tbsp pear or apple juice
30ml/2 tbsp sunflower oil
1 large or 2 small ripe pears
115g/4oz/1 cup self-raising (self-rising) flour
115g/4oz/¾ cup sultanas (golden raisins)
2.5ml/½ tsp baking powder
10ml/2 tsp mixed (apple pie) spice
1 egg

1 Preheat the oven to 180°C/350°F/Gas 4. Line a 450g/1lb loaf tin (pan) with baking parchment.

2 Put the oats in a bowl with the sugar, and pour over the pear or apple juice and oil.

3 Mix the ingredients together well using a wooden spoon or electric whisk. Leave to stand for 15 minutes.

4 Quarter, core and grate the pear(s). Add to the bowl with the flour, sultanas, baking powder, spice and egg. Using a wooden spoon, mix thoroughly.

5 Spoon the tea bread mixture into the prepared loaf tin. Bake for 55–60 minutes, or until a skewer inserted into the centre comes out clean.

6 Invert the tea bread on a wire rack and remove the lining paper. Leave to cool.

Cook's Tips

- *Health-food stores sell concentrated pear juice, ready for diluting as required.*
- *You will also find some good-quality sultanas there and organic oats if you want to make a really healthy treat.*

Energy 184kcal/780kJ; Fat 4g, Saturated Fat 0.6g; Carbohydrate 36.3g, Fibre 1.8g

Banana and Ginger Teabread

The creaminess of the banana is given a delightful lift with chunks of stem ginger in this tasty teabread. If you like a strong ginger flavour add 5ml/1 tsp ground ginger with the flour.

Serves 6 – 8

175g/6oz/1½ cups self-raising (self-rising) flour
5ml/1 tsp baking powder
40g/1½oz/3 tbsp soft margarine
50g/2oz/¼ cup soft light brown sugar
50g/2oz/⅓ cup drained preserved stem ginger, chopped
60ml/4 tbsp skimmed milk
2 ripe bananas

1 Preheat the oven to 180°C/350°F/Gas 4. Line and grease a 450g/1lb loaf tin (pan).

2 Sift the flour and baking powder into a large bowl.

3 Using your fingertips or a pastry cutter rub the margarine into the dry ingredients until the mixture resembles breadcrumbs, then stir in the sugar.

4 Peel and mash the bananas in a separate bowl.

5 Add the preserved stem ginger, milk and mashed bananas to the mixture and mix to a soft dough. Spoon into the prepared tin and bake for 40–45 minutes.

6 Run a metal spatula around the edges of the cake to loosen them, then turn the teabread on to a wire rack and leave to cool completely.

Variation

To make Banana and Walnut Teabread, add 5ml/1 tsp mixed (apple pie) spice and omit the chopped stem ginger. Stir in 50g/2oz/½ cup chopped walnuts and add 50g/2oz/⅓ cup sultanas (golden raisins).

Energy 162kcal/685kJ; Fat 4.5g, Saturated Fat 0.1g; Carbohydrate 29.7g, Fibre 1g

Angel Cake

This heavenly cake contains virtually no fat and tastes simply divine! Serve in slices with fresh fruit for a delicious healthy dessert

Makes one 25cm/10in cake

130g/4½oz/generous 1 cup sifted plain (all-purpose) flour
30ml/2 tbsp cornflour (cornstarch)
285g/10½oz/1½ cups caster (superfine) sugar
10 egg whites
6.5ml/1¼ tsp cream of tartar
1.5ml/¼ tsp salt
5ml/1 tsp vanilla extract
1.5ml/¼ tsp almond extract
icing (confectioners') sugar, for dusting

1 Preheat the oven to 160°C/325°F/Gas 3. Sift the flours before measuring, then sift them four times together with 90g/3½oz/½ cup of the sugar.

2 Beat the egg whites until foamy. Sift over the cream of tartar and salt and beat until the egg whites form soft peaks.

3 Add the remaining sugar in three batches, beating well after each addition.

4 Stir in the vanilla and almond extracts. Fold in the flour mixture in two batches.

5 Transfer to an ungreased 25cm/10in cake tin (pan) and bake until just browned on top, about 1 hour.

6 Turn the tin upside-down on to a wire rack and cool for 1 hour. Then invert on to a serving plate. Lay a star-shaped template on top of the cake, sift over some icing sugar and remove the template.

Cook's Tip
For an exceptionally light sponge cake such as this one it is important to sift the dry ingredients several times to help incorporate air into the batter. Be careful to fold in the flour to the wet ingredients so that the air will not be lost.

Energy 131kcal/558kJ; Fat 0.1g, Saturated Fat 0g; Carbohydrate 30.3g, Fibre 0.1g

Peach Roll

This is the perfect light cake for a summer afternoon tea in the garden.

Serves 6–8

3 eggs
115g/4oz/generous ½ cup caster (superfine) sugar
75g/3oz/⅔ cup plain (all-purpose) flour, sifted
15ml/1 tbsp boiling water
90ml/6 tbsp peach jam
icing (confectioners') sugar, for dusting (optional)

1 Preheat the oven to 200°C/400°F/Gas 6. Line and grease a 30 x 20cm/12 x 8in Swiss roll tin (jelly roll pan).

2 Combine the eggs and sugar in a bowl. Beat with a hand-held electric whisk until thick and mousse-like: when the whisk is lifted a trail should remain on the surface of the mixture for at least 30 seconds.

3 Carefully fold in the flour with a large metal spoon, then add the boiling water in the same way.

4 Spoon the mixture into the prepared tin, spread evenly to the edges and bake for 10–12 minutes, or until the cake springs back when lightly pressed.

5 Spread a sheet of baking parchment on a flat surface and sprinkle it with caster sugar. Carefully invert the cake on top and peel off the lining paper.

6 Make a neat cut two-thirds of the way through the cake, about 1cm/½in from the short edge nearest you – this will make it easier for you to roll the sponge cake. Trim the remaining edges to give a neat finish to the cake.

7 Spread the cake with the peach jam and roll up quickly from the partially cut end. Hold in position for a minute, making sure the join is underneath.

8 Cool on a wire rack. Dust with icing sugar, if you like.

Energy 146kcal/618kJ; Fat 2.2g, Saturated Fat 0.6g; Carbohydrate 30.1g, Fibre 0.3g

Peach and Amaretto Cake

Try this delicious cake for dessert, with reduced-fat fromage frais, or serve it solo for afternoon tea.

Serves 8

3 eggs, separated
175g/6oz/¾ cup caster (superfine) sugar
grated rind and juice of 1 lemon
50g/2oz/½ cup semolina
40g/1½oz/scant ½ cup ground almonds
25g/1oz/¼ cup plain (all-purpose) flour

For the syrup
75g/3oz/6 tbsp caster (superfine) sugar
90ml/6 tbsp water
30ml/2 tbsp amaretto liqueur
2 peaches or nectarines, halved and stoned (pitted)
60ml/4 tbsp apricot jam, sieved, to glaze

1 Preheat the oven to 180°C/350°F/Gas 4. Grease a 20cm/8in round loose-based cake tin (pan). Whisk the egg yolks, caster sugar, lemon rind and juice in a bowl until thick, pale and creamy, then fold in the semolina, almonds and flour until the mixture is smooth.

2 Whisk the egg whites in a grease-free bowl until fairly stiff. Using a metal spoon, stir a generous spoonful of the whites into the semolina mixture to lighten it, then fold in the remaining egg whites. Spoon into the prepared cake tin.

3 Bake for 30–35 minutes, then remove the cake from the oven and carefully loosen the edges. Prick the top with a skewer and leave to cool slightly in the tin.

4 Meanwhile, make the syrup. Heat the sugar and water in a small pan, stirring until dissolved, then boil without stirring for 2 minutes. Add the amaretto liqueur and drizzle slowly over the cake. Leave to cool in the tin.

5 Remove the cake from the tin and transfer it to a serving plate. Slice the peaches or nectarines and arrange them in concentric circles over the top of the cake. Brush the fruit with the glaze.

Energy 244kcal/1034kJ; Fat 5g, Saturated Fat 0.8g; Carbohydrate 46.7g, Fibre 0.9g

Chestnut and Orange Roulade

A very moist roulade with a sweet and creamy filling – ideal to serve as an impressive low-fat dessert.

Serves 8

3 eggs, separated
115g/4oz/generous ½ cup caster (superfine) sugar
½ x 439g/15½ oz can unsweetened chestnut purée
grated rind and juice of 1 orange
icing (confectioners') sugar, for dusting

For the filling
225g/8oz/1 cup low-fat soft cheese
15ml/1 tbsp clear honey
1 orange

1 Preheat the oven to 180°C/350°F/Gas 4. Line and grease a 30 x 20cm/12 x 8in Swiss roll tin (jelly roll pan).

2 Whisk the egg yolks and sugar in a bowl until thick. Put the chestnut purée into a separate bowl. Whisk the orange rind and juice into the purée, then whisk into the egg mixture.

3 Whisk the egg whites until fairly stiff. Stir a spoonful into the chestnut mixture, then fold in the remaining egg whites.

4 Spoon the mixture into the prepared tin and bake for 30 minutes, or until firm. Cool for 5 minutes in the tin, then cover with a clean damp dish towel and leave until completely cold.

5 Meanwhile, make the filling. Put the soft cheese in a bowl with the honey. Finely grate the orange rind and add to the bowl. Using a sharp knife, cut away all the peel and pith from the orange. Cut the fruit into segments, cutting either side of the membrane so that you have only the flesh. Chop roughly and set aside. Add any juice to the bowl, then beat until smooth. Mix in the orange segments.

6 Sprinkle a sheet of baking parchment with icing sugar. Turn the roulade out on to the paper; peel off the lining paper. Spread the filling over the roulade and roll up like a Swiss roll (jelly roll). Transfer to a plate and dust with icing sugar.

Energy 176kcal/741kJ; Fat 5.1g, Saturated Fat 2.2g; Carbohydrate 28.1g, Fibre 1.1g

Cinnamon and Apple Gateau

Make this lovely moist gateau as a guilt-free autumn teatime treat.

Serves 8

3 eggs
115g/4oz/½ cup caster (superfine) sugar
75g/3oz/¾ cup plain (all-purpose) flour
5ml/1 tsp ground cinnamon

For the filling and topping

4 large eating apples
15ml/1 tbsp water
60ml/4 tbsp clear honey
75g/3oz/½ cup sultanas (golden raisins)
2.5ml/½ tsp ground cinnamon
350g/12oz/1½ cups low-fat soft cheese
60ml/4 tbsp reduced-fat fromage frais or low-fat cream cheese
10ml/2 tsp lemon juice

1 Preheat the oven to 190°C/375°F/Gas 5. Line and grease a 23cm/9in shallow round cake tin (pan). Whisk the eggs and sugar until thick, then sift the flour and cinnamon over the surface and carefully fold in with a large metal spoon.

2 Pour into the prepared tin and bake for 25–30 minutes, or until the cake springs back when lightly pressed. Leave on a wire rack to cool completely.

3 To make the filling, peel, core and slice three of the apples and cook them in a covered pan with the water and half the honey until softened. Add the sultanas and cinnamon, stir well, replace the lid and leave to cool.

4 Put the soft cheese in a bowl with the fromage frais, the remaining honey and half the lemon juice; beat until smooth. Split the sponge cake in half, place the bottom half on a plate and drizzle over any liquid from the apples.

5 Spread with two-thirds of the cheese mixture, then top with the apple filling. Fit the top of the cake in place.

6 Swirl the remaining filling over the top of the sponge. Quarter, core and slice the remaining apple, dip the slices in the remaining lemon juice and use to decorate the edges.

Energy 239kcal/1010kJ; Fat 5.8g, Saturated Fat 2.9g; Carbohydrate 39.9g, Fibre 1.1g

Lemon Chiffon Cake

Tangy lemon mousse makes a delicious filling in this light cake, which is surprisingly low in saturated fat.

Serves 8

1 lemon sponge cake mix
lemon glacé icing
shreds of blanched lemon rind

For the filling

2 eggs, separated
75g/3oz/6 tbsp caster (superfine) sugar
grated rind and juice of 1 small lemon
20ml/4 tsp water
10ml/2 tsp powdered gelatine
120ml/4fl oz/½ cup reduced-fat fromage frais or crème fraîche

1 Preheat the oven to 180°C/350°F/Gas 4. Line and grease a 20cm/8in loose-based cake tin (pan).

2 Add the sponge mixture and bake for 20–25 minutes, or until firm and golden. Cool on a wire rack, then split the cake in half. Return the lower half of the cake to the clean cake tin and set aside.

3 To make the filling, whisk the egg yolks, sugar, lemon rind and juice in a bowl until thick, pale and creamy. In a grease-free bowl, whisk the egg whites until they form soft peaks.

4 Sprinkle the gelatine over the water in a heatproof bowl. When the gelatine has become spongy, place the bowl over a pan of simmering water and dissolve the gelatine, stirring occasionally. Cool slightly, then whisk into the yolk mixture. Fold in the fromage frais.

5 When the mixture begins to set, fold in a generous spoonful of the egg whites to lighten it, then fold in the remaining whites.

6 Spoon the lemon mousse over the sponge in the cake tin. Set the second layer of sponge on top and chill until set.

7 Carefully transfer the cake to a serving plate. Pour the glacé icing over the cake and spread it evenly to the edges. Decorate with the lemon shreds.

Energy 356kcal/1491kJ; Fat 18.4g, Saturated Fat 4g; Carbohydrate 43.6g, Fibre 0.6g

Strawberry Gateau

It is difficult to believe that a cake that tastes so delicious can be low fat. It is the perfect way to enjoy the first locally grown strawberries of the season.

Serves 6

2 eggs
75g/3oz/6 tbsp caster (superfine) sugar
grated rind of ½ orange
50g/2oz/½ cup plain (all-purpose) flour

For the filling

275g/10oz/1¼ cups low-fat soft cheese
grated rind of ½ orange
30ml/2 tbsp caster (superfine) sugar
60ml/4 tbsp reduced-fat fromage frais or crème fraîche
225g/8oz/2 cups strawberries, halved and chopped
25g/1oz/¼ cup chopped almonds, toasted

1 Preheat the oven to 190°C/375°F/Gas 5. Line a 30 × 20cm/12 × 8in Swiss roll tin (jelly roll pan) with baking parchment.

2 In a bowl, whisk the eggs, sugar and orange rind until thick and mousse-like, then lightly fold in the flour.

3 Turn into the prepared tin. Bake for 15–20 minutes, or until the surface is firm to the touch and golden.

4 Turn the cake out on to on a wire rack to cool. When cold, remove the lining paper.

5 Meanwhile, make the filling. In a bowl, mix the soft cheese with the grated orange rind, sugar and fromage frais until smooth. Divide the mixture between two bowls.

6 Add half the strawberries to one bowl. Cut the sponge horizontally into three equal pieces and sandwich together with the strawberry filling. Place the gateau on a serving plate.

7 Spread the plain filling over the top and sides of the cake. Press the toasted almonds over the sides and decorate the top with the remaining strawberry halves.

Energy 305kcal/1288kJ; Fat 7.6g, Saturated Fat 1.1g; Carbohydrate 35.7g, Fibre 7.2g

Tia Maria Gateau

A feather-light coffee sponge with a creamy liqueur-flavoured filling spiked with preserved stem ginger.

Serves 8

75g/3oz/¾ cup plain (all-purpose) flour
30ml/2 tbsp instant coffee powder
3 eggs
115g/4oz/½ cup caster (superfine) sugar

For the filling

175g/6oz/generous ¾ cup low-fat soft cheese
15ml/1 tbsp clear honey
15ml/1 tbsp Tia Maria
50g/2oz/⅓ cup preserved stem ginger, chopped

For the icing

225g/8oz/2 cups icing (confectioners') sugar, sifted
10ml/2 tsp coffee extract
5ml/1 tsp fat-reduced cocoa
coffee beans (optional)

1 Preheat the oven to 190°C/375°F/Gas 5. Line and grease a 20cm/8in round cake tin (pan). Sift the flour and coffee powder together into a bowl.

2 Whisk the eggs and sugar in a bowl until thick and mousse-like, then fold in the flour mixture lightly. Turn the mixture into the prepared tin. Bake for 30–35 minutes, or until firm and golden. Leave to cool on a wire rack.

3 To make the filling, mix the soft cheese with the honey in a bowl. Beat until smooth, then stir in the Tia Maria and preserved stem ginger. Split the cake in half horizontally and sandwich together with the Tia Maria filling.

4 To make the icing, mix the icing sugar and coffee extract in a bowl with enough water to make an icing which will coat the back of a wooden spoon. Pour three-quarters of the icing over the cake.

5 Stir the cocoa into the remaining icing, spoon it into a piping (icing) bag fitted with a writing nozzle and drizzle the mocha icing over the coffee icing. Decorate with coffee beans, if you like.

Energy 247kcal/1050kJ; Fat 2.5g, Saturated Fat 1.5g; Carbohydrate 54.7g, Fibre 0.5g

Chocolate Banana Cake

Fresh fruit is especially good for making a moist cake mixture. Here is a delicious sticky chocolate cake, moist enough to eat without the icing if you want to cut down on the calories.

Serves 8

225g/8oz/2 cups self-raising (self-rising) flour
45ml/3 tbsp reduced-fat unsweetened cocoa powder
115g/4oz/½ cup soft light brown sugar
30ml/2 tbsp malt extract
30ml/2 tbsp golden (light corn) syrup
2 eggs, beaten
60ml/4 tbsp skimmed milk
60ml/4 tbsp sunflower oil
2 large ripe bananas

For the icing

175g/6oz/1½ cups icing (confectioners') sugar, sifted
30ml/2 tbsp reduced-fat unsweetened cocoa powder, sifted
15–30ml/1–2 tbsp warm water

1 Preheat the oven to 160°C/325°F/Gas 3. Line and grease a deep 20cm/8in round cake tin (pan). Sift the flour into a mixing bowl with the cocoa powder. Stir in the sugar.

2 Make a well in the centre of the dry ingredients and add the malt extract, golden syrup, eggs, milk and oil. Mix well.

3 Mash the bananas thoroughly and stir them into the mixture until thoroughly combined.

4 Spoon the cake mixture into the prepared tin and bake for 1–1¼ hours, or until the centre of the cake springs back when lightly pressed.

5 Remove from the tin and turn on to a wire rack to cool.

6 To make the icing, put the icing sugar and cocoa in a mixing bowl and gradually add enough water to make a mixture thick enough to coat the back of a wooden spoon.

7 Pour over the top of the cake and ease to the edges, allowing the icing to dribble down the sides.

Energy 352kcal/1487kJ; Fat 9.4g, Saturated Fat 2.3g; Carbohydrate 64.4g, Fibre 2.3g

Spiced Apple Cake

As grated apple and dates give this cake a natural sweetness, it may not be necessary to add all the sugar.

Serves 8

225g/8oz/2 cups self-raising (self-rising) wholemeal (whole-wheat) flour
5ml/1 tsp baking powder
10ml/2 tsp ground cinnamon
175g/6oz/1 cup chopped dates
75g/3oz/scant ½ cup soft light brown sugar
15ml/1 tbsp pear and apple spread
120ml/4fl oz/½ cup apple juice
2 eggs, beaten
90ml/6 tbsp sunflower oil
2 eating apples, cored and grated
15ml/1 tbsp chopped walnuts

1 Preheat the oven to 180°C/350°F/Gas 4. Line and grease a 20cm/8in deep round cake tin (pan).

2 Sift the flour, baking powder and cinnamon into a mixing bowl, then mix in the dates and make a well in the centre.

3 Mix some of the sugar with the pear and apple spread in a small bowl. Gradually stir in the apple juice.

4 Add to the dry ingredients with the eggs, oil and apples. Mix thoroughly. Taste and add the rest of the sugar if necessary.

5 Spoon into the prepared cake tin, sprinkle with the walnuts and bake for 60–65 minutes, or until a skewer inserted into the centre of the cake comes out clean.

6 Invert on a wire rack, remove the lining paper and leave to cool.

Cook's Tip
It is not necessary to peel the apples – the skin adds extra fibre and softens on cooking.

Energy 282kcal/1186kJ; Fat 11.3g, Saturated Fat 1.5g; Carbohydrate 42.8g, Fibre 1.6g

Irish Whiskey Cake

This moist rich fruit cake is drizzled with whiskey as soon as it comes out of the oven. It is high in fibre and full of flavour.

Serves 10

115g/4oz/¾ cup sultanas (golden raisins)
115g/4oz/scant 1 cup raisins
115g/4oz/½ cup currants
115g/4oz/½ cup glacé (candied) cherries
175g/6oz/1¼ cups soft light brown sugar
300ml/½ pint/1¼ cups cold tea
1 egg, beaten
300g/11oz/2⅔ cups self-raising (self-rising) flour, sifted
45ml/3 tbsp Irish whiskey

1 Mix the sultanas, raisins, currants, cherries, sugar and tea in a large bowl. Leave to soak overnight until the tea has been absorbed.

2 Preheat the oven to 180°C/350°F/Gas 4. Line and grease a 1kg/2¼lb loaf tin (pan).

3 Add the egg and flour to the fruit mixture and beat thoroughly until well mixed.

4 Pour into the prepared tin and bake for 1½ hours or until a skewer inserted into the centre comes out clean.

5 Prick over the top of the cake with a skewer and drizzle over the whiskey while the cake is still hot.

6 Allow to stand for 5 minutes, then remove from the tin and cool completely on a wire rack.

Variation
For a tangy finish, drizzle with lemon icing. Mix the juice of 1 lemon with 225g/8oz/2 cup icing (confectioners') sugar and enough warm water for the icing to have a thin consistency. Drizzle the icing over the cooled cake and decorate with crystallized lemon slices, if you like.

Energy 311kcal/1323kJ; Fat 1.1g, Saturated Fat 0.2g; Carbohydrate 73g, Fibre 1.7g

Fruit and Nut Cake

A rich, fibrous fruit cake that matures with keeping. Omit the fruit and nut decoration from the top if you want to ice it for a Christmas cake.

Serves 12–14

175g/6oz/1½ cups self-raising (self-rising) wholemeal (whole-wheat) flour
175g/6oz/1½ cups self-raising (self-rising) white flour
10ml/2 tsp mixed (apple pie) spice
15ml/1 tbsp apple and apricot spread
45ml/3 tbsp clear honey
15ml/1 tbsp molasses
90ml/6 tbsp sunflower oil
175ml/6fl oz/¾ cup orange juice
2 eggs, beaten
675g/1½lb/4 cups luxury mixed dried fruit
115g/4oz/½ cup glacé (candied) cherries, halved
45ml/3 tbsp split almonds

1 Preheat the oven to 160°C/325°F/Gas 3. Line and grease a deep 20cm/8in cake tin (pan). Tie a band of newspaper around the outside of the tin and stand it on a pad of newspaper on a baking sheet.

2 Combine the flours in a mixing bowl. Stir in the mixed spice and make a well in the centre.

3 Put the apple and apricot spread in a small bowl. Gradually stir in the honey and molasses. Add to the bowl with the oil, orange juice, eggs and mixed fruit. Stir with a wooden spoon to mix thoroughly.

4 Scrape the mixture into the prepared tin and smooth the surface. Arrange the cherries and almonds in a decorative pattern over the top. Bake for 2 hours, or until a skewer inserted into the centre of the cake comes out clean. Turn on to a wire rack to cool, then remove the lining paper.

Cook's Tip
For a less elaborate cake, omit the cherries, chop the almonds roughly and sprinkle them over the top.

Energy 327kcal/1384kJ; Fat 7.8g, Saturated Fat 1g; Carbohydrate 63g, Fibre 2.2g

White Bread

There is nothing quite like the smell and taste of home-baked bread, eaten while still warm.

Makes two 23 x 13cm/ 9 x 5in loaves

50ml/2fl oz/¼ cup lukewarm water
15ml/1 tbsp active dried yeast
30ml/2 tbsp caster (superfine) sugar
475ml/16fl oz/2 cups lukewarm milk
25g/1oz/2 tbsp butter or margarine, at room temperature
10ml/2 tsp salt
about 900g/2lb/8 cups strong white bread flour

1 Combine the water, yeast and 15ml/1 tbsp of the sugar in a measuring jug (cup) and leave for 15 minutes, or until frothy.

2 Pour the milk into a large bowl. Add the remaining sugar, the butter or margarine, and salt.

3 Stir in the yeast mixture, then stir in the flour, 150g/5oz/1¼ cups at a time, until a stiff dough is obtained.

4 Transfer the dough to a floured surface. Knead the dough until it is smooth and elastic, then place it in a large greased bowl, cover with clear film (plastic wrap), and leave to rise in a warm place until doubled in volume, about 2–3 hours.

5 Grease two 23 x 13cm/9 x 5in loaf tins (pans). Knock back (punch down) the dough and divide in half.

6 Form into loaf shapes and place in the tins, seam down. Cover and leave to rise again until almost doubled in volume, about 45 minutes. Meanwhile, preheat the oven to 190°C/375°F/Gas 5.

7 Bake the loaves until firm and brown, about 45–50 minutes. Turn out and tap the base of a loaf: if it sounds hollow the loaf is done. If necessary, return to the oven and bake for a few minutes longer. (Turn the loaf upside down in the tin if the top is done but the base is not.) Turn out and cool on a wire rack.

Energy 1796kcal/7623kJ; Fat 20.2g, Saturated Fat 10g; Carbohydrate 376.6g, Fibre 14g

Braided Loaf

It doesn't take much effort to turn an ordinary dough mix into this work of art.

Makes one loaf

15ml/1 tbsp active dried yeast
5ml/1 tsp honey
250ml/8fl oz/1 cup lukewarm milk
50g/2oz/¼ cup butter, melted
425g/15oz/3⅔ cups strong white bread flour
5ml/1 tsp salt
1 egg, lightly beaten
1 egg yolk, beaten with 5ml/1 tsp milk, to glaze

1 Combine the yeast, honey, milk and butter in a small bowl. Stir and leave for 15 minutes to dissolve and for the yeast to become frothy.

2 In a large bowl, mix together the flour and salt. Make a central well in the flour, and add the yeast mixture and egg. With a wooden spoon, stir from the centre, gradually incorporating the flour into the liquid, to obtain a rough dough.

3 Transfer the dough to a floured surface and knead until smooth and elastic. This will take about 10 minutes.

4 Place in a clean bowl, cover with clear film (plastic wrap) and leave to rise in a warm place until doubled in volume, about 1½ hours.

5 Grease a baking sheet. Punch down (knock back) the dough and divide into three equal pieces.

6 Roll each piece into a long thin strip. Begin braiding with the centre strip, tucking in the ends neatly when you reach the end of the braid. Cover loosely with clear film and leave to rise in a warm place for 30 minutes.

7 Meanwhile, preheat the oven to 190°C/375°F/Gas 5. Brush the bread with the egg and milk glaze and bake until it is golden, about 40–45 minutes. Turn the loaf out on to a wire rack to cool.

Energy 2033kcal/8584kJ; Fat 56.4g, Saturated Fat 31.1g; Carbohydrate 348.4g, Fibre 13.2g

Wholemeal Bread

A simple wholesome bread to be enjoyed by the entire family at any time.

Makes one 23 x 13cm/ 9 x 5in loaf

525g/1lb 5oz/5¼ cups strong wholemeal (whole-wheat) bread flour
10ml/2 tsp salt
20ml/4 tsp active dried yeast
450ml/¾ pint/scant 2 cups lukewarm water
30ml/2 tbsp honey
30ml/2 tbsp oil
40g/1½oz wheatgerm
milk, to glaze

1 Warm the flour and salt in a bowl in the oven at its lowest setting for 10 minutes.

2 Meanwhile, combine the yeast with half of the water in a bowl and leave to dissolve and for the yeast to become frothy.

3 Make a central well in the flour. Pour in the yeast mixture, the remaining water, honey, oil and wheatgerm. Stir in the flour from the centre, incorporating it as you go, until smooth.

4 Grease a 23 x 13cm/9 x 5in loaf tin (pan). Knead the dough just enough to shape into a loaf. Put it in the tin and cover with clear film (plastic wrap). Leave in a warm place until the dough is about 2.5cm/1in higher than the tin rim, about 1 hour.

5 Preheat the oven to 200°C/400°F/Gas 6. Brush the loaf with milk, and bake until the base sounds hollow when tapped, about 35–40 minutes. Cool on a wire rack.

Cook's Tip

For all yeast recipes use strong bread flours and not plain (all-purpose) or self-raising (self-rising) flours. Strong bread flours have a high gluten content, which is important to allow the yeast to rise well. Breads made with strong flours are light and have an airy crumb. Soda breads or any other breads not made with yeast do not use strong flours, however.

Energy 1997kcal/8459kJ; Fat 37.2g, Saturated 4.7g; Carbohydrate 361g, Fibre 53.5g

Multigrain Bread

Try different flours, such as rye, cornmeal, buckwheat or barley to replace the wheatgerm and the soya flour used here.

Makes two 21 x 12cm/ 8½ x 4½in loaves

15ml/1 tbsp active dried yeast
50ml/2fl oz/¼ cup lukewarm water
65g/2½oz/¾ cup rolled oats
475ml/16fl oz/2 cups milk
10ml/2 tsp salt
50ml/2fl oz/¼ cup oil
50g/2oz/¼ cup soft light brown sugar
30ml/2 tbsp honey
2 eggs, lightly beaten
25g/1oz wheatgerm
175g/6oz/1½ cups soya flour
350g/12oz/3 cups strong wholemeal (whole-wheat) flour
about 450g/1lb/4 cups strong white bread flour

1 Combine the yeast and water in a small bowl, stir, and leave for about 15 minutes to dissolve and for the yeast to become frothy. Place the oats in a large bowl. Boil the milk, then pour over the rolled oats. Stir in the salt, oil, sugar and honey. Leave until lukewarm.

2 Stir in the yeast mixture, eggs, wheatgerm, soya and wholemeal flours. Gradually stir in enough strong white bread flour to obtain a rough dough.

3 Transfer the dough to a floured surface and knead, adding flour if necessary, until smooth and elastic. This will take about 10 minutes. Return to a clean bowl, cover with clear film (plastic wrap) and leave to rise in a warm place until doubled in volume, about 2½ hours.

4 Grease two 21 x 12cm/8½ x 4½in loaf tins (pans). Knock back (punch down) the risen dough and knead briefly. Then divide the dough into quarters. Roll each quarter into a cylinder 4cm/1½in thick. Twist together two cylinders and place in a tin; repeat for the remaining cylinders. Cover with clear film and leave to rise until doubled in volume again, about 1 hour. Meanwhile, preheat the oven to 190°C/375°F/Gas 5.

5 Bake until the bases sound hollow when tapped lightly, about 45–50 minutes. Turn out and cool on a wire rack.

Energy 2266kcal/9595kJ; Fat 43.1g, Saturated Fat 8g; Carbohydrate 389.3g, Fibre 38.7g

Country Bread

A filling bread made with a mixture of wholemeal and white flour.

Makes two loaves

350g/12oz/3 cups strong wholemeal (whole-wheat) bread flour
350g/12oz/3 cups plain (all-purpose) flour
150g/5oz/1¼ cups strong white bread flour
20ml/4 tsp salt
50g/2oz/¼ cup butter, at room temperature
475ml/16fl oz/2 cups lukewarm milk

For the starter

15ml/1 tbsp active dried yeast
250ml/8fl oz/1 cup lukewarm water
150g/5oz/1¼ cups plain (all-purpose) flour
1.5ml/¼ tsp caster (superfine) sugar

1 To make the starter, mix the yeast, water, plain flour and sugar in a bowl. Cover and leave in a warm place for 2–3 hours.

2 Place the flours, salt and butter in a food processor and process until just blended, about 1–2 minutes.

3 Stir together the milk and starter, then slowly pour into the processor, with the motor running, until the mixture forms a dough. Knead the dough until smooth. This will take about 10 minutes.

4 Place in an ungreased bowl, cover with clear film (plastic wrap), and leave to rise in a warm place until doubled in size, about 1½ hours. Knock back (punch down) and then return to the bowl and leave until tripled in size, about 1½ hours.

5 Grease a baking sheet. Divide the dough in half. Cut off one-third of the dough from each half and shape all the pieces into balls. Top each large ball with a small ball and press the centre with the handle of a wooden spoon to secure. Cover with oiled clear film, slash the top, and leave the dough to rise once again.

6 Preheat the oven to 200°C/400°F/Gas 6. Dust the loaves with flour and bake until browned and the bases sound hollow when tapped, 45–50 minutes. Cool on a wire rack.

Energy 1760kcal/7482kJ; Fat 12.1g, Saturated Fat 3.7g; Carbohydrate 375.5g, Fibre 25.8g

Oatmeal Bread

A healthy, rustic-looking bread made with rolled oats as well as flour.

Makes two loaves

475ml/16fl oz/2 cups milk
25g/1oz/2 tbsp butter
50g/2oz/¼ cup cup soft dark brown sugar
10ml/2 tsp salt
15ml/1 tbsp active dried yeast
50ml/2fl oz/¼ cup lukewarm water
400g/14oz/4 cups rolled oats
675–900g/1½–2lb/6–8 cups strong white bread flour

1 Put the milk in a small pan and bring to boiling point. Quickly remove from the heat and stir in the butter, brown sugar and salt. Leave the mixture to cool until lukewarm.

2 Combine the yeast and warm water in a large bowl and leave for about 15 minutes until frothy.

3 Stir in the milk mixture. Add 275g/10oz/3 cups of the rolled oats and enough flour to obtain a soft dough.

4 Transfer the dough to a floured surface and knead until smooth and elastic.

5 Place in a greased bowl, cover with clear film (plastic wrap) and leave until doubled in volume, about 2–3 hours.

6 Grease a large baking sheet. Transfer the dough to a lightly floured surface and divide in half. Shape into rounds.

7 Place on the baking sheet, cover with a dish towel or oiled clear film and leave to rise until doubled in volume, about 1 hour.

8 Preheat the oven to 200°C/400°F/Gas 6. Score the tops of the loaves and sprinkle with the remaining oats.

9 Bake until the bases sound hollow when tapped, about 45–50 minutes. Turn out on to wire racks to cool.

Energy 2254kcal/9556kJ; Fat 36.1g, Saturated Fat 9.8g; Carbohydrate 445.2g, Fibre 24.1g

Two-tone Bread

A tasty, malty bread that, when cut, reveals an attractive swirled interior.

Makes two 350g/12oz loaves

25ml/1½ tbsp active dried yeast
120ml/4fl oz/½ cup warm water
55g/2¼oz/generous ¼ cup caster (superfine) sugar
675g/1½lb/6 cups strong white bread flour
7.5ml/1½ tsp salt
600ml/1 pint/2½ cups warm milk
65g/2½oz/5 tbsp butter or margarine, melted and cooled
45ml/3 tbsp black treacle (molasses)
275g/10oz/2½ cups strong wholemeal (whole-wheat) bread flour

1 In a small bowl, dissolve the yeast in the water with 5ml/1 tsp of the sugar. Sift 350g/12oz/3 cups of the white bread flour, the salt and remaining sugar. Make a well in the centre and add the yeast, milk and butter or margarine. Mix in gradually to form a smooth soft batter.

2 Divide the batter into two bowls. To one bowl, add 275g/10oz/2½ cups of the strong white flour and mix together to a soft dough. Knead until smooth. This will take about 10 minutes. Shape into a ball, put into a greased bowl and rotate to grease all over. Cover with clear film (plastic wrap).

3 Mix the treacle and wholemeal flour into the second bowl. Add enough of the remaining white flour to make a soft dough. Knead until smooth. Shape into a ball, put in a greased bowl and cover with oiled clear film. Leave the doughs to rise in a warm place for about 1 hour, or until doubled in size. Grease two 22 x 11cm/ 8½ x 4½in loaf tins (pans).

4 Preheat the oven to 220°C/425°F/Gas 7. Knock back (punch down) the dough and divide each ball in half. Roll out half of the light dough to a 30 x 20cm/12 x 8in rectangle. Roll out half of the dark dough to the same size. Set the dark dough rectangle on the light one. Roll up tightly from a short side. Set in a loaf tin. Repeat for the other loaf. Cover the tins and leave the dough to rise until doubled in size. Bake for 30–35 minutes.

Energy 2123kcal/8994kJ; Fat 39.3g, Saturated Fat 20.8g; Carbohydrate 408.3g, Fibre 22.9g

Cheese Bread

This flavoured bread is ideal to serve with hot soup for a hearty snack lunch.

Makes one 23 x 13cm/ 9 x 5in loaf

15ml/1 tbsp active dried yeast
250ml/8fl oz/1 cup lukewarm milk
25g/1oz/2 tbsp butter
425g/15oz/3⅔ cups strong white bread flour
10ml/2 tsp salt
90g/3½oz/scant 1 cup grated mature (sharp) Cheddar cheese

1 Combine the yeast and milk in a small bowl. Stir and leave for 15 minutes to dissolve and for the yeast to become frothy.

2 Meanwhile, melt the butter, leave to cool, then add it to the yeast mixture.

3 Mix the flour and salt together in a large bowl. Make a central well in the flour and pour in the yeast mixture. With a wooden spoon, stir from the centre to obtain a rough dough. If the dough seems too dry, add 30–45ml/2–3 tbsp water.

4 Transfer to a floured surface and knead until smooth and elastic. This will take about 10 minutes. Return to the bowl, cover and leave to rise in a warm place until doubled in volume, about 2–3 hours.

5 Grease a 23 x 13cm/9 x 5in loaf tin (pan). Knock back (punch down) the dough and knead in the cheese to distribute it evenly.

6 Twist the dough, form into a loaf shape and place in the tin, tucking the ends underneath. Leave in a warm place until the dough rises above the rim of the tin, about 1½ hours.

7 Meanwhile, preheat the oven to 200°C/400°F/Gas 6. Bake the bread for 15 minutes, then lower the heat to 190°C/375°F/Gas 5 and bake until the base sounds hollow when tapped, about a further 30 minutes.

Energy 93kcal/394kJ; Fat 2.4g, Saturated Fat 1.3g; Carbohydrate 16.5g, Fibre 0.6g

Rye Bread

Rye bread is popular in Northern Europe and makes an excellent base for open sandwiches.

Makes 2 loaves, each serving 10

350g/12oz/3 cups strong wholemeal (whole-wheat) flour
225g/8oz/2 cups rye flour
115g/4oz/1 cup strong white bread flour
7.5ml/1½ tsp salt
1 sachet easy-blend (rapid-rise) dried yeast
30ml/2 tbsp caraway seeds
475ml/16fl oz/2 cups hand-hot water
30ml/2 tbsp molasses
30ml/2 tbsp sunflower oil

1 Grease a baking sheet. Put the flours in a bowl with the salt and yeast. Set aside 5ml/1 tsp of the caraway seeds and add the remainder to the bowl. Mix well, then make a well in the centre.

2 Add the water to the bowl with the molasses and oil. Stir from the centre outwards, gradually incorporating the flour and mixing to a soft dough, and adding a little extra water if necessary.

3 Turn the dough on to a floured surface and knead for 5 minutes until smooth and elastic. Divide the dough in half and shape into two 23cm/9in long oval loaves.

4 Flatten the loaves slightly and place them on the prepared baking sheet. Brush them with water and sprinkle with the remaining caraway seeds. Cover and leave in a warm place until doubled in size, about 1½ hours. Meanwhile, preheat the oven to 220°C/425°F/Gas 7.

5 Bake the loaves for 30 minutes, or until they sound hollow when tapped underneath. Allow to cool on a wire rack.

Cook's Tip
Using warm rather than cold liquid helps the yeast to start working, as it is a living organism that thrives in warm and moist conditions.

Energy 127kcal/540kJ; Fat 1.8g, Saturated Fat 0.2g; Carbohydrate 25.7g, Fibre 3.1g

Caraway Rye Bread

To bring out the flavour of the caraway seeds, toast them lightly in the oven first, if you like.

Makes one loaf

200g/7oz/scant 1¾ cups rye flour
475ml/16fl oz/2 cups boiling water
120ml/4fl oz/½ cup black treacle (molasses)
65g/2½oz/5 tbsp butter, cut into pieces
15ml/1 tbsp salt
30ml/2 tbsp caraway seeds
15ml/1 tbsp active dried yeast
120ml/4fl oz/½ cup lukewarm water
about 850g/1lb 14oz/7½ cups strong white bread flour
semolina or flour, for dusting

1 Mix the rye flour, boiling water, treacle, butter, salt and caraway seeds in a large bowl. Leave to cool.

2 In another bowl, mix the yeast and lukewarm water and leave to dissolve and for the yeast to become frothy.

3 Stir into the rye flour mixture. Stir in just enough strong white bread flour to obtain a stiff dough. If it becomes too stiff to mix with the spoon, stir with your hands. Transfer to a floured surface and knead until the dough is no longer sticky and is smooth and shiny. This will take about 10 minutes.

4 Place in a greased bowl, cover with clear film (plastic wrap), and leave in a warm place until doubled in volume, about 1½ hours.

5 Knock back (punch down) the dough, cover, and leave to rise again for 30 minutes.

6 Preheat the oven to 180°C/350°F/Gas 4. Dust a baking sheet with semolina or flour.

7 Shape the dough into a ball. Place on the sheet and score several times across the top. Bake until the base sounds hollow when tapped, about 40 minutes. Cool on a wire rack.

Energy 4323kcal/18332kJ; Fat 64.4g, Saturated Fat 33.6g; Carbohydrate 893.3g, Fibre 49.8g

Austrian Three-Grain Bread

A mixture of grains gives this close-textured bread a delightful nutty flavour.

Makes 1 large loaf

225g/8oz/2 cups strong white bread flour
7.5ml/1½ tsp salt
225g/8oz/2 cups malted brown flour
225g/8oz/2 cups rye flour
75g/3oz/½ cup medium oatmeal
1 sachet easy-blend (rapid-rise) dried yeast
45ml/3 tbsp sunflower seeds
30ml/2 tbsp linseeds
475ml/16fl oz/2 cups hand-hot water
30ml/2 tbsp malt extract

1 Sift the plain flour and salt into a mixing bowl and add the remaining flours, oatmeal, yeast and sunflower seeds. Set aside 5ml/1 tsp of the linseeds and add the rest to the flour mixture. Make a well in the centre.

2 Add the water to the bowl with the malt extract. Gradually incorporate the flour and mix to a soft dough, adding extra water if necessary.

3 Flour a baking sheet. Turn the dough on to a floured surface and knead for 5 minutes, or until smooth and elastic.

4 Divide it in half. Roll each half into a sausage about 30cm/12in in length. Twist the two pieces together, dampen each end and press together firmly.

5 Lift the loaf on to the prepared baking sheet. Brush with water, sprinkle with the remaining linseeds and cover loosely with clear film (plastic wrap) (balloon it to trap the air inside). Leave in a warm place until doubled in size, about 1½ hours. Meanwhile, preheat the oven to 220°C/425°F/Gas 7.

6 Bake the bread for 10 minutes, then lower the oven temperature to 200°C/400°F/Gas 6 and cook for 20 minutes more, or until the loaf sounds hollow when tapped underneath.

7 Transfer the cooked loaf to a wire rack to cool completely.

Energy 3076kcal/13051kJ; Fat 54.1g, Saturated Fat 5.2g; Carbohydrate 592g, Fibre 57.3g

Sesame Seed Bread

This delicious bread with its nutty flavour breaks into individual rolls. It is ideal for entertaining.

Makes one 23cm/9in loaf

10ml/2 tsp active dried yeast
300ml/½ pint/1¼ cups lukewarm water
200g/7oz/1¾ cups strong white bread flour
200g/7oz/scant 1¾ cups strong wholemeal (whole-wheat) bread flour
10ml/2 tsp salt
65g/2½oz/5 tbsp toasted sesame seeds
milk, to glaze
30ml/2 tbsp sesame seeds, for sprinkling

1 Combine the yeast and 75ml/5 tbsp of the water in a small bowl and leave to dissolve and for the yeast to become frothy.

2 Mix the flours and salt in a large bowl. Make a central well in the flour and pour in the yeast and water. Stir from the centre to obtain a rough dough.

3 Transfer to a floured surface and knead until smooth and elastic. This will take about 10 minutes. Return to the bowl and cover with clear film (plastic wrap). Leave in a warm place until the dough has doubled in size, about 1½–2 hours.

4 Grease a 23cm/9in round cake tin (pan). Knock back (punch down) the dough and knead in the sesame seeds.

5 Divide the dough into 16 balls and place in the tin. Cover with clear film (plastic wrap) and leave in a warm place until risen above the rim, about 1½ hours.

6 Preheat the oven to 220°C/425°F/Gas 7. Brush the loaf with milk and sprinkle with the sesame seeds. Bake for 15 minutes. Lower the heat to 190°C/375°F/Gas 5 and bake until the base sounds hollow when tapped, about 30 minutes. Turn the loaf out on a wire rack and leave to cool before breaking into individual rolls and serving.

Energy 1691kcal/7142kJ; Fat 44.7g, Saturated Fat 6.4g; Carbohydrate 283.8g, Fibre 29.3g

Dill Bread

Tasty herb breads such as this are expensive to buy ready-made – and hard to find – and they never taste as good as home-made.

Makes two loaves

20ml4 tsp active dried yeast
475ml/16fl oz/2 cups lukewarm water
30ml/2 tbsp caster (superfine) sugar
1.05kg/2lb 5½oz/scant 9½ cups strong white bread flour
½ onion, chopped
60ml/4 tbsp oil
a large bunch of dill, finely chopped
2 eggs, lightly beaten
150g/5oz/⅔ cup cottage cheese
20ml/4 tsp salt
milk, to glaze

1 Mix together the yeast, water and sugar in a large bowl and leave for 15 minutes to dissolve and for the yeast to become frothy. Stir in about half of the flour. Cover and leave to rise in a warm place for 45 minutes.

2 In a frying pan, cook the onion in 15ml/1 tbsp of the oil until soft, about 5 minutes. Set aside to cool, then stir into the yeast mixture.

3 Stir the dill, eggs, cottage cheese, salt and the remaining oil into the yeast. Gradually add the remaining flour until the dough is too stiff to stir.

4 Transfer to a floured surface and knead until smooth and elastic. This will take about 10 minutes. Place in a bowl, cover with clear film (plastic wrap) and leave to rise until doubled in volume, about 1–1½ hours.

5 Grease a large baking sheet. Cut the dough in half and shape into two rounds. Place on the sheet and leave to rise in a warm place for 30 minutes.

6 Preheat the oven to 190°C/375°F/Gas 5. Score the tops of the loaves, brush with the milk to glaze and bake until browned, about 50 minutes. Transfer to a wire rack to cool.

Energy 2207kcal/9346kJ; Fat 37.4g, Saturated Fat 6.9g; Carbohydrate 428.3g, Fibre 16.7g

Rosemary Bread

Sliced thinly, this herb bread is delicious with cheese or soup for a light meal.

Makes one 23 x 13cm/ 9 x 5in loaf

1 sachet easy-blend (rapid-rise) dried yeast
175g/6oz/1½ cups strong wholemeal (whole-wheat) bread flour
175g/6oz/1½ cups self-raising (self-rising) flour
25g/1oz/2 tbsp butter
50ml/2fl oz/¼ cup warm water
250ml/8fl oz/1 cup milk, at room temperature
15ml/1 tbsp sugar
5ml/1 tsp salt
15ml/1 tbsp sesame seeds
15ml/1 tbsp dried chopped onion
15ml/1 tbsp fresh rosemary leaves
115g/4oz/1 cup cubed Cheddar cheese
rosemary leaves and coarse salt, to decorate

1 Mix the yeast with the wholemeal and self-raising flours in a large mixing bowl. Melt the butter in a small pan, then stir the warm water, milk, sugar, butter, salt, sesame seeds, onion and rosemary into the flour.

2 Knead thoroughly until quite smooth. This will take about 10 minutes. Flatten the dough, then add the cheese cubes. Knead them in until they are well combined.

3 Place the dough in a large clean bowl. Cover the bowl with a dish towel or clear film (plastic wrap) and put it in a warm place for 1½ hours, or until the dough has doubled in size.

4 Grease a 23 x 13cm/9 x 5in loaf tin (pan) with butter. Knock back (punch down) the dough and shape it into a loaf.

5 Place in the tin, cover with the dish towel or oiled clear film and leave for about 1 hour, or until doubled in size. Preheat the oven to 190°C/375°F/Gas 5.

6 Bake for 30 minutes. Cover the loaf with foil for the last 5–10 minutes of baking. Turn the bread out on to a wire rack to cool. Garnish with some rosemary leaves and coarse salt sprinkled on top.

Energy 1999kcal/8422kJ; Fat 68.7g, Saturated Fat 41.5g; Carbohydrate 280.2g, Fibre 22g

Olive and Oregano Bread

Fresh herbs are fabulous in loaves. This is an excellent accompaniment to all salads and is very good with grilled (broiled) goat's cheese.

Serves 8–10

15ml/1 tbsp olive oil
1 onion, chopped
450g/1lb/4 cups strong white bread flour
10ml/2 tsp easy-blend (rapid-rise) dried yeast
5ml/1 tsp salt
1.5ml/¼ tsp ground black pepper
50g/2oz/½ cup pitted black olives, roughly chopped
15ml/1 tbsp black olive paste
15ml/1 tbsp chopped fresh oregano
15ml/1 tbsp chopped fresh parsley
300ml/½ pint/1¼ cups hand-hot water

1 Lightly oil a baking sheet. Heat the olive oil in a frying pan and fry the onion until golden brown.

2 Sift the flour into a mixing bowl. Add the yeast, salt and pepper. Make a well in the centre.

3 Add the fried onion (with the oil), the olives, olive paste, chopped oregano and parsley, and the water. Stir from the centre outwards and gradually incorporate the flour. Mix to a soft dough, adding a little extra water if necessary.

4 Turn the dough on to a floured surface and knead for 5 minutes until smooth and elastic.

5 Shape into a 20cm/8in round and place on the baking sheet.

6 Using a sharp knife, make criss-cross cuts over the top, cover and leave in a warm place until doubled in size, about 1½ hours. Preheat the oven to 220°C/ 425°F/Gas 7.

7 Bake the olive and oregano loaf for 10 minutes, then lower the oven temperature to 200°C/400°F/Gas 6. Bake for 20 minutes more, or until the loaf sounds hollow when tapped underneath. Cool on a wire rack.

Energy 172kcal/727kJ; Fat 2.3g, Saturated Fat 0.4g; Carbohydrate 35.4g, Fibre 1.7g

Spiral Herb Bread

When you slice this unusual loaf, its herbal secret is revealed inside.

Makes two 23 x 13cm/ 9 x 5in loaves

30ml/2 tbsp active dried yeast
600ml/1 pint/2½ cups lukewarm water
30ml/2 tbsp caster (superfine) sugar
425g/15oz/3⅔ cups strong white bread flour
500g/1¼lb/5 cups strong wholemeal (whole-wheat) bread flour
15ml/1 tbsp salt
25g/1oz/2 tbsp butter
a large bunch of parsley, finely chopped
a bunch of spring onions (scallions), chopped
1 garlic clove, finely chopped
1 egg, lightly beaten
milk, for glazing
salt and ground black pepper

1 Combine the yeast and 50ml/2fl oz/¼ cup of the water with the sugar, stir and leave for 15 minutes to dissolve.

2 Combine the flours and salt in a large bowl. Make a central well and pour in the yeast mixture and the remaining water. With a wooden spoon, stir to a rough dough. Transfer to a floured surface; knead until smooth. Return to the bowl, cover with clear film (plastic wrap), and leave until doubled in size.

3 Meanwhile, combine the butter, parsley, spring onions and garlic in a large frying pan. Cook over a low heat, stirring, until softened. Season and set aside.

4 Grease two 23 x 13cm/9 x 5in loaf tins (pans). When the dough has risen, cut in half and roll each half into a rectangle 35 x 23cm/14 x 9in. Brush with the beaten egg and spread with the herb mixture. Roll up to enclose the filling, and pinch the short ends to seal. Place in the tins, seam-sides down. Cover and leave in a warm place until the dough rises above the tin rims, about 1½ hours.

5 Preheat the oven to 190°C/375°F/Gas 5. Brush the loaves with milk and bake until the bases sound hollow when tapped, about 55 minutes. Cool on a wire rack.

Energy 1726kcal/7323kJ; Fat 21.9g, Saturated Fat 8.6g; Carbohydrate 345.9g, Fibre 30.6g

Focaccia

This Italian flatbread makes a delicious snack with olives and feta cheese.

Serves 8

450g/1lb/4 cups strong white bread flour
5ml/1 tsp salt
1.5ml/¼ tsp ground black pepper
10ml/2 tsp easy-blend (rapid-rise) dried yeast
a pinch of sugar
300ml/½ pint/1¼ cups hand-hot water
15ml/1 tbsp pesto
115g/4oz/⅔ cup pitted black olives, chopped
25g/1oz/½ cup drained sun-dried tomatoes in oil, chopped, plus 15ml/1 tbsp oil from the jar
5ml/1 tsp coarse sea salt
5ml/1 tsp chopped fresh rosemary

1 Lightly oil a 30 x 20cm/12 x 8in Swiss roll tin (jelly roll pan). Sift the flour, salt and pepper into a bowl. Add the yeast and sugar, and make a well in the centre.

2 Add the water with the pesto, olives and sun-dried tomatoes to the dry ingredients (reserve the oil). Mix to a soft dough, adding a little extra water if necessary. Turn on to a floured surface and knead for 5 minutes until smooth and elastic.

3 Roll into a rectangle measuring 33 x 23cm/13 x 9in. Drape over the rolling pin and place in the prepared tin. Leave to rise until doubled in size, about 1½ hours. Meanwhile, preheat the oven to 220°C/425°F/Gas 7.

4 Using your fingertips, make indentations all over the dough. Brush with the oil from the sun-dried tomatoes, then sprinkle over the salt and chopped rosemary. Bake for 20–25 minutes, or until golden. Remove to a wire rack and serve warm.

Variation
Try adding 15ml/1 tbsp fresh chopped sage and half a chopped onion to the dough and the same again sprinkled over the top before baking.

Energy 230kcal/973kJ; Fat 4.3g, Saturated Fat 0.9g; Carbohydrate 44.2g, Fibre 2.3g

Rosemary Focaccia

Italian flat bread is easy to make using a packet mix. Additions include olives and sun-dried tomatoes.

Makes two loaves

450g/1lb packet white bread mix
60ml/4 tbsp extra virgin olive oil
10ml/2 tsp dried rosemary, crushed
8 sun-dried tomatoes, chopped
12 black olives, pitted and chopped
200ml/7fl oz/scant 1 cup lukewarm water
sea salt flakes, for sprinkling

1 Following the instructions on the pack, combine the bread mix with half the oil, the rosemary, tomatoes, olives and enough water to form a firm dough.

2 Knead the dough on a lightly floured surface for about 5 minutes.

3 Return to the mixing bowl and cover with a piece of oiled clear film (plastic wrap). Leave the dough to rise in a warm place until doubled in size, about 1 hour.

4 Meanwhile, lightly grease two baking sheets and preheat the oven to 220°C/425°F/Gas 7.

5 Knock back (punch down) the dough and knead again. Divide into two and shape into flat rounds. Place on the baking sheet, and make indentations with your fingertips. Trickle over the remaining olive oil and sprinkle with sea salt flakes.

6 Bake the focaccia for 12–15 minutes until golden brown and cooked. Turn out on to wire racks to cool. This bread is best eaten slightly warm.

Cook's Tip
A bread mix is quick but you can also make focaccia dough by mixing 500g/1lb/3 cups strong white bread flour with 5ml/1 tsp salt and 5ml/1 tsp easy-blend (rapid-rise) yeast. Then follow the recipe as above.

Energy 1001kcal/4225kJ; Fat 27.2g, Saturated Fat 4g; Carbohydrate 177.7g, Fibre 8.1g

Saffron Focaccia

A dazzling yellow bread that is both light in texture and distinctive in flavour. The olive oil drizzled over the top makes the bread moist and it keeps well.

Makes one loaf

a pinch of saffron threads
150ml/¼ pint/⅔ cup boiling water
225g/8oz/2 cups strong white bread flour
2.5ml/½ tsp salt
5ml/1 tsp easy-blend (rapid-rise) dried yeast
15ml/1 tbsp olive oil

For the topping
2 garlic cloves, sliced
1 red onion, cut into thin wedges
rosemary sprigs
12 black olives, pitted and coarsely chopped
15ml/1 tbsp olive oil

1 Place the saffron in a heatproof jug (pitcher) and pour in the boiling water. Leave to infuse (steep) until lukewarm.

2 Place the flour, salt, yeast and olive oil in a food processor. Turn on and gradually add the saffron and its liquid. Process until the dough forms a ball. Alternatively, use your hands to incorporate the liquid into the flour.

3 Turn out on to a floured surface and knead for 10–15 minutes. Place in a bowl, cover with clear film (plastic wrap) and leave to rise until doubled in size, about 30–40 minutes.

4 Knock back (punch down) the dough and roll into an oval shape about 1cm/½in thick. Place on a lightly greased baking sheet and leave to rise for 30 minutes.

5 Preheat the oven to 200°C/400°F/Gas 6. With your fingers, press indentations over the surface of the bread.

6 To make the topping cover the dough with the sliced garlic, onion wedges, rosemary sprigs and chopped olives.

7 Brush lightly with olive oil and bake for 25 minutes, or until the loaf sounds hollow when tapped on the base. Leave to cool on a wire rack.

Energy 1018kcal/4292kJ; Fat 28.3g, Saturated Fat 4.1g; Carbohydrate 179.6g, Fibre 8.7g

Cheese and Onion Herb Stick

An extremely tasty bread which is very good with soup or salads. Use a strong cheese to give the bread plenty of flavour.

Makes 2 sticks, each serving 4–6

15ml/1 tbsp sunflower oil
1 red onion, chopped
450g/1lb/4 cups strong white bread flour
5ml/1 tsp salt
5ml/1 tsp mustard powder
10ml/2 tsp easy-blend (rapid-rise) dried yeast
45ml/3 tbsp chopped fresh herbs, such as thyme, parsley, marjoram or sage
75g/3oz/¾ cup grated reduced-fat Cheddar cheese
300ml/½ pint/1¼ cups hand-hot water

1 Lightly oil two baking sheets. Heat the oil in a frying pan and fry the onion until well browned.

2 Sift the flour, salt and mustard powder into a mixing bowl. Stir in the yeast and herbs.

3 Set aside 30ml/2 tbsp of the cheese. Add the remainder to the flour mixture and make a well in the centre. Add the water and the fried onions and their oil. Stir the ingredients working from the inside outwards, gradually incorporating the flour, and mix to a soft dough, adding a little extra water if necessary.

4 Turn the dough on to a floured surface and knead for 5 minutes until smooth and elastic. Divide the mixture in half and roll each piece into a stick 30cm/12in in length.

5 Place each bread stick on a baking sheet, make diagonal cuts along the top and sprinkle with the reserved cheese. Cover and leave until doubled in size, about 1½ hours. Meanwhile, preheat the oven to 220°C/425°F/Gas 7.

6 Bake the loaves for 25 minutes, or until the bread sounds hollow when tapped underneath. Leave on a wire rack to cool completely.

Energy 154kcal/653kJ; Fat 2.4g, Saturated Fat 0.8g; Carbohydrate 29.5g, Fibre 1.2g

Potato Bread

Vegetables incorporated into loaves make a moist crumb and help to keep the bread longer. You could try this recipe with cooked and mashed carrot instead.

Makes two 23 x 13cm/ 9 x 5in loaves

20ml/4 tsp active dried yeast
250ml/8fl oz/1 cup lukewarm milk
225g/8oz potatoes, boiled (reserve 250ml/8fl oz/1 cup of the cooking liquid)
30ml/2 tbsp oil
20ml/4 tsp salt
850–900g/1lb 4oz–2lb/ 7½–8 cups strong white bread flour

1 Combine the yeast and milk in a large bowl and leave to dissolve and for the yeast to become frothy, about 15 minutes. Meanwhile, mash the potatoes.

2 Add the potatoes, the oil and the salt to the yeast mixture and mix to combine thoroughly.

3 Stir in the reserved cooking water, then stir in the flour, in six separate batches, to form a stiff dough.

4 Knead on a lightly floured surface until smooth. This will take about 10 minutes. Return to the bowl, cover with clear film (plastic wrap), and leave in a warm place until doubled in size, about 1–1½ hours.

5 Knock back (punch down), then leave to rise again for 40 minutes, or until almost doubled in size.

6 Grease two 23 x 13cm/9 x 5in loaf tins (pans). Roll the dough into 20 small balls. Place two rows of balls in each tin. Leave until the dough has risen above the rims of the tins, about 1½ hours.

7 Meanwhile, preheat the oven to 200°C/400°F/Gas 6. Bake the dough for 10 minutes, then lower the heat to 190°C/375°F/Gas 5. Bake until the bases of the loaves sound hollow when tapped, about 40 minutes. Cool on a wire rack.

Energy 1693kcal/7186kJ; Fat 19g, Saturated Fat 3.6g; Carbohydrate 356.3g, Fibre 14.5g

Soda Bread

Finding the bread bin empty need never be a problem when your repertoire includes a recipe for soda bread. It takes only a few minutes to make and needs no rising or proving.

Serves 8

450g/1lb/4 cups plain (all-purpose) flour
5ml/1 tsp salt
5ml/1 tsp bicarbonate of soda (baking soda)
5ml/1 tsp cream of tartar
350ml/12fl oz/1½ cups buttermilk

1 Preheat the oven to 220°C/425°F/Gas 7 and lightly flour a baking sheet.

2 Sift the flour, salt, bicarbonate of soda and cream of tartar into a mixing bowl and make a well in the centre.

3 Add the buttermilk to the dry ingredients and mix quickly to form a soft dough. Turn the dough on to a floured surface and knead lightly.

4 Shape into a round about 18cm/7in in diameter, and place on the baking sheet.

5 Cut a deep cross on top of the loaf and sprinkle it with a little flour.

6 Bake the soda bread for 25–30 minutes, then transfer to a wire rack to cool.

Cook's Tips

- *Soda bread needs a light hand. The ingredients should be bound together quickly in the bowl and kneaded very briefly. The aim is just to get rid of the largest cracks, as the dough becomes tough if handled for too long.*
- *If possible, eat soda bread warm from the oven as it does not keep well.*

Energy 206kcal/875kJ; Fat 0.9g, Saturated Fat 0.2g; Carbohydrate 45.6g, Fibre 1.7g

Irish Soda Bread

Easy to make, this distinctive bread goes well with soup, cheese and traditional, rustic-style dishes.

Makes one loaf

275g/10oz/2½ cups plain (all-purpose) flour
150g/5oz/1¼ cups plain (all-purpose) wholemeal (whole-wheat) flour
5ml/1 tsp bicarbonate of soda (baking soda)
5ml/1 tsp salt
25g/1oz/2 tbsp butter or margarine, at room temperature
300ml/½ pint/1¼ cups buttermilk
15ml/1 tbsp plain (all-purpose) flour, for dusting

1 Preheat the oven to 200°C/400°F/Gas 6. Grease a baking sheet. Sift together the flours, bicarbonate of soda and salt.

2 Make a central well and add the butter or margarine and buttermilk. Working from the centre, stir to combine the ingredients until a soft dough is formed.

3 With floured hands, gather the dough into a ball. Knead for up to 3 minutes. Shape the dough into a large round.

4 Place on the baking sheet. Cut a cross in the top with a sharp knife and dust with the flour. Bake until brown, about 40–50 minutes. Transfer to a wire rack to cool.

Cook's Tips

- *It is the acid in buttermilk that acts with the bicarbonate of soda to make traditional soda bread rise. Because the bread does not include yeast it is not given any rising time. In fact, it is important to put the bread into the oven as soon as the liquid is added, as the gases start to form immediately and the loaf will be heavy if you don't put it straight in the oven.*
- *Soured cream or milk with 15ml/1 tbsp lemon juice can be used instead of buttermilk, but do not substitute plain milk for the buttermilk as this will not produce a successful loaf.*

Energy 1778kcal/7532kJ; Fat 32.7g, Saturated Fat 17.3g; Carbohydrate 335.4g, Fibre 22.5g

Sage Soda Bread

This wonderful loaf, quite unlike bread made with yeast, has a velvety texture and a powerful sage aroma.

Makes one loaf

225g/8oz/2cups plain (all-purpose) wholemeal (whole-wheat) flour
115g/4oz/1 cup plain (all-purpose) flour
2.5ml/½ tsp salt
5ml/1 tsp bicarbonate of soda (baking soda)
30ml/2 tbsp shredded fresh sage
300–450ml/½–¾ pint/1¼–scant 2 cups buttermilk

1 Preheat the oven to 220°C/425°F/Gas 7. Lightly grease a baking sheet and set aside.

2 Sift the wholemeal and white flours with the salt and bicarbonate of soda into a large bowl.

3 Stir in the fresh sage and add enough buttermilk to make a soft dough. Do not overmix or the bread will be heavy.

4 Shape the dough into a round loaf and place on the lightly greased baking sheet.

5 Cut a cross in the top, cutting deep into the dough.

6 Bake in the oven for about 40 minutes, or until the loaf is well risen and sounds hollow when tapped on the base. Leave to cool on a wire rack.

Variations

- *Try this loaf made with all white flour rather than wholemeal (whole-wheat) and white for a finer and lighter texture.*
- *Fresh rosemary would also work well in place of the sage for this loaf.*
- *You could form the dough into two smaller loaves and bake them for 25–30 minutes.*
- *Fruit soda bread tastes great, too. In place of the sage add 150g/5oz/1 cup raisins.*

Energy 1186kcal/5041kJ; Fat 7.3g, Saturated Fat 1.3g; Carbohydrate 246.3g, Fibre 23.8g

Sun-dried Tomato Plait

This makes a marvellous centrepiece for a summer buffet. If you only have dried tomatoes, soak them in a little boiling water for 15 minutes and add 15ml/1 tbsp oil to the mixture.

Serves 8–10

225g/8oz/2 cups strong wholemeal (whole-wheat) flour
225g/8oz/2 cups strong white bread flour
5ml/1 tsp salt
1.5ml/¼ tsp ground black pepper
10ml/2 tsp easy-blend (rapid-rise) dried yeast
a pinch of sugar
300ml/½ pint/1¼ cups hand-hot water
115g/4oz/2 cups drained sun-dried tomatoes in oil, chopped, plus 15ml/1 tbsp oil from the jar
25g/1oz/⅓ cup freshly grated Parmesan cheese
30ml/2 tbsp red pesto
2.5ml/½ tsp coarse sea salt

1 Oil a baking sheet. Put the wholemeal flour in a large bowl. Sift in the white flour, salt and pepper. Add the yeast and sugar.

2 Make a well in the centre and add the water, the sun-dried tomatoes, oil, Parmesan cheese and pesto. Gradually incorporate the flour and mix to a soft dough, adding a little extra water if necessary.

3 Turn the dough on to a floured surface and knead for 5 minutes until smooth and elastic. Shape into three 33cm/13in long sausages.

4 Dampen the ends of the three sausages. Press them together at one end, braid them loosely, then press them together at the other end. Transfer to the baking sheet, and cover and leave in a warm place until doubled in size, about 1½ hours. Meanwhile, preheat the oven to 220°C/425°F/Gas 7.

5 Sprinkle the braid with coarse sea salt. Bake for 10 minutes, then lower the oven temperature to 200°C/400°F/Gas 6 and bake for a further 15–20 minutes, or until the loaf sounds hollow when tapped underneath. Leave on a wire rack to cool completely.

Energy 190kcal/804kJ; Fat 3.7g, Saturated Fat 1.4g; Carbohydrate 33.5g, Fibre 3g

Courgette Crown Bread

Adding grated courgettes and cheese to a loaf mixture will keep it tasting fresher for longer.

Serves 8

450g/1lb/2¾ cups coarsely grated courgettes (zucchini)
salt
500g/1¼lb/5 cups strong white bread flour
2 sachets easy-blend (rapid-rise) dried yeast
60ml/4 tbsp freshly grated Parmesan cheese
ground black pepper
30ml/2 tbsp olive oil
lukewarm water, to mix
milk, to glaze
sesame seeds, to garnish

1 Spoon the courgettes into a colander, sprinkling them lightly with salt. Leave to drain for 30 minutes, then pat dry with kitchen paper.

2 Mix the flour, yeast and Parmesan cheese together and season with black pepper.

3 Stir in the oil and courgettes, and add enough lukewarm water to make a firm dough.

4 Knead the dough on a lightly floured surface until smooth. This will take about 10 minutes. Return to the mixing bowl, cover it with oiled clear film (plastic wrap) and leave it to rise in a warm place, until doubled in size, about 1½ hours.

5 Meanwhile, grease and line a 23cm/9in round cake tin (pan). Preheat the oven to 200°C/400°F/Gas 6.

6 Knock back (punch down) the dough, and knead it lightly. Break into eight balls, roll each one and arrange them, touching, in the tin. Brush the tops with the milk glaze and sprinkle over the sesame seeds.

7 Allow to rise again for 1 hour, then bake for 25 minutes, or until golden brown. Cool slightly in the tin, then turn out on to a wire rack to cool completely.

Energy 271kcal/1144kJ; Fat 5.4g, Saturated Fat 1.6g; Carbohydrate 49.6g, Fibre 2.5g

Spinach and Bacon Bread

This bread is so tasty that it is a good idea to make double the quantity and freeze some of the loaves.

Makes 2 loaves, each serving 8

15ml/1 tbsp olive oil
1 onion, chopped
115g/4oz rindless smoked bacon rashers (strips), chopped
675g/1½lb/6 cups plain (all-purpose) flour
7.5ml/1½ tsp salt
2.5ml/½ tsp freshly grated nutmeg
1 sachet easy-blend (rapid-rise) dried yeast
475ml/16fl oz/2 cups hand-hot water
225g/8oz chopped spinach, thawed if frozen
25g/1oz/¼ cup grated reduced-fat Cheddar cheese

1 Lightly oil two 23cm/9in cake tins (pans).

2 Heat the oil in a frying pan and fry the onion and bacon for 10 minutes, or until golden brown.

3 Sift the flour, salt and grated nutmeg into a mixing bowl, add the yeast and make a well in the centre. Add the water.

4 Tip in the fried bacon and onion, with the oil it was cooked in, then add the well-drained thawed spinach. Stir from the centre outwards, gradually incorporating the flour, and mix to a soft dough.

5 Turn the dough on to a floured surface and knead for 5 minutes until smooth and elastic. Divide the mixture in half. Shape each half into a ball, flatten slightly and place in a prepared tin, pressing the dough so that it extends to the edges.

6 Mark each loaf into six wedges and sprinkle with the cheese. Cover loosely with oiled clear film (plastic wrap) and leave in a warm place until each loaf has doubled in size, about 1½ hours. Meanwhile, preheat the oven to 200°C/400°F/Gas 6.

7 Bake the loaves for 25–30 minutes, or until they sound hollow when tapped underneath. Leave on a wire rack to cool completely.

Energy 160kcal/680kJ; Fat 1.6g, Saturated Fat 0.3g; Carbohydrate 32.6g, Fibre 1.7g

Prosciutto and Parmesan Bread

This nourishing bread can be made very quickly, and makes a delicious meal when served with a tomato and feta cheese salad.

Serves 8

225g/8oz/2 cups self-raising (self-rising) wholemeal (whole-wheat) flour
225g/8oz/2 cups self-raising (self-rising) flour
5ml/1 tsp salt
5ml/1 tsp ground black pepper
75g/3oz prosciutto, chopped
30ml/2 tbsp chopped fresh parsley
25g/1oz/2 tbsp freshly grated Parmesan cheese
45ml/3 tbsp Meaux mustard
350ml/12fl oz/1½ cups buttermilk
skimmed milk, to glaze

1 Preheat the oven to 200°C/400°F/Gas 6 and lightly flour a baking sheet.

2 Put the wholemeal flour in a bowl and sift in the plain flour, salt and pepper. Stir in the ham and parsley. Set aside about half of the grated Parmesan cheese and add the rest to the flour mixture. Make a well in the centre.

3 Mix the mustard and buttermilk in a jug (pitcher), pour into the bowl and quickly mix to a soft dough.

4 Turn on to a well-floured surface and knead very briefly. Shape into an oval loaf and place on the baking sheet.

5 Brush the loaf with milk, sprinkle with the reserved Parmesan cheese and bake for 25–30 minutes, or until golden brown. Cool on a wire rack.

Cook's Tip

When chopping the ham, sprinkle it with flour so that it does not stick together. Do not knead the mixture as for a yeast dough, or it will become tough. It should be mixed quickly and kneaded very briefly before shaping.

Energy 229kcal/972kJ; Fat 2.9g, Saturated Fat 1g; Carbohydrate 42.4g, Fibre 3.4g

Walnut Bread

This rich bread could be served at a dinner party with soup or the cheese course, or with a rustic ploughman's lunch.

Makes one loaf

420g/15oz/3⅔ cups strong wholemeal (whole-wheat) bread flour
150g/5oz/1¼ cups strong white bread flour
12.5ml/2½ tsp salt
550ml/18fl oz/2¼ cups lukewarm water
15ml/1 tbsp clear honey
15ml/1 tbsp active dried yeast
150g/5oz/1 cup walnut pieces, plus more to decorate
1 beaten egg, to glaze

1 Combine the wholemeal and white flours and salt in a large bowl. Make a well in the centre and add 250ml/8fl oz/1 cup of the water, the honey and the yeast. Set aside until the yeast dissolves and becomes frothy.

2 Add the remaining water. With a wooden spoon, stir from the centre, incorporating flour with each turn, to obtain a smooth dough. Add more flour if the dough is too sticky and use your hands if the dough becomes too stiff to stir.

3 Transfer to a floured board and knead, adding flour if necessary, until the dough is smooth and elastic. This will take about 10 minutes. Place in a greased bowl and roll the dough around in the bowl to coat thoroughly on all sides. Cover with clear film (plastic wrap) and leave in a warm place until doubled in volume, about 1½ hours. Knock back (punch down) the dough and knead in the walnuts evenly.

4 Grease a baking sheet. Shape the dough into a round loaf and place on the baking sheet. Press in walnut pieces to decorate the top. Cover loosely with a damp cloth or clear film and leave to rise in a warm place until doubled in size, 25–30 minutes.

5 Preheat the oven to 220°C/425°F/Gas 7. With a sharp knife, score the top of the loaf. Brush with the egg glaze. Bake for 15 minutes. Lower the heat to 190°C/375°F/Gas 5 and bake until the base sounds hollow when tapped, about 40 minutes.

Energy 2786kcal/11722kJ; Fat 107g, Saturated Fat 9.4g; Carbohydrate 393.2g, Fibre 47g

Pecan Nut Rye Bread

A tasty homespun loaf that recalls the old folk-cooking of the United States.

Makes two 21 x 11cm/ 8½ x 4½in loaves

25ml/1½ tbsp active dried yeast
700ml/22fl oz/2¾ cups lukewarm water
675g/1½lb/6 cups strong white bread flour
500g/1¼lb/5 cups rye flour
30ml/2 tbsp salt
15ml/1 tbsp clear honey
10ml/2 tsp caraway seeds, (optional)
115g/4oz/½ cup butter, at room temperature
225g/8oz pecan nuts, chopped

1 Combine the yeast and 120ml/4fl oz/½ cup of the water. Stir and leave for 15 minutes for the yeast to dissolve entirely and become frothy.

2 In the bowl of an electric mixer, combine the white and rye flours, salt, honey, caraway seeds and butter. With the dough hook, mix on low speed until well blended. Alternatively, use your hands to incorporate the liquid into the flour.

3 Add the yeast mixture and the remaining water and mix on medium speed, or use your hands, until the dough forms a ball. Transfer to a floured surface and knead in the chopped pecan nuts.

4 Return the dough to the bowl, cover with clear film (plastic wrap) and leave in a warm place until doubled, about 2 hours.

5 Grease two 21 x 11cm/8½ x 4½in loaf tins (pans). Knock back (punch down) the risen dough.

6 Divide the dough in half and form into two loaves. Place in the tins, seam sides down. Dust the tops with flour. Cover with oiled clear film and leave to rise in a warm place until doubled in volume, about 1 hour.

7 Preheat the oven to 190°C/375°F/Gas 5. Bake until the bases sound hollow when tapped, 45–50 minutes. Transfer to wire racks to cool completely.

Energy 3213kcal/13513kJ; Fat 135.5g, Saturated Fat 37.8g; Carbohydrate 464.6g, Fibre 45g

Banana and Cardamom Bread

The combination of banana and fragrant cardamom is delicious in this soft-textured moist loaf.

Serves 6

10 cardamom pods
400g/14oz/3½ cups strong white bread flour
5ml/1 tsp salt
5ml/1 tsp easy-blend (rapid-rise) dried yeast
150ml/¼ pint/⅔ cup hand-hot water
30ml/2 tbsp malt extract
2 ripe bananas, mashed
5ml/1 tsp sesame seeds

1 Grease a 450g/1lb loaf tin (pan). Split the cardamom pods, and remove the seeds and then chop the pods finely.

2 Sift the flour and salt into a large bowl, add the yeast and make a well in the centre. Add the water with the malt extract, chopped cardamom pods and bananas. Stir from the centre outwards, gradually incorporating the flour and mixing to a soft dough, and adding a little extra water if necessary.

3 Turn the dough on to a floured surface and knead for 5 minutes until smooth and elastic. Shape into a braid and place in the prepared tin. Cover loosely with clear film (plastic wrap) (ballooning it to trap the air) and leave in a warm place until well risen, about 1½ hours. Meanwhile, preheat the oven to 220°C/425°F/Gas 7.

4 Brush the braid lightly with water and sprinkle with the sesame seeds. Bake for 10 minutes, then lower the oven temperature to 200°C/400°F/Gas 6. Cook for 15 minutes more, or until the loaf sounds hollow when tapped underneath. Remove to a wire rack to cool.

Cook's Tip
Cardamom is a green or white seed pod containing tiny black seeds. It has a distinctive warm and pronounced scent that really works well in cakes, pastries and desserts.

Energy 279kcal/1185kJ; Fat 1.5g, Saturated Fat 0.2g; Carbohydrate 63.5g, Fibre 2.5g

Swedish Sultana Bread

A lightly sweetened bread that goes very well with a selection of cheeses and that is also excellent toasted at teatime.

Serves 10

225g/8oz/2 cups strong wholemeal (whole-wheat) bread flour
225g/8oz/2 cups strong white bread flour
5ml/1 tsp easy-blend (rapid-rise) dried yeast
5ml/1 tsp salt
115g/4oz/⅔ cup sultanas (golden raisins)
50g/2oz/½ cup walnuts, chopped
15ml/1 tbsp clear honey
150ml/¼ pint/⅔ cup hand-hot water
175ml/6fl oz/¾ cup hand-hot skimmed milk, plus extra for glazing

1 Grease a baking sheet. Put the flours in a bowl with the yeast, salt and sultanas.

2 Set aside 15ml/1 tbsp of the walnuts and add the remainder to the bowl. Mix the ingredients lightly and make a well in the centre.

3 Dissolve the honey in the water and add the mixture to the bowl with the milk. Stir from the centre outwards, gradually incorporating the flour, and mixing to a soft dough, and adding a little extra water if necessary.

4 Turn the dough on to a floured surface and knead for 5 minutes, or until smooth and elastic. Shape into a 28cm/11in long sausage shape. Place on the prepared baking sheet.

5 Make diagonal cuts down the length of the loaf. Brush the top with milk, sprinkle with the remaining walnuts and leave in a warm place until doubled in size, about 1½ hours. Meanwhile, preheat the oven to 220°C/ 425°F/Gas 7.

6 Bake the loaf for 10 minutes, then lower the oven temperature to 200°C/400°F/Gas 6 and bake for 20 minutes more or until the loaf sounds hollow when tapped underneath. Remove to a wire rack to cool.

Energy 225kcal/953kJ; Fat 4.1g, Saturated Fat 0.4g; Carbohydrate 43.9g, Fibre 1.8g

Malt Loaf

This is a rich and sticky loaf. If it lasts long enough to go stale, try toasting it for a delicious teatime treat.

Serves 8

350g/12oz/3 cups strong white bread flour
1.5ml/¼ tsp salt
5ml/1 tsp easy-blend (rapid-rise) dried yeast
a pinch of caster (superfine) sugar
30ml/2 tbsp soft light brown sugar
175g/6oz/1 cup sultanas (golden raisins)
150ml/¼ pint/⅔ cup hand-hot skimmed milk
15ml/1 tbsp sunflower oil
45ml/3 tbsp malt extract

To glaze

30ml/2 tbsp caster (superfine) sugar
30ml/2 tbsp water

1 Sift the flour and salt into a mixing bowl, and stir in the yeast, the pinch of sugar, brown sugar and sultanas.

2 Make a well in the centre of the dry ingredients. Add the hot milk with the oil and malt extract. Stir from the centre outwards, gradually incorporating the flour and mixing to a soft dough, and adding a little extra milk if necessary.

3 Turn on to a floured surface and knead for about 5 minutes until smooth and elastic. Lightly oil a 450g/1lb loaf tin (pan).

4 Shape the dough and place it in the prepared tin. Cover with a damp dish cloth or some oiled clear film (plastic wrap) and leave in a warm place until doubled in size, about 1½ hours. Meanwhile, preheat the oven to 190°C/375°F/Gas 5.

5 Bake the loaf for 30–35 minutes, or until it sounds hollow when tapped underneath.

6 While the loaf is baking, make the glaze by dissolving the sugar in the water in a small pan. Bring to the boil, stirring, then lower the heat and simmer for 1 minute.

7 Brush the loaf while hot, then transfer it to a wire rack to cool.

Energy 259kcal/1101kJ; Fat 2.1g, Saturated Fat 0.3g; Carbohydrate 58.4g, Fibre 1.8g

Prune Bread

Moist inside, with a crusty walnut topping.

Makes 1 loaf

225g/8oz/1 cup dried prunes
15ml/1 tbsp active dried yeast
75g/3oz/⅔ cup strong wholemeal (whole-wheat) bread flour
400–425g/14–15oz/3½–3⅔ cups strong white bread flour
2.5ml/½ tsp bicarbonate of soda (baking soda)
5ml/1 tsp salt
5ml/1 tsp pepper
25g/1oz/2 tbsp butter, at room temperature
175ml/6fl oz/¾ cup buttermilk
50g/2oz/½ cup walnuts, chopped
milk, for glazing

1 Simmer the prunes in water to cover until soft, about 20 minutes, or soak overnight. Drain, reserving 60ml/4 tbsp of the soaking liquid. Pit and chop the prunes.

2 Combine the yeast and the reserved prune liquid, stir and leave for 15 minutes to dissolve and so that the yeast becomes frothy.

3 In a large bowl, stir together the wholemeal and white flours, bicarbonate of soda, salt and pepper. Make a well in the centre. Add the prunes, butter and buttermilk. Pour in the yeast mixture. With a wooden spoon, stir from the centre, folding in more flour with each turn, to obtain a rough dough.

4 Transfer to a floured surface and knead until smooth and elastic. This will take about 10 minutes. Return to the bowl, cover with clear film (plastic wrap) and leave to rise in a warm place until doubled in volume, about 1½ hours. Grease a baking sheet.

5 Knock back (punch down) the dough with your fist, then knead in the walnuts. Shape the dough into a long, cylindrical loaf. Place on the baking sheet, cover loosely, and leave to rise in a warm place for 45 minutes. Preheat the oven to 220°C/425°F/Gas 7. With a sharp knife, score the top. Brush with milk and bake for 15 minutes. Lower to 190°C/375°F/Gas 5 and bake for 35 minutes more, or until the base sounds hollow. Cool.

Energy 2520kcal/10639kJ; Fat 70.4g, Saturated Fat 19.9g; Carbohydrate 433.3g, Fibre 33.4g

Raisin Bread

Enjoy this with savoury or sweet dishes.

Makes 2 loaves

15ml/1 tbsp active dried yeast
450ml/¾ pint/1¾ cups lukewarm milk
150g/5oz/1 cup raisins
65g/2½oz/½ cup currants
15ml/1 tbsp sherry or brandy
2.5ml/½ tsp freshly grated nutmeg
grated rind of 1 large orange
60g/2¼oz/generous ¼ cup caster (superfine) sugar
15ml/1 tbsp salt
115g/4oz/½ cup butter, melted
700–850g/1lb 8oz–1lb 14oz/6–7½ cups strong white bread flour
1 egg beaten with 15ml/1 tbsp single (light) cream, to glaze

1 Stir the yeast with 120ml/4fl oz/½ cup of the milk and leave to stand for 15 minutes to dissolve. Mix the raisins, currants, sherry or brandy, nutmeg and orange rind together.

2 In another bowl, mix the remaining milk, sugar, salt and half the butter. Add the yeast mixture. With a wooden spoon, stir in half the flour, 150g/5oz at a time, until blended. Add the remaining flour as needed to form a stiff dough. Transfer to a floured surface and knead until smooth and elastic. This will take about 10 minutes. Place in a greased bowl, cover and leave to rise in a warm place until doubled in volume, about 2½ hours.

3 Knock back (punch down) the dough, return to the bowl, cover and leave to rise in a warm place for 30 minutes. Grease two 21 x 11cm/8½ x 4½in loaf tins (pans). Divide the dough in half and roll each half into a 50 x 18cm/20 x 7in rectangle.

4 Brush the rectangles with the remaining melted butter. Sprinkle over the raisin mixture, then roll up tightly, tucking in the ends slightly as you roll. Place in the prepared tins, cover, and leave to rise until almost doubled in volume, about 1 hour. Preheat the oven to 200°C/400°F/Gas 6. Brush the loaves with the egg glaze. Bake for 20 minutes. Lower to 180°C/350°F/Gas 4 and bake until golden, 25–30 minutes more. Cool on racks.

Energy 2187kcal/9239kJ; Fat 58.9g, Saturated Fat 33.9g; Carbohydrate 388.3g; Fibre 13g

Coconut Bread

This bread is delicious served with a cup of hot chocolate or a glass of fruit punch.

Makes 1 loaf

175g/6oz/¾ cup butter
115g/4oz/½ cup demerara (raw) sugar
225g/8oz/2 cups self-raising (self-rising) flour
200g/7oz/1¾ cups plain (all-purpose) flour
115g/4oz/1⅓ cups desiccated (dry unsweetened shredded) coconut
5ml/1 tsp mixed (apple pie) spice
10ml/2 tsp vanilla extract
15ml/1 tbsp rum
2 eggs
about 150ml/¼ pint/⅔ cup milk
15ml/1 tbsp caster (superfine) sugar, blended with 30ml/2 tbsp water, to glaze

1 Preheat the oven to 180°C/350°F/Gas 4. Grease two 450g/1lb loaf tins (pans).

2 Place the butter and sugar in a large bowl and sift in the flour. Rub the ingredients together using your fingertips or a pastry cutter until the mixture resembles fine breadcrumbs.

3 Add the coconut, mixed spice, vanilla extract, rum, eggs and milk to the butter and sugar mixture, and mix together well with your hands. If you think that the mixture is too dry, moisten with milk. Turn out on to a floured board and knead until firm and pliable.

4 Halve the mixture and place in the prepared loaf tins. Glaze with sugared water and bake for 1 hour, or until the loaves are cooked. Test with a skewer; the loaves are ready when the skewer comes out clean.

Cook's Tips

This coconut bread is a cross between a teabread and a yeast bread. It is quick to make and needs no rising time. It is also delicious spread with butter or a fruit preserve.

Energy 4148kcal/17357kJ; Fat 234.3g, Saturated Fat 158.1g; Carbohydrate 465.9g, Fibre 28.9g

Danish Wreath

This is a delicious sweet loaf for tea.

Serves 10–12

5ml/1 tsp active dried yeast
175ml/6fl oz/¾ cup milk
50g/2oz/½ cup caster (superfine) sugar
450g/1lb/4 cups strong white bread flour
2.5ml/½ tsp salt
2.5ml/½ tsp vanilla extract
1 egg, beaten
225g/8oz/1 cup unsalted (sweet) butter
1 egg yolk beaten with 10ml/2 tsp water
115g/4oz/1 cup icing (confectioners') sugar

For the filling

200g/7oz/scant 1 cup soft dark brown sugar
5ml/1 tsp ground cinnamon
50g/2oz/⅓ cup walnuts or pecans, plus extra to decorate

1 Mix the yeast, milk and 2.5ml/½ tsp of the sugar in a small bowl. Leave for 15 minutes to dissolve. Mix the flour, sugar and salt. Make a well and add the yeast, vanilla and egg to make a rough dough. Knead until smooth, wrap in clear film (plastic wrap) and chill. Roll the butter between sheets of baking parchment to form two 15 x 10cm/6 x 4in rectangles. Roll the dough to a 30 x 20cm/12 x 8in rectangle. Place one butter rectangle in the centre. Fold the bottom third of dough over and seal the edge. Place the other butter rectangle on top and cover with the top third of the dough.

2 Roll the dough into a 30 x 20cm/12 x 8in rectangle. Fold into thirds. Wrap and chill for 30 minutes. Repeat twice more. After the third fold, chill for 1–2 hours. Grease a baking sheet. Roll out the dough to a 62 x 15cm/25 x 6in strip. Mix the filling ingredients and spread over, leaving a 1cm/½in edge. Roll the dough into a cylinder, place on the baking sheet in a circle and seal the edges. Cover and leave to rise for 45 minutes.

3 Preheat the oven to 200°C/400°F/Gas 6. Slash the top every 5cm/2in, cutting 1cm/½in deep. Brush with the egg and milk. Bake for 35–40 minutes, or until golden. Cool. To serve, mix the icing sugar with a little water, then drizzle over the wreath. Sprinkle with some nuts.

Energy 361kcal/1520kJ; Fat 11.9g, Saturated Fat 5.6g; Carbohydrate 61.8g, Fibre 1.3g

Kugelhopf

A traditional round moulded bread from Germany, flavoured with Kirsch or brandy.

Makes one ring loaf

100g/3¾oz/¾ cup raisins
15ml/1 tbsp Kirsch or brandy
15ml/1 tbsp easy-blend (rapid-rise) dried yeast
120ml/4fl oz/½ cup lukewarm water
115g/4oz/½ cup unsalted (sweet) butter, at room temperature
90g/3½oz/½ cup caster (superfine) sugar
3 eggs, at room temperature
grated rind of 1 lemon
5ml/1 tsp salt
2.5ml/½ tsp vanilla extract
425g/15oz/3⅔ cups strong white bread flour
120ml/4fl oz/½ cup milk
25g/1oz/¼ cup flaked (sliced) almonds
80g/3¼oz/generous ½ cup whole blanched almonds, chopped
icing (confectioners') sugar, for dusting

1 In a bowl, combine the raisins and Kirsch or brandy. Combine the yeast and water, stir and leave for 15 minutes until the yeast becomes frothy.

2 Cream the butter and sugar until thick and fluffy. Beat in the eggs, one at a time. Add the lemon rind, salt and vanilla extract. Stir in the yeast mixture.

3 Add the flour, alternating with the milk, until well blended. Cover and leave to rise in a warm place until doubled in volume, about 2 hours.

4 Grease a 2.75 litre/4½ pint/11¼ cup kugelhopf mould, then sprinkle the flaked almonds evenly over the base. Work the raisins and chopped almonds into the dough, then spoon into the mould.

5 Cover with clear film (plastic wrap), and leave to rise in a warm place until the dough almost reaches the top of the tin, about 1 hour.

6 Preheat the oven to 180°C/350°F/Gas 4. Bake until golden brown, about 45 minutes. If the top browns too quickly, cover with foil. Cool in the tin for 15 minutes, then turn out on to a wire rack. Dust the top lightly with icing sugar.

Energy 3828kcal/16069kJ; Fat 175.7g, Saturated Fat 70.1g; Carbohydrate 501.5g, Fibre 22.9g

Individual Brioches

These buttery rolls with their distinctive topknots are delicious served with jam at coffee time.

Makes 8

15ml/1 tbsp active dried yeast
15ml/1 tbsp caster (superfine) sugar
30ml/2 tbsp warm milk
2 eggs
about 200g/7oz/1¾ cups strong white bread flour
2.5ml/½ tsp salt
75g/3oz/6 tbsp butter, cut into six pieces, at room temperature
1 egg yolk, beaten with 10ml/2 tsp water, to glaze

1 Butter eight individual brioche tins (pans) or muffin cups. Put the yeast and sugar in a small bowl, add the milk and stir until dissolved. Leave the yeast mixture to stand for 5 minutes so that the yeast begins to work, then beat in the eggs.

2 Put the flour and salt into a food processor, then, with the machine running, slowly pour in the yeast mixture. Scrape down the sides and process until the dough forms a ball.

3 Add the butter and pulse to blend. Alternatively, use your hand to incorporate the flour into the liquid.

4 Transfer the dough to a lightly buttered bowl and cover with a clean dish towel or clear film (plastic wrap). Leave to rise in a warm place for about 1 hour, then knock back (punch down) the dough.

5 Shape three-quarters of the dough into eight balls and place them into the prepared tins. Shape the last quarter into eight small balls, make a depression in the top of each large ball and set a small ball into it.

6 Leave the brioches to rise in a warm place for 30 minutes. Preheat the oven to 200°C/400°F/Gas 6.

7 Brush the brioches with the egg glaze. Bake for about 15–18 minutes, or until golden brown. Transfer to a wire rack and leave to cool completely.

Energy 183kcal/765kJ; Fat 9.5g, Saturated Fat 5.4g; Carbohydrate 21.6g, Fibre 0.8g

Dinner Milk Rolls

Making bread especially for your dinner guests is not only a wonderful gesture, it is also quite easy to do.

Makes 12–16

750g/1lb 10oz/6½ cups strong white bread flour
10ml/2 tsp salt
25g/1oz/2 tbsp butter
1 sachet easy-blend (rapid-rise) dried yeast
450ml/¾ pint/1¾ cups lukewarm milk
cold milk, to glaze
poppy, sesame and sunflower seeds, or sea salt flakes, for sprinkling

1 Sift together the flour and salt into a large bowl. Rub in the butter, then stir in the yeast. Mix to a firm dough with the lukewarm milk (you may not need it all).

2 Knead the dough for 5 minutes on a lightly floured surface, then return it to the bowl, cover with a clean dish towel or clear film (plastic wrap), and leave to rise until doubled in volume, about 1½ hours.

3 Grease a baking sheet. Knock back (punch down) the dough and knead again, then divide into 12–16 pieces and form into shapes of your choice.

4 You can make mini-cottage loaves by setting a small ball on to a larger one and pressing a finger in the top; use three lengths of dough to make a braid; one long length can be made into a simple knot; or make three cuts in a round roll for an easier decoration.

5 Place the rolls or mini-cottage loaves on the baking sheet, glaze the tops with milk, and sprinkle over your chosen seeds or sea salt flakes.

6 Leave in a warm place to start rising again. Meanwhile, preheat the oven to 230°C/450°F/Gas 8. Bake the rolls for 12 minutes, or until golden brown and cooked. Turn out on to a wire rack, and leave to cool. (Eat the rolls the same day as they will not keep well.)

Energy 247kcal/1047kJ; Fat 3.2g, Saturated Fat 1.6g; Carbohydrate 50.4g, Fibre 1.9g

Pleated Rolls

Fancy home-made rolls show that every care has been taken to ensure a welcoming dinner party.

Makes 48 rolls

15ml/1 tbsp active dried yeast
475ml/16fl oz/2 cups lukewarm milk
115g/4oz/½ cup margarine
50g/2oz/¼ cup caster (superfine) sugar
10ml/2 tsp salt
2 eggs
985g–1.2kg/2lb 3oz–2½lb/ scant 7–8 cups strong white bread flour
50g/2oz/¼ cup butter

1 Combine the yeast and 120ml/4fl oz/½ cup milk in a large bowl. Stir and leave for 15 minutes. Scald the remaining milk, leave to cool for 5 minutes, then beat in the margarine, sugar, salt and eggs. Leave until lukewarm.

2 Pour the milk mixture into the yeast mixture. Stir in half the flour with a wooden spoon. Add the remaining flour, 150g/5oz/ 1¼ cups at a time, to obtain a rough dough.

3 Transfer the dough to a floured surface and knead until elastic. This will take about 10 minutes. Place in a clean bowl, cover with clear film (plastic wrap) and leave to rise in a warm place until doubled in volume. Melt the butter and set aside.

4 Lightly grease two baking sheets. Knock back (punch down) the dough and divide into four equal pieces. Roll each piece into a 30 x 20cm/12 x 8in rectangle, about 5mm/¼in thick. Cut each of the rectangles into four long strips, then cut each strip into three 10 x 5cm/4 x 2in rectangles.

5 Brush each rectangle with the melted butter, then fold the rectangles in half, so that the top extends about 1cm/½in over the bottom. Place the rectangles slightly overlapping on the baking sheet, with the longer sides facing up.

6 Cover and chill for 30 minutes. Preheat the oven to 180°C/ 350°F/Gas 4. Bake until golden, 18–20 minutes. Cool slightly before serving.

Energy 107kcal/452kJ; Fat 3.5g, Saturated 0.8g; Carbohydrate 17.5g, Fibre 0.6g

Clover Leaf Rolls

These rolls are delightful for a dinner party. For a witty touch, make one "lucky four-leaf clover" in the batch.

Makes 24

300ml/½ pint/1¼ cups milk
30ml/2 tbsp caster (superfine) sugar
50g/2oz/¼ cup butter, at room temperature
10ml/2 tsp active dried yeast
1 egg
10ml/2 tsp salt
450–500g/1–1¼lb/4–5 cups strong white bread flour
melted butter, to glaze

1 Heat the milk to lukewarm in a small pan, pour into a large bowl and stir in the sugar, butter and yeast. Leave for 15 minutes to dissolve and for the yeast to become frothy.

2 Stir the egg and salt into the yeast mixture. Gradually stir in 475g/1lb 2oz/4½ cups of the flour, and then add just enough extra flour to obtain a rough dough.

3 Knead the dough on a lightly floured surface until smooth. This will take about 10 minutes.

4 Place the dough in a greased bowl, cover with clear film (plastic wrap) and leave in a warm place until doubled in size, about 1½ hours.

5 Grease two 12-cup bun trays. Knock back (punch down) the dough, and divide to make 72 equal-size balls.

6 Place three balls, in one layer, in each bun cup. Cover the trays loosely with a clean dish towel and leave to rise in a warm place, until doubled in size, about 1½ hours.

7 Meanwhile, preheat the oven to 200°C/400°F/Gas 6. Brush the rolls with the melted butter glaze.

8 Bake the rolls for about 20 minutes, or until they are lightly browned. Carefully turn out on to a wire rack and allow to cool slightly before serving.

Energy 2125kcal/8967kJ; Fat 59.8g, Saturated Fat 36.1g; Carbohydrate 342.2g, Fibre 13.2g

Wholemeal Rolls

To add interest, make these individual rolls into different shapes if you wish.

Makes 12

15ml/2 tbsp active dried yeast
50ml/2fl oz/¼ cup lukewarm water
5ml/1 tsp caster (superfine) sugar
175ml/6fl oz/¾ cup lukewarm buttermilk
1.5ml/¼ tsp bicarbonate of soda (baking soda)
5ml/1 tsp salt
40g/1½oz/3 tbsp butter, at room temperature
200g/7oz/scant 1¾ cups strong wholemeal (whole-wheat) bread flour
150g/5oz/1¼ cups plain (all-purpose) flour
1 beaten egg, to glaze

1 In a large bowl, combine the yeast, water and sugar. Stir, and leave for 15 minutes to dissolve and for the yeast to become frothy.

2 Add the buttermilk, bicarbonate of soda, salt and butter, and stir to blend. Stir in the strong wholemeal bread flour. Add just enough of the plain flour to obtain a rough dough.

3 Knead on a floured surface until smooth. This will take about 10 minutes. Divide into three equal parts. Roll each into a cylinder, then cut into four pieces.

4 Grease a baking sheet. Form the pieces into torpedo shapes, place on the baking sheet, cover with a clean dish towel and leave in a warm place until doubled in size, about 1 hour.

5 Preheat the oven to 200°C/400°F/Gas 6. Brush the rolls with egg. Bake until firm, about 15–20 minutes. Cool on a wire rack.

Cook's Tip
Kneading is the most important part of breadmaking, as it develops the dough and helps it to rise. You can be as rough as you like: make the dough into a ball and then press down and push it away from you with one hand, so that it stretches. Repeat until the dough is elastic.

Energy 127kcal/538kJ; Fat 3.5g, Saturated 2g; Carbohydrate 21.5g, Fibre 1.9g

Granary Baps

These baps make excellent picnic fare and are also good buns for hamburgers.

Makes 8

oil, for greasing
450g/1lb/4 cups malted brown flour
5ml/1 tsp salt
10ml/2 tsp easy-blend (rapid-rise) dried yeast
15ml/1 tbsp malt extract
300ml/½ pint/1¼ cups hand-hot water
15ml/1 tbsp rolled oats

1 Lightly oil a large baking sheet. Put the malted flour, salt and yeast in a large bowl and make a well in the centre. Dissolve the malt extract in the water and add it to the well.

2 Stir from the centre outwards, gradually incorporating the flour and mixing to a soft dough.

3 Turn the dough on to a floured surface and knead for 5 minutes, or until smooth and elastic. Divide the dough into eight pieces.

4 Shape into balls and flatten with the palm of your hand to make 10cm/4in rounds.

5 Place the rounds on the prepared baking sheet, cover loosely with oiled clear film (plastic wrap) (ballooning it to trap the air inside) and leave in a warm place until the baps have doubled in size. Preheat the oven to 220°C/425°F/Gas 7.

6 Brush the baps with water, sprinkle with the oats and bake for 20–25 minutes, or until they sound hollow when tapped underneath. Cool on a wire rack.

Variation
To make a large loaf, shape the dough into a round, flatten it slightly and bake for 30–40 minutes. Test by tapping the base of the loaf – if it sounds hollow, it is cooked.

Energy 195kcal/834kJ; Fat 1.3g, Saturated Fat 0.2g; Carbohydrate 41.4g, Fibre 3.7g

Wholemeal Herb Triangles

These make a good lunchtime snack when stuffed with ham and salad and also taste good when served with soup.

Makes 8

225g/8oz/2 cups strong wholemeal (whole-wheat) bread flour
115g/4oz/1 cup strong white bread flour
5ml/1 tsp salt
2.5ml/½ tsp bicarbonate of soda (baking soda)
5ml/1 tsp cream of tartar
2.5ml/½ tsp chilli powder
50g/2oz/¼ cup soft margarine
250ml/8fl oz/1 cup skimmed milk
60ml/4 tbsp chopped mixed fresh herbs
15ml/1 tbsp sesame seeds

1 Preheat the oven to 220°C/425°F/Gas 7. Lightly flour a baking sheet.

2 Put the wholemeal flour in a large bowl. Sift in the strong white bread flour, the salt, bicarbonate of soda, cream of tartar and the chilli powder, then rub in the margarine.

3 Add the milk and herbs and mix quickly to a soft dough. Turn on to a lightly floured surface. Knead only very briefly or the dough will become tough.

4 Roll out to a 23cm/9in circle and place on the prepared baking sheet. Brush lightly with water and sprinkle with the sesame seeds.

5 Cut the dough round into 8 wedges, separate slightly and bake for 15–20 minutes. Transfer the triangles to a wire rack to cool. Serve warm or cold.

Variation
Sun-dried Tomato Triangles: replace the mixed herbs with 30ml/2 tbsp chopped, drained sun-dried tomatoes in oil, and add 15ml/1 tbsp mild paprika, 15ml/1 tbsp chopped fresh parsley and 15ml/1 tbsp chopped fresh marjoram.

Energy 204kcal/858kJ; Fat 7.1g, Saturated Fat 0.3g; Carbohydrate 30.6g, Fibre 3.1g

Poppy Seed Knots

The poppy seeds look attractive and add a slightly nutty flavour to these rolls.

Makes 12

300ml/½ pint/1¼ cups lukewarm milk
50g/2oz/¼ cup butter, at room temperature
5ml/1 tsp caster (superfine) sugar
10ml/2 tsp active dried yeast
1 egg yolk
10ml/2 tsp salt
500–575g/1¼lb–1lb 6oz/5–5½ cups strong white bread flour
1 egg beaten with 10ml/2 tsp water, to glaze
poppy seeds, for sprinkling

1 In a large bowl, stir together the milk, butter, sugar and yeast. Leave for 15 minutes to dissolve and for the yeast to become frothy.

2 Stir in the egg yolk, salt and 275g/10oz/2½ cups of the flour. Add half the remaining flour and stir to obtain a soft dough.

3 Transfer the dough to a floured surface and knead, adding flour if necessary, until smooth and elastic. This will take about 10 minutes.

4 Place in a bowl, cover with clear film (plastic wrap) and leave in a warm place until the dough doubles in volume, about 1½–2 hours.

5 Grease a baking sheet. Knock back (punch down) the dough with your fist and cut into 12 pieces the size of golf balls.

6 Roll each piece into a rope, twist to form a knot and place 2.5cm/1in apart on the prepared baking sheet. Cover loosely and leave to rise in a warm place until doubled in volume, about 1–1½ hours.

7 Meanwhile, preheat the oven to 180°C/350°F/Gas 4. Brush the knots with the egg glaze and sprinkle over the poppy seeds. Bake until the tops are lightly browned, about 30 minutes. Cool slightly on a wire rack before serving.

Energy 191kcal/807kJ; Fat 4.9g, Saturated Fat 2.7g; Carbohydrate 33.9g, Fibre 1.3g

Poppy Seed Rolls

Pile these soft rolls in a basket and serve them for breakfast or with dinner.

Makes 12

oil, for greasing
450g/1lb/4 cups strong white bread flour
5ml/1 tsp salt
5ml/1 tsp easy-blend (rapid-rise) dried yeast
300ml/½ pint/1¼ cups hand-hot skimmed milk
1 egg, beaten

For the topping

1 egg, beaten
poppy seeds

1 Lightly grease two baking sheets with oil. Sift the flour and salt into a mixing bowl.

2 Add the yeast. Make a well in the centre and pour in the milk and the egg. Stir from the centre outwards, gradually incorporating the flour and mixing to a soft dough.

3 Turn the dough on to a floured surface and knead for 5 minutes, or until smooth and elastic. Cut into 12 pieces and shape into rolls (make a variety of shapes or just simple round rolls if you prefer).

4 Place the rolls on the prepared baking sheets, cover loosely with clear film (plastic wrap), ballooning it to trap the air inside, and leave in a warm place until the rolls have doubled in size, about 1½ hours. Meanwhile, preheat the oven to 220°C/425°F/Gas 7.

5 Glaze the rolls with beaten egg, sprinkle with poppy seeds and bake for 12–15 minutes, or until golden brown. Transfer to a wire rack to cool completely.

Variations
Vary the toppings. Linseed, sesame and caraway seeds all look good; try adding caraway seeds to the dough, too, for extra crunch and flavour.

Energy 142kcal/603kJ; Fat 1g, Saturated Fat 0.2g; Carbohydrate 30.2g, Fibre 1.2g

French Bread

For truly authentic bread you should use flour grown and milled in France.

Makes 2 loaves

15ml/1 tbsp active dried yeast
475ml/16fl oz/2 cups lukewarm water
15ml/1 tbsp salt
850–900g/1lb 14oz–2lb/ 7½–8 cups strong white bread flour
semolina or flour, for sprinkling

1 In a large bowl, combine the yeast and water, stir, and leave for 15 minutes for the yeast to dissolve and become frothy. Stir in the salt.

2 Add the flour, 150g/5oz/1¼ cups at a time, to obtain a smooth dough. Knead for 5 minutes.

3 Shape into a ball, place in a greased bowl and cover with clear film (plastic wrap). Leave to rise in a warm place until doubled in size, about 2–4 hours.

4 Knock back (punch down) the dough. On a lightly floured surface, shape the dough into two long loaves. Place on a baking sheet sprinkled with semolina or flour and leave to rise for 5 minutes.

5 Score the tops of the loaves diagonally with a sharp knife. Brush with water and place in a cold oven. Place an ovenproof pan of boiling water on the base of the oven and set the oven to 200°C/400°F/Gas 6. Bake the loaves until crusty and golden, about 40 minutes. Cool on a wire rack.

Cook's Tip
A pan of boiling water placed in the oven will ensure that you will get the traditional crusty top for your French bread. Bake the loaves at the top of the oven and use proper French bread tins (pans) if you can, as these keep the loaves in shape and are perforated to aid cooking.

Energy 1559kcal/6626kJ; Fat 9.6g, Saturated Fat 3.4g; Carbohydrate 341.4g, Fibre 13.2g

Breadsticks

If you prefer, use other seeds, such as poppy seeds, in these sticks.

Makes 18–20

15ml/1 tbsp active dried yeast
300ml/½ pint/1¼ cups lukewarm water
425g/15oz/3⅔ cups strong white bread flour
10ml/2 tsp salt
5ml/1 tsp caster (superfine) sugar
30ml/2 tbsp olive oil
1 egg, beaten, to glaze
150g/5oz/10 tbsp sesame seeds, toasted
coarse salt, for sprinkling

1 Combine the yeast and water in a small bowl, stir and leave for about 15 minutes for the yeast to dissolve and become frothy.

2 Place the flour, salt, sugar and olive oil in a food processor. With the motor running, slowly pour in the yeast mixture and process until the dough forms a ball. Alternatively, use your hand to incorporate the liquid into the flour.

3 Knead until smooth. This will take about 10 minutes. Place in a bowl, cover with clear film (plastic wrap) and leave to rise in a warm place for 45 minutes. Grease two baking sheets.

4 Roll the dough into 18–20 30cm/12in sticks. Place on the baking sheets, brush with the egg glaze then sprinkle with toasted sesame seeds and coarse salt. Leave to rise, uncovered, for 20 minutes.

5 Preheat the oven to 200°C/400°F/Gas 6. Bake until golden, about 15 minutes. Turn off the heat but leave in the oven for a further 5 minutes. Serve warm or cool.

Variation
For Rye and Caraway Breadsticks, substitute 200g/7oz/scant 2 cups rye flour for 200g/7oz/scant 2 cups of the strong white bread flour. Sprinkle with caraway seeds instead of sesame seeds.

Energy 128kcal/538kJ; Fat 5.7g, Saturated Fat 0.8g; Carbohydrate 16.8g, Fibre 1.3g

Caraway Bread Sticks

Ideal to nibble with drinks, these can be made in a wide variety of flavours, including cumin seed, poppy seed and celery seed, as well as the coriander and sesame variation given below.

Makes about 20

225g/8oz/2 cups plain (all-purpose) flour
2.5ml/½ tsp salt
2.5ml/½ tsp easy-blend (rapid-rise) dried yeast
10ml/2 tsp caraway seeds
150ml/¼ pint/⅔ cup hand-hot water
a pinch of sugar

1 Grease two baking sheets. Sift the flour, salt, yeast and sugar into a large bowl, stir in the caraway seeds and make a well in the centre.

2 Add the water and stir from the centre outwards, gradually mixing the flour to make a soft dough, and adding a little extra water if necessary.

3 Turn the dough on to a lightly floured surface and knead for 5 minutes until smooth and elastic.

4 Divide the mixture into 20 pieces and roll each one into a 30cm/12in stick.

5 Arrange the bread sticks on the baking sheets, leaving room to allow for rising. Leave for 30 minutes, or until well risen. Meanwhile, preheat the oven to 220°C/425°F/Gas 7.

6 Bake the bread sticks for 10–12 minutes, or until golden brown. Cool on the baking sheets.

Variation
To make Coriander and Sesame Sticks: replace the caraway seeds with 15ml/1 tbsp crushed coriander seeds. Dampen the bread sticks lightly and sprinkle them with sesame seeds before baking.

Energy 41kcal/176kJ; Fat 0.4g, Saturated Fat 0.1g; Carbohydrate 8.7g, Fibre 0.4g

Tomato Breadsticks

Once you've tried this exceptionally simple recipe you'll never buy manufactured breadsticks again.

Makes 16

225g/8oz/2 cups strong white bread flour
2.5ml/½ tsp salt
7.5ml/½ tbsp easy-blend (rapid-rise) dried yeast
5ml/1 tsp honey
5ml/1 tsp olive oil
150ml/¼ pint/⅔ cup warm water
6 halves sun-dried tomatoes in olive oil, drained and chopped
15ml/1 tbsp milk
10ml/2 tsp poppy seeds

1 Place the flour, salt and yeast in a food processor. Add the honey and olive oil and, with the machine running, gradually pour in the water until the dough starts to cling together (you may not need all the water).

2 Process for a further 1 minute. Alternatively, use your hand to incorporate the liquid into the flour.

3 Turn out the dough on to a floured surface and knead for 3–4 minutes, until springy and smooth. Knead in the sun-dried tomatoes.

4 Form the dough into a ball and place in a lightly oiled bowl. Cover with clear film (plastic wrap). Place in a warm position and leave to rise for 5 minutes.

5 Preheat the oven to 150°C/300°F/Gas 2. Lightly grease a baking sheet. Divide the dough into 16 pieces and roll each piece into a 28 x 1cm/11 x ½in stick.

6 Place on the lightly greased baking sheet and leave to rise in a warm place for 15 minutes.

7 Brush the breadsticks with milk and sprinkle with poppy seeds. Bake for 30 minutes. Leave the breadsticks to cool on a wire rack.

Energy 53kcal/227kJ; Fat 0.4g, Saturated Fat 0.1g; Carbohydrate 11.7g, Fibre 0.5g

Croissants

Enjoy breakfast Continental-style with these melt-in-the-mouth croissants.

Makes 18

15ml/1 tbsp active dried yeast
325ml/11fl oz/1⅓ cups lukewarm milk
10ml/2 tsp caster (superfine) sugar
12.5ml/1½ tsp salt
450g/1lb/4 cups strong white bread flour
225g/8oz/1 cup cold unsalted (sweet) butter
1 egg, beaten with 10ml/2 tsp water, to glaze

1 In a large bowl, stir together the yeast and milk. Leave for about 15 minutes for the yeast to become frothy. Stir in the sugar and salt, and about 150g/5oz/1¼ cups of the flour.

2 Slowly add the remaining flour. Mix well until the dough pulls away from the sides of the bowl. Cover and leave to rise in a warm place until doubled in size, about 1½ hours.

3 Turn out on to a lightly floured surface and knead until smooth. Wrap in baking parchment and chill for 15 minutes.

4 Roll out the butter between two sheets of baking parchment to make two 15 x 10cm/6 x 4in rectangles. Roll out the dough to a 30 x 20cm/12 x 8in rectangle.

5 Interleave the butter with the dough. With a short side facing you, roll it out again to 30 x 20cm/12 x 8in. Fold in thirds again, wrap and chill for 30 minutes. Repeat this procedure twice, then chill for 2 hours.

6 Roll out the dough to a rectangle about 3mm/⅛in thick. Trim the sides, and then cut into 18 equal-size triangles. Roll up from the base to the point. Place point-down on baking sheets and curve to form crescents. Cover and leave to rise in a warm place until more than doubled in size, about 1–1½ hours.

7 Preheat the oven to 240°C/475°F/Gas 9. Brush with egg glaze. Bake for 2 minutes. Lower the heat to 190°C/375°F/Gas 5 and bake until golden, about 10–12 minutes. Serve warm.

Energy 189kcal/789kJ; Fat 10.9g, Saturated Fat 6.8g; Carbohydrate 20.9g, Fibre 0.8g

Quick-mix Sponge Cake

Choose either chocolate or lemon flavouring for this light and versatile sponge cake, or leave it plain.

Makes 1 x 20cm/8in round or ring cake

115g/4oz/1 cup self-raising (self-rising) flour
5ml/1 tsp baking powder
115g/4oz/½ cup soft margarine
115g/4oz/½ cup caster (superfine) sugar
2 eggs

For the flavourings
Chocolate: 15ml/1 tbsp unsweetened cocoa powder blended with 15ml/1 tbsp boiling water
Lemon: 10ml/2 tsp grated lemon rind

1 Preheat the oven to 160°C/325°F/Gas 3. Grease a 20cm/8in round cake tin (pan), line the base with baking parchment and grease the paper.

2 Sift the flour and baking powder into a bowl. Add the margarine, sugar and eggs with the chosen flavourings, if using.

3 Beat with a wooden spoon for 2–3 minutes. The mixture should be pale in colour and slightly glossy.

4 Spoon the mixture into the cake tin and smooth the surface. Bake in the centre of the oven for 30–40 minutes, or until a skewer inserted into the centre of the cake comes out clean. Turn out on to a wire rack, remove the lining paper and leave to cool completely.

Cook's Tips
• *This sponge cake is ideal for a celebration cake that will be simply iced, but do not use it for a cake that needs to be carved into an intricate shape. Madeira cake is best for that purpose.*
• *Always leave any cake to cool completely before decorating it. It is best to leave it overnight in a sealed, airtight container to settle if possible.*

Energy 1504kcal/6260kJ; Fat 110g, Saturated Fat 5.3g; Carbohydrate 107.8g, Fibre 6g

Genoese Sponge Cake

This light sponge cake has a firm texture due to the addition of butter and is suitable for cutting into layers for gateaux.

Makes 1 x 20cm/8in round cake

4 eggs
115g/4oz/generous ½ cup caster (superfine) sugar
75g/3oz/6 tbsp unsalted (sweet) butter, melted and cooled slightly
75g/3oz/⅔ cup plain (all-purpose) flour

For the flavourings
Citrus: 10ml/2 tsp grated orange, lemon or lime rind
Chocolate: 50g/2oz plain (semisweet) chocolate, melted
Coffee: 10ml/2 tsp coffee granules, dissolved in 5ml/1 tsp boiling water

1 Preheat the oven to 180°C/350°F/Gas 4. Base line and grease a 20cm/8in round cake tin (pan).

2 Whisk the eggs and caster sugar together in a heatproof bowl until thoroughly blended.

3 Place the bowl over a pan of simmering water and continue to whisk the mixture until thick and pale.

4 Remove the bowl from the pan and continue to whisk until the mixture is cool and leaves a thick trail on the surface when the beaters are lifted.

5 Pour the butter carefully into the mixture, leaving any sediment behind.

6 Sift the flour over the surface and add your chosen flavouring, if using. Using a plastic spatula, carefully fold the flour, butter and any flavourings into the mixture until smooth and evenly blended.

7 Scrape the mixture into the prepared tin, tilt to level and bake for 30–40 minutes, until firm to the touch and golden. Cool on a wire rack and decorate as you like.

Energy 1736kcal/7280kJ; Fat 89.6g, Saturated Fat 48.1g; Carbohydrate 212.5g, Fibre 3.2g

Madeira Cake

Enjoy this cake in the traditional way by serving it with a large glass of Madeira or sherry.

Serves 6–8
225g/8oz/2 cups plain (all-purpose) flour
5ml/1 tsp baking powder
225g/8oz/1 cup butter or margarine, at room temperature
225g/8oz/generous 1 cup caster (superfine) sugar
grated rind of 1 lemon
5ml/1 tsp vanilla extract
4 eggs

1 Preheat the oven to 160°C/325°F/Gas 3. Base line and grease a 20cm/8in cake tin (pan).

2 Sift the plain flour and baking powder into a bowl.

3 Cream the butter or margarine, adding the caster sugar about 30ml/2 tbsp at a time, until light and fluffy. Stir in the lemon rind and vanilla extract. Add the eggs one at a time, beating for 1 minute after each addition. Add the flour mixture and stir until just combined.

4 Pour the cake mixture into the prepared tin and tap lightly to level. Bake for about 1¼ hours, or until a metal skewer inserted in the centre comes out clean.

5 Cool in the tin on a wire rack for 10 minutes, then turn the cake out on to a wire rack and leave to cool completely.

Cook's Tips
- *Madeira cake is ideal for using as a celebration cake as it keeps better than a sponge cake and so will last for longer while you decorate it. It also has a firm texture that will be easy to ice with butter icing and sugarpaste.*
- *Level the domed top before icing the cake by putting a deep cake board inside the cake tin (pan) the cake was baked in and placing the cake on top. Cut the part of the cake that extends above the top of the tin using a sharp knife.*

Energy 453kcal/1894kJ; Fat 26.3g, Saturated Fat 15.5g; Carbohydrate 51.4g, Fibre 0.9g

Sponge Roll

Vary the flavour of the roll by adding a little grated orange, lime or lemon rind to the mixture, if you like.

Serves 6–8
4 eggs, separated
115g/4oz/½ cup caster (superfine) sugar, plus extra for sprinkling
115g/4oz/1 cup plain (all-purpose) flour
5ml/1 tsp baking powder

For a chocolate flavouring
Replace 25ml/1½ tbsp of the flour with 25ml/1½ tbsp unsweetened cocoa powder

1 Preheat the oven to 180°C/350°F/Gas 4. Base line and grease a 33 x 23cm/13 x 9in Swiss roll tin (jelly roll pan).

2 Whisk the egg whites until stiff peaks form and then beat in 30ml/2 tbsp of the caster sugar.

3 Beat the egg yolks with the remaining caster sugar and 15ml/1 tbsp water for about 2 minutes, or until the mixture is pale and leaves a thick ribbon trail.

4 Sift together the flour and baking powder into another bowl. Carefully fold the beaten egg yolks into the egg whites, then fold in the flour mixture.

5 Pour the mixture into the prepared tin and gently smooth the surface with a plastic spatula.

6 Bake in the centre of the oven for 12–15 minutes, or until the cake starts to come away from the edges of the tin.

7 Turn the cake out on to a piece of baking parchment lightly sprinkled with caster sugar. Peel off the lining paper and cut off any crisp edges.

8 Spread with jam, if you like, and roll up, using the baking parchment to help you.

9 Leave to cool on a wire rack, then dust with icing sugar.

Energy 142kcal/603kJ; Fat 3g, Saturated Fat 0.8g; Carbohydrate 26.2g, Fibre 0.5g

Rich Fruit Cake

This is an ideal recipe for a celebration cake. Make this cake a few weeks before icing, wrap and store in an airtight container to mature.

Makes 1 x 20cm/8in round or 18cm/7in square cake

375g/13oz/1½ cups currants
250g/9oz/1½ cups sultanas (golden raisins)
150g/5oz/1 cup raisins
90g/3½oz/scant ½ cup glacé (candied) cherries, halved
90g/3½oz/generous ½ cup almonds, chopped
65g/2½oz/scant ½ cup mixed (candied) peel
grated rind of 1 lemon
40ml/2½ tbsp brandy
250g/9oz/2¼ cups plain (all-purpose) flour, sifted
6.5ml/1¼ tsp mixed (apple pie) spice
2.5ml/½ tsp freshly grated nutmeg
65g/2½oz/generous ½ cup ground almonds
200g/7oz/scant 1 cup soft margarine or butter
225g/8oz/1¼ cups soft light brown sugar
15ml/1 tbsp black treacle (molasses)
5 eggs, beaten

1 Preheat the oven to 140°C/275°F/Gas 1. Grease a deep 20cm/8in round or 18cm/7in square cake tin (pan), line the base and sides with a double thickness of baking parchment and grease the paper.

2 Combine the ingredients in a large mixing bowl. Beat with a wooden spoon for 5 minutes, or until well mixed.

3 Spoon the mixture into the prepared cake tin. Make a slight depression in the centre.

4 Bake in the centre of the oven for 3–3½ hours. Test the cake after 3 hours. If it is ready it will feel firm and a skewer inserted into the centre will come out clean. Cover the top loosely with foil if it starts to brown too quickly.

5 Leave the cake to cool completely in the tin. Then turn out. The lining paper can be left on until you are ready to ice or serve, to help keep the cake moist.

Energy 7388kcal/31049kJ; Fat 320.2g; Saturated Fat 124.8g; Carbohydrate 1047.9g; Fibre 39.1g

Light Fruit Cake

This slightly less dense fruit cake is still ideal for marzipanning and icing.

Makes 1 x 20cm/8in round or 18cm/7in square cake

225g/8oz/1 cup soft margarine or butter
225g/8oz/generous 1 cup caster (superfine) sugar
grated rind of 1 orange
5 eggs, beaten
300g/11oz/2⅔ cups plain (all-purpose) flour
2.5ml/½ tsp baking powder
10ml/2 tsp mixed (apple pie) spice
175g/6oz/¾ cup currants
175g/6oz/generous 1 cup raisins
175g/6oz/1 cup sultanas (golden raisins)
50g/2oz/¼ cup dried, ready-to-eat apricots
115g/4oz/⅔ cup mixed (candied) peel

1 Preheat the oven to 150°C/300°F/Gas 2. Grease a deep 20cm/8in round or 18cm/7in square cake tin (pan), line the base and sides with a double thickness of baking parchment and grease the paper.

2 Beat the margarine and sugar together in a large bowl until soft. Add the orange rind and then the eggs, one at a time, beating after each addition and adding a spoonful of flour to stop them curdling. Sift the remaining flour with the baking powder and mixed spice. Stir in the currants, raisins and sultanas.

3 Cut up the apricots in strips, using kitchen scissors, and add to the mixture. Beat thoroughly with a wooden spoon for 3–4 minutes, until thoroughly mixed.

4 Spoon the mixture into the cake tin. Make a slight depression in the centre. Bake in the centre of the oven for 2½–3¼ hours. Test the cake after 2½ hours. If it is ready it will feel firm and a skewer inserted into the centre will come out clean. Test at intervals if necessary. Cover the top loosely with foil if it starts to brown too quickly.

5 Leave the cake to cool completely in the tin, then turn out. The lining paper can be left on until you are ready to ice or serve, to help keep the cake moist.

Energy 5719kcal/24077kJ; Fat 218.7g; Saturated Fat 8.5g; Carbohydrate 918.1g; Fibre 28.3g

Marzipan Roses

To decorate a cake, shape the roses in a variety of colours and sizes then arrange on top.

1 Form a small ball of coloured marzipan into a cone shape. This forms the central core which supports the petals.

2 Take a piece of marzipan about the size of a large pea, and make a petal shape that is thicker at the base.

3 Wrap the petal around the cone, pressing the petal to the cone to secure. Bend back the ends of the petal to curl. Repeat with more petals, each overlapping. Make some petals bigger until the required size is achieved.

Marzipan

Marzipan can be used on its own, under an icing or for modelling decorations.

Makes 450g/1lb/3 cups
225g/8oz/2 cups ground almonds
115g/4oz/generous ½ cup caster (superfine) sugar
115g/4oz/1 cup icing (confectioners') sugar, sifted
5ml/1 tsp lemon juice
a few drops of almond extract
1 egg or 1 egg white

1 Stir the ground almonds and sugars together in a bowl until evenly mixed. Make a well in the centre and add the lemon juice, almond extract and enough egg or egg white to mix to a soft but firm dough, using a wooden spoon.

2 Form the marzipan into a ball. Lightly dust a surface with icing sugar and knead the marzipan until smooth. Wrap in clear film (plastic wrap) or store in a plastic bag until needed. Tint with food colouring if required.

Energy 2357kcal/9874kJ; Fat 131.1g, Saturated Fat 11.5g; Carbohydrate 255.9g, Fibre 16.6g

Sugarpaste Icing

Sugarpaste icing is wonderfully pliable and can be coloured, moulded and shaped in imaginative ways.

Makes 350g/12oz/2¼ cups
1 egg white
15ml/1 tbsp liquid glucose, warmed
350g/12oz/3 cups icing (confectioners') sugar, sifted

1 Put the egg white and glucose in a mixing bowl. Stir them together to break up the egg white.

2 Add the icing sugar and mix together with a metal spatula, using a chopping action, until well blended and the icing begins to bind together.

3 Knead the mixture with your fingers until it forms a ball.

4 Knead the sugarpaste on a work surface that has been lightly dusted with icing sugar for several minutes until it is smooth, soft and pliable.

5 If the icing is too soft, knead in some more sifted sugar until it reaches the right consistency.

Cook's Tips

- *Sugarpaste icing is sometimes known as rolled fondant and is available ready made in sugarcraft stores. It is easy to make yourself but if you are using a large quantity and are in a hurry you could purchase it ready made. It is available in a variety of colours.*
- *If you want to make the sugarpaste in advance wrap it up tightly in a plastic bag. The icing will keep for about three weeks.*
- *The paste is easy to colour with paste colours; add a little at a time using the tip of a knife.*
- *Roll out sugarpaste on a surface lightly sprinkled with icing (confectioners') sugar or a little white vegetable fat (shortening) to avoid the paste sticking.*

Energy 1435kcal/6123kJ; Fat 0g, Saturated Fat 0g; Carbohydrate 377.6g, Fibre 0g

Royal Icing

Royal icing gives a professional finish. This recipe makes enough icing to cover the top and sides of an 18cm/7in cake.

Makes 675g/1½lb/4½ cups

3 egg whites
about 675g/1½lb/6 cups icing (confectioners') sugar, sifted
7.5ml/1½ tsp glycerine
a few drops of lemon juice
food colouring (optional)

1 Put the egg whites in a bowl and stir lightly with a fork to break them up.

2 Add the sifted icing sugar gradually, beating well with a wooden spoon after each addition.

3 Add enough icing sugar to make a smooth, shiny icing that has the consistency of very stiff meringue.

4 Beat in the glycerine, lemon juice and food colouring, if using.

5 Leave for 1 hour before using, covered with damp clear film (plastic wrap), then stir to burst any air bubbles.

Cook's Tips

• The icing will keep for up to three days in a refrigerator, stored in a plastic container with a tight-fitting lid.
• This recipe is for an "icing" consistency suitable for flat-icing a marzipanned rich fruit cake. When the spoon is lifted, the icing should form a sharp point, with a slight curve at the end, known as "soft peak". For piping, the icing needs to be slightly stiffer. It should form a fine sharp peak when the spoon is lifted.
• Royal icing is not appropriate for a sponge cake, as its stiff consistency would easily drag on the surface.
• Never use royal icing direct on to the cake's surface; a layer of marzipan will make a smooth surface for icing and stop cake crumbs mixing with the icing.

Energy 2694kcal/11494kJ; Fat 0g, Saturated Fat 0g; Carbohydrate 705.4g, Fibre 0g

Butter Icing

The creamy rich flavour and silky smoothness of butter icing is popular with both children and adults.

Makes 350g/12oz/1½ cups

75g/3oz/6 tbsp soft margarine or butter, softened
225g/8oz/2 cups icing (confectioners') sugar, sifted
5ml/1 tsp vanilla extract
10–15ml/2–3 tsp milk

For the flavourings

Chocolate: blend 15ml/1 tbsp unsweetened cocoa powder with 15ml/1 tbsp hot water. Cool before beating into the icing.

Coffee: blend 10ml/2 tsp coffee powder with 15ml/1 tbsp boiling water. Omit the milk. Cool before beating the mixture into the icing.

Lemon, orange or lime: substitute the vanilla extract and milk with lemon, orange or lime juice and 10ml/2 tsp of finely grated citrus rind. Omit the rind if using the icing for piping. Lightly tint the icing with food colouring, if you like.

1 Put the margarine or butter, icing sugar, vanilla extract and 5ml/1 tsp of the milk in a bowl.

2 Beat with a wooden spoon or an electric mixer, adding sufficient extra milk to give a light, smooth and fluffy consistency. For flavoured butter icing, follow the instructions above for the flavour of your choice.

Cook's Tips

• The icing will keep for up to three days in an airtight container stored in a refrigerator.
• Butter icing can be coloured with paste colours. Add a little at a time using a cocktail stick (toothpick) until you reach the desired shade.
• You can apply butter icing with a knife and make a smooth finish, or you can pipe the icing on to your cake using a plain or fluted nozzle, or use a serrated scraper for a ridged finish.

Energy 1461kcal/6149kJ; Fat 62g, Saturated Fat 0.5g; Carbohydrate 238g, Fibre 0g

Fudge Frosting

A darkly delicious frosting, this can transform a simple sponge cake into one worthy of a very special occasion.

Makes 350g/12oz/1½ cups
50g/2oz plain (semisweet) chocolate
225g/8oz icing (confectioners') sugar, sifted
50g/2oz/4 tbsp butter
45ml/3 tbsp milk or single (light) cream
5ml/1 tsp vanilla extract

1 Break or chop the chocolate into small pieces. Put the chocolate, icing sugar, butter, milk or cream and vanilla extract in a heavy pan.

2 Stir over a very low heat until both the chocolate and the butter have melted. Remove the mixture from the heat and stir until it is evenly blended.

3 Beat the icing frequently as it cools until it thickens sufficiently to use for spreading or piping.

4 Use the icing immediately and work as quickly as possible once it has reached the right consistency. If you let it cool too much it will become too thick to work with.

Cook's Tips

- *Spread fudge frosting smoothly over the cake or swirl it. Or be even more elaborate with a little piping – it really is very versatile.*
- *This recipe makes enough to fill and coat the top and sides of a 20cm/8in or 23cm/9in round sponge cake.*
- *This icing should be used immediately.*
- *Use a good quality chocolate so that you achieve a pronounced flavour for this frosting.*
- *As the frosting contains cream it is best to keep the finished cake in the refrigerator until ready to serve.*

Energy 1534kcal/6468kJ; Fat 55.9g, Saturated Fat 34.9g; Carbohydrate 269.3g, Fibre 1.3g

Crème au Beurre

The rich, smooth texture of this icing makes it ideal for spreading, filling or piping on to cakes and gateaux.

Makes 350g/12oz/1½ cups
60ml/4 tbsp water
75g/3oz/6 tbsp caster (superfine) sugar
2 egg yolks
150g/5oz/10 tbsp unsalted (sweet) butter, softened

For the flavourings
Citrus: replace water with orange, lemon or lime juice and 10ml/2 tsp grated rind
Chocolate: add 50g/2oz plain (semisweet) chocolate, melted
Coffee: add 10ml/2 tsp instant coffee granules, dissolved in 5ml/1 tsp boiling water, cooled

1 Put the water in a pan and bring to the boil, then stir in the sugar. Heat gently, stirring, until the sugar has dissolved.

2 Boil rapidly until the mixture becomes syrupy, or reaches the "thread" stage (107°C/225°F on a sugar thermometer). To test, place a little syrup on the back of a dry teaspoon. Press a second teaspoon on to the syrup and gently pull apart. The syrup should form a fine thread. If not, return to the heat, boil rapidly and re-test a minute later.

3 Whisk the egg yolks together in a bowl. Continue to whisk while slowly adding the sugar syrup in a thin stream. Whisk until thick, pale and cool. Beat the butter until light and fluffy. Add the egg mixture gradually, beating well after each addition, until thick and fluffy.

4 For Chocolate or Coffee Crème au Beurre, fold in the flavouring at the end.

Cook's Tip

It is important that the syrup reaches the correct stage and does not cook any further, as it will become too firm and you will not be able to whisk it into the egg yolks smoothly.

Energy 1534kcal/6354kJ; Fat 134.3g, Saturated Fat 81.3g; Carbohydrate 79.3g, Fibre 0g

American Frosting

A light marshmallow icing which crisps on the outside when left to dry, this versatile frosting may be swirled or peaked into a soft coating.

Makes 350g/12oz/1½ cups
1 egg white
30ml/2 tbsp water
15ml/1 tbsp golden (light corn) syrup
5ml/1 tsp cream of tartar
175g/6oz/1½ cups icing (confectioners') sugar, sifted

1 Place the egg white with the water, golden syrup and cream of tartar in a heatproof bowl. Whisk together until blended.

2 Stir the icing sugar into the mixture and place the bowl over a pan of simmering water. Whisk until the mixture becomes thick and white.

3 Remove the bowl from the pan and continue to whisk the frosting until cool and thick, and the mixture stands up in soft peaks. Use immediately to fill or cover cakes.

Caramel Icing

A rich-tasting icing that makes a lovely cake topping.

Makes 450g/1lb/2 cups
75ml/5 tbsp creamy milk
75g/3oz/6 tbsp butter
30 ml/2 tbsp caster (superfine) sugar
350g/12oz/3 cups icing (confectioners') sugar

1 Warm the milk and butter in a pan. Heat the caster sugar in another pan over medium heat until it turns golden. Immediately remove from the heat before the caramel darkens.

2 Pour the milk mixture over the caramel and return the pan to a low heat. Heat the mixture until the caramel has dissolved, stirring occasionally. Sift in the icing sugar a little at a time, and beat with a wooden spoon until the icing is smooth. Use immediately.

Top: Energy 746kcal/3181kJ; Fat 0g, Saturated Fat 0g; Carbohydrate 194.7g, Fibre 0g
Above: Energy 2070kcal/8850kJ; Fat 604g, Saturated Fat 38.2g; Carbohydrate 404.5g, Fibre 0g

Glacé Icing

An instant icing for quickly finishing the tops of large or small cakes.

Makes 350g/12oz/1½ cup
225g/8oz/2 cups icing (confectioners') sugar
30–45ml/2–3 tbsp hot water
food colouring (optional)

For the flavourings
Citrus: replace the water with orange, lemon or lime juice
Chocolate: sift 10ml/2 tsp unsweetened cocoa powder with the icing (confectioners') sugar
Coffee: replace the water with strong, liquid coffee

1 Sift the icing sugar into a bowl. Using a wooden spoon, gradually stir in enough of the hot water to obtain the consistency of thick cream.

2 Beat until white and smooth, and the icing thickly coats the back of the spoon. Tint with a few drops of food colouring, if you wish, or flavour the icing as suggested above. Use immediately to cover the top of the cake.

Simple Piped Flowers

Bouquets of iced blooms, such as roses, pansies and bright summer flowers, make colourful cake decorations.

Makes 350g/12oz/1½ cup
225g/8oz/2 cups icing (confectioners') sugar
30–45ml/2–3 tbsp hot water

1 For a rose, make a fairly firm icing. Colour the icing. Fit a petal nozzle into a paper piping (icing) bag, half-fill with icing and fold over the top to seal. Hold the piping bag so that the wider end is pointing at what will be the base of the rose and hold a cocktail stick (toothpick) in the other hand.

2 Pipe a small cone shape around the tip of the stick, pipe a petal halfway around the cone, lifting it so that it is at an angle and curling outwards, turning the stick at the same time. Repeat with more overlapping petals. Remove from the stick and leave to dry.

Top: Energy 887kcal/3782kJ; Fat 0g, Saturated Fat 0g; Carbohydrate 235.1g, Fibre 0g
Above: Energy 887kcal/3782kJ; Fat 0g, Saturated Fat 0g; Carbohydrate 235.1g, Fibre 0g

Honey Icing

A simple and tasty topping for cakes.

Makes 275g/10oz/1¼ cups
75g/3oz/6 tbsp butter, softened
175g/6oz/1½ cups icing (confectioners') sugar
15ml/1 tbsp clear honey
15ml/1 tbsp lemon juice

1 Put the softened butter into a bowl and gradually sift over the icing sugar, beating well after each addition.

2 Beat in the honey and lemon juice and combine well. Spread over the cake immediately.

Butterscotch Frosting

Soft light brown sugar and treacle make a rich and tempting frosting for cakes.

Makes 675g/1½lb/3 cups
75g/3oz/6 tbsp unsalted (sweet) butter
45ml/3 tbsp milk
25g/1oz/2 tbsp soft light brown sugar
15ml/1 tbsp black treacle (molasses)
350g/12oz/3 cups icing (confectioners') sugar, sifted

For the flavourings
Citrus: replace the treacle with golden (light corn) syrup and add 10ml/2 tsp finely grated orange, lemon or lime rind
Chocolate: sift 15ml/1 tbsp unsweetened cocoa powder with the icing (confectioners') sugar
Coffee: replace the treacle (molasses) with 15ml/1 tbsp coffee granules

1 Place the butter, milk, sugar and treacle in a bowl over a pan of simmering water. Stir until the butter melts and the sugar dissolves completely.

2 Remove from the heat and stir in the icing sugar. Beat until smooth. For different flavourings, follow the instructions above. Pour over the cake, or cool for a thicker consistency.

Chocolate Fudge Icing

A rich glossy icing which sets like chocolate fudge, this is versatile enough to smoothly coat, swirl or pipe, depending on the temperature of the icing when it is used.

Makes 450g/1lb/2 cups
115g/4oz plain (semisweet) chocolate, in squares
50g/2oz/¼ cup unsalted (sweet) butter
1 egg, beaten
175g/6oz/1½ cups icing (confectioners') sugar, sifted

1 Place the chocolate and butter in a heatproof bowl over a pan of hot water.

2 Stir the mixture occasionally with a wooden spoon until both the chocolate and butter are melted. Add the egg and beat well until thoroughly combined.

3 Remove the bowl from the pan and stir in the icing sugar, then beat until smooth and glossy.

4 Pour immediately over the cake for a smooth finish, or leave to cool for a thicker spreading or piping consistency.

Chocolate Curls

These tasty curls look spectacular on a gateau.

Makes around 20 curls
115g/4 oz plain (semisweet) chocolate

1 Melt the chocolate, then pour on to a smooth surface, such as marble or plastic laminate. Spread evenly over the surface with a palette knife. Leave to cool slightly.

2 Hold a large, sharp knife at a 45° angle to the chocolate and push it along the chocolate in short sawing movements from right to left to make curls. Lift off with the knife and leave to cool.

Top: Energy 1291Kcal/5420kJ; Fat 61.6g; Saturated fat 39.1g; Carbohydrate 194.8g; Fibre 0g
Above: Energy 2095kcal/8850kJ; Fat 62.4g, Saturated Fat 39.5g; Carbohydrate 404.5g; Fibre 0g

Top: Energy 1722kcal/7235kJ; Fat 78.8g, Saturated Fat 46.9g; Carbohydrate 256.2g, Fibre 2.9g
Above: Energy 29Kcal/123kJ; Fat 1.6g; Saturated fat 1g; Carbohydrate 3.7g; Fibre 0.1g

Apricot Glaze

It is a good idea to make a large quantity of apricot glaze, especially when making celebration cakes.

Makes 450g/1lb/1½ cups
450g/1lb/generous 1½ cups apricot jam
45ml/3 tbsp water

1 Place the jam and water in a pan. Heat gently, stirring occasionally, until the jam has melted.

2 Boil the jam rapidly for 1 minute, then rub through a sieve, pressing the fruit against the sides of the sieve with the back of a wooden spoon.

3 Discard the skins left in the sieve.

4 Use the warmed glaze to brush cakes before applying marzipan, or use for glazing fruits on gateaux and cakes.

Pastillage

This paste sets very hard and is used for making firm decorative structures from icing sugar.

Makes 350g/12oz/1¼ cups
300g/11oz icing (confectioners') sugar
1 egg white
10ml/2 tsp gum tragacanth

1 In a large bowl, sift most of the icing sugar over the egg white, a little at a time, stirring continuously until the mixture sticks together.

2 Add the gum tragacanth and transfer the mixture to a work surface which has been dusted with icing sugar.

3 Knead the mixture well until the ingredients are thoroughly combined and the paste has a smooth texture.

4 Knead in the remaining icing sugar and mix until stiff.

Top: Energy 1175kcal/5022kJ; Fat 0g, Saturated Fat 0g; Carbohydrate 311.9g, Fibre 0g
Above: Energy 1453Kcal/6190kJ; Fat 5.5g; Saturated fat 1.6g; Carbohydrate 365.8g; Fibre 0g

Sugar-frosting Flowers

Choose edible flowers such as pansies, primroses, violets, roses, freesias, apple blossom, wild bergamot (monarda), borage, carnations, honeysuckle, jasmine and marigolds.

Makes 10–15 flowers, depending on their size
1 egg white
caster (superfine) sugar
10–15 edible flowers

1 Lightly beat an egg white in a small bowl and sprinkle some caster (superfine) sugar on a plate.

2 Wash the flowers then dry on kitchen paper. Evenly brush both sides of the petals with the egg white. Hold the flower by its stem over a plate lined with kitchen paper, sprinkle it evenly with the sugar, then shake off any excess. Place on a wire rack covered with kitchen paper and leave to dry in a warm place.

Glossy Chocolate Icing

A rich smooth glossy icing, this can be made with plain or milk chocolate.

Makes 350g/12oz/1¼ cups
175g/6oz plain (semisweet) chocolate
150ml/¼ pint/⅔ cup single (light) cream

1 Break up the chocolate into small pieces and place it in a pan with the cream.

2 Heat gently, stirring occasionally, until the chocolate has melted and the mixture is smooth.

3 Allow the icing to cool until it is thick enough to coat the back of a wooden spoon. Use it at this stage for a smooth glossy icing, or allow it to thicken to obtain an icing which can be swirled or patterned with a cake decorating scraper.

Top: Energy 6Kcal/24kJ; Fat 0g; Saturated fat 0g; Carbohydrate 1.1g; Fibre 0.1g
Above: Energy 1182kcal/4937kJ; Fat 77.7g, Saturated Fat 47.6g, Carbohydrate 114.4g, Fibre 4.4g

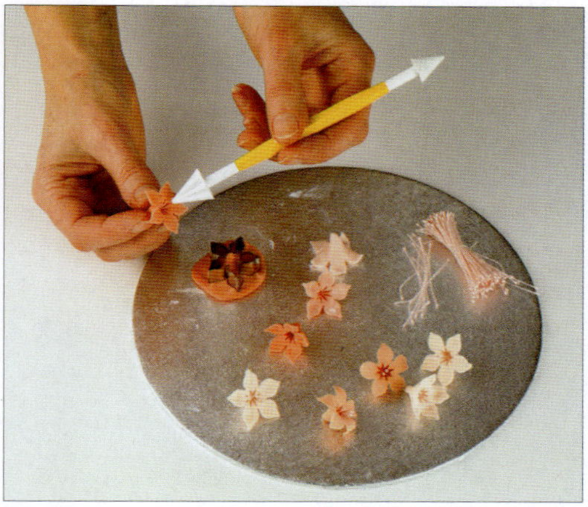

Petal Paste

Makes 500g/1¼lb
10ml/2 tsp powdered gelatine
25ml/1½ tbsp cold water
10ml/2 tsp liquid glucose
10ml/2 tsp white vegetable fat (shortening)
450g/1lb/4 cups icing (confectioners') sugar, sifted
5ml/1 tsp gum tragacanth
1 egg white

1 Place the gelatine, water, liquid glucose and white fat in a heatproof bowl set over a pan of hot water until melted, stirring occasionally.

2 Remove the bowl from the heat.

3 Sift the icing sugar and gum tragacanth into a large bowl. Make a well in the centre and add the egg white and the gelatine mixture.

4 Thoroughly combine the ingredients to form a soft malleable white paste.

5 Knead the paste on a surface dusted with icing sugar until smooth, white and free from cracks.

6 Place in a plastic bag or wrap in clear film (plastic wrap), sealing well to exclude all the air.

7 Leave the paste for about two hours before using, then knead again and use small pieces at a time, leaving the remaining petal paste well sealed.

Piping Twisted Ropes

Fit nozzles nos 43 or 44, or a writing nozzle, into a baking parchment piping (icing) bag and half-fill with royal icing. Hold the bag at a slight angle and pipe in a continuous line with even pressure, twisting the bag as you pipe.

Energy 1888kcal/8044kJ; Fat 8.2g, Saturated Fat 3.6g; Carbohydrate 478.3g, Fibre 0g

Marbling

Sugarpaste lends itself to tinting in all shades and marbling is a good way to colour the paste.

1 Using a cocktail stick (toothpick), add a little of the chosen edible food colour to some sugarpaste icing. Do not knead the food colouring fully into the icing.

2 When the sugarpaste is rolled out, the colour is dispersed in such a way that it gives a marbled appearance.

Meringue Frosting

This wonderfully light and delicate frosting needs to be used immediately.

Makes 450g/1lb/1½ cups
2 egg whites
115g/4oz/1 cup icing (confectioners') sugar, sifted
150g/5oz/⅔ cup unsalted (sweet) butter, softened

For the flavourings
Citrus: 10ml/2 tsp finely grated orange, lemon or lime rind.
Chocolate: 50g/2oz plain (semisweet) chocolate, melted
Coffee: 10ml/2 tsp coffee granules, blended with 5ml/1 tsp boiling water, cooled

1 Whisk the egg whites in a clean, heatproof bowl, add the icing sugar and gently whisk to mix well. Place the bowl over a pan of simmering water and whisk until thick and white. Remove the bowl from the pan and continue to whisk until cool when the meringue stands up in soft peaks.

2 Beat the butter in a separate bowl until light and fluffy. Add the meringue gradually, beating well after each addition, until thick and fluffy. Fold in the chosen flavouring, using a metal spatula, until evenly blended. Use immediately for coating, filling and piping on to cakes.

Energy 1592kcal/6620kJ; Fat 123.3g, Saturated Fat 78.1g; Carbohydrate 121.1g, Fibre 0g

Index

Notes

Notes

Notes

Notes

Notes

Notes

Notes

Notes